THE CAMBRIDGE COMPANION TO LITERATURE AND DISABILITY

This Companion analyzes the representation of disability in literatures in English, including American and postcolonial writing, across all major time periods and through a variety of critical approaches. Through the alternative ideas of mind and embodiment generated by physiological and psychological impairments, an understanding of disability narrative changes the way we read literature. With contributions from major figures in literary disability studies, *The Cambridge Companion to Literature and Disability* covers a wide range of impairments, including cognitive difference, neurobehavioral conditions, and mental and chronic illnesses. This book shows how disability demands innovation in literary form and aesthetics, challenges the notion of a human "norm" in the writing of character, and redraws the ways in which writing makes meaning of the broad spectrum of humanity. It will be a key resource for students and teachers of disability and literary studies.

Clare Barker is Lecturer in English Literature (Medical Humanities) at the University of Leeds. She is the author of *Postcolonial Fiction and Disability: Exceptional Children, Metaphor and Materiality* (2011), and has co-edited two special issues of the *Journal of Literary and Cultural Disability Studies*, on 'Disabling Postcolonialism' (with Stuart Murray, 2010) and 'Disability and Indigeneity' (with Siobhan Senier, 2013). Her research focuses on representations of disability, health, and biomedicine in postcolonial literatures and film.

Stuart Murray is Professor of Contemporary Literatures and Film at the University of Leeds, where he is also Director of the Leeds Centre for Medical Humanities. He began working in disability studies following the diagnosis of his two sons with autism in 2002, taught the first course in a UK university on representations of disability in literature and film, and was the founding editor of the UK's first publishing series focused on representations of health and disability: Representations: Health, Disability, Culture and Society. His book *Representing Autism* (2008) was the first critical monograph on the topic, while *Autism* (2012) was the launch book in Routledge's Integrating Science and Culture series.

A complete list of books in the series is at the back of this book.

THE CAMBRIDGE COMPANION TO LITERATURE AND DISABILITY

EDITED BY
CLARE BARKER
University of Leeds
STUART MURRAY
University of Leeds

CAMBRIDGE
UNIVERSITY PRESS

University Printing House, Cambridge CB2 8BS, United Kingdom

One Liberty Plaza, 20th Floor, New York, NY 10006, USA

477 Williamstown Road, Port Melbourne, VIC 3207, Australia

314–321, 3rd Floor, Plot 3, Splendor Forum, Jasola District Centre, New Delhi – 110025, India

79 Anson Road, #06–04/06, Singapore 079906

Cambridge University Press is part of the University of Cambridge.

It furthers the University's mission by disseminating knowledge in the pursuit of education, learning, and research at the highest international levels of excellence.

www.cambridge.org
Information on this title: www.cambridge.org/9781107087828
DOI: 10.1017/9781316104316

First published 2018

Printed in the United States of America by Sheridan Books, Inc.

A catalogue record for this publication is available from the British Library.

Library of Congress Cataloging-in-Publication Data
NAMES: Barker, Clare, 1980– editor. | Murray, Stuart, 1967– editor.
TITLE: The Cambridge companion to literature and disability / edited by Clare Barker, University of Leeds ; Stuart Murray, University of Leeds.
DESCRIPTION: Cambridge, United Kingdom ; New York, NY: Cambridge University Press, 2017. | Includes bibliographical references and index.
IDENTIFIERS: LCCN 2017024675 | ISBN 9781107087828
SUBJECTS: LCSH: People with disabilities in literature.
CLASSIFICATION: LCC PN56.5.H35 C36 2017 | DDC 809/.933527–dc23
LC record available at https://lccn.loc.gov/2017024675

ISBN 978-1-107-08782-8 Hardback
ISBN 978-1-107-45813-0 Paperback

CONTENTS

PART II ACROSS CRITICAL METHODS

CONTRIBUTORS

CLARE BARKER is Lecturer in English Literature (Medical Humanities) in the School of English at the University of Leeds. She is the author of *Postcolonial Fiction and Disability: Exceptional Children, Metaphor, and Materiality* (2011) and has coedited two special issues of the *Journal of Literary and Cultural Disability Studies*, on "Disabling Postcolonialism" (with Stuart Murray, 2010) and "Disability and Indigeneity" (with Siobhan Senier, 2013). Her research focuses on representations of disability, health, and biomedicine in postcolonial literatures and film, and she is currently working on a Wellcome Trust–funded research project entitled "Genetics and Biocolonialism in Contemporary Literature and Film."

RIA CHEYNE is Lecturer at Liverpool Hope University. Her research focuses on representations of disability in contemporary literature and culture, particularly popular genre fiction, and bridges the fields of literary studies, disability studies, and the medical humanities. She has published on disability and/or genre in the *Journal of Modern Literature*, *Journal of Literary and Cultural Disability Studies*, *Science Fiction Studies*, and *Extrapolation*, as well as in *Disability in Science Fiction: Representations of Technology as Cure*, edited by Kathryn Allan (2013). She also guest-edited a special issue of the *Journal of Literary and Cultural Disability Studies*, "Popular Genres and Disability Representation," published in 2012. She is currently completing a book on disability and affect in post-1970 genre fiction, examining representations of disability in science fiction, fantasy, horror, crime fiction, and romance.

G. THOMAS COUSER got his BA in English at Dartmouth College (1968) and his PhD in American Studies at Brown University (1977). He taught English and American Studies at Connecticut College in New London before moving on to Hofstra University on Long Island, where he taught American Literature and American Studies, and founded and directed the Disability Studies Program. He retired from Hofstra in 2011.

His books include *American Autobiography: The Prophetic Mode* (1979), *Altered Egos: Authority in American Autobiography* (1989), *Recovering Bodies: Illness, Disability, and Life Writing* (1997), *Vulnerable Subjects: Ethics and Life Writing* (2004), *Signifying Bodies: Disability in Contemporary Life Writing* (2009), and *Memoir: An Introduction* (2012).

In addition to over sixty articles and book chapters, he has published personal essays in the *Hudson Review*, the *New Haven Review*, and the *Southwest Review*. He recently completed a memoir of his father, *Letter to My Father: A Memoir*.

MICHAEL DAVIDSON is Distinguished Professor Emeritus of Literature at the University of California, San Diego. He is the author of *The San Francisco Renaissance: Poetics and Community at Mid-Century* (Cambridge University Press, 1989), *Ghostlier Demarcations: Modern Poetry and the Material Word* (1997), and *Guys Like Us: Citing Masculinity in Cold War Poetics* (2003). He has written extensively on disability issues, most recently *Concerto for the Left Hand: Disability and the Defamiliar Body* (2008). His most recent critical book, *On the Outskirts of Form: Practicing Cultural Poetics*, was published in 2011. He is currently completing *Invalid Modernism*, a book on interconnections between disability and modernist aesthetics.

JAY DOLMAGE is Associate Professor and Associate Chair of English at the University of Waterloo. He is the founding editor of the *Canadian Journal of Disability Studies* and is the author of *Disability Rhetoric* (2014), which won a PROSE Award from the Association of American Publishers in 2015. His essays on rhetoric, writing, and disability studies have appeared in edited collections and journals, including *Cultural Critique*, *Disability Studies Quarterly*, *Pedagogy*, and *Rhetoric Review*. He grew up in the disability rights movement in Canada and remains committed to promoting greater access within higher education and across society.

ALLISON P. HOBGOOD is Associate Professor of English and Women's and Gender Studies at Willamette University. She is the author of *Passionate Playgoing in Early Modern England* (Cambridge University Press, 2014) and has coedited with David Houston Wood two collections on early modern disability studies, *Recovering Disability in Early Modern England* (2013) and "Disabled Shakespeares" (in *Disability Studies Quarterly*, 2009). She recently edited a special issue on disability, care work, and teaching in the journal *Pedagogy* (2015). Her other work has appeared in journals from *Disability Studies Quarterly* to *Shakespeare Bulletin*, and in *Disability, Health, and Happiness in the Shakespearean Body* (2015) and *Shakespearean Sensations* (Cambridge University Press, 2014). Her new monograph project examines how impaired bodies and minds helped construct early modern cultural perceptions of what constituted humanness, and articulates how disability was a key shaping force in the Renaissance, from science to politics to art to religion.

MICHELLE JARMAN is Associate Professor of Disability Studies at the Wyoming Institute for Disabilities at the University of Wyoming, where she directs the undergraduate Minor in Disability Studies. Dr. Jarman received her PhD in English from the University of Illinois at Chicago. Her broad research interests focus upon intersecting literary and cultural representations of disability, gender, and ethnicity. She is coeditor of *Barriers and Belonging: Personal Narratives of Disability* (2017). Jarman's essays have appeared in journals such as the *Journal of Literary and Cultural Disability Studies*, *Disability Studies Quarterly*, *Feminist Formations*, and the *Journal of American Culture*, as well as in literary and disability studies anthologies.

ESSAKA JOSHUA is Associate Dean for Undergraduate Studies in the College of Arts and Letters at the University of Notre Dame, having been Senior Lecturer at the Department of English, University of Birmingham (UK). She is the author of *The Romantics and the May Day Tradition* (2007) and *Pygmalion and Galatea: The History of a Narrative in English Literature* (2001). Joshua has published widely on eighteenth- and nineteenth-century literature and on disability studies. In 2012, she was the winner of the Society for Disability Studies' Tyler Rigg Award for literature and literary analysis.

ALISON KAFER is Professor of Feminist Studies at Southwestern University, where she also teaches in the environmental studies and race and ethnicity studies programs. She is the author of *Feminist, Queer, Crip* (2013). Her work has also appeared in a number of journals and anthologies, including *Disability Studies Quarterly*, *Feminist Disability Studies*, the *Journal of Literary and Cultural Disability Studies*, and *Sex and Disability*.

EUNJUNG KIM is Assistant Professor in the Department of Women's and Gender Studies and the Disability Studies Program at Syracuse University. She is the author of *Curative Violence: Rehabilitating Disability, Gender, and Sexuality in Modern Korea* (2017). Her work has appeared in several journals and anthologies, such as *GLQ*, *Disability and Society*, *Sexualities*, *Intersectionality and Beyond*, *Against Health*, and *Asexualities*.

PETRA KUPPERS is Professor of English, Art and Design, Theatre and Drama, and Women's Studies at the University of Michigan. She has authored numerous academic publications with a disability focus, including *Studying Disability Arts and Culture: An Introduction* (2014), *Disability Culture and Community Performance: Find a Strange and Twisted Shape* (2011), *The Scar of Visibility: Medical Performance and Contemporary Art* (2007), and *Disability and Contemporary Performance: Bodies on Edge* (2003). She is the artistic director of The Olimpias, a disability arts collective, and is a poet and performance artist. Her collections include *Cripple Poetics: A Love Story* (with Neil Marcus, 2008) and, most recently, *Pearl Stitch* (2016).

ROBERT MCRUER is Professor of English at The George Washington University, where he teaches queer theory, disability studies, and twentieth- and twenty-first-century American studies. He is the author of *Crip Theory: Cultural Signs of Queerness and Disability* (2006), which was awarded the Alan Bray Memorial Book Award by the GL/Q Caucus of the Modern Language Association, and of *The Queer Renaissance: Contemporary American Literature and the Reinvention of Lesbian and Gay Identities* (1997). With Abby L. Wilkerson, he coedited "Desiring Disability: Queer Theory Meets Disability Studies," a special issue of the journal *GLQ: A Journal of Lesbian and Gay Studies* (2003); and with Anna Mollow, he coedited *Sex and Disability* (2012). Most recently, he coedited with Merri Lisa Johnson two special issues of the *Journal of Literary and Cultural Disability Studies* on "Cripistemologies" (2014). His forthcoming book is titled *Crip Times: Disability, Globalization, and Resistance.*

STUART MURRAY is Professor of Contemporary Literatures and Film in the School of English at the University of Leeds, where he is also Director of the University's Centre for Medical Humanities. He is the author of *Representing Autism: Culture, Narrative, Fascination* (2008) and *Autism* (2012), and has published articles on disability in modern and contemporary British, American, and postcolonial writing, as well as contemporary cinema. His latest work is on the intersection between disability and ideas of the posthuman, and his next book is *Disability and the Posthuman: Bodies, Minds, and Cultural Futures.*

SAMI SCHALK is Assistant Professor of Gender and Women's Studies at University of Wisconsin–Madison. Her research focuses on the representation of disability, race, and gender in contemporary American literature and culture, especially African American and women's literature. Her work has appeared in *Disability Studies Quarterly*, *Journal of Modern Literature*, *Journal of Literary and Cultural Disability Studies*, *Journal of Popular Culture*, and elsewhere. Her first book, *Bodyminds Reimagined: (Dis)ability, Race, and Gender in Black Women's Speculative Fiction*, is forthcoming in 2018.

MARTHA STODDARD HOLMES is Associate Dean of Humanities, Arts, Behavioral and Social Sciences at California State University, San Marcos, where she is also Professor of Literature and Writing Studies. Author of *Fictions of Affliction: Physical Disability in Victorian Culture* (2004), she has published extensively on the cultural history of the body from the Victorian era to the present, from representations of disability to the public culture of cancer. Her current projects include a graphic narrative of ovarian cancer.

EDWARD WHEATLEY is Professor of English at Loyola University, Chicago. His book, *Stumbling Blocks before the Blind: Medieval Constructions of a Disability* (2010), was published in the series *Corporealities: Discourses of Disability*. He has received fellowships from the National Endowment for the Humanities and the American Council of Learned Societies and was also an Andrew W. Mellon Faculty Fellow in the Humanities at Harvard University. His articles on disability in the literature and culture of the Middle Ages have appeared in such journals as *Exemplaria: A Journal of Theory in Medieval and Renaissance Studies*, *The Journal of the Warburg and Courtauld Institutes*, and *Comparative Drama*, and he has also published in and served on the editorial board of *Disability Studies Quarterly*.

DAVID HOUSTON WOOD serves as Distinguished Professor of English and Honors Program Director at Northern Michigan University. The author of *Time, Narrative, and Emotion in Early Modern England* (2009), and coeditor, with Allison P. Hobgood, of two essay collections – "Disabled Shakespeares" (*Disability Studies Quarterly*, 2009) and *Recovering Disability in Early Modern England* (2013) – he has also published widely in journals and collections such as *Disability Studies Quarterly*, *Shakespeare Yearbook*, *Renaissance Drama*, *Prose Studies*, and *Interfaces*, with work on early modern disability forthcoming in *Companion to Renaissance Drama* (2nd edn.).

ACKNOWLEDGMENTS

There is a human story behind how every book comes into being, and this one more than most has been touched by illness, disability, and major life events. During the course of creating this book, the editors have experienced disability personally or cared for disabled family members, and have gone through the illness and loss of Clare's partner Anthony at the age of thirty-five. Given these experiences, this book feels more important than ever to us: it is important to properly think through the place of disability in the world around us, in our own lives, and in the books we read. It is important to find ways of bringing disability as often as possible into our classrooms, our students' consciousness, and our critical vocabularies. We hope this Companion helps to enable these conversations.

Clare would like to thank the Barker and Carrigan families for providing childcare that allowed me peace and space to write during a very difficult time. And thank you to Anthony who always inspired me in my work and pushed me to make it as good as it could be; he talked this book over with me many times with his typical energy and enthusiasm, and I hope he would be proud of how it has turned out. Stuart would like to thank everyone who helped facilitate his son's move to assisted independent living. Our biggest thanks goes to our wonderful team of contributors, for their great collective wisdom and insight about disability and representation but also for their kindness, support, patience, and compassion as the editing process met with delays and was put on hold altogether for a period. Thank you to everyone involved in this book's production for working on it with so much care.

CHRONOLOGY OF LITERARY AND CULTURAL DISABILITY STUDIES

This chronology sets out the major milestones in the establishment of literary and cultural disability studies as an academic field. It charts how the field has come into being, developed, and diversified over time, as well as listing book-length publications and journal special issues on literary, cultural, and critical approaches to disability. We do not include literary texts with a significant disability theme since, as the essays in this volume attest, disability is everywhere in literature.

Year	Events	Major Publications
1963		Erving Goffman, *Stigma: Notes on the Management of Spoiled Identity*.
1971		Peter L. Hayes, *The Limping Hero: Grotesques in Literature*. An early precursor to disability studies criticism.
1975	In the UK, the Union of the Physically Impaired Against Segregation published its *Fundamental Principles of Disability*, a document that distinguishes between "impairment" and "disability," asserting that it is society that disables people with impairments. These ideas came to be known as the social model of disability, and remain at the foundation of disability studies research and activism.	
1978		Susan Sontag, *Illness as Metaphor*. An influential work of cultural criticism that anticipates literary disability studies' interest in unpacking disability metaphors.

1980 First issue of *The Disability Newsletter*, which was to become, in 1985, *Disability Studies Quarterly* (*DSQ*). This interdisciplinary journal was the first in the field of disability studies, and is an open access publication available at www.dsq-sds.org.

1986 The Section for the Study of Chronic Illness, Impairment, and Disability (SSCIID) of the Social Science Association was renamed the Society for Disability Studies (SDS), a US-based interdisciplinary scholarly organization. *DSQ* is the official journal of the SDS.

1987 Alan Gartner and Tom Joe (eds.), *Images of the Disabled, Disabling Images*. An early text analyzing disability stereotypes and stock characters, which anticipates some of the concerns of literary and cultural disability studies;

William Paulson, *Enlightenment, Romanticism and the Blind in France*.

1988 Michelle Fine and Adrienne Asch (eds.), *Women with Disabilities: Essays in Psychology, Culture, and Politics*;

Arthur Kleinman, *The Illness Narratives: Suffering, Healing, and the Human Condition*.

1990 Americans with Disabilities Act (US). Foundational legislation enforcing standards of accessibility and reasonable accommodation in public services and employment, and prohibiting discrimination on the basis of disability. The ADA brought disability in line with other civil rights legislation in the United States.

Opening of the Disability Research Unit at the University of Leeds (UK), a major research center for disability research and teaching in the social sciences. This became the interdisciplinary Centre for Disability Studies in 2000, home to the Disability Archive UK (http://disability-studies.leeds.ac.uk/library/), and continues to do important work in promoting the social model of disability.

1991		Jenny Morris, *Pride Against Prejudice: A Personal Politics of Disability.*
1994	The first disability studies program in the US launches at Syracuse University.	
1995	Disability Discrimination Act (UK). The UK's foundational disability rights legislation, requiring reasonable adjustments to be made for disabled people in education, employment, public services, and transport. Since replaced by the 2010 Equality Act.	Lennard J. Davis, *Enforcing Normalcy: Disability, Deafness, and the Body.* One of the founding texts that marked the emergence of literary and cultural disability studies. Theorizing and interrogating normalcy remains a primary concern within the field. Arthur Frank, *The Wounded Storyteller: Body, Illness, and Ethics*; Athena Vrettos, *Somatic Fictions: Imagining Illness in Victorian Culture.*
1996		Rosemarie Garland-Thomson (ed.), *Freakery: Cultural Spectacles of the Extraordinary Body*; Susan Wendell, *The Rejected Body: Feminist Philosophical Reflections on Disability.*
1997		G. Thomas Couser, *Recovering Bodies: Illness, Disability, and Life Writing*; Lennard J. Davis (ed.), *The Disability Studies Reader* (1st edn.), a cornerstone text in humanities-based disability studies that has subsequently gone through four further editions (2006, 2010, 2013, and 2017); Rosemarie Garland-Thomson, *Extraordinary Bodies: Figuring Physical Disability in American Culture and Literature.* Another highly influential text that established the idea of the "normate"; David T. Mitchell and Sharon L. Snyder (eds.), *The Body and Physical Difference: Discourses of Disability.*
1999		Eli Clare, *Exile and Pride: Disability, Queerness, and Liberation*; Mairian Corker and Sally French (eds.), *Disability Discourse.*
2000	Launch of the University of Michigan Press's *Corporealities: Discourses of Disability* book series, which is dedicated to cultural and representational approaches to disability.	Helen Deutsch and Felicity Nussbaum (eds.), *Defects: Engendering the Modern Body*; David T. Mitchell and Sharon L. Snyder, *Narrative Prosthesis: Disability and the Dependencies of Discourse.*

"Narrative prosthesis" has become one of the key ideas within literary disability studies;

Henri-Jacques Stiker, *A History of Disability*;

Allen Thiher, *Revels in Madness: Insanity in Medicine and Literature*.

2001 Special issue of *European Romantic Review* on "Byron and Disability." This is the first disability-oriented special issue of a journal focused on a single author.

2002 Mairian Corker and Tom Shakespeare (eds.), *Disability/Postmodernity: Embodying Disability Theory*;

Lennard J. Davis, *Bending over Backwards: Disability, Dismodernism, and Other Difficult Positions*;

Sharon L. Snyder, Brenda Jo Brueggemann, and Rosemarie Garland-Thomson (eds.), *Disability Studies: Enabling the Humanities*.

2003 Petra Kuppers, *Disability and Contemporary Performance: Bodies on Edge*;

Felicity Nussbaum, *The Limits of the Human: Fictions of Anomaly, Race, and Gender in the Long Eighteenth Century*;

Martha L. Rose, *The Staff of Oedipus: Transforming Disability in Ancient Greece*;

Paul Youngquist, *Monstrosities: Bodies and British Romanticism*;

special issue of *GLQ: A Journal of Lesbian and Gay Studies* on "Desiring Disability: Queer Theory Meets Disability Studies."

2004 Lois Bragg, *Oedipus Borealis: The Aberrant Body in Old Icelandic Myth and Saga*;

G. Thomas Couser, *Vulnerable Subjects: Ethics and Life Writing*;

Maria Frawley, *Invalidism and Identity in Nineteenth-Century Britain*;

Martha Stoddard Holmes, *Fictions of Affliction: Physical Disability in Victorian Culture*;

		Bonnie G. Smith and Beth Hutchinson (eds.), *Gendering Disability*.
2005	The Modern Language Association designates disability studies a division of study.	Carrie Sandahl and Philip Auslander (eds.), *Bodies in Commotion: Disability and Performance*.
2006		Gary L. Albrecht (ed.), *Encyclopedia of Disability* (5 vols.);
		Robert McRuer, *Crip Theory: Cultural Signs of Queerness and Disability*;
		Irina Metzler, *Disability in Medieval Europe: Thinking about Physical Impairment during the High Middle Ages*;
		Tom Shakespeare, *Disability Rights and Wrongs*;
		Sharon L. Snyder and David T. Mitchell, *Cultural Locations of Disability*;
		David M. Turner and Kevin Stagg (eds.), *Social Histories of Disability, and Deformity*;
		special issue of *MELUS: Multi-Ethnic Literature of the United States* on "Race, Ethnicity, Disability, and Literature."
2007	Launch of the *Journal of Literary and Cultural Disability Studies* (initially called the *Journal of Literary Disability*), edited by David Bolt. Published in the UK by Liverpool University Press, this is the first journal devoted to humanities-based disability research, and runs special issues focusing on a wide range of disability topics in literature, culture, and critical theory. See http://online.liverpooluniversitypress.co.uk/loi/jlcds for a full list of issues.	Ato Quayson, *Aesthetic Nervousness: Disability and the Crisis of Representation*; special issue of *Wagadu: A Journal of Transnational Women's and Gender Studies* on "Intersecting Gender and Disability Perspectives in Rethinking Postcolonial Identities."
2008	Launch of Liverpool University Press's *Representations: Health, Disability, Culture, and Society* book series.	Michael Davidson, *Concerto for the Left Hand: Disability and the Defamiliar Body*;
	The Society for Disability Studies' Tyler Rigg Prize is established, for outstanding disability studies scholarship in literature and literary analysis.	Patrick McDonagh, *Idiocy: A Cultural History*; Stuart Murray, *Representing Autism: Culture, Narrative, Fascination*;

Mark Osteen (ed.), *Autism and Representation*;

Tobin Siebers, *Disability Theory*;

Marlene Tromp (ed.), *Victorian "Freaks": The Social Context of Freakery in the Nineteenth Century*;

special issue of *Nineteenth-Century Gender Studies* on "Critical Transformations: Disability and the Body in Nineteenth-Century Britain."

2009

Susan Antebi, *Carnal Inscriptions: Spanish American Narratives of Corporeal Difference and Disability*;

Fiona Kumari Campbell, *Contours of Ableism: The Production of Disability and Abledness*;

G. Thomas Couser, *Signifying Bodies: Disability in Contemporary Life Writing*;

Lennard J. Davis, *Obsession: A History*;

Rosemarie Garland-Thomson, *Staring: How We Look*;

Mark Mossman, *Disability, Representation and the Body in Irish Writing: 1800–1922*;

Susan M. Schweik, *The Ugly Laws: Disability in Public*;

special issue of *Victorian Review* on "Victorian Disability";

special issue of *Disability Studies Quarterly* on "Disabled Shakespeares."

2010

Joshua Eyler (ed.), *Disability in the Middle Ages: Reconsiderations and Reverberations*;

Tory Vandeventer Pearman, *Women and Disability in Medieval Literature*;

Tobin Siebers, *Disability Aesthetics*;

Jeannette Stirling, *Representing Epilepsy: Myth and Matter*;

Wendy J. Turner and Tory Vandeventer Pearman (eds.), *The Treatment of Disabled Persons in Medieval Europe: Examining Disability in the Historical, Legal, Literary, Medical, and Religious Discourses of the Middle Ages*;

		Edward Wheatley, *Stumbling Blocks before the Blind: Medieval Constructions of a Disability.*
2011		Gary L. Albrecht, Katherine D. Seelman, and Michael Bury (eds.), *Handbook of Disability Studies*; Clare Barker, *Postcolonial Fiction and Disability: Exceptional Children, Metaphor, and Materiality*; Chris Bell (ed.), *Blackness and Disability: Critical Examinations and Cultural Interventions*; Nirmala Erevelles, *Disability and Difference in Global Contexts*; Dan Goodley, *Disability Studies: An Interdisciplinary Introduction*; Kim Q. Hall (ed.), *Feminist Disability Studies*; Margaret Price, *Mad at School: Rhetorics of Mental Disability and Academic Life*; special issue of *Disability Studies Quarterly* on "Disability and Rhetoric."
2012	Publication of the first issue of the *Canadian Journal of Disability Studies.*	David Bolt, Julia Miele Rodas, and Elizabeth Donaldson (eds.), *The Madwoman and the Blindman:* Jane Eyre, *Discourse, Disability* – the first literary disability studies book devoted to a single text; Mel Y. Chen, *Animacies: Biopolitics, Racial Mattering, and Queer Affect*; Alice Hall, *Disability and Modern Fiction: Faulkner, Morrison, Coetzee and the Nobel Prize for Literature*; Robert McRuer and Anna Mollow (eds.), *Sex and Disability*; Kristina Richardson, *Difference and Disability in the Medieval Islamic World: Blighted Bodies*; David M. Turner, *Disability in Eighteenth-Century England: Imagining Physical Impairment.*
2013		Kathryn Allen (ed.), *Disability in Science Fiction: Representations of Technology as Cure*;

		David Bolt, *The Metanarrative of Blindness: A Re-Reading of Twentieth-Century Anglophone Writing*; Lennard J. Davis, *The End of Normal: Identity in a Biocultural Era*; Jennifer Esmail, *Reading Victorian Deafness: Signs and Sounds in Victorian Literature and Culture*; Allison P. Hobgood and David Houston Wood (eds.), *Recovering Disability in Early Modern England*; Alison Kafer, *Feminist, Queer, Crip*; China Mills, *Decolonizing Global Mental Health: The Psychiatrization of the Majority World*; Susannah B. Mintz, *Hurt and Pain: Literature and the Suffering Body*; Sarah Jaquette Ray, *The Ecological Other: Environmental Exclusion in American Culture*; Tom Shakespeare, *Disability Rights and Wrongs Revisited.*
2014	Launch of Palgrave Macmillan's *Literary Disability Studies* book series.	Jay Dolmage, *Disability Rhetoric*; Petra Kuppers, *Studying Disability Arts and Culture: An Introduction*; Rebecca Mallett and Katherine Runswick-Cole, *Approaching Disability: Critical Issues and Perspectives*; Chris Mounsey (ed.), *The Idea of Disability in the Eighteenth Century*; Ellen Samuels, *Fantasies of Identification: Disability, Gender, Race.*
2015	The Tobin Siebers Prize for Disability Studies in the Humanities is established by the University of Michigan Press and University of Michigan Department for English Language and Literature. This prize, honoring the late Tobin Siebers's contribution to disability studies, is awarded for the best book-length manuscript on a humanities-focused disability topic.	Karen Bourrier, *The Measure of Manliness: Disability and Masculinity in the Mid-Victorian Novel*; Sujata Iyengar (ed.), *Disability, Health, and Happiness in the Shakespearean Body*; Irina Metzler, *A Social History of Disability in the Middle Ages: Cultural Considerations of Physical Impairment*; Julie Avril Minich, *Accessible Citizenships: Disability, Nation, and the Cultural Politics of Greater Mexico*;

	David T. Mitchell with Sharon L. Snyder, *The Biopolitics of Disability: Neoliberalism, Ablenationalism, and Peripheral Embodiment*;
	Rebecca Sanchez, *Deafening Modernism: Embodied Language and Visual Poetics in American Literature*.
2016	David Bolt and Claire Penketh (eds.), *Disability, Avoidance and the Academy: Challenging Resistance*;
	Michael Bradshaw (ed.), *Disabling Romanticism: Body, Mind, and Text*;
	Alice Hall, *Literature and Disability*;
	Kirsty Johnston, *Disability Theatre and Modern Drama: Recasting Modernism*;
	Irina Metzler, *Fools and Idiots? Intellectual Disability in the Middle Ages*.
2017	Michelle Jarman, Leila Monaghan, and Alison Quaggin Harkin (eds.), *Barriers and Belonging: Personal Narratives of Disability*;
	Eunjung Kim, *Curative Violence: Rehabilitating Disability, Gender, and Sexuality in Modern Korea*.

I

CLARE BARKER AND STUART MURRAY

Introduction

On Reading Disability in Literature

Disability is everywhere in literature. Whether in the bodies that populate countless narratives containing physical disability, or in the mental difference that informs so much detail about character and psychology, disability features in literary production as a constant presence. And it does so across all time periods, from the earliest expressions of European poetry to the contemporary global novel, and all points in between. In the seventy-first verse of "Hávamál" or "Sayings of the High One," part of the *Poetic Edda*, a collection of Old Norse mythological and heroic poems written in the thirteenth century, the speaker notes that

> The lame can ride horses, the handless drive herds;
> the deaf can fight and do well;
> better blind than to be burnt;
> no one has use for a corpse[1]

Like most literary descriptions of disability, that in the *Poetic Edda* is accompanied by a value judgment. The "sayings" of "Hávamál" run to around 165 stanzas (depending on the edition consulted) and are attributed to the Norse god Odin. They comprise a guide to wisdom and proper living, with the first seventy-nine verses focused in particular on how an individual should conduct themselves when a traveler or a guest. Here, then, the positive attributes recognized in those with disabilities take the form of an instruction to consider the full value of living and the appropriate relationship between a visitor and a host. Disability, it is implied here, can illuminate the truths of human complexities because of the manner in which its difference revises expectations of behavior.

Disability is not a running theme in "Hávamál," and the verses before and after the one cited here do not mention it. It is an unexpected topic in the context of the poem, and unusual in its positive assessment of how disability functions. It is typical of much disability representation, however, in that it connects the fact of disability to an extension of how that fact might be read: it is rare to encounter an account of, say, a physically different body that does not extend to a comment on what that body does or, crucially, *means*. In this book, we will see that such judgments proliferate across many kinds of writing, from ideas of medieval monsters or the sentimental figures of the realist nineteenth-century novel to modernist fixations with eugenics and contemporary patterns of racialization or obsessions with mental health. In each, disability is figured in complex contexts: it taps into ideas about what it means to be "human"; arouses notions of "deviance" or, conversely, being "special"; provides an example that shocks, creates fear, or invites pity; or functions as the subject of spiritual or philosophical contemplation. It appears that we rarely represent disability without making automatic connections to the various stories we feel it might, as the consequence of its very existence, tell.

But if it is true that disability pervades literature across the ages, it is also true that it is frequently not seen. That this is the case is, as the above examples of context suggest, less to do with the texts themselves than the reading practices that have been brought to them. Precisely because disability appears to signal the possibility of so many connections to other topics, it can easily be lost or subsumed in what are presumed to be more "important" (and nearly always nondisabled) questions. To take what is probably the most famous example of such transfiguration, when in his opening soliloquy, Richard – in William Shakespeare's *Richard III* (c. 1592) – tells us that he is "not shaped for sportive tricks," but rather is "rudely stamped" and "Deformed, unfinished, sent before my time / Into this breathing world scarce half made up," he does so to explain why he is, as a consequence, "determinèd to prove a villain / And hate the idle pleasure of these days."[2] Richard's villainy and hatred are, in his own words, directly connected to his physical disabilities, but in a manner such that the *actual* disabilities seem clearly less important than the function they serve to underscore: here, the fact that he will be, as he puts it, "subtle, false and treacherous" throughout the rest of the play.[3] In the end, it is treachery, rather than disability, that Richard's "deformed" body ultimately signifies.

There are numerous other examples from the literary canon that follow a similar logic: in Herman Melville's *Moby-Dick* (1851), Ahab's missing leg clearly signals ideas of his obsession and maniacal behavior; Rochester's blindness, in Charlotte Brontë's *Jane Eyre* (1847), allows that novel to explore questions of romance and care; Lenny, in John Steinbeck's *Of Mice and Men* (1937), conveys the text's reflections on innocence through the representation of his assumed "simplicity." In these and many other examples, disability is made to work primarily as a metaphor, a textual device that, precisely because of the ways in which it reconfigures what disability means, ultimately has little to say about the actual lives experienced by those with disabilities.

In part, it was the need to unpack the complexities of these metaphors, and the prejudices of the representations that often accompanied them, that led to the rise of literary disability studies as a critical discipline in the 1990s. Within sociology, disability studies had already become an established subject area, with scholars and activists involved in the push for independent living from the 1970s onwards.[4] While sociological disability studies sought to uncover the social and institutional prejudices that created environments that disempowered and discriminated against people with disabilities, the subject's literary and cultural critiques drew from these social model methodologies and worked in the wake of the waves of feminist, queer, postcolonial, and critical race studies scholarship that had produced oppositional and revisionist reading strategies, offering up new accounts of canonical texts and bringing new critical paradigms through which to consider disability representation.

In the mid-1990s, Lennard J. Davis's *Enforcing Normalcy* (1995) and Rosemarie Garland-Thomson's *Extraordinary Bodies* (1997) were both foundational texts in the development of the new subject area. Each brought analytical tools from literary studies and critical and cultural theory to bear on disability representation, and each established core critical terms that helped shape the development of the discipline. Both Davis and Garland-Thomson focused on the power of the idea of the normal – "normalcy" in Davis, "the normate" in Garland-Thomson – in definitions of disability. If disability was judged to be a state of negative difference, then the normal was the central mode from which it deviated. As both showed, normalcy and the normate are ideological and bureaucratic constructions, defining a subject position that might appear to be straightforward and understood by all, but in fact is a fabricated state that disavows difference. As Davis asserted, "[t]o understand the disabled body, one must return to the concept of the norm, the normal body."[5] And it is the *idea* of the normal body, developed through methods of measurement, testing, and their bureaucratization, that – for Davis – sets up the implication that "the majority of the population must or should somehow be part of the norm." In turn, "with the concept of the norm comes the concept of deviations or extremes," and as a consequence, "when we think of bodies, in a society where the concept of the norm is operative, then people with disabilities will be thought of as deviants."[6] In a memorable phrase, Davis then concluded that "the 'problem' is not the person with disabilities: the problem is the way that normalcy is constructed to create the 'problem' of the disabled person."[7]

Garland-Thomson, outlining her concept of the normate, noted that something that seems as if it should be everywhere – the normal – is in fact almost impossible to find. The normate is, she observes, "the constructed identity of those who, by way of the bodily configurations and cultural capital they assume, can step into a position of authority and wield the power it grants them." But, she goes on, if any attempt is made to actually define what this position or identity is, "what emerges is a very narrowly defined profile that describes only a minority of actual people."[8] The normal is, then, a set of rules that is always disappearing over the horizon, an illusion masquerading as fact. As a result, Garland-Thomson notes, disability is "not so much a property of bodies as a product of cultural rules about what bodies should be or do."[9]

Many of the metaphors that accompanied literary representations of characters with disabilities were, this new scholarship made clear, invested in these ideas of rules or of a deviation from the norm. Every character in popular fiction who was understood to be criminal because of, say, a facial disfigurement, or heroic because they challenged the perceived limitations that come with living "confined to" a wheelchair, could now be seen to be the products of ableist cultural assumptions about what kind of body or mind was normal and what were seen to be the terms of any difference from such norms. These new critical approaches made it clear that, in such thinking, disability is figured as deficit, defined by what it is *not*, rather than understood as its own mode of being.

Ableism thus took its place alongside patriarchy, sexism, racism, homophobia, and colonialism; and literary/cultural disability studies formed part of the ongoing critical description, and deconstruction, of these power systems and the ways in which they produced cultural narratives that wrote disability. In 2000, David Mitchell and Sharon Snyder's book *Narrative Prosthesis: Disability and the Dependencies of Discourse* unpacked how such ableist assumptions operated in the specific arena of narrative. Their key term "narrative prosthesis" highlighted how texts use and rely on disability to make narrative work. The phrase, they wrote, "is meant to indicate that disability has been used throughout history as a crutch upon which literary narratives lean for their representational power, disruptive potentiality, and analytical insight." Such a process was, Mitchell and Snyder asserted, a "perpetual discursive dependency," and they noted that "disability pervades literary narrative, first as a stock feature of characterization and, second, as an opportunistic metaphorical device."[10] Here, then, was disability representation seen through a specific critical disability logic. Mitchell and Snyder know full well that their own use of the idea of narrative relying on disability as a "crutch" is exactly the kind of metaphorical usage to which their work draws attention. But this self-awareness, coming from within a disability studies perspective, redefines the critical parameters through which literature is read. Thinking in the terms of Lennard Davis or Rosemarie Garland-Thomson, it offers a revised idea of the critical "normal."

Since the publication of these seminal books, in which a politicized engagement with disability representation forces revisions of even the most foundational critical practices, we have seen a huge amount of growth in the field of literary and cultural disability studies. Both Tobin Siebers, in *Disability Aesthetics* (2010), and Ato Quayson, in *Aesthetic Nervousness: Disability and the Crisis of Representation* (2007), point to disability's pivotal role in complicating and enriching notions of the aesthetic because of the difference disabled bodies and minds bring to the processes of representation. Quayson, for instance, observes a kind of dissonance or "nervousness" at the level of form itself when disability enters a narrative: working as part of a text's structural and symbolic apparatus, with specific narrative functions, disability also accesses the "active ethical core" of a text since it can have "a direct effect on social views of people with disability in a way that representations of other literary details, tropes, and motifs do not offer."[11] The relationship between the aesthetic, the political, and the ethical implications of disability representation is an ongoing concern within literary and cultural disability studies, but such work on aesthetics and narrative theory has pushed the field beyond making distinctions between "positive" and "negative" representations toward a better understanding of the complex nature of many disability narratives. And as several chapters in this book show, a focus on disability can also help us to understand how the process of writing, reading, or performing a work of literature (or indeed a work of criticism) is an embodied one, encountered differently according to variances in attention, energy, and technologies of reading, speaking, and writing. As disability critics have helped show, narrative structure and style may be shaped directly by disabled embodiment – whether that be a stammer, a cognitive difference, or the discrete grammars and conventions of sign languages or digital assistive devices. Thinking about "disability aesthetics"[12] can fundamentally change our understandings of literature: what a story looks like; how a poem should sound; what we consider to be beautiful.

In other ways, too, literary and cultural disability studies is rethinking and nuancing the premises and norms of disability studies scholarship. At the heart of sociological disability studies is the social model of disability, the assertion that disability is not a feature of "dysfunctional" bodies and minds, but instead is created by the inaccessible architectural and social infrastructures that typify contemporary living environments.[13] The social model still remains the single most influential idea within disability studies and activism – a highly effective political tool that has underpinned productive change in legislation, education, and social understandings of disability across many countries and regions of the world. But literary and cultural scholars have sought to flesh out this actually very simple premise to theorize in more depth the relationships between impaired bodies and their social worlds: a common concern with the social model is that, by shifting the focus from biomedical understandings of disability toward a social construction approach, it leaves little room for thinking about the body itself. In *Disability Theory* (2008), Siebers puts forward the notion of "complex embodiment," showing how "the body and its representations [are] mutually transformative,"[14] while in a similar vein Snyder and Mitchell offer their "cultural model of disability" in *Cultural Locations of Disability* (2006), emphasizing the "potentially meaningful materiality" of disabled embodiment, which can be "a source of embodied revelation," providing unique insights into cultural formations and social experiences.[15] Current discourse around "disability gain" – the recognition of the many ways in which disability can enrich human experience – is an extension of this kind of thinking.[16] These approaches follow a general movement, led by the humanities, toward acknowledging the exclusions of the politically focused "no pity" stance of the early disability rights movement. Literary and cultural scholarship is keen to recognize and validate the embodied and emotional aspects – the *human* aspects, whether painful, pleasurable, distressing, or celebratory – of disability experience.[17] More recently still, Merri Lisa Johnson and Robert McRuer's playful neologism "cripistemologies" seeks to unsettle (in a spirit of "collaboration and conviviality") "what we think we know about disability, and how we know around and through it," continually interrogating ideas that are in danger of becoming all-too-comfortable commonplaces in the field.[18] Although these approaches come from diverse disciplinary backgrounds, the insights they provide have proved hugely enabling in the development of an ongoing critical sophistication in the way disability in literature is read and understood.

Literary disability studies is rapidly diversifying in terms of its reach across literatures, embodied conditions, and interdisciplinary engagements. Since 2007, the *Journal of Literary and Cultural Disability Studies*, edited by David Bolt, has provided a dedicated platform for publishing new work in the field and has contributed greatly to this transformation, helping to establish a critical mass of literary disability scholarship and consolidate a transatlantic community of researchers and students. From the revisionary focus on a handful of canonical American and European writers and texts that marked the 1990s, along with work that looked for disability in perhaps the more obvious historical and literary settings such as the hospital and the freak show, there now exists a burgeoning corpus of studies – reflected in this Companion – exploring disability representations in depth across a range of national and cultural literatures, periods, and genres. Increasing numbers of books are being published on how disability operates in narrative, not only in general theoretical terms (as with narrative prosthesis or aesthetic nervousness), but how it functions specifically in, say, the romance novel, autism narratives, or in television comedy writing; and in indigenous literatures, medieval English religious texts, or twentieth-century Irish writing. All of these more focused studies provide new insights into their particular literary field, while also helping to increase understanding of disability's relationships to particular historical and cultural contexts; to generic experimentation, audiences, and trends within the literary marketplace; and to medical advances, health policy, and political/economic imperatives in their given contexts.

In turn, thinking about disability and literature has broadened to not only consider a far wider spectrum of what might be considered "disability" itself (where early criticism focused heavily on the body, contemporary criticism considers mental health, as well as other cognitive and intellectual states, for example), but also to situate disability within new networks and intersections. As Alison Kafer and Eunjung Kim show in their essay in this volume, intersectionality has emerged as a theoretical term in its own right within disability studies, and intersectional approaches to disability representation demonstrate that disability can never be extricated from questions surrounding race, sexuality, gender, or class. It is important here to stress that this is not a process of simply lining up what might be perceived of as minority identity positions to find common cause, but rather it is a critical process that examines the subtleties of the ways in which disability is "fully enmeshed" (to use Kafer and Kim's term) in the multiple experiences and manifestations of accompanying subject positions. Disability narratives never stand alone, but interweave around and through other codes and contexts for writing. So, for example, it is impossible to read the multiple disabled characters in Truman Capote's fiction without also considering their queerness; or to read the powerful representation of physical difference in a novel such as Toni Morrison's *Beloved* (1987) and not understand it as a process inherently connected to the text's depiction of race. Intersectional criticism not only highlights such connections; by doing so it continues the process by which disability in literature is brought in from the critical margins and shows the ways in which disability representation is central to many of the core concerns of writing.

Some of the most exciting developments in contemporary disability theory and criticism come from intersectional and interdisciplinary engagements. Garland-Thomson's work following *Extraordinary Bodies* focused increasingly on the commonality between disability and visual modes of representation, and her 2010 book, *Staring: How We Look*, theorizes a common disability experience – being stared at – with ideas taken from multiple critical disciplines across both the arts and sciences.[19] Robert McRuer's *Crip Theory: Cultural Signs of Queerness and Disability* (2006) and Alison Kafer's *Feminist, Queer, Crip* (2013) each develop the link between disability and queer experiences and identities through a process of "cripping," an intersectional critique that opens writing up to new points of critical interpretation.[20] We are also beginning to see important new engagements between disability studies and ecocriticism, animal studies, and the environmental humanities, connections that have brought topics such as toxicity and environmentally produced diseases (and the novels, memoirs, poems, and plays about them) under the purview of disability scholarship. Straddling all of these areas (queer, disability, and environmental studies), we find startling insights, such as Mel Y. Chen's work on "animacies," regarding how life itself – in all its manifestations – is constructed in multiple oppressive discourses.[21]

Thinking across the intersections between disability and postcolonial studies has drawn attention to "western" biases and assumptions that pertain even in politically engaged disability scholarship, as well as enabling better understandings of how colonial histories and globalization have shaped disability experiences around the world. From a different perspective, Jasbir Puar's work on "debility" highlights how the supposed singularity of "disability" as a minority identity position, and the "civil rights" focus of disability politics, do not adequately capture the precarious nature of existence for the vast majority of disabled global citizens, and proposes alternative frameworks for understanding corporeal vulnerability in conditions of poverty or precarity.[22] Related to this, one of the most pressing concerns for disability scholars in the aftermath of the 2008 global financial crisis is how austerity regimes and budget cuts to crucial health and welfare services are affecting disabled people. This has led to increased critical scrutiny, with a disability slant to it, of capitalism and neoliberal economics; of work, labor conditions, and the concept of "productivity"; of diversity initiatives, inclusion agendas, and changing understandings of citizenship; and of how academia, the university, and the production of academic writing itself (for academics and students alike) fit into these paradigms.[23] These kinds of contemporary cultural studies are often methodologically hybrid in nature, combining literary analysis with critical theory, qualitative research, and cultural commentary. As these examples show, literary disability studies has established a place at the heart of contemporary critical thinking and the forefront of intellectual activity that seeks to reach across disciplinary boundaries. The difference of disability, frequently so derided, has emerged as a wonderful prompt to create fresh approaches in both literature and the criticism that seeks to map its meanings.

The essays in this Companion work in the wake of all this revisionary research. They explore the proliferation and meaning of disability representation across literatures and time periods, and they do so through what Michael Davidson has usefully called a "disability optic." Such an optic, in Davidson's words, shows how "considerations of disability deconstruct or 'crip' discourses of compulsory able-bodiedness that underwrite epistemological claims." He goes on: "What would it mean for the humanities to think through the body and reimagine curricula not around 'the history of ideas' but through an armless Venus de Milo, a crippled Oedipus, or a madwoman in the attic?"[24] This book is committed to such thinking and reimagining, and to recognizing that, as Alice Hall notes, "disability has the potential to be a transformative critical category for the humanities."[25] The contents that follow are full of examples of how literature and culture look when we use the kind of lens Davidson suggests to trace the transformations Hall predicts.

We have deliberately structured this Companion to provide a wide range of critical perspectives on the ways in which literary representations of disability function, in part to do justice to the many kinds of critical positions just mentioned, but also to ensure that the contents are as useful to the reader as is possible. In line with Davidson, we want this Companion to assist in reimagining curricula, in this case English literature programs, where disability is often still "avoided" despite the subject's now well-established engagement with other "minority" literatures,[26] or tends to sit on the margins of mainstream literary studies as a minor or final year option module. With this in mind, the essays in the first half of the book cover the major periods and subject areas of writing in English – those that usually make up core courses on undergraduate degree programs.[27] They provide a resource for including a consideration of disability in these key curricular areas, aiming to ground the reader in the ways in which disability representation has worked in specific temporal moments and geocultural locations. It is always vital to see disability in the context of the time in which it is being lived, and indeed the very idea of what the word "disability"' means in the medieval period or the eighteenth century differs – often profoundly – from, say, that found in modern or contemporary writing. Similarly, disability in postcolonial literatures takes very different forms from depictions found in European or American texts. In each essay in the first half of this volume, the author outlines arguments about what disability is made to mean in the particular moment of the writing in question. In order to do this, the critical arguments in these essays range across texts that exemplify the cultural perceptions and literary formations of the time. They seek to show that disability representation can be a focus of, or a useful and fascinating lens onto, any major period or area of literary study, and that for those inclined to do so, the critical strategies exemplified in these essays can be brought to bear on any kind of literature being studied or researched.

The material in the second half of the book organizes its investigations not through time and period, but rather takes approaches suggested by the core *critical* ideas that currently animate literary disability studies. So, the essays here respond to the particular directions and parameters of contemporary disability representation. G. Thomas Couser's chapter on disability life writing, for example, recognizes that autobiography has been a major vehicle for the expression of disability identities since the popular emergence of life writing as a significant commercial publishing category in the 1990s. Equally, disabled bodies and minds are common in genre literature, from science fiction to romance, and Ria Cheyne's essay captures how we, as readers, might understand such representations. The focus on race, queer cultural production, intersectionality, women's writing, and rhetoric in this half of the Companion marks similar crucial moments where thinking critically about disability in literature intersects with other theoretical and activist categories that have been seminal in exploring how identities and aesthetics interact in writing.

But the essays in the volume also take a critical stance on the very construction of the idea of disability itself. Even the briefest of contemplations makes it clear that the single word and concept – disability – cannot hope to be an effective term to convey the vast multiplicity of subject positions and experiences that make up the lives of those with disabilities. For Ellen Samuels, the idea that such a label might be able to undertake such work is a "fantasy." She observes: "The overmastering fantasy of disability identification is that disability is a knowable, obvious, and unchanging category. Such a fantasy permeates all levels of discourse regarding disabled bodies and minds, even as it is repeatedly and routinely disproved by the actual realities of those bodies' and minds' fluctuating abilities."[28] Literature is singularly well placed to explore the complexities of such identification; the plasticity of the ways in which literary texts make meaning – the combination of (among others) formal aesthetics, characterization, generic affiliation, and narrative playfulness – creates rich webs of content that allow for a thorough exploration of the "actual realities" of which Samuels writes.

Further, as Snyder and Mitchell point out, in contrast with the "people-based" methodologies of much contemporary disability research, the *textual* study of disability has the advantage of not making demands on the "time, liberty, and energies" of disabled people themselves – who have, after all, been continually subjected to medical scrutiny, social surveillance, and time-consuming research studies.[29] Since texts "inevitably filter disability through the reigning ideologies of their day," they "supply windows onto social contexts (including present ones) for our scrutiny."[30] This does not mean, of course, that literature gives direct, unmediated representations of social realities. But neither is it at a remove from "reality" due to its craftedness and origins in the imagination: as this brief overview of disability criticism has shown, it is precisely *through* its creative and aesthetic practices that literature can get us to the heart of beliefs and activities surrounding the human body and mind. As the contents of this book show, literary representations of disability, whether realist or non-realist, social/political or fantastical, open up our understanding of the multiplicities inherent within disability experiences.

In ending this Introduction, we would like to suggest that "companion" might be thought of productively as a disability term. It suggests connections to ideas of "care," a word that carries much baggage when connected to disability. But while care can signal the worst kinds of institutionalization, it can also productively be constituted as an understanding of, and advocacy for, the difference that disability brings. Reading and writing, whether as leisure or critical practices, are made better by caring. Seen in these terms, the idea of a "companion" that has the capacity to learn and understand, to counter ignorance, or to promote links across life experiences can be a powerful force for recognition and justice. We want to offer this Companion in such terms.

NOTES

1. *The Elder Edda: A Book of Viking Lore*, trans. by Andy Orchard (London: Penguin, 2011), p. 25. We are grateful to Yann Steunou-Murray for bringing details of the *Edda* to our attention.
2. William Shakespeare, *The Tragedy of King Richard the Third,* in *The Norton Shakespeare*, ed. by Stephen Greenblatt (New York: Norton, 1997), I.1.14–31.
3. Ibid., I.1.37.
4. See, for example, Dan Goodley, *Disability Studies: An Interdisciplinary Introduction* (London: SAGE, 2011).
5. Lennard J. Davis, *Enforcing Normalcy: Disability, Deafness, and the Body* (London: Verso, 1995), p. 23.
6. Ibid., p. 29.
7. Ibid., p. 24.

8. Rosemarie Garland-Thomson, *Extraordinary Bodies: Figuring Physical Disability in American Culture and Literature* (New York: Columbia University Press, 1997), p. 8.
9. Ibid., p. 6.
10. David T. Mitchell and Sharon L. Snyder, *Narrative Prosthesis: Disability and the Dependencies of Discourse* (Ann Arbor: University of Michigan Press, 2000), p. 49; p. 47.
11. Ato Quayson, *Aesthetic Nervousness: Disability and the Crisis of Representation* (New York: Columbia University Press, 2007), p. 19.
12. Tobin Siebers, *Disability Aesthetics* (Ann Arbor: University of Michigan Press, 2010).
13. On the social model of disability and its critiques, see Tom Shakespeare, "The Social Model of Disability," in *The Disability Studies Reader*, 4th edn., ed. by Lennard J. Davis (New York and London: Routledge, 2013), pp. 214–21.
14. Tobin Siebers, *Disability Theory* (Ann Arbor: University of Michigan Press, 2008), p. 25.
15. Sharon L. Snyder and David T. Mitchell, *Cultural Locations of Disability* (Chicago and London: University of Chicago Press, 2006), p. 10.
16. Rosemarie Garland-Thomson, "Disability Gain," paper presented at *Avoidance in/and the Academy: The International Conference on Disability, Culture, and Education*, Liverpool Hope University, September 11, 2013.
17. See Joseph P. Shapiro, *No Pity: People with Disabilities Forging a New Civil Rights Movement* (New York: Three Rivers Press, 1994), and, for example, Elizabeth Donaldson and Catherine Prendergast (eds.), "Disability and Emotion," special issue of *Journal of Literary and Cultural Disability Studies*, 5.2 (2011).
18. Merri Lisa Johnson and Robert McRuer, "Cripistemologies: Introduction," *Journal of Literary and Cultural Disability Studies*, 8.2 (2014), 127–47.
19. Rosemarie Garland-Thomson, *Staring: How We Look* (Oxford and New York: Oxford University Press, 2009).
20. Robert McRuer, *Crip Theory: Cultural Signs of Queerness and Disability* (New York and London: New York University Press, 2006); Alison Kafer, *Feminist, Queer, Crip* (Bloomington and Indianapolis: Indiana University Press, 2013).
21. Mel Y. Chen, *Animacies: Biopolitics, Racial Mattering, and Queer Affect* (Durham, NC: Duke University Press, 2012). On disability and environment, see also Sarah Jaquette Ray, *The Ecological Other: Environmental Exclusion in American Culture* (Tucson: University of Arizona Press, 2013).
22. Jasbir K. Puar, "The Cost of Getting Better: Ability and Debility," in *The Disability Studies Reader*, 4th edn., pp. 177–84.
23. See David T. Mitchell with Sharon L. Snyder, *The Biopolitics of Disability: Neoliberalism, Ablenationalism, and Peripheral Embodiment* (Ann Arbor: University of Michigan Press, 2015); Robert McRuer, *Crip Times: Disability, Globalization, and Resistance* (New York: NYU Press, forthcoming 2018); Johnson and McRuer, "Introduction: Cripistemologies"; Dan Goodley, Rebecca Lawthom, and Katherine Runswick-Cole, "Dis/ability and Austerity: Beyond Work and Slow Death," *Disability and Society*, 29.6 (2014), 980–84; Lennard J. Davis, *The End of Normal: Identity in a Biocultural Era* (Ann Arbor:

University of Michigan Press, 2013); and Margaret Price, *Mad at School: Rhetorics of Mental Disability and Academic Life* (Ann Arbor: University of Michigan Press, 2011).

24. Michael Davidson, *Concerto for the Left Hand: Disability and the Defamiliar Body* (Ann Arbor: University of Michigan Press, 2008), p. 4. The notions of "cripping" and "compulsory able-bodiedness" are drawn from the work of Robert McRuer; see *Crip Theory.*
25. Alice Hall, *Literature and Disability* (New York and London: Routledge, 2016), p. 14. See also pp. 18–29 for Hall's "Introduction to Disability Studies."
26. For more on the "avoidance" of disability in higher education, see David Bolt and Claire Penketh (eds.), *Disability, Avoidance and the Academy: Challenging Resistance* (Abingdon and New York: Routledge, 2016); and Mitchell and Snyder, *The Biopolitics of Disability*, Chapter 2, where the argument is made that inclusion and diversity initiatives in higher education are often "purposefully insufficient" (p. 67).
27. Of course, the focus in this Companion on literatures in English (or translated into English) means this book's approach to the topic of "literature and disability" is inevitably partial, and there is much work still to be done on literary disability representations emerging from other linguistic traditions and cultural contexts.
28. Ellen Samuels, *Fantasies of Identification: Disability, Gender, Race* (New York: New York University Press, 2014), p. 121.
29. Snyder and Mitchell, *Cultural Locations of Disability*, p. 193.
30. Ibid., p. 201.

PART I

Across Literatures

2

EDWARD WHEATLEY

Monsters, Saints, and Sinners

Disability in Medieval Literature

There is a certain degree of linguistic anachronism in writing about disability in medieval literature, because the term "disability" itself did not exist in English in the Middle Ages. Its absence from the language until the mid-sixteenth century meant that conceptually, medieval people would probably not have thought of people with disabilities as a group but would have differentiated among them, especially on the basis of recognizable disabilities for which terminology existed (blindness, deafness, lameness, and so forth). Recognition of less easily identifiable disabilities such as cognitive disabilities or mental illness would also have been problematic in this period because medicine as it developed through later centuries was only beginning to appear. So if scholars of medieval literature are sometimes uncertain about how to identify and analyze what appear to be disabilities in medieval texts, such uncertainty can nevertheless yield fruitful readings that contextualize the history of and social responses to apparently non-normate characters and historical figures.[1]

What must be acknowledged before turning to the literature of this period is that historically, not all disabled people were considered monsters, and not all of the people who could cure or aid them were considered saints. Disabilities ranging from minor to severe must have been very common in an era when medicine was only beginning to develop, and therefore they must have been understood and accepted as part of daily life. But if medieval *society* found most disabilities unremarkable, such was not usually the case with medieval *literature*. As David Mitchell and Sharon Snyder have theorized, disability in literature generally requires a narrative explanation of its origin or a narrative of its eradication, whether through cure or social exclusion.[2] Even so, with historical contextualization, we can move beyond the sometimes extreme representations of disabilities to a greater understanding of their place in medieval culture.

If the saints and monsters of this chapter's title were relatively rare, sinners were not: in medieval Christian culture, everyone, both disabled and normate, was considered sinful. The institution that defined sin, the Catholic Church, also exercised a good deal of control over disability-related discourse. This control grew directly out of the Gospel stories of Jesus curing people with disabilities, including blindness, lameness, and apparent mental illness, and the thaumaturgic (that is, miracle-working) power provided by the New Testament God was reproduced in numerous lives of saints who, in imitation of Jesus, also cured disabilities. The persuasive power of these narratives was reinforced by the Catholic practice of visiting holy sites, including not only those in Palestine where Jesus had lived but also the sites of the miraculous activities and martyrdom of saints. Churches were often built on these sites in honor of these locally important saints and housed relics associated with them; disabled pilgrims touched or otherwise venerated these relics in the hope of miraculous cure (and of course a steady stream of pilgrims provided a parish or a monastic organization with a steady income from those visitors).

Another important aspect of disability in both the religious and economic spheres of European culture was the giving of money to support disabled people who could not work, whether through personal alms-giving to beggars or the foundation of hospices or other institutions. People with disabilities who begged for a living often did so either at a church door or even within the church during mass, practices that indicated to alms-givers that their donations had spiritual significance. Obviously the financial means of the giver determined the amount of money that could be given, but both the small personal gesture and the more visible public intervention were considered spiritually efficacious.

As a field, and as is made clear throughout this volume, disability studies relating to the modern era has posited important models for considering disability: these include the medical model, in which disability is considered pathological and in need of a cure, and the social model, in which disability is accepted as belonging to society as a whole, not just people with disabilities (see Chapter 1). Social responses to disability acknowledge it as merely a category of difference and not a pathology. In order for us to understand the place of disability in medieval culture, a third category is necessary: the religious model of disability, whereby people understand disability largely through the institutional practices of the Church and its doctrine, including the possibility of miraculous cure. The religious model overlaps to a certain extent with the social model because, through alms-giving and church-related hospices and hospitals devoted to the disabled, medieval society helped to care for people with disabilities. But if the religious model of disability was the norm in deeply religious medieval Europe, it was not always apparent in its literature. Indeed, it might be argued that certain nonrealistic genres of literature such as the romance and the fabliau offered medieval writers and their readers the opportunity to consider disabilities in imagined environments over which the Church did not exercise control.[3]

A significant aspect of the religious model is the degree to which Christians might have believed that a disability was divine punishment for sinful behavior. In some medieval texts, the origins of characters' disabilities are not described; they are simply aspects of the human condition. However, other texts show sinners whose disabilities are clearly represented as divine punishment. Indeed, hagiographies include both types of characters: there are those whose disabilities appear natural and who might therefore be eligible for miraculous cure if they venerate a saint or perform other Christian rites; but there are also those who are disabled for offending saints, most frequently by working on a particular saint's day or committing crimes against an institution named for that saint.[4] Miracles of cure greatly outnumber miracles of chastisement in medieval hagiographies, but nevertheless the association of sin with disability in the latter category must have raised doubts in people's minds about why or how other people became disabled.

The examples below, which represent only a small sampling of instances of disability in medieval literature, have been chosen in order to show both the variety of disabilities in texts of this era and the variety of responses that writers have to them.

Monsters

In the medieval literary imagination, monsters can be difficult to categorize in relation to disability. Some of them, such as the best-known monsters in Old English literature, Grendel and his mother from the epic *Beowulf*, are clearly nonhuman, supernatural beings rather than people with disabilities. Giants appear frequently in medieval romances, but inasmuch as they are inevitably strong, fierce fighters, should their gigantism (if we choose to call their condition by that name) be considered a disability?

In other instances, however, authors construct clear relationships between monstrosity and humanity that allow us to consider a character's monstrous difference as a disability. For example, in her *Lais*, a collection of romances that often feature supernatural elements, the twelfth-century Anglo-Norman writer Marie de France includes *Bisclavret*, the story of a baron of that name who becomes a werewolf and disappears into the forest for three days a week. His wife asks about these disappearances, and he reluctantly tells her the truth, adding that he leaves his clothes near an old chapel and that should he not be able to retrieve them, he would remain a werewolf permanently. The shocked wife begins an affair with a knight whom she persuades to steal Bisclavret's clothing. A year later, the king and his hunting party come upon the werewolf Bisclavret, who shows remarkably noble, genteel behavior and becomes a court favorite. Later, however, Bisclavret wreaks vengeance on his wife and her new husband, tearing the nose off her face and attacking him. She reveals what she has done to Bisclavret, his clothes are restored to him, and once again he becomes human. The wife's punishment has long-term effects: "Many of the women in the family ... were born without noses and lived noseless."[5] If we consider Bisclavret's lycanthropic state as a disability (which his wife certainly does), then disability theory suggests that his clothing serves as a prosthesis, hiding his disability and allowing him to "pass" in normate culture.[6] His revenge upon his wife effectively disables her by disfiguring her and her female descendants, because physical – and particularly facial – disfigurement made women damaged goods in the medieval marriage market.

Although the readers of Marie's *Lais* never learn the cause of Bisclavret's lycanthropy, in some medieval texts monstrosity was blamed on sin. An Anglo-Norman contemporary of Marie's, Giraldus Cambrensis or Gerald of Wales, lived from about 1146 to 1223 and was, like her, an aristocrat. One of his works, *The Topography of Ireland*, is often complimentary about the qualities of the land itself but is more often scathing about the people, accusing them of bestiality and other unnatural practices that result in the birth of monsters. Among other monstrous creatures are werewolves who have had to give up their human form because of the curse of one Saint Natalis, as well as such hybrid creatures as a woman with a beard and a mane on her back, and a man who was half-ox.[7] The people are ill-tempered, Gerald says, and "so in eternal death the saints of this land that have been elevated by their merits are more vindictive than the saints of any other region" (91). He continues:

> I have never seen among any other people so many blind by birth, so many lame, so many maimed in body, and so many suffering from some natural defect ... And it is not surprising if nature sometimes produces such beings contrary to her ordinary laws when dealing with a people that is adulterous, incestuous, unlawfully conceived and born outside the law, and shamefully abusing nature herself in spiteful and horrible practices. It seems a just punishment from God that those who do not look on him with the interior light of the mind should often grieve in being deprived of the gift of the light that is bodily and external.
>
> (118)

Here we see a complex connection between the religious and the political. While Gerald uses the religious model of disability to explain why Ireland is so full of monsters and disabled people, his is ostensibly a political project. His book ends with an envoy to Henry II of England, whom Gerald praises as the first foreign king in centuries to conquer Ireland, a "western Alexander," and on the basis of the *Topographia Hibernica*, Gerald hopes to win a commission to write of Henry's role in the Crusades.

Medieval literature frequently represents monstrous deformity as a genuine physical disability resulting in social ostracism. One such conventional figure is the "loathly lady," a threatening representation of monstrous female sexuality and earthly appetites who appears in several late medieval romances. Readers of medieval literature know this figure in Geoffrey Chaucer's "The Wife of Bath's Tale" in *The Canterbury Tales*, but there her loathliness is simply her age: she is too old to wed the knight whom she demands to marry. She is much more monstrous in analogous romances such as *The Wedding of Sir Gawain and Dame Ragnelle*. When she first appears, the poet devotes more than fifteen lines to her ugliness: her red, snotty nose; her wide mouth; her yellow teeth; her cheeks, broad as women's hips; and her saggy breasts.[8] The poet returns repeatedly to her loathliness, later adding:

> She had two tethe on every* syde — *each*
> As borys* tuskes, I wolle nott hyde,* — *boar's / dissemble*
> Of lengthe a large handfulle.* — *hand's breadth*
> The one tusk went up and the other doun. (ll. 549–52)

The animalistic nature represented by her tusks is reinforced by her appetite at the wedding feast: she eats three capons, three curlews, roasted meats, and any other food set before her (ll. 611–16).

The loathly lady, characterized by both her hideousness and her ravenous appetites, exemplifies the type of the grotesque described by Mikhail Bakhtin, a type that fits many representations of people with disabilities in medieval literature. The grotesque body transgresses corporeal boundaries in such a way that it is always "in the act of becoming. It is never finished, never completed; it is continually built, created, and builds and creates another body."[9] Bakhtin also writes that "[t]he artistic logic of the grotesque image ignores the closed, smooth, and impenetrable surface of the body and retains only its excrescences (sprouts, buds) and orifices, only that which leads beyond the body's limited space or into the body's depths. Mountains and abysses, such is the relief of the grotesque body."[10] This vision maps convincingly onto the loathly lady, with her snotty nose, her physical excrescences, and her enormous mouth. Carnivalesque misrule, the inversion of the normal social order often instigated by grotesques, is also apparent in this narrative in the lady's inappropriate desire to marry Sir Gawain, but because carnival allows for only a temporary challenge to social norms, order must be restored,[11] as it is when the loathly lady turns into a beautiful young woman fit to be the wife of a knight (which she does in the analogues to this story as well). The disability of her deformity is miraculously eradicated.[12]

Saints

At the heart of the religious model of disability are saints and the practices associated with them. As previously noted, during their lives, religious figures who would later become saints were to cure people with illnesses and disabilities in imitation of Jesus' miraculous cures; indeed, proof of miracles associated with holy figures was necessary for them to be canonized. Previous to canonization, their cases could also benefit from proof of miracles, curative and otherwise, that were performed by or near their relics. Then after they were designated saints, the sites of their burial or the institutional repository of their relics often became pilgrimage sites to which people with disabilities would go in the hope of a cure. The work of André Vauchez, the influential scholar of hagiography, shows the changes in types of miraculous cures of disabilities recorded in canonization proceedings from the early thirteenth to the early fifteenth centuries; these records show that on the whole, disabilities (paralysis, motor problems, sensory disabilities, mental illness) appear more frequently in hagiographic texts written in the thirteenth century than in those written between 1301 and 1417, though of course the earlier hagiographies survived into the later century and would have continued to exert religious influence.[13] Although such statistics were unavailable in the Middle Ages, they show that the Church emphasized saints' connections to disability theologically, and this theological emphasis made itself apparent in religious discourse of all kinds: sermons, the visual arts, drama, and of course vernacular literature.

The cults of numerous saints were established in England during the Anglo-Saxon period, so it is not surprising that the Venerable Bede includes them in his *History of the English Church and People*, written in the early eighth century. The initial chapters of Book Five are devoted to some of the miracles performed by John, Bishop of Hexham, the first of which is the cure of a man who had been mute since birth. John makes the sign of the cross on the man's tongue and tells him to speak.

> "Pronounce some word," he said: "Say *yea*," which is the English word of agreement and assent, i.e., "Yes." The lad's tongue was loosed, and at once he did what he was told. The Bishop then proceeded to the names of the letter: "Say A." And he said "A." Now say "B," he said, which the youth did.[14]

This miracle shows greater involvement by the saint than most miracles: John is not only curing the disability, but he is teaching the newly cured boy, helping with his integration into educated Christian society. The episode has received scholarly attention not only for the way the young man's tongue is liberated but also for its validation of the English language as worthy of being taught via Latin pedagogical methods.[15]

In the later Middle Ages, the stories of Christian saints who cured disabilities appeared in a number of different genres, but many of them can be traced back to the highly influential compilation entitled *Legenda Aurea* (*The Golden Legend*) by the thirteenth-century Dominican monk Jacobus de Voragine. More than 1,000 medieval manuscripts of the work have survived, and printing, which began in Europe in the 1450s, allowed it to reach an even wider audience through hundreds of early editions, not only in Latin but in every major western European language as well.[16] It was popular enough in English to be among the books printed by England's first printer, William Caxton, in 1483, within seven years of the establishment of his press in London; he mentions that his text came from an earlier translation, so *The Golden Legend* was clearly circulating in English before that date.[17] It remains probably the most important work in the medieval canon for the study of miraculous interventions relating to disability.

Potentially the most widely available literature in the Middle Ages for teaching about miraculous Christian cures was the drama. A great deal of evidence exists relating to the performance history of cycle drama, the plays that presented episodes of biblical history from the creation of the world to Doomsday, usually as part of a religious festival but with heavy civic involvement. The three complete extant cycles – York, Chester, and N-Town[18] – emphasize the life of Jesus, some of whose miraculous cures are presented in the texts and therefore become models for cures by later saints. However, Jesus' most significant cure, which is heavily emphasized in all the cycles, confronts not disability but death: the raising of Lazarus from the dead not only shows the power of Christian belief over death but also prefigures Jesus' own resurrection. (In imitating Jesus later, only the most powerful saints are capable of raising the dead.) In the Chester cycle, the playwright combines the raising of Lazarus and Jesus' cure of the blind man at Siloe in a single play, thus juxtaposing his two most impressive miracles, and the cure of the blind man is given the full scriptural addendum of nonbelievers refusing to put their faith in the miracle.[19] In addition, Simon the Leper thanks Jesus for curing him (251), though this cure is not staged. And finally, Jesus restores the ear of Malchus, which the disciple Peter angrily strikes off with his sword at the time of Jesus' betrayal (282–83). The York cycle devotes less stage time to the blind man and adds a lame man, presenting short, generalized cures for both, and also presents the restoration of Malchus' ear.[20] The N-Town Cycle does not stage any of the lesser miracles; instead, at the beginning of the Passion Play, a demon states that Jesus has cured the "crooked" (lame or physically disabled), the blind, and the mute, after which he mentions the raising of Lazarus.[21] Here the playwright may be drawing on the notion that disabilities are within the purview of demons, since in the Bible mental illness in particular is sometimes blamed on demonic possession, as it is in Matthew 8:28–34 and Mark 5:1–20.

The importance of saints and miracles in medieval culture was also felt in vernacular romance, a genre that sometimes used Christian themes. In these texts, characters might be given the power to perform miracles or achieve spiritual states generally reserved for saints. In the Chaucerian corpus, the legendary Custance of "The Man of Law's Tale" both aids in performing and benefits from miracles, including the cure of a blind man and the divine blinding of a perjurer against her in a murder trial.[22] Both Chaucer and the author of his main source text were clearly invested in showing how miracles contributed to the full conversion of Northumberland, making it a part of the Christian England of the late Middle Ages. Sir Thomas Malory's *Le Morte Darthur*, a translated compendium of earlier Arthurian literature written around 1470, includes two knights, Lancelot and his son Galahad, who are characterized as saintly partly because they cure disabilities. When Galahad achieves the Holy Grail, he receives the Eucharist from Jesus himself in the presence of a disabled man called the Maimed King. Jesus then tells Galahad to take the bloody spear which had pierced Jesus' side when he was crucified (which at that time was instrumental in curing the blind Longinus) and use the blood to anoint the Maimed King in order to heal him, which Galahad does.[23] Although Lancelot is not as morally spotless as Galahad, mainly because of his affair with Guinevere, he is given curative powers in an episode that does not come from earlier Arthurian literature. Malory adds a short original episode just before the final unraveling of the Round Table in which a Hungarian knight, Sir Urry, has been cursed so that "ever his wounds should one time fester and another time bleed, so that he should never be whole until the best knight of the world had searched his wounds" (460). After King Arthur and all of the knights of the Round Table fail to cure Urry, Arthur asks Lancelot to try. Initially he modestly demurs, but then he touches Urry's wounds one by one and they "seemed as they had been whole seven years" (465).[24] Malory clearly means for the speed and efficacy with which Lancelot cures such serious wounds to strongly reinforce his spiritual superiority; not even fully canonized saints always demonstrate such power.

Although the cure of disabilities by religious figures received the lion's share of attention in medieval religious discourse, they also used disabilities to punish sinners. Miracles of chastisement appear frequently in medieval hagiography. Perhaps the best known in the New Testament is God's blinding of Saul as he is on his way to persecute Christians in Damascus; instead, he converts to Christianity, regains his vision, and later changes his name to Paul.[25] In the fifteenth century, these events were dramatized in a short play entitled "The Conversion of Saint Paul."[26] Saints also frequently disabled people who offended them, whether by passively failing to venerate them or by actively working against them.[27] The presence of such miracles in many hagiographies must have raised the suspicions of medieval people that sin brought disability as punishment in real life, as Gerald of Wales says of Ireland in the passage quoted above.

Sinners

In representing the "sinners" discussed in this section, medieval writers generally deployed the religious model of disability, though the Wife of Bath is a notable exception because she knows that her disability had a clearly human cause. In some instances the disability is interpreted as punishment for sin, but in many, religion is only brought into it after the disability appears, when it is examined as a manifestation of God's will or a cure is sought through religious means. The variety of disabilities here also elicits various social responses, whether in fiction or in accounts of historical figures, that probably resembled the lived experiences of people with disabilities in the Middle Ages.

Surely the best-known disability in all of medieval English literature is the hearing impairment of the Wife of Bath in Chaucer's *Canterbury Tales*. When introducing her in the General Prologue, the pilgrim narrator emphasizes her deafness by mentioning it in the first two lines about her: "A good Wif was ther of biside Bathe, / But she was somdel [somewhat] deef, and that was scathe [a pity]."[28] In the prologue to her tale the Wife recounts how she became disabled. Her fifth husband, Jankyn, reads to her frequently from a "book of wikked wyves" (III, l. 685) filled with misogynistic texts, and ultimately she becomes so angry that she tears three leaves out of the book and knocks him to the floor; in return he strikes her on her ear, deafening it (III, ll. 634–36, 788–96). Recent criticism informed by disability studies has read her deafness in a number of ways: the hearing impairment is merely emblematic of the Wife's more serious disability, her aging female body;[29] her deployment of experience and orality accommodates her deafness and creates a satisfying world for her;[30] and the Wife's aggressive sexuality is what produces her narrative, while her deafness represents a punishment for it that seeks to curb her deviance.[31] However her deafness is interpreted, it is clear that it is more of an impairment than an actual disability: she is one of only a handful of Canterbury pilgrims who engages in lively dialogue with her fellow travelers, and she clearly understands what they have to say. Thus deafness is an element of her characterization but by no means the dominant one.

While Chaucer was creating the Wife of Bath, his contemporary William Langland was addressing difficult social issues relating to disability and poverty in his lengthy allegorical dream vision *Piers Plowman*, which he revised three times. Langland believed strongly that in order for society to function properly, people needed to do the work that God put them on the earth to do, but he also confronted the question of how to support those who cannot work, including people with disabilities, the "blynde and bedredne [bedridden] and broken in here [their] membres."[32] According to Langland, if these and other unfortunate people accept these "mischiefs" meekly, they will benefit spiritually by suffering their purgatory on earth rather than later. These people are truly deserving of alms from their Christian brethren. Langland also mentions another terrible aspect of disability, the purposeful mutilation of children in order for them to receive more alms from sympathetic givers: he says that immoral parents break their children's backs or other bones in order to disable them (Passus 9, l. 94). While his concern for people with disabilities is palpable, Langland is also deeply concerned about a disability-related social problem that appears repeatedly in medieval literature: able-bodied people who feign disabilities in order not to have to work. When the eponymous character is preparing to plow a half-acre field, "faytours... fayned hem blynde / And leyde her legges alery [Idlers... pretended to be blind / And twisted their legs backward]" (Passus 8, ll. 128–29). They claim to be unable to work until Piers calls the allegorical figure of Hunger to seize them by the stomach; thereby, "Blynde and broke-legged he botened [cured] a thousend" (Passus 8, l. 188), a miraculous cure indeed.[33] The social anxieties about feigned disabilities that Langland addresses here gave normates yet another reason to be suspicious about people with disabilities: to what extent might they be pretending?

The marginalization of people with disabilities sometimes resembled the marginalization of Jews, and several anti-Semitic tropes deployed disability. In a late fifteenth-century play called *The Croxton Play of the Sacrament*, sin is clearly associated with both literal and metaphorical disability. The play presents the desecration of sanctified Eucharistic bread that supposedly took place in Spain in 1461, when a group of Jews led by one Jonathas pays a Christian merchant named Aristorius to steal the sacrament from the church so that they can "put Hym to a new passyoun [passion]."[34] The pronoun "him" is used because of the medieval Christian belief in transubstantiation, that is, that consecrated bread was truly the body of Christ. The Jews stab the bread five times, and like a real body, it begins to bleed. Frightened, Jonathas picks up the host in order to throw it into boiling oil, but it adheres to his hand. The other men nail the bread to a post and try to pull Jonathas off it, but though his body comes away, his hand remains attached. Symbolically, Jonathas' dismemberment suggests the incompleteness of the Jews in their unwillingness to believe in Christ. Ultimately, the men throw both hand and bread into an oven from which Jesus emerges to ask why they are blasphemously subjecting the host to such desecration; the Jews then convert to Christianity, and Jonathas' hand is restored. Beyond Jonathas' literal disability is the metaphorical use of blindness, which was frequently deployed in medieval religious discourse to describe Jews' refusal to see the divinity of Jesus. Before his conversion Jonathas twice blames the bread for the "conceit" of making the Jews blind (ll. 203, 388).[35]

In contrast to the very public art of the drama, three people with disabilities undertook what might be called in modern terms "life writing" in the fifteenth century, and all three deploy the religious model of disability. Thomas Hoccleve, a poet active during the first three decades of the century, was affected by a form of mental illness in 1416 and did not write for five years.[36] Thereafter, in "The Complaint of Hoccleve" he wrote about his experience, saying that his "memorie / Wente to pleie [play] as for a certein space [time]" and calling himself "brainseke."[37] He was so disabled that his friends went on pilgrimages on his behalf. He writes poignantly of the aftereffects of the illness, which are largely social; some friends rejected him when he was ill and stayed away from him after his recovery, while others never again trusted him fully because they feared the illness would return.[38]

Mental illness also appears in *The Book of Margery Kempe*, in which Margery begins having mystical visions after suffering from what resembles postpartum depression: after giving birth to her first child, "she despaired of her life, thinking she might not live."[39] For periods of her life she is overtaken by uncontrollable fits of loud crying and weeping, particularly when she meditates on the suffering of Jesus: "she fell down and cried with loud voice, wonderfully turning and twisting her body on every side, spreading her arms abroad as if she should have died, and could not keep herself from crying or from these bodily movings, for the fire of love that burnt so fervently in her soul with pure pity and compassion" (51–52). Although Margery's book constructs her behavior as the result of her mystical visions, some of her contemporaries believed her to be insane. Even so, she acquires such sanctity that later in life she is able to cure a young woman who was "newly delivered of a child and she was out of her mind" (130) – in other words, a woman who strongly resembled Margery in her time of difficulty earlier. The cure represents the mystic coming full circle spiritually from a point at which she could not help herself to a point at which she could help others. The scribe who wrote down Margery's story even goes so far as to say, "[The cure] was, as they thought who knew it, a right great miracle" (131). It is likely that he was hopeful that such nomenclature would help if Margery were ever considered for canonization and needed a miracle or two to make her case.

The poet John Audelay, a chantry priest who wrote during the first quarter of the fifteenth century, names himself in his poetry eighteen times, and in sixteen of those instances he calls himself blind. Although he does not write about his blindness per se, he states that God is chastising him; he presumably believed this because he had been party to an incident on Easter Sunday of 1417 in which families inimical to each other had a violent confrontation in church and one man was killed, a serious desecration of sacred space on the holiest day of the year. Audelay's misery is also indicated by his repeated comparison of himself to "blind Bayard," an unruly blind horse that is mentioned in several medieval proverbs.[40] Given Audelay's belief that God was using blindness to punish him, his frequent focus on his blindness along with the Bayard trope represents a form of spiritual self-castigation: he relived and presumably repented of the traumatic event that he believed to have been the root of his disability every time he mentioned it. His occupation as a chantry priest would have given him ample time to consider his sinfulness.

The pervasiveness of religion in medieval Europe had profound effects on the cultural understanding of disability, and if in one sense it limited the kinds of legitimate responses that Christians could have to it, in another sense it kept disability very much in the public eye. However, literature offered a space in which disability's connection to religious views and practices could be largely determined by the interests of the author. The connection was central in hagiographies and *The Book of Margery Kempe*, tangential in *Le Morte Darthur* and Hoccleve's "Complaint," and vestigial in *Bisclavret* and "The Wife of Bath's Tale." Texts including disabilities during the Middle Ages also demonstrate a basic understanding of a kind of a social model in which disabilities are the responsibility of society as a whole, though this frequently overlaps with religious practices, as in *Piers Plowman*. The medical model was, not surprisingly, the least discursively powerful of this triumvirate in this period, but its relative absence from literature is in certain ways a boon for readers who are invited to find interpretations based in the details of the texts rather than beginning with a diagnosis that delimits such interpretations.

NOTES

1. The term "normate" was coined by Rosemarie Garland-Thomson in *Extraordinary Bodies: Figuring Physical Disability in American Culture and Literature* (New York: Columbia University Press, 1997). The "normate" is the socially constructed ideal image whereby "people can represent themselves as definitive human beings," in contrast to people with disabilities (p. 8).
2. David T. Mitchell and Sharon L. Snyder, *Narrative Prosthesis: Disability and the Dependencies of Discourse* (Ann Arbor: University of Michigan Press, 2000), pp. 1–10.
3. For a more detailed discussion of the religious model of disability, see Edward Wheatley, *Stumbling Blocks before the Blind: Medieval Constructions of a Disability* (Ann Arbor: University of Michigan Press, 2010), pp. 9–19.
4. See, for example, the miracle in which a blacksmith's tools adhere to his hands in Rosalind C. Love (ed. and trans.), *Three Eleventh-Century Anglo-Latin Saints' Lives* (Oxford: Clarendon Press, 1996), pp. 77–79, and the adhesion of a cutting tool to the hands of a harvesting girl on St. Ethelthryth's Day in Goscelin of Saint-Bertin, *The Hagiography of the Female Saints of Ely*, ed. and trans. by Rosalind C. Love (Oxford: Clarendon Press, 2004), pp. 119–23.
5. Marie de France, *Bisclavret,* in *The Lais of Marie de France*, trans. by Glyn S. Burgess and Keith Busby (London: Penguin, 1986), pp. 68–72 (p. 72).
6. See Gillian Nelson Bauer, "The Werewolf's Closet: Clothing as Prosthesis in Marie de France's *Bisclavret*," in *The Treatment of Disabled Persons in Medieval Europe: Examining Disability in the Historical, Legal, Literary, Medical, and Religious Discourses of the Middle Ages*, ed. by Wendy J. Turner and Tory Vandeventer Pearman (Lewiston, NY: Edwin Mellen Press, 2010), pp. 259–90.
7. Giraldus Cambrensis, *The History and Topography of Ireland (Topographia Hiberniae)*, trans. by John J. O'Meara (Atlantic Highlands, NJ: Humanities Press, 1982), pp. 69–74. Further page references to primary texts will be given parenthetically in the body of the chapter.
8. *The Wedding of Sir Gawain and Dame Ragnelle*, ed. by Thomas Hahn (TEAMS Middle English Texts; Kalamazoo, MI: Medieval Institute Publications, 1995), ll. 232–52.
9. Mikhail Bakhtin, *Rabelais and His World*, trans. by Hélène Iswolsky (Bloomington: Indiana University Press, 1984), p. 317.
10. Ibid., pp. 317–18.
11. For Bakhtin's discussion of the social dynamics of the carnivalesque, see Chapter 3 of *Rabelais and His World*, "Popular-Festive Forms and Images in Rabelais," pp. 196–277.
12. For an overview of the figure of the loathly lady as disabled, see Tory Vandeventer Pearman, "Disruptive Dames: Disability and the Loathly Lady in *The Tale of Florent, The Wife of Bath's Tale*, and *The Weddynge of Sir Gawain and Dame Ragnelle*," in Turner and Vandeventer Pearman (eds.), *The Treatment of Disabled Persons in Medieval Europe*, pp. 291–312.
13. Reproduced in Irina Metzler, *Disability in Medieval Europe: Thinking about Physical Impairment in the High Middle Ages, c. 1100–1400* (London: Routledge, 2006), p. 130.

14. Bede, *A History of the English Church and People*, trans. by Leo Sherley-Price (Harmondsworth: Penguin, 1955), p. 272.
15. Irina Dumitrescu, "Bede's Liberation Theology: Releasing the English Tongue," *PMLA*, 128.1 (2013), 40–56.
16. Jacobus de Voragine, *The Golden Legend*, vol. 1, intro. and trans. by William Granger Ryan (Princeton, NJ: Princeton University Press, 1993), p. xiii.
17. Ibid., p. xiv.
18. The N-Town cycle, which in its introduction states only that it will be performed in "N-Town," has not been conclusively linked to any city in Britain and may not have been performed at all. A partial fourth cycle associated with Wakefield reproduces the material from the York cycle that is discussed here.
19. R. M. Lumiansky and David Mills (eds.), *The Chester Mystery Cycle* (EETS SS 3; Oxford: Oxford University Press, 1974), pp. 23–50.
20. Clifford Davidson (ed.), *The York Corpus Christi Plays* (TEAMS Middle English Texts; Kalamazoo, MI: Medieval Institute Publications, 2011): Play 25, "The Entry into Jerusalem," ll. 288–390; Play 29, "The Trial Before Cayphas and Annas," ll. 272–93.
21. Douglas Sugano (ed.), *The N-Town Plays* (TEAMS Middle English Texts; Kalamazoo, MI: Medieval Institute Publications, 2007): Play 26, "Conspiracy; Entry into Jerusalem," ll. 37–38.
22. Larry Benson (ed.), *The Riverside Chaucer* (Boston: Houghton Mifflin, 1987), II, ll. 533–66, 659–79.
23. Sir Thomas Malory, *Le Morte Darthur: The Winchester Manuscript*, ed. by Helen Cooper (Oxford: Oxford University Press, 1998), p. 398. For the background of the Maimed King's disability, see Malory, p. 377.
24. Lancelot's saintliness is reaffirmed after he dies, when his body exudes the odor of sanctity and remains incorruptible for more than two weeks (525).
25. Acts 9:1–27.
26. F. J. Furnivall (ed.), *The Digby Plays with an Incomplete "Morality" of Wisdom, Who Is Christ* (London: K. Paul, Trench, Trubner, 1896), pp. 25–52.
27. For examples of blinding as miraculous chastisement, see Wheatley, *Stumbling Blocks before the Blind*, pp. 157–72.
28. Benson (ed.), *The Riverside Chaucer*, I, ll. 445–46. Elsewhere in *The Canterbury Tales*, disability figures prominently in "The Merchant's Tale," in which the main character, January, goes blind.
29. Mikee Delony, "Alisoun's Aging, Hearing Impaired Female Body: Gazing at the Wife of Bath in Chaucer's *Canterbury Tales*," in Turner and Vandeventer Pearman (eds.), *The Treatment of Disabled Persons in Medieval Europe*, pp. 313–44.
30. Edith Edna Sayers, "Experience, Authority, and the Mediation of Deafness: Chaucer's Wife of Bath," in Joshua R. Eyler (ed.), *Disability in the Middle Ages: Reconsiderations and Reverberations* (Farnham: Ashgate, 2010) pp. 81–92.
31. Tory Vandeventer Pearman, *Women and Disability in Medieval Literature* (New York: Palgrave Macmillan, 2010), pp. 60–71.
32. William Langland, *Piers Plowman: A New Annotated Edition of the C-Text*, ed. by Derek Pearsall (Exeter: University of Exeter Press, 2008), Passus 9, l. 178. For a discussion of disability in the poem see Jennifer M. Gianfalla, "'Ther is moore

mysshapen amonges thise beggeres': Discourses of Disability in *Piers Plowman*," in Eyler (ed.), *Disability in the Middle Ages*, pp. 119–34.

33. For another instance of feigned disability that is justified because it takes place in a society populated by liars and thieves, see the character Geffrey in *The Tale of Beryn*, in John M. Bowers (ed.), *The Canterbury Tales: Fifteenth-Century Continuations and Additions* (Kalamazoo, MI: Medieval Institute Publications, 1992), pp. 79–196.
34. *The Croxton Play of the Sacrament*, ed. by John T. Sebastian (TEAMS Middle English Texts; Kalamazoo, MI: Medieval Institute Publications, 2012), l. 38.
35. For a discussion of this pervasive metaphor see Wheatley, *Stumbling Blocks before the Blind*, pp. 63–89.
36. M. C. Seymour (ed.), *Selections from Hoccleve* (Oxford: Clarendon Press, 1981), p. xvii.
37. Ibid., "The Complaint of Hoccleve," pp. 75–87; ll. 50–51, 129.
38. For a discussion of Hoccleve's mental illness see Matthew Boyd Goldie, "Psychosomatic Illness and Identity in London, 1416–1421: Hoccleve's Complaint and Dialogue with a Friend," *Exemplaria*, 11.1 (1999), 23–52.
39. Lynn Staley (trans. and ed.), *The Book of Margery Kempe* (New York: W. W. Norton, 2001), p. 6.
40. Wheatley, *Stumbling Blocks before the Blind*, pp. 212–18.

3

ALLISON P. HOBGOOD
AND
DAVID HOUSTON WOOD

Early Modern Literature and Disability Studies

When we tell people that we work in early modern disability studies, they invariably respond, "Oh, you mean Richard III, right?"[1] "Of course," we reply, "but he's just the tip of the iceberg." We open our essay with this anecdote not to invalidate its logic – the infamous Yorkist king is an obvious figure for examining disability in the late medieval and early modern periods – but to broaden our scopes of study and our literary imaginations when it comes to premodern disability and its representations. To that end, our chapter contributes to the growing body of work represented in this volume by articulating conceptions of disability specific to early modernity and theorizing the myriad ways disability operated (and was operationalized) in pre-Enlightenment England. We illuminate how varied embodiments and lived experiences of disabled individuals in the Renaissance functioned representationally in literature of the period and, further, cultivated unique aesthetic modes in early modern English texts. Our essay covers a wide array of genres – we explore well-known medico-philosophical treatises by Michel de Montaigne and Robert Burton alongside lesser known, noncanonical poetry and drama from the seventeenth century – to show both the diversity and ubiquity of Renaissance disability and its attendant literary discourses. The first part of our essay outlines some discourses of disability and their literary manifestations to reveal various "ideologies of ability" at work in the Renaissance.[2] The second section offers a case study in which we engage early modern humoral theory as one way bodily dys/function was configured in the sixteenth and seventeenth centuries. Part three explores how, on both the page and stage, early modern disability generates what contemporary disability theorists have called a disability aesthetic,[3] in this case, a compelling ethical and aesthetic desire for disability produced by the performance of impairment on the English Renaissance stage.

Early Modern Ideologies of Ability

In his seminal study, *Disability Theory*, Tobin Siebers aims to "define the ideology of ability and to make its workings legible and familiar, despite how imbricated it may be in our thinking and practices, and despite how little we notice its patterns, authority, contradictions, and influence as a result."[4] Similarly, our goal in early modern disability studies is to examine literature to devise how the able body served as an underpinning for countless social norms and ideological postures in early modern England: "the ideology of ability," Siebers further explains, "is at its simplest the preference for able-bodiedness. At its most radical, it defines the baseline by which humanness is determined."[5] In a similar vein, Rosemarie Garland-Thomson coins the concept of the normate: "the veiled subject position of cultural self, the figure outlined by the array of deviant others whose marked bodies shore up the normate's boundaries."[6] In these various iterations, ideologies of ability sediment unachievable ideals and norms about humanness, and uphold untenable fantasies of ability. In early modernity, these taken-for-granted, pervasive principles were part and parcel of what we might term "ability logics": foundational cultural logics that privileged able-bodiedness and, in so doing, energized a range of approaches to medicine, education, civic engagement, theology, and social performance.

We illustrate throughout this essay how ability logics and normative baselines operated within Elizabethan and Jacobean cultures, but of course with their own specifically early modern parameters. Consider briefly how Shakespearean drama is filled with ostensible normates: think Orlando or Romeo, for example.[7] These normates are nonetheless often given over, among other things, to deviant passions and wildly vacillating humors.[8] This volatility meant that even wealthy, white, young Renaissance males were susceptible to emotional and behavioral eruptions like, say, the murderous monstrousness of Leontes in Shakespeare's *The Winter's Tale* (c. 1610–11). Such psychosomatic outbursts within the context of Renaissance humoralism were not perceived as wholly unusual, then, but rather as inevitable deviations from a psychophysiological standard. Put differently, perfect somatic balance – known as eukrasia – was a method for denoting typical human functionality in the Renaissance, even as it anticipated the impossibility of individuals ever fully measuring up.[9] As we detail below, this failure was absolutely stigmatizing insofar as it meant straying from a norming baseline and idealized type. That said, we further explain that non-normativity – humoral and others kinds too – was not exclusively stigmatic in the period; it was also productive. Our work strives to uncover theories of disability embodiment that challenge uniquely premodern ideologies of ability, and our interests lie at the seemingly paradoxical juncture where early modern difference was policed yet productive, controlled yet cultivated, deviant yet desirable.

To undertake this kind of work in the most ethical way possible, early modernists must address head-on what one might call the "problem of models" in our field of study. Even as we rely on contemporary disability theory for our historical work, we must realize that an easy, backwards importation of contemporary models of disability – the medical, social, and cultural models, for example – is not wholly sufficient for reading disability in the Renaissance. As Julie Singer has explained regarding medieval disability studies, scholars intent on disability analysis must identify terms, tropes, and modes for understanding impairment that are explicit to their period.[10] Without dismissing the invaluable importance of contemporary disability studies to our own project, we similarly assert that representations of disability in early modern literature conjure and clarify all kinds of specifically premodern schemas for grasping disability, each one underpinned by an ideology of ability.

In exploring how literary discourses participated in the standardization of human bodies and minds in early modernity, we trouble the now conventional sense in contemporary disability studies that norms were instantiated in the late eighteenth century and hence that disability is a wholly modern invention.[11] Following Elizabeth Bearden, we find that classical and premodern conceptions of *ideal* and *natural* bodies in the Renaissance constructed – and privileged – both normalcy and ability; more specifically, they produced what Bearden calls "norming effects." The ideal, when put into practice, set its own system of normalcy, while the natural enabled totalizing categories of standard and deviant.[12] Further, narrowly normalizing ideologies of ability common in the classical and medieval periods took on new shapes in Renaissance England. Early modern medical, philosophical, and literary texts rescripted mental and physical differences previously deemed *unnatural* and *monstrous* as *abnormal* or *imperfect* corporeality, and did so to their own norming ends. Valerie Traub clarifies that, in particular, early modern anatomy and cartography "crafted a spatialized idiom that rendered newly thinkable a representative conceptual model, a stable secular standard, against which commonalities and differences could be measured."[13] At play, then, across early modern literary texts is a deliberate, discursive process of physical and mental standardization of the human form and its behaviors.[14] Natural, monstrous, perfect, defective, deformed: all of these premodern concepts exacted some kind of norming effect.

During this era, diverse kinds of non-normativity were identifiable upon a continuum ranging from welcome exception to notable deficiency to radical deviancy, which produced profound sociocultural terror. In each instance, though, disability was very rarely itself alone: it had to mean something. For instance, cases of visible bodily deviation from ideal forms garnered the label *monstrous*, a concept stemming from a moral model of disability and drawing upon medieval beliefs that impairment was divinely sanctioned by God or supernaturally manifested by nature. Inspired by classical authors like Herodotus and Pliny the Elder, medieval writers like Bartholomew Anglicanus and John Mandeville conditioned early modern English views of the exoticness of so-called outsiders like the Anthropophagi and the Amazons.[15] Such attitudes to embodied difference were further inculcated by a complex early modern lexicon that juxtaposed terms pertaining to excellence (*beautiful, kind, natural*, and *ideal*) with "disability" vocabulary (*ugly, unkind, unnatural*, and *monstrous*). Texts like Stephen Batman's *The Doome Warning All Men to the Judgemente* (1581) and a number of the Renaissance narratives collected and reprinted in the *Black-Letter Ballads and Broadsides* (1870) specifically offer early modern reports of "monsterous births."[16] For example, tales from *Black-Letter Ballads* like "The True Description of a Monsterous Chylde, Borne in the Ile of Wight...," "The Forme and Shape of a Monsterous Child, Borne at Maydstone...," and "The True Description of Two Monsterous Children, Laufully Begotten between George Steuens and Margerie His Wife ... " all narrate congenital deformity as a form of otherness and monstrosity within, and exemplify how the highly metaphorical term *monster* reflected definitively early modern English anxieties, mores, and meanings.[17]

Notably, however, against the metaphorical impulse inherent in a moral model of disability burgeoned what Hobgood elsewhere has termed a protomedical model of disability.[18] This schema often looked to both natural causation and physiological cure for congenital deformities and other impairments; thus, it simultaneously reflected moralizing fears and dangerously palpable, more scientifically driven rationalizations. While the scientific logic at the heart of the protomedical model was fundamentally incorrect in many ways, its instantiation was well underway by the late sixteenth century and symptomatically shows itself in numerous literary texts composed during the Renaissance. Take, for instance, John Lamport's 1685 treatise, *A Direct Method of Ordering and Curing People of That Loathsome Disease, the Small-Pox*, which typically evinces this burgeoning conception of impairment as medical crisis.[19] The text endeavors to "prevent the usual Deformity of Marks and Scars," claims to offer prevention and cure (especially to "Instruct the poor ignorant tenders of the sick, and such poor Wretches as are not able to hire a Tender"), and promotes "the Medicines herein mentioned" as they may be "truly prepared by the

Author at Reasonable Rates" (13, 16). Lamport's treatise medicalizes, stigmatizes, and economically capitalizes upon pockmarked "Deformity" as a fate to be avoided at all costs, and touts medicine as an empirically verifiable cure-all: "I have not Wrote from bare Conjecture," Lamport explains, "but from undeniable Experiments" (n. pag.; see "The Epistle to the Reader").

A 1603 English translation of Michel de Montaigne's *Essayes* offers another, perhaps more nuanced, example of this protomedical model narrated through an intimate, first-person treatise that blends Renaissance philosophy with historical anecdote and autobiographical detail.[20] In a chapter entitled "Of a Monstrous Childe" (2.30), Montaigne, via a medicalizing gaze, describes encountering "a childe, whom two men and a nurce (which named themselves to be his father, his Unckle, and his Aunt) carried about with intent to get some money with the sight of him, by reason of his strangenes" (409). The child was what we would now term a conjoined twin who,

> Under his paps... was fastned and joyned to an other childe, but had no head, and who had the conduite of his body stopped, the rest whole.... They were joyned face to face, and as if a little child would embrace another somewhat bigger.... Thus, what of the imperfect one was not joyned, as armes, buttockes, thighes and legges, did hang and shake upon the other, whose length reached to the middle-leg of the other perfect. (409)

In this passage, Montaigne juxtaposes the contrasting physical forms of the two boys in a depiction of what he later in the essay calls the "double body"; in so doing, he makes hypervisible the beholdenness of perfection to imperfection and reifies an ideology of ability that privileges bodily wholeness. In this instance, the boy and his twin are equally early-modern medical specimens to be closely observed and marvels to be read according to the logic of a medieval era gone by. Furthermore, the fully developed child, in spite of being fused to another "incomplete" being and "strange" enough for kin to exploit him for a fee, is nonetheless "perfect."[21] The dichotomous proximity of perfection to imperfection is absolutely case specific for Montaigne, and here the two terms retain a kind of flexible, reciprocal plasticity even as they ultimately have the norming effect of stigmatizing the boy (and his twin) as "monstrous." The ideology of ability at work in Montaigne anticipates a cure or kill mentality inherent in the modern medical model of disability and works in tandem with emergent sixteenth- and early seventeenth-century discourses that articulated previously so-called natural phenomena in more clinical, mechanistic terms.

"Strange Alterations": Adustion, Ability, and *The Winter's Tale*

Any discussion of "normal" and "abnormal" within early modern medical science requires examination of the formal humoral categories Renaissance medical theorists identified as the *natural* and the *unnatural*. This bifurcated classification system demonstrates disability as an operational category of difference by another name in early modernity: again, as Elizabeth Bearden argues, "[b]efore normal, there was natural."[22] While humoral logic understood a certain amount of radical or vital heat as requisite to facilitate a body's general solubility (the healthy flow of the bodily fluids to the various bodily members), Renaissance philosophers and physicians considered excesses in heat to be especially dangerous. Such excesses could lead to *adustion*, the irregular scorching of the humors responsible for transforming natural humors into an unnatural state, and thereby producing dangerous byproducts – humoral excrements and vapors – that could have severe behavioral implications.

This model of the unnatural and natural thus presents a uniquely early modern schema for norming bodily function. Timothy Bright, writing in 1586 on melancholy, observes that the melancholic humor is

> of two sorts: natural, or vnnaturall: [the] natural is ... the grosser part of the bloud ordained for nourishment, which surchargeth the bodie .... The vnnaturall is an humour rising of melancholie before mentioned ... wholly changed into an other nature by an vnkindly heate, which turneth these humours, which before were raunged vnder natures gouernment, and kept in order, into a qualitie wholly repugnant, whose substance and vapor giueth such annoyance to all partes, that as it passeth or is seated maketh strange alterations in our actions.[23]

Bright's distinction between the two forms of the melancholic humor explicitly configures early modern disability categories, wherein the unnatural functions as a stigmatized marker of inward affective impairment often shamefully externalized through aberrant behaviors and "strange alterations in our actions." Bright locates this inward trauma in the adust humor's effects upon the organs, observing that "excessive distemper of heat ... raiseth the greatest tempest of perturbations and most of all destroyeth the braine with all his faculties, and disposition of action" (111). This inward humoral alteration from the natural to the unnatural via the influence of excessive heat thus explains sudden behavioral shifts from typical melancholy sadness to choleric rage, for instance.

Behavioral shifts derived from the abnormal, explosive transformation of the melancholic humor through the psychosomatic interaction between heart and brain were typified by an array of period-specific symptoms ranging from innocuous eye-rolling and lip-chewing to far more serious and stigmatized behavioral indicators such as hallucinations and heart palpitations. As Bright observes of the interaction between the heart and the brain, unnatural melancholy produces terrifying hallucinations as it

> counterfetteth terrible obiectes to the fantasie, and polluting both the substance, and spirites of the brayne, causeth it without externall occassion, to forge monstrous fictions . . . whiche the iudgement taking as they are presented by the disordered instrument, deliuer over to the hart, which . . . giuing credite to the mistaken report of the braine breaketh out into that inordinate passion, against reason. (113, 110, 102)

Such unnatural, aberrant humoral interplay between these two organs, he notes, includes the false interpretation of outward events, "monstrous fictions," which themselves can relay false report such that "the hart may be abused from the brayne" (94).

As Stephen Batman observes in a similar context in 1582, while individual emotional health relies significantly on the heart's ability to maintain proper, timely "movement," if the vital, natural heat becomes overheated to the extreme, then a second major symptom of unnatural melancholy can result: heart palpitations.[24] "The bloud of the heart," Batman explains, "boyleth and moveth, and so the vitall spirite is grieved . . . Also the heart sometime quaketh . . . And so it seemeth to a sicke man, [as] yf the heart moveth from place to place" (Book 5, Section 36). This activity Batman calls "*Cardiaca passio*," in which the *moving* of the heart, or the strong emotion directed toward like or dislike, turns to *movement* of the heart, which causes its errant beating. Robert Burton, too, confirms in his famous *The Anatomy of Melancholy* (1628) that a common effect of this transformation toward unnatural melancholy is the "palpitation of the heart," and he further identifies unnatural melancholy as the cause for a series of similarly sudden, deleterious behavioral changes.[25] Burton observes that when fear stokes unnatural melancholy, "Many lamentable effects this fear causeth in men . . . it makes sudden cold and heat to come over all the body, palpitation of the heart, syncope, &c" (1.2.3.5). Such transformations, he insists, "causeth oftentimes sudden madness," as well as a condition in which the impaired individual is both "tormented in mind" and often suspects "treason . . . of their dearest and nearest friends" (1.2.3.5, 1.3.1.2).

Such disabling conversion from natural to unnatural humoral embodiment might be explored best in the context of Leontes' ostensibly sudden derangement as it manifests in Shakespeare's late romance, *The Winter's Tale*.[26] Among other things, the play depicts in Act One, Scene Two the idealized boyhood of the two friends, Leontes and Polixenes, as "twinned lambs that did frisk i'th'sun" (I.2, 69), their nostalgic misogyny through which their association with women serves as cause of their ostensible fall, and the troubling image of Polixenes grasping hands with Leontes' nine-months-pregnant wife. Amid this complex unfolding of character relationships, Leontes glares in horror and exclaims:

> *[Aside.]* Too hot, too hot:
> To mingle friendship farre is mingling bloods.
> I have *tremor cordis* on me. My heart dances,
> But not for joy, not joy. (I.2, 110–13; emphasis in original)

While Leontes' language reflects his torment at having been cuckolded, his specific lexicon ("Too hot, too hot") evidences an awareness of the psychosomatic volatility inherent in the humoral paradigm and expresses a variety of early modern anxieties about aberrant embodiment and vehement emotion. Leontes' felt realization of a sudden, unnatural influx of heat, his articulation of the heart palpitation he calls "*tremor cordis*," and his subsequent identification of his heart's interaction with the "infection of [his] brains" (I.2, 147) narrates the inward processes of his derangement and outlines his dominance by unnatural humors that are typified by the stigmatizing behaviors early modern humoral theorists, as we have seen just above, aimed to diagnose.

The "clinical specificity" of Leontes' self-diagnosis, as Derek Cohen calls it, is a "brilliant dramatic stroke"[27] that can redirect our attention to disability, here an impairment which derives from the unnaturalness of Leontes' humorality and its symptomatology both inwardly and outwardly configured. In other words, Leontes' shift from the status of ostensibly rich, married, healthy, twenty-something normate, at the play's outset, to that of an unnaturally constituted humoral monster displays a form of Bright's "melancholie madnesse" that is demonstrably both early modern and stable in definition as a pre-Enlightenment disability sensibility. While scholarship runs rife with all kinds of explanations for Leontes' derangement,[28] disability theory and methodology open up new, innovative frameworks for reading this scene. By engaging humoral treatises – early modern disability discourses – which correlate in marked ways with Shakespeare's play, the advent of Leontes' derangement in Act One, Scene Two, is so startling not just because of its roots in the radical skepticism, cuckoldry, and anxieties born of Renaissance patriarchy, but because it serves as an example of disability deployed, narrated, and pursued both literally *and* metaphorically as narrative prosthetic.[29] More crucially, it functions as a form of period-specific, character-driven realism in which the stigmatization of Leontes' psychosomatic derangement becomes a keen example of how the protomedical model of disability starts to obtain in early modern England.

Drama, Desire, and Disability Aesthetics

Exploring the norming effects mobilized by premodern disability clarifies not just underpinning ideologies of ability at play in the Renaissance but likewise reveals key counterdiscourses – disability theories and logics – made possible only in opposition to fantasies of ability and with keen sensibility toward non-normative embodiment. Take, for example, early modern writer Thomas Traherne's "Dumnesse," a lyric poem whose counterdiscourse, or disability aesthetic, manifests an intense *desire for* disability.[30] Traherne crafts a poem about how "Man was born to Meditat on Things, /. . . And therfore Speechless made at first" (ll. 1–5). While in certain instances Traherne employs impairment as an opportunistic form of rhetorical disability, he simultaneously writes his poem *against* an ability logic, cultivating a resistant counterlogic that embraces impairment (lack of speech, for our purposes, though notably also deafness in the poem) as the condition for spiritual and poetic accomplishment.[31] "Dumnesse," in fact, evidences not just a celebration of disability but a real longing for it; the inability to communicate orally is a "Blessed Case" (l. 17) that we all should hope for: "*I then my Bliss did, when my Silence, break*" (l. 20; emphasis in original). In Traherne's aesthetic, impairment is something to be held close, kept integral, and invited to thrive; "My Non-Intelligence of Human Words," the speaker admits, "Ten thousand Pleasures unto me affords" (ll. 21, 22). Being "pent within" (l. 53) allows the narrator to find spiritual guidance and inspiration everywhere; "All things did com / With Voices and Instructions" (ll. 67–8). And although speech ultimately "destroyed / The Oracle, and all I there enjoyd" (ll. 74–5), muteness instills into the poet speaker a godliness that "got such a root / Within my Heart . . . / It may be Trampld on, but still will grow" (ll. 82–4). In "Dumnesse," impaired speech is an epistemological benefit not a deficit. It is the fundamental condition of possibility for the narrator's spiritual life and a distinct *in*ability he wishes he might never have lost; further, it is the root of the poet's aesthetic.

Traherne's poem begins to imagine an alternative understanding of early modern bodies and minds that both welcomes and needs disability, and thus anticipates what Rosemarie Garland-Thomson recently posed as "the bioethical question of why we might want to conserve rather than eliminate disability from the human condition."[32] Bearing this query in mind, we turn, finally, to an anonymous play called *Looke about You* for discussion of its distinct disability aesthetic, one premised, like Traherne's, upon the deliberate desire for and conservation of disability.[33] Performed circa 1600, the play is a madcap romp through Henry II's England that features a stutterer named Redcap, "The po po Porters Sonne of the F Fl Fleete, going to Stepney about businesse to the La La Lady Fa Fa Faukenbridge" (C), who becomes enmeshed in court intrigue. The action of this "pleasant commodie" centers upon a series of nobles (as well as a character named Skinke, progenitor of chaos in the play) adopting Redcap's clothes and affecting his stutter in order to negotiate fracturing sympathies among the royal family. Frequent recourse to stuttering (both genuine, for the sympathetic Redcap; and feigned, by his numerous imitators) highlights many other representations of disability also staged in this play: from jokes about "lameness" and "halting" (limping) to "madness" and blindness; and from stigmas associated with the plague to those involving habitual drunkenness.

Amongst these myriad disability representations, Redcap's speech impairment stands out as one of the play's main interests. In fact, we read *Looke about You* as revealing and reveling in an aesthetic that deliberately incorporates the body's limits into composition. Speech impairment is produced and used in the play not just as a narrative prosthetic, but it quite literally is the mode of embodiment *through which the drama makes meaning*. In this alternate formulation, the play both calls attention to and lives out nonnormative embodiment and its contingent relationship to early modern psychophysiological ideals.

On the one hand, *Looke about You* certainly typifies early modern stigma against atypical locution[34] as various characters in the play compare Redcap to base animals and imply that stuttering is coincident with cognitive impairment: "Farewell and be hang'd good stammering ninny [simpleton or fool]," mocks Skinke, for example; "I thinke I have set your Redcaps heeles arunning, wold your Pyanet [magpie; also figurative for chatterer or gossip] chattering humour could as sa safely se set mee fr from the searchers walkes" (C). That said, stuttering in *Looke about You* does more than just codify an ideology of linguistic ability insofar as it also functions as a narrative prosthesis. Although Redcap's stutter does not get centralized dramatically in order to be explained (away), it *does* become paramount insofar as it enables the disguise plot of the play and provides the drama with narrative momentum. Simultaneously, though, Redcap's speech patterning operates as "the textual obstacle that causes the literary operation of open-endedness to close down or stumble."[35] Even in its formal necessity, then, stuttering is still an undesirable mode of embodiment that the play must either cure or exterminate. And, sure enough, just before the tidy close of the comedy, Redcap is expelled from the narrative: "A f fo fore I go goe I b b be s s seech you let Sk Skinke and gl Gloster be lo lo looked too, for they have p p playd the k k knaves to to to b b bad," begs Redcap, only to be "Put forth" by King Henry who curtly commands, "Take hence that stuttering fellow, shut them forth" (L).

While the drama's use of Redcap's stutter certainly evidences early modern sociocultural stigma as well as a formal, narrative need for and yet repulsion toward disability, on the other hand, it concurrently, and somewhat paradoxically, indicates a profound desire for it. As in Traherne's "Dumnesse," speech impairment drives the narrative, but not simply prosthetically to enable the drama's plot devices or genre obligation. Instead, in various characters' imitative embracing of Redcap's vocal patterning, we see a deliberate reproduction and conservation of disability that is as enabling and agential as it is stigmatizing. The play's diction is marked by obsessive word and sound repetition, and audible breaks, pauses, and interjectional utterances abound. Redcap is not merely given full voice in *Looke about You*, but his atypical speech serves as a linguistic template in the play; his distinctive voice is replicated so intently and ubiquitously that it becomes the drama's dominant aesthetic mode.

Looke about You, thus, harnesses speech impairment as a distinctive resource and aesthetic template. Note, for example, the unlucky pursuivant who fails to carry out his heraldic duties and subsequently laments strictly in assonant ejaculations and recurrent phrases: "O O O not too fast; O I am sicke, O very sicke. ... But I, but I, but I, O my head, O my heart. ... O my box, my box, with the Kings armes, O my box,. .. O my box, it cost me, O Lord every penny O, my box" (F3). Take too, Blocke's aside commentary about his mistress's dubious actions: "Hem, these women, these women, and she bee not in love eyther with Prince Richard or this lad, let blocks head be made a chopping blocke" (C2). Here, as Old Richard Faukenbridge's servant puns on the high stakes of his job, he repeats "block" not only for witty emphasis but in a final echo that mirrors the doubled-up phrasing at the start of the line in "these women, these women." Blocke, like numerous other characters throughout the play, also begins his sentence with a "Hem," an indistinct, initial hesitation or clearing of the throat that can function very much like a stutter. So too, Old Richard Faukenbridge utters lines whose singsong sound springs from repetitive diction – "Ile make you laugh, ile make you laugh yfaith; / Come, come, he's ready, O come, come away" (K2-K3). This diction reminds readers and listeners of how Redcap's reiterated initial consonants, for instance, have their own distinctive melodiousness: "Go go god ye, go god s speed ye" (K3). As even these few examples attest, stammering dominates *Looke about You*'s acoustic landscape and, thereby, likely forced players and playgoers to both confront and reconsider conventional aesthetic expectations they held about early modern theater and stageplaying.

Interestingly, the play desires and conserves disability in concomitant modes, not just via uncharacteristic aurality in performance but *typographically* in the printed playtext itself: the words on the page strive to sustain performed stuttering and aestheticize it further. The fact that Redcap stumbles over any and every word the author finds dramatically or metrically useful points to how staged stuttering in *Looke about You* extends beyond performative utility into a durable, expressly textual, aesthetic mode. A line like Redcap's "I am g g glad of th th that, my fa fa father the p p porter sha shall ge ge get a f f fee by you" (B3) deliberately marks and reproduces in print each and every locution presumably uttered by an actor on stage. On first reading, as it might have been for early modern listening audiences as well, this typographical incompleteness is both unexpected and jarring in its deliberate fragmentation. As these typographical fragments accrue, however, they become something *more than* complete; on the page and taken together, they prosthetically supplement staged speech impairment to conserve formally an aural variation that, in performance, is ephemeral. The printed phrase "La La Lady Fa Fa Faukenbridge," for example, apprehends indistinct and impermanent speech and, ironically, distinctly demonstrates it on the page. The play's type allows – perhaps even forces – readers to linger longer in the space of linguistic difference, in spaces marked by stammering print and forceful gaps between single, repeated letters.

Following Ato Quayson, we posit that the disability conservation work evident in *Looke about You* is highly efficacious.[36] Atypical speech in *Looke about You* functions as far more than (play)textual detail; it is an unavoidable disruption marking "a threshold that opens up to other questions of a textual and also ethical kind."[37] The play's artistic stutter, especially instantiated typographically, embraces a kind of aesthetic nervousness that, like a stutter itself, short-circuits normative modes of reading, seeing, hearing, and interacting.[38] Further, acknowledging the always transitory nature of performance, it preserves the live staging of disability by textually re-embodying it in an exceptional typography that celebrates linguistic difference. As students and scholars continue to interrogate early modern ideologies of ability and explore new prehistories of stigma and their norming effects, *Looke about You* and other Renaissance disability narratives can serve not only to exemplify how variant embodiment made meaning in the English Renaissance but also facilitate humane conversation about disability ethics, aesthetics, and the ways that early modern literature captured and conserved an undeniable desire for disability difference.

NOTES

1. See William Shakespeare, *The Tragedy of King Richard the Third*, in *The Norton Shakespeare*, ed. by Stephen Greenblatt (New York: Norton, 1997).
2. On this term, see Tobin Siebers, *Disability Theory* (Ann Arbor: University of Michigan Press, 2008), especially the introduction, pp. 1–33.

3. See Michael Davidson, *Concerto for the Left Hand: Disability and the Defamiliar Body* (Ann Arbor: University of Michigan Press, 2008), and Tobin Siebers, *Disability Aesthetics* (Ann Arbor: University of Michigan Press, 2010).
4. Siebers, *Disability Theory*, p. 9.
5. Ibid., p. 8.
6. Rosemarie Garland-Thomson, *Extraordinary Bodies: Figuring Physical Disability in American Culture and Literature* (New York: Columbia University Press, 1997), p. 8.
7. For more on these characters, see *As You Like It* and *Romeo and Juliet* in Greenblatt (ed.), *The Norton Shakespeare*.
8. The four humors – blood, phlegm, choler, and melancholy – were produced by the body's internal organs and passed through the bloodstream delivering cold, heat, moistness, and dryness to the rest of the body. Character traits and personality qualities were associated with an excess of one or the other of these humors. See Gail Kern Paster, *The Body Embarrassed: Drama and the Disciplines of Shame in Early Modern England* (Ithaca, NY: Cornell University Press, 1993); and Gail Kern Paster, Katherine Rowe, and Mary Floyd-Wilson (eds.), *Reading the Early Modern Passions: Essays in the Cultural History of Emotion* (Philadelphia: University of Pennsylvania Press, 2004).
9. Eukrasia occurred when a perfect elemental equilibrium was achieved, and a dearth or excess of any one humor could provoke illnesses from consumption to dropsy to dysentery. See F. D. Hoeniger, *Medicine and Shakespeare in the English Renaissance* (Newark: University of Delaware Press, 1992), pp. 181–83.
10. Julie Singer, "Disability and the Social Body," *postmedieval*, 3.2 (2012), 135–41 (pp. 135–36).
11. See Lennard J. Davis, *Enforcing Normalcy: Disability, Deafness, and the Body* (London: Verso, 1995), Chapter 2.
12. Elizabeth B. Bearden, "Before Normal, There Was Natural: John Bulwer, Disability, and Natural Signing in Early Modern England and Beyond," *PMLA*, 132.1 (2017), 33–50.
13. Valerie Traub, "The Nature of Norms in Early Modern England: Anatomy, Cartography, *King Lear*," *South Central Review*, 26.1–2 (2009), 42–81 (p. 57).
14. For numerous examples and further reading on early modern disability, from court dwarfs in Spenser's *Faerie Queene* to Jonson's *Volpone* to the philosophies of Hobbes and Locke, see Allison P. Hobgood and David Houston Wood, *Recovering Disability in Early Modern England* (Columbus: Ohio State University Press, 2013).
15. See Margaret T. Hodgen, *Early Anthropology in the Sixteenth and Seventeenth Centuries* (Philadelphia: University of Pennsylvania Press, 1964), pp. 49–74.
16. Stephen Batman, *The Doome Warning All Men to the Judgemente* (London, 1581) and *Black-Letter Ballads and Broadsides* (London: Joseph Lilly, 1870).
17. See, in *Black-Letter Ballads and Broadsides*, "The True Description of a Monsterous Chylde, Borne in the Ile of Wight . . . " (London, 1562), pp. 63–66; "The Forme and Shape of a Monsterous Child, Borne at Maydstone . . . "

(London, 1568), pp. 194–97; and "The True Description of Two Monsterous Children, Laufully Begotten between George Steuens and Margerie His Wife … " (London, 1566), pp. 217–20. These texts are cited in Ian Frederick Moulton, "'A Monster Great Deformed': The Unruly Masculinity of *Richard III*," *Shakespeare Quarterly*, 47.3 (1996), 251–68 (pp. 262–64).

18. See Allison Hobgood, "Caesar Hath the Falling Sickness: The Legibility of Early Modern Disability in Shakespearean Drama," *Disability Studies Quarterly*, 29.4 (2009), n. pag., http://dsq-sds.org/article/view/993/1184, accessed May 24, 2017; and "Teeth Before Eyes: Illness and Invisibility in Shakespeare's *Richard III*," in *Disability, Health, and Happiness in the Shakespearean Body*, ed. by Sujata Iyengar (New York: Routledge, 2015), pp. 23–40.
19. John Lamport, *A Direct Method of Ordering and Curing People of That Loathsome Disease, the Small-Pox* (London: Printed by J. Gain, 1685). Further page references to primary texts will be given parenthetically in the body of the chapter.
20. Michel de Montaigne, *The Essayes or Morall, Politike and Millitarie Discourses* (London: By Val. Sims for Edward Blount, 1603).
21. For more on the complex meanings of "perfect," see *The Oxford English Dictionary Online*. 2017. Willamette University Library. www.oed.com.ezproxy .app.willamette.edu/, accessed May 24, 2017.
22. Bearden, "Before Normal," p. 33.
23. Timothy Bright, *A Treatise of Melancholie* (London: Thomas Vautrolloer, 1586), pp. 1–3.
24. Stephen Batman, *Batman upon Bartholome, His Booke De Proprietatibus Rerum* (London: Thomas East, 1582).
25. See Robert Burton, *The Anatomy of Melancholy* (Oxford: Henry Cripps, 1628), 1.2.3.5, 1.3.1.1, 1.3.2.2.
26. For an examination of this scene with relation to time, narrative, and emotion – one that fails to account for disability reading strategies – see David Houston Wood, *Time, Narrative, and Emotion in Early Modern England* (Farnham: Ashgate, 2009), pp. 103–31. All citations from *The Winter's Tale* refer to *The Norton Shakespeare*.
27. Derek Cohen, "Patriarchy and Jealousy in *Othello* and *The Winter's Tale*," *Modern Language Quarterly*, 48.3 (1987), 207–23 (p. 211).
28. For an overview of the various scholarly positions regarding the ostensible cause of Leontes' derangement maintained by Harold Bloom, Frank Kermode, J. H. P. Pafford, Sir Arthur Quiller-Couch, Roger Trienens, and Dover Wilson, see Wood, *Time, Narrative, and Emotion*, especially pp. 104–05.
29. On narrative prosthesis, see David T. Mitchell and Sharon Snyder, *Narrative Prosthesis: Disability and the Dependencies of Discourse* (Ann Arbor: University of Michigan Press, 2001), p. 52.
30. *The Poetical Works of Thomas Traherne*, ed. by Gladys Wade (New York: Cooper Square Publishers, 1965), pp. 23–25. For the most recent and nearly complete compilation of Traherne's writings, see *The Works of Thomas Traherne*, ed. by Jan Ross (Cambridge: D. S. Brewer, 2005), 5 vols. Traherne's works were lost for over two centuries, discovered in manuscript in 1896–97, and initially attributed to Henry Vaughan.

31. On opportunistic rhetorical disability in Traherne, see Susannah B. Mintz, "An Collins and the Disabled Self" in *An Collins and the Historical Imagination*, ed. Scott W. Howard (Farnham; Burlington, VT: Ashgate, 2014), pp. 53–69; and "Strange Bodies: Thomas Traherne's Disabled Subject" in *Re-Reading Thomas Traherne: A Collection of New Critical Essays*, eds. Jacob Blevins and Arizona Center for Medieval and Renaissance Studies (Tempe, AZ: Arizona Center for Medieval and Renaissance Studies, 2007), pp. 1–20.
32. Rosemarie Garland-Thomson, "The Case for Conserving Disability," *Journal of Bioethical Inquiry*, 9.3 (2012), 339–55 (p. 341).
33. *A Pleasant Commodie Called Looke about You* (London: Printed [by Edward Allde] for William Ferbrand, 1600). The 1600 playtext was reprinted in facsimile by the Malone Society in 1913 and published by Richard S. M. Hirsch as *A Pleasant Commedie Called Looke about You: A Critical Edition* (New York: Garland, 1980).
34. See Carla Mazzio, *The Inarticulate Renaissance: Language Trouble in an Age of Eloquence* (Philadelphia: University of Pennsylvania Press, 2009), p. 3.
35. Mitchell and Snyder, *Narrative Prosthesis*, p. 50.
36. Ato Quayson, *Aesthetic Nervousness: Disability and the Crisis of Representation* (New York: Columbia University Press, 2007), Chapter 1, especially p. 19.
37. Ibid., p. 208.
38. Ibid., p. 17.

4

ESSAKA JOSHUA

Disability and Deformity

Function Impairment and Aesthetics in the Long Eighteenth Century

Discussion of disability in the long eighteenth century (1660–1832) is made difficult by the fact that the conventional concept of disability was not properly in place – neither as a medical description, nor as a feature of a group, nor as a personal identity. Instead, disability studies scholars who investigate disability historically explore ancestral and analogous concepts. There are further difficulties with the study of impairment in the literature of this period. Firstly, it is not always clear which impairments are present. Sometimes, however, the ambiguities surrounding the presentation of an impairment are important. Indeed, challenging the certainty of diagnosis is an important part of the disability studies approach. Secondly, the personal circumstances of characters change the way in which an impairment is conceptualized. Concepts of impairment are affected by whether the impairment is acquired or congenital, visible or hidden, function-based or aesthetic, and, importantly, by gender, race, class, sexuality, and socioeconomic status. Thirdly, individual impairments have cultural histories of their own, and it is important to investigate these cultural meanings since they inflect the way in which authors use particular impairments.

When the term "disability" is used in the long eighteenth century, it describes any kind of incapacity in a person or thing. Samuel Johnson defines the noun "disability" as the "[w]ant of power to do any thing; weakness; impotence," and the verb "to disable" as "[t]o deprive of natural force; to weaken; to crush."[1] But, "disability" is not a common word in the period. "Deformity," however, is frequently used and is the dominant heterogeneous category used to describe congenital and acquired impairments that are visible: these conditions are as diverse as freckles, smallpox scarring, having one eye, having no teeth, dwarfism, and limb loss. Deformities are usually understood in aesthetic terms, without explicitly referencing function. There are a few other important terms. Natural historians in the period refer to people with unusual deformities by using the term *lusus naturae* (a sport of nature). People with unusual deformities are sometimes referred to as "monsters," a term used widely but which is also present in natural history. According to Johnson, "defect," another common word in the eighteenth-century discourse of disability, describes a perceived deficiency or an absence of something deemed necessary.

Function Impairment

We see something of the conceptual difference between function impairment and deformity in Frances Burney's *Camilla* (1796), a novel that explores Eugenia Tyrold's transition from perceiving herself as having a function impairment to understanding that she is perceived by others as having a deformity. The novel includes several characters with impairments. Sir Hugh Tyrold limps because of gout, and Eugenia, his niece, limps because of a spinal impairment acquired after she is dropped by her uncle from a seesaw. She also has smallpox scars and is of small stature. Both characters use a garden chair and lean on people for support, and Sir Hugh uses walking sticks. The narrator says in one striking moment of resemblance: "They proceeded very slowly, the baronet leaning upon Dr. Marchmont, and Eugenia upon Dr. Orkborne."[2] Sir Hugh is an elderly baronet whose limp is presented as a function impairment rather than a deformity. Old men are usually not held to a standard of beauty and so are not deemed deficient in this regard. Eugenia's situation is more complex. The visible impairments of high-ranking female characters are usually treated as aesthetic rather than functional, because beauty is highly valued by suitors. The plain-speaking, lower-ranking Mr. Dubster offers Eugenia his observations on the gendered and class dimensions of function impairment, saying that "it's but a hard thing upon a man to be a cripple in the middle of life. It's no such great hindrance to a lady, so I don't say it out of disrespect; because ladies can't do much at the best" (289). Mr. Dubster suggests that impaired function is not a problem for women who do not work. His extensive derogatory reference to Eugenia's appearance confirms that he conceptualizes her impairments aesthetically, and he implies that a deficiency of this kind *is* a problem for women who do not work.

Eugenia is kept in ignorance of the aesthetic implications of deformity until they are revealed to her by accident when she is fourteen, in an encounter with verbally abusive market women. Until this point, she has recognized her physical difference, but not its aesthetic significance. Characters who conceptualize Eugenia's impairments as functional rather than aesthetic are presented as having moral worth. For instance, Edgar Mandlebert is not concerned with how dancing with Eugenia will appear, and he politely asks whether Eugenia is interested in dancing. Camilla, her sister, treats this as an implied question about ability and responds that Eugenia's "lameness is no impediment; for she never thinks of it" (64). The sisters' vain cousin, Clermont Lynmere, who has been chosen to marry Eugenia, is, however, concerned about her appearance. When Clermont rejects the proposed marriage, Camilla comments that "though she had seen with concern the inequality of their outward appearance, Clermont had seemed to her, in all else, so inferior to her sister, that she had repined at his unworthiness, but never doubted the alliance" (630). *Camilla* criticizes the inflated social currency of physical beauty and promotes moral beauty as deserving of higher value, while demonstrating that concepts of impairment, whether aesthetic or functional, shift in different contexts.

Mr. Dubster raises the possibility that function impairment is irrelevant to women of rank. The novelist and political scientist Mary Wollstonecraft argues, in *A Vindication of the Rights of Woman* (1792), that the assumption that women are merely decorative amounts to social oppression. The economic and social dependence of women is generated, in part, she suggests, by the cultural suppression of their intellectual and physical utility. Wollstonecraft attacks what she sees as a fashion for women imitating and acquiring function impairment, or "that lovely weakness," and for men wasting their lives by engaging in pointless fashionable pursuits.[3] She also addresses what she believes to be some common misconceptions about impaired bodies. It is usually thought, she points out, that those with impaired function must have intellectual superiorities. Wollstonecraft counters this myth with the observation that "strength of mind has, in most cases, been accompanied by superior strength of body, – natural soundness of constitution" and insists that "dependence of body naturally produces dependence of mind" (111). She calls women who court weakness of body "infatuated" because they are "proud of a defect," and she laments that they see incapacity as a goal (107). A "defect," she asserts, can never "become an excellence" (107). In exposing the constructedness of gender, Wollstonecraft conceptualizes function impairment in terms of inutility and degradation. This idea also circulates in the feminist novel of the late eighteenth century.

Wollstonecraft's ideas on function impairment accord with those of her husband, William Godwin. In his *Enquiry Concerning Political Justice* (1793/1798), Godwin outlines his theory of a politically just society.[4] He promotes the idea of acting in the interests of the greater good rather than according to personal interest. Godwin's famous example of saving the person deemed most useful to society when rescuing one of two people from a burning building suggests that lives are valuable only through work. Godwin makes physical and intellectual utility the driver behind his theory of moral action, idealizing intellectual independence and autonomy in decision-making, and even speculating that, when reason is fully in control of human life, people will be able to heal their own bodies with their minds. The case of the burning building suggests that Godwin's theory of political justice is conceptually dependent on people being nonimpaired and that he defines utility in terms of a particular range of physical and intellectual abilities. Moreover, Godwin uses physical function impairment to characterize a decadent and effeminate aristocracy, the nature of evil, and a corrupt body politic; and he links both intellectual and physical function impairment with limitation, ignorance, and exclusion. Sometimes function impairment is conspicuously absent from Godwin's consideration, and at other times it is present in incongruous contexts, revealing a deep anxiety about bodily difference.

Elizabeth Hamilton, in her satirical novel, *Memoirs of Modern Philosophers* (1800), finds Godwin's version of political justice to be at odds with sympathy. Hamilton uses function impairment as a way to challenge Godwin's ideas on social contribution, by suggesting that providing for people with function impairments, through acts of personal charity, is both virtuous and essential. Mrs. Biggs, a "bed-ridden" widow with a broken back, and her son, who has intellectual impairments, are financially supported by Mrs. Biggs's daughters. Dr. Orwell praises "their filial piety, their sisterly affection, their kind and humane attention to their unfortunate brother, and the many self-denials they must have undergone in the performance of these duties"; he regards them as "an example of virtue as is not to be contemplated without bettering the heart," and as being "of greater consequence to society, than volumes of philosophy."[5] Bridgetina Botherim, who expounds a parodied version of Godwin's system, rejects this lesson, responding that the daughters should do more for "general utility" (345). The novel implies that family members have a duty to look after each other and that judgments made solely on the basis of reason are at odds with sensibility, benevolence, and familial love. Hamilton has no solution for the exclusion of people with disabilities from political justice, however, and her novel implies, problematically, that people with function impairments are to be pitied or treated as the occasion for the nonimpaired to demonstrate their moral worth. Nevertheless, Hamilton destigmatizes function impairment in the context of the family, and considers some of the practical consequences of favoring nonimpaired people.

Sentimental literature frequently depicts function impairment as pitiable, often using children in this context and focusing on loss. Charles Lamb's encounter poem "Blindness," for instance, narrates a stagecoach encounter between a beautiful blind girl, her mother, and a sighted old man.[6] Unaware of her impairment, the man points to the view and suggests she turn her "pretty eyes" on it (375). The girl responds plainly, "I cannot see the prospect, I am blind." The sighted passenger is emotionally affected by this ("Never did tongue of child utter a sound / So mournful, as her words fell on my ear"), and the circumstances generate pity even as the blind girl demonstrates her acceptance of her condition (375). The poem derives its sentiment in part from the irony of the beautiful girl's being unable to experience scenic beauty visually and in part from the coupling of her seemingly perfect beauty with a supposed defect, blindness.

William Wordsworth often uses an encounter between an impaired person and a seemingly nonimpaired person to explore the complex emotions raised in situations of charitable giving. "Andrew Jones" describes the meeting between the eponymous character and an unnamed beggar with a mobility impairment.[7] Andrew takes the two pennies that the beggar attempts to retrieve from the ground, thrown for him by a man on horseback. Wordsworth's pejorative terminology – he calls the man a "cripple" (l. 10) and a "poor crawling helpless wretch" (l. 11) – places an emphasis on pity that is patronizing and shocking to the modern ear, but his speaker firmly argues for the beggar's right to independence and fair treatment. The speaker regards Andrew's appropriation of the money intended for the beggar as more socially discordant than excessive drinking or swearing. The poem appears to begin with a charitable model of disability (which requires us to see people with function impairments as a social problem), but Wordsworth subverts this by presenting Andrew as socially deviant.

Charitable situations introduce problematic hierarchies between people with impairments and the charity-givers. But there are many examples where these hierarchies are challenged. Wordsworth offers a dynamic interaction between the speaker and a function-impaired veteran in "The Discharged Soldier" (1798). The poet builds a close connection between the soldier and the speaker through a series of images that explore their common ground, often contrasting impairment and nonimpairment only to dismantle the distinctions later on. Wordsworth begins by having his speaker appear to embrace ability in the declamatory and truncated first line, "I love to walk," followed, with enjambment, by the clause "Along the public way."[8] Though meant as a continuation, the line change creates a moment when the reader is forced to manage the transition. The pause may anticipate the walker's difficulties in that it is a moment when a leap is accommodated. Wordsworth, whose work contains much wordplay, may hint at the etymology of "enjambment" in his use of it. It means "to stride over," and the word contains the French for "leg" (*jambe*). The pause may also ironize the first clause, as the speaker rejoices in an able-bodiedness that is temporary and contextual. The opening statement is more than a simple identification of activity and location; it is a celebration of pedestrianism, mobility, and independence that is quickly countered by the opposite. The expectation of vigor is replaced with a description of the speaker "slowly" mounting "up a steep ascent" on a road so waterlogged that it "seemed before my eyes another stream" (ll. 6 and 9). The watery road leaks into the brook in the valley. The muddy road and streams unite, anticipating the meeting of the impaired and nonimpaired people. The union of the dissident, marginal, and transient watery road and the central brook that belongs in the valley exemplify the superficiality of the division of a normative and non-normative binary. In self-identifying as a "worn out" and "exhausted" worker, the speaker universalizes the condition of weakness, bringing us into an understanding of it as a common way of being (l. 17). In his struggle up the muddy hill, his body is made more akin to that of the soldier he has yet to meet. The soldier, though he is encouraged by the speaker, does not perform the expected role of telling an emotional story of his impairments, and the speaker is careful not to assume that help is needed. The speaker of the poem invites the veteran to become and to remain visible to the public: begging is the soldier's social entitlement, and the speaker does not regard this as a shameful pursuit.

Wollstonecraft's concern about imitating function impairment highlights a major anxiety in the period. David Turner and Tim Hitchcock both comment that people were anxious about the counterfeiting of function impairment, especially in the case of begging and extortion.[9] Duncan Campbell, a deaf clairvoyant who became the subject of a biography, *The History of the Life and Adventures of Mr. Duncan Campbell* (1720), was frequently accused of imposture, and the controversies over his deafness continue.[10] The credibility of Campbell's deafness was as much an issue for his contemporaries as his claim to possess second sight (premonitions), given that there was a popular assumption that deaf people could not be educated. While Joseph Addison describes Campbell as a London spectacle to be viewed alongside dancing monkeys and moving pictures, Campbell's autobiography, *Secret Memoirs* (1732), reveals an educated man with a circle of hearing friends who conversed with him in sign language and via written notes.[11] Campbell inspired a huge amount of writing that gives us insight into one of the earliest deaf celebrities and into the cultural attitudes expressed toward his impairment.[12] Much of the biographical material in these publications, however, may be colored by the demand for an extraordinary life that is worthy of a biography, and the truth about his deafness may never be known.

Acting-theory manuals give a sense of the simulation of function impairment as it was portrayed on the stage. They also help us understand how the rhetoric of stage movement and embodied characterization responded to the impaired body. Much acting theory in the long eighteenth century alludes to philosophical discussions about the emotional body and to the pseudoscience of physiognomy, making close links between physical and mental states. The question of whether an actor needed to have experienced something in order to imitate it is a prominent one. Actors with impairments were universally deemed to be problematic, and the attributes of the ideal actor's body were widely discussed. For instance, David Lyddal suggests, in his notes to his poem *The Prompter* (1810), that "An actor that we knew to be actually deformed; would be an intolerable representative of our third King Richard."[13] The eighteenth-century stage had its own language of impairment; and impairment embodies some surprising things, such as kingship. Robert Lloyd remarks, in his poem *The Actor* (1760), that the theatrical portrayal of monarchs requires the actor to drag one foot behind him: "One Foot put forward in Position strong, / The other like its Vassal dragg'd along."[14] Less surprisingly, physical impairment is frequently used to signal intellectual impairment. This conjunction is particularly conspicuous in accounts of comic acting. According to the *Theatrical Preceptor* (1811), the clown should have "an open mouth, arms dangling, yet the shoulders raised, the toes turned inward, a shambling gait with a heavy step, great slowness of conception, and apparent stupidity of mind and manner."[15]

The performance of function impairment is used as a disguise for homosexuality in Tobias Smollett's *Roderick Random* (1748). Smollett, a physician who included many accounts of medicine and doctors in his novels, uses Captain Whiffle as the occasion for the exploration of an effeminized masculinity that is also a masquerade of physical delicacy. By designating his perfumes, mask, chintz wrap, silk, lace, and bed rest as medical interventions, Whiffle intends to deflect attention from their associations with the feminine. Whiffle's physical impairment affords him the opportunity to conduct a relationship with his physician, Dr. Simper. Whiffle also attempts to deflect attention from his sexuality by ascribing a non-normative body to Mr. Morgan, a surgeon's first mate who wishes to be promoted. Whiffle calls Morgan "a monster and a stinkard" whose stench of tobacco will kill him, and he demands that the room be fumigated with perfume.[16] Morgan retaliates by calling Whiffle "disguised and transfigured, and transmogrified with affectation and whimsies" in such a fashion as to make him baboon-like, whereas Morgan believes his own body to be as nature intended (196). Whiffle is quickly exposed by the crew and is accused "of maintaining a correspondence with his surgeon, not fit to be named" (199). Captain Whiffle's masculinity is presented as normative in a medical context, but is defined by the crew as unnatural. His attack on Morgan recalls Alexander Pope's attack on Lord Hervey (as Sporus) in his "Epistle to Dr Arbuthnot" (1735). Pope portrays Hervey's bisexuality in terms of a disordered and grotesque body, and symbolizes Hervey's political influence as toothless and impotent.[17] In describing Sporus as grotesque, Pope deflects attention from his own impairments and deformities, positioning himself as a virtuous and manly character who has been unfairly ridiculed.

Oliver Goldsmith's *The Vicar of Wakefield* (1766) exemplifies something of the complexity of theological and metaphysical uses of function impairment. The novel equates impairment with suffering, suggesting that suffering is rewarded in the afterlife and that impairment is a form of religious trial. The vicar, Dr. Primrose, acquires a function impairment when he is burnt in a fire that destroys his home and nearly kills his two youngest children. Job-like in his suffering, Primrose presents himself as having been guilty of little more than family pride and as being punished disproportionately for it. These associations between impairment and disadvantage connect to the novel's wider interest in the body as a reflection of moral status – seen in the links between Primrose's daughter's illness and her temporary status as a suspected fallen woman – and in the use of ability as a metaphor for social advantage. Primrose, fearful that mixing ranks and social climbing is dangerous to those who are socially vulnerable, admires a quest story about a nameless dwarf and a giant. The dwarf, disadvantaged by his size, ends the journey as a sight-impaired double-amputee, and the giant gains the quest's prizes. The vicar implies, through a link between height and rank, that the socially inferior receive disadvantages, while the socially superior reap the rewards. The tale foreshadows the main narrative in that the vicar becomes the dwarf, incapacitated by the fire and socially disadvantaged by his lack of wealth; and, like the dwarf, he labors on beyond the point at which it would be prudent to stop. The novel links social disadvantage with non-normative body politics in more direct ways, too. On the first page, Primrose reveals that he does not welcome relatives he describes as "the blind, the maimed, and the halt," and Mrs. Primrose is forced to insist that "as they were the same *flesh and blood*, they should sit with us at the same table."[18]

Engagement with function impairments and experiences of temporary impairment sometimes enables writers to think from the position of impairment in ways that are transformational. When Samuel Taylor Coleridge is temporarily prevented, by a burn, from walking with his friends William and Dorothy Wordsworth, he is reminded, in "This Lime Tree Bower My Prison" (1797), of the imaginative gains that may come from impairment. His disablement brings an enriched understanding of his companionship with William and Dorothy as he walks with them in imagination.[19] Furthermore, some function impairments gain iconic status. Admiral Lord

Nelson, a partially sighted amputee, is celebrated in a poem on his death in which his impairments are close to super-abilities:

> Oh England has lost her right-hand,
> Of NELSON her Champion bereft;
> Yet Ocean she still can command,
> And like him, beat the French with her left.[20]

Nelson's physical impairments are often an embodiment of national pride. Function impairment in a military context is often different from function impairment in a nonmilitary context, in that the impairments can have honorific value and are symbolic in enigmatic ways.

Deformity and Aesthetics

Deformity was most commonly conceptualized as a set of characteristics that are the opposite of beauty. Philosophers of the period usually characterize deformity negatively, and standardize it as something that exhibits irregularity, disproportion, disharmony, asymmetry, peculiarity, sickness, and decay. From the beginning of aesthetics as a distinct philosophical discipline, looking at people or objects with deformities is regarded as causing the viewer to experience "pain" (Hume), "disgust" (Burke), and "disappointment" (Hutcheson).[21] Shaftesbury describes deformity as unnatural and Addison calls it "disagreeable."[22] In eighteenth-century accounts of the "picturesque," however, we see the beginnings of an affirmative deformity aesthetics. The picturesque, an aesthetic introduced as an alternative to the sublime and the beautiful, describes real and represented objects whose appearance conforms to standard philosophical definitions of deformity, but without the negative evaluation. The picturesque appears in books on art, travel, and gardening, and in poetry and novels. Theorists of the picturesque reject symmetry, harmony, proportion, and the ideals of perfection, celebrating instead architectural ruins, irregular landscapes, and people whose appearance does not accord with the usual standards for beauty. William Gilpin, Uvedale Price, and Richard Payne Knight discuss the ways in which art can remove the negative evaluation of deformity.[23] Addison's suggestion that we find pleasure in the "Agreeableness of the Objects to the Eye, and from their Similitude to other Objects," and that this similitude provides a possibility for taking aesthetic pleasure in deformity, is an important mechanism for the picturesque theorists' justification of the appeal of deformity.[24] We also see this maneuver in Romantic aesthetics. Wordsworth, for instance, uses this reasoning in the Preface to *Lyrical Ballads* (1802) when he defends his inclusion of mad people, an "idiot," old people, and several people with mobility impairments in *Lyrical Ballads* (1798). He argues that the mind derives pleasure in many cases, such as in ordinary conversation, artistic representations, and the differences of the sexes, "from the perception of similitude in dissimilitude, and dissimilitude in similitude."[25] Pleasure comes from reflecting on the relationships between an object and its similarities to, and differences from, something else – and not from identifying the characteristics of beauty.

Aside from deformities, intellectual impairments are often presented in aesthetic terms. In *Camilla*, Eugenia Tyrold's father takes her to a cottage to view a beautiful woman, as part of his attempt to make her accept her new understanding of her appearance. Initially, Eugenia is dismayed at the insensitivity; but when it becomes apparent that the woman "was born an idiot," Eugenia understands that she is to consider herself as more fortunate (310). Burney's engagement with Shaftesbury's views on beauty and deformity is relevant to the aestheticization of intellectual impairment that we find in *Camilla*. Shaftesbury asserts that beautiful people are beautiful because their appearance conforms to a standard of harmony, proportion, and order, and, importantly, because their beauty reveals the presence of the human mind. Even though we may think that we admire the "outward features" of someone, Shaftesbury argues, we are really admiring "a mysterious expression and a kind of shadow of something *inward* in the temper."[26] This inner beauty is the soul, or mind, or the effect of moral action. Shaftesbury is so committed to the idea of the enhancing power of the human mind on beauty that he deems it the thing that makes art beautiful: "the beautifying, not the beautified, is the really beautiful."[27] The importance of the effect of the mind means that, according to Shaftesbury, people with intellectual impairments can neither produce beautiful objects nor be beautiful themselves: "It is mind alone which forms. All which is void of mind is horrid and matter formless is deformity itself."[28] The narrator of *Camilla* suggests that the beautiful woman's beauty diminishes as her intellectual impairment becomes visible: "the slaver driveled unrestrained from her mouth, rendering utterly disgusting a chin that a statuary might have wished to model" (309). When defending the subject matter of "The Idiot Boy" (*Lyrical Ballads*), Wordsworth offers an alternative view. The critic John Wilson regarded the poem as generating disgust, but Wordsworth responded that he intended the boy to be handsome, and the poem's pace had prevented him from including this detail. For Wordsworth, beauty can diminish the distaste that people might feel when seeing people with intellectual impairments.[29]

The experience of being deformed is something that is considered by philosophers only occasionally. Hume, for example, suggests in *A Treatise of Human Nature* (1739–40), that deformity causes self-dissatisfaction. For Hume, being deformed causes us to think of ourselves, and, when we think of ourselves, we experience either pride or "humility" (his word for dissatisfaction). Deformity causes dissatisfaction because it is "peculiar" to a person; this Hume contrasts with short-term illness, which he sees as so various and as experienced so frequently by so many people that it is "in a manner separated from us" and we never consider it "as connected with our being and existence."[30] Hume decides, however, that long-term illness, like deformity, is "an object of humility" because it engages our sense of self.[31] David Hartley, unusually, suggests that the disadvantages associated with deformity originate in the social context of the person. In *Observations on Man* (1749), Hartley dismisses the worries one might have about being deformed as merely concerns about how one is seen by the world: "Beauty and Deformity are not attended with their respective pleasing or displeasing Associates, except when they are made apparent to, and taken notice of, by the World."[32] Hartley's point is brief but significant in that it anticipates the social model of disability.

William Hay offers one of the fullest and most remarkable accounts of deformity in his autobiographical reflection on life with a deformity, "Deformity: An Essay" (1754). Hay claims an affinity with other deformed people, calling them "brother[s] in blood," and suggests that deformity is "visible to every eye; but the effects of it are known to very few."[33] Hay challenges a number of assumptions about deformity, taking issue, for instance, with Francis Bacon's view, in "Of Deformity" (1612), that deformity aids advancement. Hay asserts that it is more likely that deformed people are at a disadvantage, because they have to contend with prejudice, while beautiful people are rewarded "at first sight" (I, 19). Hay observes that some deformities are treated more cruelly than others, and that the mob finds more to mock in "a crooked man, than one that is deaf, lame, squinting, or purblind" (I, 22). He is puzzled that people comment openly about his body shape, but not about his smallpox scars. He settles on the answer that, as his shape "is more uncommon, it is more remarkable" (I, 22). We see similar reactions to these deformities in Smollett's *Peregrine Pickle* (1751), a novel that has an extraordinary number of characters with impairments and deformities. The principal master at one of Peregrine's schools, Mr. Keypstick, is described as having "certain ridiculous peculiarities in his person, such as a hunch upon his back, and distorted limbs, that seemed to attract the satirical notice of Peregrine."[34] Whereas Keypstick is tripped and stuck with pins, the smallpox scars of Peregrine's friend Godfrey Gauntlet, "of which he bore a good number," lend a "peculiar manliness to the air of his countenance" (148). Smollett also considers the common association between deformity and bad character. The narrator implies that Peregrine's mother is perverse in preferring her son Gammy, who "though remarkably distorted in his body, [is] much more crooked in his disposition," to the handsome and charming Peregrine (107).

Hay observes that deformed people in higher social ranks tend to spend time studying and cultivating their minds rather than engaging in social pursuits. Deformity is, he suggests, associated with wits and intellectuals. Burney's Eugenia is an example of the deformed female intellectual. In addition to money, Sir Hugh gives her a classical education. Although personally rewarding, this is shown to be a social disadvantage that various characters regard as adding to her deformity or causing it. Smollett's *Roderick Random* explores the deformed female wit through the character of Miss Snapper, whom Roderick describes as "being bent sideways into the figure of an S, so that her progression very much resembled that of a crab" (331). Walking with her into the long room at Bath, Roderick observes that "we no sooner entered, than the eyes of every body present were turned upon us; and when we had suffered the martyrdom of their looks for some time, a whisper circulated at our expence, which was accompanied with many contemptuous smiles, and tittering observations, to my utter shame and confusion" (335). Miss Snapper, however, has experienced this before, and displays what Roderick calls "astonishing composure" (335). She wins the acceptance of the assembly, after an encounter with the verbally abusive Beau Nash, and is "applauded to the skies, for the brilliancy of her wit, and her acquaintance [is] immediately courted by the best people of both sexes in the room" (336). Miss Snapper's wit does not enfreak her in this brief vignette, as it does other female intellectuals of the period, but opens the way to the public acceptance of her deformities.

Conclusion

Function impairments and deformities, while conceptualized very differently, have much in common in the way they are used in the literature of the long eighteenth century. Narratives about function impairment and deformity often contain similar components: the acquisition of an impairment or deformity or of the knowledge of its social significance; an adverse social response; the wish to remove the impairment or deformity; the association of the impairment or deformity with significant qualities or gifts (such as superior strength, clairvoyance, intellectual ability, and money); and the conclusions of death, downfall, withdrawal, or acceptance. Both function impairment and deformity are used to explore impediments to work as well as reasons for employment. They are both associated with the supernatural, they are used as religious tests, as prompts for the nonimpaired to demonstrate virtue, as occasions for moral enrichment, and as prompts toward studious retirement from the world. Function impairment and deformity both offer transformational possibilities for imaginative and intellectual gain.

In spite of these congruities in narrative arrangements, function impairments and deformities are separate phenomena and there are some major differences. Deformity aesthetics is celebrated in the form and subject matter of the Romantic fragment poem, in the picturesque, and in Gothic literature. Function impairment plays an important role in feminist challenges to particular forms of femininity and masculinity; and the case is made that weak women are celebrated for a function impairment that appears incongruously to be aesthetically appealing. Deformity is more often associated with bad character than function impairment, and deformities are more often described as generating fear, self-dissatisfaction, ruthless ambition, and ridicule. Function impairments, but not deformities, are counterfeited for economic gain, used to signal the dignity of royalty, to represent the dissipated aristocrat, and the recipient of charity. Sometimes, as in the case of Admiral Nelson, function impairments are not impairments; and sometimes, as in the case of Eugenia's early life, deformities are not deformities.

NOTES

1. Samuel Johnson, *A Dictionary of the English Language*, 2nd edn., 2 vols. (London, 1755–56). Eighteenth Century Collections Online. Gale. University of Notre Dame. Accessed December 30, 2011.
2. Fanny Burney, *Camilla*, ed. by Edward A. Bloom and Lillian D. Bloom (Oxford: Oxford University Press, 1983), p. 142. Further page references to primary texts will be given parenthetically in the body of the chapter.
3. Mary Wollstonecraft, *A Vindication of the Rights of Men; A Vindication of the Rights of Woman; An Historical and Moral View of the French Revolution*, ed. by Janet Todd (Oxford: Oxford University Press, 1993), p. 105.
4. William Godwin, *An Enquiry Concerning Political Justice*, ed. by Mark Philp (Oxford: Oxford University Press, 2013).
5. Elizabeth Hamilton, *Memoirs of Modern Philosophers*, ed. by Claire Grogan (Peterborough, Ontario: Broadview, 2000), pp. 344–45.
6. Charles Lamb, *The Works of Charles and Mary Lamb*, ed. by E. V. Lucas, 5 vols. (London: Methuen, 1903), III, p. 375. The poem belongs to the volume *Poetry for Children* (1809).
7. William Wordsworth and Samuel Taylor Coleridge, *Lyrical Ballads*, ed. by Michael Mason (London: Longman, 1992), pp. 273–74.
8. William Wordsworth, *William Wordsworth. The Major Works*, ed. by Stephen Gill (Oxford: Oxford University Press, 1984), pp. 45–49.

9. David M. Turner, *Disability in Eighteenth-Century England: Imagining Physical Impairment* (New York: Routledge, 2012), p. 103, and Tim Hitchcock, *Down and Out in Eighteenth-Century London* (London: Hambledon and London, 2004), pp. 110–12.
10. *The History of the Life and Adventures of Mr. Duncan Campbell* (London: E. Curll et al., 1720). This biography has been attributed to Daniel Defoe, to Eliza Haywood, and to Defoe with the assistance of William Bond. The consensus is now that it is by Bond, but the work refers to the author as an elderly man, whereas Bond was a near contemporary of Campbell's. The most likely candidate is John Beaumont, whose work *The History* extensively plagiarizes and whose initials appear in a now obscure 1717 announcement "that it [*The History*] was shortly to be published, and that it was written by J. B. (i.e. Defoe)." John Robert Moore, *A Checklist of the Writings of Daniel Defoe*, 2nd edn. (Hamden, CT: Archon, 1971), p. 173. (Moore assumes "J. B." to have been one of Defoe's pseudonyms.) The *History* is particularly significant in that it contains the earliest known printing of a finger-spelling chart in an English book.
11. Joseph Addison, "No. 31, 5 April, 1711" in *The Spectator*, ed. by Donald Bond, 5 vols. (Oxford: Clarendon Press, 1965), I, pp. 127–32. Duncan Campbell, *Secret Memoirs of the Late Mr. Duncan Campbell, The Famous Deaf and Dumb Gentleman, Written By Himself* (London: J. Millan and J. Chrichley, 1732). Eighteenth Century Collections Online. Gale. Accessed November 14, 2013.
12. Works that focus on Campbell include Anon., *Mr Campbell's Packet, For the Entertainment of Gentlemen and Ladies* (London: T. Bickerton, 1720); Eliza Fowler Haywood, *A Spy Upon the Conjurer: Or, A Collection of Surprising Stories, with Names, Places, and Particular Circumstances Relating to Mr. Duncan Campbell, Commonly Known by the Name of the Deaf and Dumb Man; and the Astonishing Penetration and Event of His Predictions* (London: Mr. Campbell, 1724); Anon., *The Dumb Projector: Being a Surprizing Account of a Trip to Holland Made by Mr. Duncan Campbell* (London: W. Ellis, 1725). Campbell may also have been the inspiration for Cadwallader, a hearing character who impersonates a deaf fortune-teller, in Tobias Smollett's *Peregrine Pickle* (1751).
13. Lisa Zunshine (ed.), *Acting Theory and the English Stage, 1700–1830*, 5 vols. (London: Pickering and Chatto, 2009), IV, p. 191.
14. Robert Lloyd, *The Actor: A Poetical Epistle to Bonnell Thornton, Esq.* (London: R. and J. Dodsley, 1760), p. 6. Eighteenth Century Collections Online. Gale. Accessed October 3, 2013.
15. *The Theatrical Preceptor* (1811) in Zunshine (ed.), *Acting Theory*, IV, p. 239.
16. Tobias Smollett, *The Adventures of Roderick Random*, ed. by Paul-Gabriel Boucé (Oxford: Oxford University Press, 1979), p. 196.
17. The grotesque combines animals and humans.
18. Oliver Goldsmith, *The Vicar of Wakefield*, ed. by Arthur Friedman and Robert L. Mack (Oxford: Oxford University Press, 2006), pp. 9–10 (emphasis in original).
19. Samuel Taylor Coleridge, *The Collected Works of Samuel Taylor Coleridge: Poems: Part 1*, ed. by J. C. C. Mays, Bollingen Series, 16 vols. (Princeton, NJ: Princeton University Press, 2001), 16, pp. 349–54.

20. Anon., "On the Death of Lord Nelson," *The Times*, November 23, 1805, p. 3. Times Digital Archive: 1785–1985. Accessed August 28, 2012.
21. David Hume, *A Treatise of Human Nature*, ed. by Ernest C. Mossner (London: Penguin, 1985), p. 349; Edmund Burke, *A Philosophical Enquiry into the Origin of Our Ideas of the Sublime and Beautiful*, ed. by Adam Phillips (Oxford: Oxford University Press, 1990), p. 94; Francis Hutcheson, *An Inquiry into the Original of Our Ideas of Beauty and Virtue; in Two Treatises. I. Concerning Beauty, Order, Harmony, Design. II. Concerning Moral Good and Evil*, 2nd edn. (London: J. Darby et al., 1726), Treatise I, Sect. VI, Art. 1, pp. 72–73. Eighteenth Century Collections Online. Gale. Accessed January 3, 2012.
22. Anthony Ashley Cooper [Lord Shaftesbury], *Characteristics of Men, Manners, Opinions, Times*, ed. by Lawrence E. Klein (Cambridge: Cambridge University Press, 1999), pp. 414–15; Joseph Addison, "No. 418 Monday, June 30, 1712," in *The Spectator*, ed. by Donald Bond, 5 vols. (Oxford: Clarendon Press, 1965), III, pp. 566–70 (p. 566).
23. See William Gilpin, *Three Essays: On Picturesque Beauty; On Picturesque Travel; and On Sketching Landscape* (London: R. Blamire, 1792); Uvedale Price, *An Essay on the Picturesque* (London: J. Robson, 1794); Uvedale Price, *A Dialogue on the Distinct Characters of the Picturesque and the Beautiful in Answer to the Objections of Mr. Knight* (London: J. Robson, 1801); and Richard Payne Knight, *An Analytical Inquiry into the Principles of Taste*, 3rd edn. (London: Luke Hansard, T. Payne, and J. White, 1806).
24. Joseph Addison, "No. 414 Wednesday, June 25, 1712," in *The Spectator*, ed. by Donald Bond, 5 vols. (Oxford: Clarendon Press, 1965), III, pp. 548–53 (p. 550).
25. William Wordsworth, "Preface (1802)," in *Lyrical Ballads*, ed. by Michael Mason (London: Longman, 1992), pp. 55–87 (p. 82).
26. Shaftesbury, *Characteristics*, p. 63 (emphasis in original).
27. Ibid., p. 322.
28. Ibid.
29. For a discussion of Wilson's letter and Wordsworth's response see Patrick McDonagh, *Idiocy: A Cultural History* (Liverpool: Liverpool University Press, 2009), pp. 24–48.
30. Hume, *A Treatise of Human Nature*, p. 353.
31. Ibid.
32. David Hartley, *Observations on Man: His Frame, His Duty, and His Expectations*, ed. by Theodore L. Huguelet (Gainesville, FL: Scholars' Facsimiles and Reprints, 1966), p. 447.
33. William Hay, "Deformity: An Essay [1754]," in *The Works of William Hay, Esq.*, 2 vols. (London: J. Nichols, 1794), I, pp. 5–48 (I, pp. 12 and 5). For further discussion of this text, see G. Thomas Couser's chapter in this volume.
34. Tobias Smollett, *The Adventures of Peregrine Pickle, in which are included Memoirs of a Lady of Quality*, ed. by James L. Clifford and Paul-Gabriel Boucé (Oxford: Oxford University Press, 1993), p. 57.

5

MARTHA STODDARD HOLMES

Embodying Affliction in Nineteenth-Century Fiction

Physical and mental disabilities are everywhere in nineteenth-century literature. The long nineteenth century (1789–1914) generated iconic characters who still contribute to the ways we think, talk, and feel about disability in the twenty-first century, such as Charles Dickens's "crippled" boy Tiny Tim Cratchit from *A Christmas Carol* (1843) and "madwoman" Bertha Mason from Charlotte Brontë's *Jane Eyre* (1847). Along with characters readily identifiable as disabled, many other familiar figures are worth considering in terms of disability: the outsize, visually extraordinary creature of Mary Shelley's *Frankenstein* (1818); the mysteriously embodied Geraldine of Coleridge's narrative poem *Christabel* (1816); consumptive and angelic Little Nell, of Dickens's *The Old Curiosity Shop* (1840–41); Edward Hyde, whose "imprint of deformity and decay" haunts Robert Louis Stevenson's *The Strange Case of Dr Jekyll and Mr Hyde* (1886);[1] or Count Dracula, chronically disabled by the physical and social distinctions of his vampirism in Bram Stoker's *Dracula* (1897). Dickens, the Brontë sisters, George Eliot, Elizabeth Gaskell, and Thomas Hardy all engage disability in multiple fictional works, as do many less canonical writers including Wilkie Collins, Dinah Mulock Craik, Charlotte Mary Yonge, Mary Elizabeth Braddon, and Ellen Price Wood.

Why are there so many disabled characters in nineteenth-century fiction? One answer is the fact that their real-life referents peopled London's streets and workhouses, "special" schools and institutions, and the homes of every socioeconomic class. There were many ways of becoming disabled, and most disabilities were acquired in the course of a lifetime rather than recognized or diagnosed at birth. The rise of industrialization and the factory system created new types of disabilities through nonfatal accidents and injuries. Medical interventions that transformed acute, formerly fatal, conditions into chronic ones presented additional modes of "making disability." These factors increased disability's overall incidence in nineteenth-century British life.

The presence of disabilities, however, includes not just how many people experience them but also a broader range of issues including where disabled people live, who sees them and in what context, how and where they are written and spoken about by others, and how disabled people represent themselves. Within this larger discourse, despite the growth of institutions that tended to remove them from public view (like the asylum, the school, and the workhouse), disabled people were an increasingly visible aspect of Victorian British culture. Popular fiction and mainstream journalism, as well as medical, educational, and social reform treatises, all participated in "materializing" disabled people in texts and images.

"Disabled people" or "people with disabilities" were not usual descriptors of the period; more common labels were "the afflicted" or, increasingly, "the defective" – resonant words still frequently used as adjectives, but rarely as nouns, in the twenty-first century, even as noun phrases like "the disabled" or "the blind" persist.[2] These shifts in terminology and usage signal that the meaning of disability is never fixed or static. To give an example, mental disability is a condition common to all times. In some historical, social, physical, and political contexts, however, mental disability is articulated as incompatible with work; elsewhere, it is considered no barrier to a range of occupations or accomplishments an individual desires, even if it may constrain some of those options; and in still other contexts, some mental differences (autism spectrum disorder, for example) are recognized as contributing exceptional skills to particular tasks or disciplines. Deafness, in some social, cultural, physical, and historical contexts, is a disability; in others, it is a potentially desirable cultural attribute.

The meaning of disability was constructed and reconstructed throughout the nineteenth century in a wide range of explorations and debates. What caused disabling illnesses and impairments, if not injury or accident? Were they inherited, "caught" from tactile or even visual contact with others? Was learning to sign an acceptable route for deaf children, or should they be forced to vocalize? Could blind adults work? If they could, but could not earn enough from that work, did they deserve charity? Or, was a working person's request for help a shameless act of begging? Nineteenth-century fiction, while it recycled and repurposed figures of disability from earlier texts (scripture, classical texts, and Shakespearean drama),[3] implicitly addresses such questions, collaborating with texts by physicians and surgeons, "special" educators, social reformers, journalists, and disabled men and women themselves to create a new discourse that theorized able and disabled cultural identities and constructed relationships among the "afflicted" and the "whole."

Nineteenth-century fiction writers often drew on other significant forms of cultural difference such as gender/sexuality, race/ethnicity, age, and social class to organize disability representations. For example, distinctions between the "natural" characteristics of men and those of women are leveraged in nineteenth-century fiction to show disabled characters as exceeding or falling short of their expected social roles, often in the context of a fictional narrative of development (bildungsroman) that seems to exclude disabled boys and girls from future lives as workers, lovers, or parents. Physical vulnerability, celebrated as a feminine trait, may signal that a disabled male is not man enough, while ironically also marking a disabled female as an outlier by exceeding the norm for the conventions of courtship, love, and marriage.

Disabled Boys and Men

The first disabled character many people think of is Tiny Tim, the cheerful "cripple" who inspires the miser Scrooge to return to his lost feelings of community and charity. Whether portrayed as a Muppet, a mouse, or a human, Tim comes across as a simple reminder to keep a particular spirit of Christmas in our hearts: "God bless Us, Every One!"[4] But how simple is Tiny Tim?

From our first encounter in the text, the narrator guides us to an emotional understanding of him: "Alas for Tiny Tim, he bore a little crutch, and had his limbs supported by an iron frame!" (49). The narrative literally and figuratively frames him as pitiable through its descriptive details. His "plaintive" voice singing of a lost child in the snow (53), his "feebl[e]" hurrah (51), and his "withered little hand" (52) all present him as likely to die young. This pathetic tone, however, seems at odds with other suggestions of Tim's condition. In comparison to his working-class peers, injured and killed in occupations particularly and ironically suited to little bodies, such as climbing up chimneys or unclogging the moving parts of factory machines, Tim seems to live well. He does not express pain or suffering; he is central to a lively and loving family; and he is mobile, with an "active little crutch" (50).

That the source of Tim's disabilities and his lifetime prognosis are also unclear is logical enough; this is neither a clinical case study nor a social commentary on the working lives of children. And yet, an overwhelming tone emerges to take the place of the grounding such details might offer to anchor or substantiate our emotional responses to this character. By the time the Ghost of Christmas Future has envisioned Tim's elaborately mourned death, generating tears for characters and readers alike, the statement at the story's close that "Tiny Tim ... did NOT die" is simply insufficient to dial back the sorrow that is so firmly attached to him (83). The sadness associated with a child dying sticks to the story of a child living with disabilities, happy and not in pain – and establishes disability as a tragedy.

The fact that we leave Tim as a child helps to preserve this effect. The delineation of disabled characters as children is actually a significant and recurrent element in nineteenth-century fiction. The fact that many children (disabled and able) in the nineteenth century did not grow up because of disease or injury may be a partial explanation. Fiction, however, is more than a record of the demographics of a time, and the representation of disability does more than one kind of cultural work. Fictional disabled children helped to organize complicated feelings about the economic and social challenges associated with a British population that doubled over the course of the century, and concerns about the patterns of health within an increasingly urbanized society. The pleasure of feeling sad about Tiny Tim's disability is facilitated by the fact that readers do not have to worry about how he will make his living.

The boundary between childhood and adulthood, famously developed and celebrated in what has been termed a "Cult of the Child," was particularly vexed in regard to children with disabilities, as it indicated an entry into a working world in which they might not be considered able to contribute.[5] As Britain found its way from the New Poor Law forward, restrictions on who could receive "outdoor" relief helped to foster a climate of scrutiny toward anyone seeking assistance, and a belief in "energetic" and "anergetic" parts of society, a binary that journalist Henry Mayhew used to structure his catalogue of the street people of London.[6] Those who might not work could be viewed as parasites. Gender role ideologies provided another intensifier of such concerns. If men in particular were expected to labor, then anyone who had crossed the line from boy to man and did not do what was recognized as work ran the risk of being classified as part of the so-called undeserving poor. Thus, the social issue of work and charity had a particular impact on fictional portrayals of all boys on the edge of adulthood, but especially boys with disabilities.

If disabled boy characters are pathos-inspiring emblems of innocence and authenticity, disabled men characters often inspire fear or repugnance.[7] The adventure narratives of Robert Louis Stevenson are rife with examples, such as the menacing amputee Long John Silver from *Treasure Island* (1883), precursor to J. M. Barrie's even more iconic Captain Hook in *Peter and Wendy* (1911). Characters' universal recoil at Edward Hyde in Stevenson's *The Strange Case of Dr Jekyll and Mr Hyde* (1886) is rationalized as a response to disability as a manifestation of all that is bad about Henry Jekyll: "Evil … had left on that body an imprint of deformity and decay"

(63). Other characterizations of men with disabilities place them anywhere along a spectrum from moral weakness to pure malignity, as exemplified by the petulant, selfish Frederick Fairlie in Wilkie Collins's *The Woman in White* (1860) or the manipulative, sadistic, and lustful Quilp, a little person in Dickens's *The Old Curiosity Shop* (1840–41). When disabled adult males are central to the plot, they are often metaphors for the failings of nondisabled others. Further, they are often presented as money-seekers who do not earn their living in a respectable way, suggesting concerns about the drain disabled people might place on society.

When disabled boys in nineteenth-century fiction approach adulthood, they present a narrative disruption whose existence and resolution has significant cultural contexts. An example is Dickens's third published novel *Nicholas Nickleby* (serialized in 1838–39). The protagonist Nicholas becomes a teacher at Dotheboys Hall, a "school" in Yorkshire that seems more like a private warehouse for disabled boys, the most abject of whom is Smike, a resident since early childhood. Smike's disablement defies classification as either physical or mental; described as "lame," he is also portrayed not simply as a "timid, broken-spirited creature" but also as a "poor half-witted creature."[8] Dickens's description of Smike among a group of "children with the countenances of old men" articulates disability as that which radically disrupts a normal human developmental cycle (88).

Smike's vulnerability is a crucial catalyst and showcase for Nicholas's moral development. Nicholas befriends Smike; ultimately assaults Squeers, the cruel headmaster who has abused his friend; and leaves the school with Smike in tow, telling the other boy, "[m]y heart is linked to yours" (256). Estranged from his wealthy uncle Ralph (later revealed to be Smike's father), Nicholas must make his own way in the world without help. Smike joins him in the adventure, trying different occupations including acting, a profession that showcases both the efficacy of Smike's body in the representation of starvation and the inefficacy of his mind in regard to memorization.

As the novel proceeds, a clear and purposeful distinction emerges between the developmental paths of nondisabled young men like Nicholas and disabled young men like Smike. Nicholas's search for work is a plot excursion appropriate to a bildungsroman or even a picaresque narrative. For Smike, however, the same search is deadly serious and would result in ruin without Nicholas's care. As a disabled adult, his only available roles are in affective labor, as a vehicle for others' cruelty or a spur to others' sympathy (a service that extends to Dickens's readers, who begged the author not to kill him off during the novel's serial publication).

Smike's limited options in work are paralleled by restrictions in his emotional and sexual life. When Nicholas returns with Smike to live with his mother and sister, Smike falls in love with Kate Nickleby. The pathos of this passion – what allows Smike's love to align with the prospectively elegiac tone of the rest of his plot – depends on the assumption that Kate cannot possibly return it. Nicholas cannot even see his friend's feelings until Smike is on his deathbed, when he realizes that "the dying boy, with all the ardour of a nature concentrated on one absorbing, *hopeless*, secret passion, loved his sister Kate" (763; emphasis added). Nicholas and Smike are again reciprocals: one's rise both furthers and depends on the other's fall. As Tiny Tim's vulnerability does for Scrooge, Smike's suffering catalyzes Nicholas's ethical development and propels the moral narrative of the bildungsroman. But Smike's own development is cut short by the narrative itself and its assumptions about disability. As Nicholas moves forward into the world of work and marriage, the narrative must leave Smike's exhausted body and ashamed love behind, in service to the novel's closure. Kate and Nicholas both marry and have children who, in the final sentences, tend to the flowers on Smike's grave, "their eyes filled with tears . . . [speaking] low and softly of their poor dead cousin" (831). The emotional labor Smike does for others continues to the end of the novel, but there is no "bildung" for boys like him (or Tim).

There are more nuanced resolutions to the representational gap between disabled boys and disabled men. In George Eliot's *The Mill on the Floss* (1860), the protagonist Maggie Tulliver's brother Tom has a "lame" classmate, Philip Wakem. A sensitive thinker who recognizes Maggie's strengths and desires, Philip declares his love. Maggie returns it, though not in kind; and Philip's father ultimately condones the match, dismissing as "stuff" any concerns about "an accidental deformity, when a girl's really attached to a man."[9] Maggie's first experience of romantic passion, however, is for Stephen Guest, who is nondisabled, and the tragic end of Maggie's bildungsroman forecloses Philip's possibilities. Where Dickens kills off Smike, Eliot removes Maggie, leaving the solitary Philip to visit her grave. The nuances aside, the same issues of work and love are neatly, if less dramatically, dispatched in comparison to Dickens; the issue of where Philip will work is defused by his father's wealth, but plotting curtails his one attempt at marriage.

Not all adult male characters with disabilities are presented as malign or inadequate. Edward Rochester of *Jane Eyre* (1847) is another complex representation – an adult male who marries *after* becoming disabled. After Rochester loses his sight and one hand in a fire set by his mentally disabled wife, he is at least as interesting as he was when she was semi-safely confined in the upper rooms of Thornfield Hall. His disabilities seem to enable his second, much happier, marriage.[10] Further, while some critics have argued that Brontë represents Rochester's disablement as a punishment and reduction of his personal power, others note the erotic charge in the portrayal of his post-accident relationship with Jane.[11] At the same time, like Philip, Rochester is presented as economically stable, potentially bracketing the social concerns that emerge around other adult male characters with disabilities.

Disabled Girls and Women

Nineteenth-century representations of disabled girls emerging into womanhood are not detached from concerns about work. Indeed, many characters, such as Margaret Jennings in Elizabeth Gaskell's *Mary Barton* (1848), are dramatized as being disabled *by* work – in Margaret's case, the eye-straining labor of needlework. A more distinctive focus in fictional portrayals of disabled women, however, is a concern with sexuality, marriage, and reproduction. Dangerous occupations were a more likely cause of disability, but fear of inherited conditions and the mother's influence on her unborn child evolved, over the course of the century, into theories of breeding and eugenics. With love, marriage, and motherhood forming the repeated trajectory of the nondisabled female's bildungsroman, the question of whether or not disabled women should marry and reproduce is engaged regularly in nineteenth-century novels through the portrayal of disabled women characters at a "marriageable" age, even when their disability seems to keep them out of the typical heroine's plot.

Such exclusions are the rule for many texts. In Dickens's *The Cricket on the Hearth* (1845), at one time nearly as popular as *A Christmas Carol*, a young blind woman named Bertha Plummer is just as susceptible to dreams of love and marriage as her two sighted friends, but one of the key turning points in the plot is her realization that the man she adores is planning to marry someone else and has never, ever considered her a possible partner.[12] Nydia, the blind adolescent flower-seller in Edward Bulwer-Lytton's *The Last Days of Pompeii* (1839), tries to poison her rival and eventually commits suicide. Similar to Smike, she is heartbroken by a passion that is not simply unrequited but not even recognized.[13] And when Elizabeth Gaskell's self-centered beauty Nest Gwynn in "The Well of Pen-Morfa" (1850) falls into a well and is spinally injured, her betrothed ends their engagement.[14]

Portrayals of women with intellectual disabilities similarly dramatize their divergence from the marriage plot, as if disability was, by definition, disablement from expected gender roles. An interesting example is Anne Catherick, the "woman in white" of Wilkie Collins's 1860 sensational novel. Anne never expresses any desire to be courted, to marry, or to have children, but she is perceived as sexual by the men in the novel. This sets up a fascinating parallel with the nondisabled woman they actually do court and (in turn) marry, Laura Fairlie, who appears identical to Anne (and is in fact her half-sister).[15] While Anne is killed off before the novel ends, other works suggest fears about mentally disabled women who do desire and partake in marriage. In *Jane Eyre*, Brontë dramatizes the "madwoman in the attic" Bertha Mason's mental disability as gendered feminine and dangerously marked by sexuality and violence, charting her madness as unfitness for the roles of wife and mother.

In many of these portrayals, disablement is not just that which excludes women characters from the marriage plot, but the direct result of that plot. Rosa Dartle in *David Copperfield* (1850) is facially disfigured by her beloved James Steerforth's careless violence. One of the angriest and most interesting women characters Dickens ever created, she survives both her love object and her perceived rival Little Em'ly, but only in a representation of disability as rage indelible as the scar on her lip.[16] Gaskell's Nest Gwynn's disabling accident is presented as the result of vanity and dangerous clothing. Clara Hewett of George Gissing's *The Nether World*, like Nest distinguished by her physical beauty, is disfigured when a rival throws acid in her face.[17] Not all of these plots end in misery – Nest finds solace in mothering an intellectually disabled child – but none of them ends in marriage.

While most nineteenth-century fiction reiterates the narrative that disabled women will not marry, several writers push the boundaries in fascinating ways. Dickens's friend, collaborator, and competitor Wilkie Collins created just as many disabled characters, but he placed them in positions central to the novel, often in versions of the bildungsroman. In *Poor Miss Finch* (1872), notably, Collins places a young blind woman, Lucilla Finch, at the center of his plot of courtship, sexual feeling, and marriage; two men fall in love with her, shifting the operative question from disability to romance, and from "should she marry at all?" to "which man will she choose?"[18]

Dinah Mulock Craik's 1850 novel *Olive* may have been written in conversation with Charlotte Brontë's *Jane Eyre* (1848), generating interesting comparative readings. Olive Rothesay, born with a visible but not physically disabling spinal anomaly, has been seen as a rewrite of Jane, who describes herself as "poor, obscure, plain, and little" (292). *Olive*, however, is a much more sustained exploration of disability, particularly in relation to courtship. The novel's central focus is the developmental process through which its heroine learns the narratives of embodiment that structure others' views of her identity and her life's potential.[19] The process includes Olive's discovery of meaningful work and culminates in her realization that she is fit to be an excellent wife and mother. Craik, a working woman (and mother) herself, imagined a complex life in work and love – production and reproduction – for a heroine with a disability.

Like many bildungsromane, *Olive* begins with the protagonist's birth, in this case, to a young beauty whose husband is on an extended business trip to the West Indies. Mrs. Rothesay's delight in her baby is disrupted by a doctor's pronouncement that the child is "deformed" (14). This kind of interpellation recurs in the novel, marking points at which others, often not recognizing the pain they cause, pronounce Olive's disabled identity as a shorthand for her life prospects. In one of the novel's most memorable scenes, the preteen Olive, happily attending a ball at the home of her beautiful neighbor Sara, overhears comments reflecting Sara's limited view of Olive's potential in the world of love and marriage. Sara's answers, when confronted, radically alter Olive's own perceptions:

> "I assure you, dear," began Sara, hesitatingly, "it does not signify to me, or to any of those who care for you; you are such a gentle little creature, we forget it all in time. But perhaps with strangers, especially with men, who think so much about beauty, this defect" –
>
> She paused, laying her arm round Olive's shoulders – even affectionately, as if she herself were much moved. But Olive, with a cheek that whitened, and a lip that quivered more and more, looked resolutely at her own shape imaged in the glass.
>
> "I see as I never saw before – so little I thought of myself. Yes, it is quite true – quite true."
>
> She spoke beneath her breath, and her eyes seemed fascinated into a hard, cold gaze. Sara became almost frightened.
>
> "Do not look so, my dear girl; I did not say that it was a positive *deformity*."
>
> Olive faintly shuddered: "Ah, that is the word! I understand it all now."
>
> (67; emphasis in original)

This moment looks backward to another overheard comment from Olive's father, who mentions her marriage portion to her and then says to himself that he has forgotten that she will never marry. It looks forward, as well, to an even crueler moment of interpellation when her father comes home drunk and, rebuffing her help, calls her a "white-faced, mean-looking hunchback" (76).

When Olive's father makes a disastrous investment and dies, Olive uses her artistic talent to support her mother and herself and to pay back her father's debts. A successful painter, she continues to work for most of the novel. If Olive is in some instances compliant with the version others render of her body and its possible and impossible life scripts, she retains a strong sense of her own worth. While she repeatedly sacrifices herself for those she loves – her parents, Sara, and many others – she remains a strong representative of Craik's belief that women should marry for love and not for convenience, social advancement, or even protection. Olive's sense of self-preservation persists through three marriage proposals (the first from her artist mentor, the second from Sara's younger brother). When she finally falls in love – pointedly, with Sara's widower – even the deeply inscribed messages of her social body do not prevent her final happy marriage and adoptive motherhood. The fact that Olive does not have a biological child, combined with some suggestions of family hereditary "taint" as a cause for her disability, might imply that this outcome is Craik's mode of narrative prophylaxis; she will allow her disabled heroine to marry, but not to reproduce. An important counter to this is biographical: Craik, who married George Craik, a disabled man who worked at the publishing house Macmillan, became an intensely happy mother through adoption of a baby girl.

Disabled adolescence, as Craik develops it, is thus not simply a highly charged plot point because it reminds readers of debates about disability, work, and reproduction, but also because adolescence is when the social body is subject to public interrogation on these registers. Rather than capitulate to social constructions of disability, work, and marriage, Craik works the reader through the protagonist's often painful experiences of the social construction of disability and on to a plausible happy ending.

Other notable examples of texts that push the boundaries of nineteenth-century disability representation come from Charlotte Mary Yonge, like Craik sometimes termed a "Christian lady novelist," who made disabled young women central to a number of her works. The best-known today is *The Clever Woman of the Family* (1865), a multi-plot novel whose central narrative focuses on Ermine Williams, disabled by burns in her adolescence, and Ermine's renewed courtship by a man who fell in love with her before her disablement.[20] As is true of Craik's novels, many people with disabilities inhabit the domestic world Yonge imagines, to the extent that disability is somewhat normalized. Both Yonge and Craik, very popular in their own time, have recently been rediscovered by scholars partly for their representations of disability. Both writers narrate love, family life, and work as persisting in the context of disability, and correspondingly, narrate disability as a normal and potentially developmental aspect of life.

Nineteenth-century fiction mediated between the lived, individual, and familial experiences of disability and debates about social welfare, medicine, heredity, and education. Such representations expressed, reinscribed, and challenged firmly held beliefs; publicized, posited, and explored new ones; and articulated and shaped for readers actual encounters with disablement in themselves or others. These literary representations are significant not only because they offer insights into nineteenth-century culture and inform later literary works, but also because they contribute to how we imagine disability, an experience we will all enter if we live long enough.

New readers of nineteenth-century fictional representations of disability may wonder at the restrictions authors place on their disabled characters' lives and conclude that many – Dickens in particular – were purveyors of outdated stereotypes. There are dangers in that conclusion. In its sheer numbers of fictional representations of disability, nineteenth-century literature affirms the importance of disability as a social identity. In imagining people with disabilities as family members, workers, lovers, and parents, writers investigated not only disability and ability, but also the social construction of work, marriage, gender, sexuality, and family. As such, these literary texts performed significant work toward the goal of articulating disability as an essential and meaningful human experience.

NOTES

1. Robert Louis Stevenson, *The Strange Case of Dr Jekyll and Mr Hyde,* in *The Strange Case of Dr Jekyll and Mr Hyde* and *Weir of Hermiston*, ed. by Emma Letley (Oxford and New York: Oxford University Press, 1987), p. 63. Further page references to primary texts will be given parenthetically in the body of the chapter.
2. On "defects" and other disability terms in currency prior to the Victorian period, see also Chapter 4 in this volume.
3. The figures of Job, Oedipus, Philoctetes, and Richard III, for example, cast long shadows over future representations of disability to this day. In this volume, see Chapter 8 for one of contemporary literature's engagements with Philoctetes, and Chapter 1 and Chapter 3 on Richard III.
4. Charles Dickens, *A Christmas Carol,* in *A Christmas Carol and Other Christmas Books*, ed. by Robert Douglas-Fairhurst (Oxford: Oxford University Press, 2006), pp. 5–83 (p. 83). Popular film adaptations of Dickens's text include *The Muppet Christmas Carol*, dir. Brian Henson (Walt Disney Pictures/Jim Henson Productions, 1992) and *Mickey's Christmas Carol*, dir. Burny Mattinson (Walt Disney Productions, 1983).
5. Childhood, as a condition of sexual innocence and a time to learn rather than labor, was, like disability, actively under construction in the nineteenth century. Cultural studies of childhood have theorized a shift between the eighteenth and nineteenth centuries from thinking of children as "imperfect adults-in-the-making [...] toward the notion that they were exemplary beings to be cherished for their primal innocence and authenticity." Marah Gubar, "Innocence," in *Keywords for Children's Literature*, ed. by Philip Nel and Lissa Paul (New York: New York University Press, 2011), pp. 121–28 (p. 122). In fact, it is often argued that childhood was invented in the nineteenth century, co-constructed by literary works that represented childhood as a state in which "heaven lies about us" and legislation that limited work and mandated education. William Wordsworth, "Ode on Intimations of Immortality from Recollections of Early Childhood," in *William Wordsworth: The Major Works including* The Prelude (Oxford: Oxford University Press, 2008), pp. 297–302 (p. 299). By mid-century, childhood was to some extent enshrined as a state of wonder, innocence, and proximity to both nature and the divine.

6. The Poor Law Amendment Act of 1834 was commonly called the "New Poor Law." It reorganized state administration of public relief to limit "outdoor" relief, or supplemental assistance that allowed people to stay in their own homes. Instead, most relief was "indoor," in parish workhouses.
7. For more on disabled boys and men in Victorian literature and culture, see Chapter 4 of Martha Stoddard Holmes, *Fictions of Affliction: Physical Disability in Victorian Culture* (Ann Arbor: University of Michigan Press, 2004). See also Karen Bourrier, *The Measure of Manliness: Disability and Masculinity in the Mid-Victorian Novel* (Ann Arbor: University of Michigan Press, 2015).
8. Charles Dickens, *Nicholas Nickleby* (Oxford: Oxford University Press, 1950), p. 96.
9. George Eliot, *The Mill on the Floss*, ed. by Gordon S. Haight (Oxford and New York: Oxford University Press, 1996), p. 543.
10. Charlotte Brontë, *Jane Eyre*, ed. by Stevie Davies (London: Penguin, 2006).
11. See the essays in David Bolt, Julia Miele Rodas, and Elizabeth Donaldson (eds.), *The Madwoman and the Blindman:* Jane Eyre*, Discourse, Disability* (Columbus: Ohio State University Press, 2012).
12. Charles Dickens, *The Cricket on the Hearth*, in *A Christmas Carol and Other Christmas Books*, ed. by Robert Douglas-Fairhurst (Oxford: Oxford University Press, 2006), pp. 163–242.
13. Sir Edward Bulwer-Lytton, *The Last Days of Pompeii*, in *Novels of Sir Edward Bulwer Lytton*, vol. 3 (Boston: Little, Brown, 1896).
14. Elizabeth Gaskell, "The Well at Pen-Morfa," in *Elizabeth Gaskell: Four Short Stories*, ed. by Anna Walters (London: Pandora, 1983).
15. Wilkie Collins, *The Woman in White*, ed. by John Sutherland (Oxford: Oxford University Press, 1998).
16. Charles Dickens, *David Copperfield* (Oxford: Oxford University Press, 1999).
17. George Gissing, *The Nether World* (Oxford: Oxford University Press, 1992).
18. Wilkie Collins, *Poor Miss Finch*, ed. by Catherine Peters (Oxford: Oxford University Press, 1995).
19. Dinah Maria Mulock Craik, *Olive*, ed. by Cora Kaplan (Oxford: Oxford University Press, 1996).
20. Charlotte Mary Yonge, *The Clever Woman of the Family* (London: Virago, 1985).

6

MICHAEL DAVIDSON

Paralyzed Modernities and Biofutures

Bodies and Minds in Modern Literature

To be ill is to produce narrative.

Athena Vrettos[1]

Although we tend to think of literary modernism as a revolution of the material word, it is less often noted that it is underwritten by the material body. The fragmentations and dislocations that we associate with modernist experimentation often accompany representations of psychological and physical trauma. It is hard to think of any major modernist work that does not, in some way, feature disease or disability as a figure for social upheavals and cultural malaise – from Charlotte Perkins Gilman's "The Yellow Wall-Paper" (1892) and Edith Wharton's *Ethan Frome* (1911) to Henry James's *The Wings of the Dove* (1902), from Ford Madox Ford's *The Good Soldier* (1915) to Joseph Conrad's *The Secret Agent* (1907), from Dostoevsky's *The Idiot* (1868) and Ibsen's *Ghosts* (1881) to Andre Gide's *L'Immoralist* (1902), from Thomas Mann's *Death in Venice* (1912) and *The Magic Mountain* (1924) to Gunter Grass's *The Tin Drum* (1959), Katherine Ann Porter's "Pale Horse Pale Ryder" (1939), and most of the plays and prose by Samuel Beckett.[2] If we were to include in this list the psychological toll of physical impairments caused by World War I, we would have to add figures such as Jake Barnes in *The Sun Also Rises* (1926), Sir Clifford Chatterley in *Lady Chatterley's Lover* (1928), and Septimus Smith in *Mrs. Dalloway* (1925). If to be ill is to produce narrative, as Athena Vrettos says in my epigraph, nothing could embody this fact more vividly than those cosmopolitan novels whose grand tours include stops at health spas, sanitaria, or the therapeutic air of the Alps.[3]

At another level, the rhetoric of disease permeates modernist cultural poetics. Matthew Arnold in "The Scholar Gypsy" (1853), speaks of "this strange disease of modern life, / With its sick hurry, its divided aims," and Søren Kierkegaard describes the unredeemed time of modernity as a "sickness unto death."[4] Dostoevsky's Underground Man in *Notes from the Underground* (1864) regards "excessive consciousness [as] a ... genuine absolute disease," and Walter Benjamin refers to Baudelaire's description of the "shock" of the metropolitan crowd as a type of nervous disorder.[5] Nietzsche's later writings on Wagner describe his music as "contagious" and "unhealthy."[6] In the era's most representative poem, T. S. Eliot's *The Waste Land* (1922), a blind, transgendered speaker laments the sickness of modern life figured through a king who is suffering from an undiagnosed disease and who fishes by a polluted stream. The speaker encounters a one-eyed merchant, a fortune-teller with a bad cold, a clerk with serious acne, a husband and wife who suffer from nervous disorders ("my nerves are bad tonight"), and listens to denizens of a pub who discuss abortion and the loss of teeth. In the distance the poem's speaker hears the sound of a young woman who has been raped and whose tongue has been severed. The poet, as Eliot confesses obliquely in the poem ("by the water of Leman there I lay down"), wrote most of it while living at a sanatorium where he was recovering from his own psychological collapse. Although *The Waste Land* is usually read as an elegy for the decline of Europe and the loss of spiritual and cultural authority, its multiple references to illness, disease, and cognitive disorders suggest that this foundational poem for modernism was *founded* on an ill body.[7]

A standard reading of this emphasis on disease and disability in modernism would see it as the result of late nineteenth-century developments in medical science, evolutionary biology, and psychology. The pseudoscience of eugenics, invented by Charles Darwin's half-cousin, Sir Francis Galton, promoted the idea that society could – and should – improve the human race by controlling reproduction and weeding out "imperfect" or "dysgenic" individuals. Selective reproduction, sterilization, and the euthanasia of infants born with mental illnesses were among the procedures advocated by eugenicists. Such practices embody what Michel Foucault calls "biopower," those forms of social control that regularize life not by imposing power from above but by inscribing power onto and through the body.[8] The attempt to contain bodies and rationalize populations produced a vast archive of illnesses and diseases, many of which were products of new forms of mobility, urbanization, and technology. Workplace injuries due to increased industrialization, the spread of tuberculosis, shell shock or what would today be diagnosed as posttraumatic stress disorder (PTSD) as a result of World War I, and various psychoanalytical categories – hysteria, neurasthenia, agoraphobia – evolved simultaneously with the modern city. Despite therapeutic advances in medical science (transfusion, inoculation, prosthetics, and psychoanalysis) an equal number of new ailments emerged as byproducts of such methods. Ian Hacking advances the fascinating (perhaps tongue-in-cheek) thesis that fugue states – conditions of unconscious wandering where an individual finds himself hundreds of miles from home – result from the invention of the bicycle and the expansion of tourism. Hacking links these instances of "mad traveling" to the European fascination with bicycle racing and, by extension, trains and other new forms of mobility. His main point is not whether there is a strict causality between bicycles and mental diseases but whether certain impairments – "transient mental illness" such as hysteria or fugue states – are the products of historically specific diagnoses. As Hacking suggests, one generation's fidgety child is another generation's ADD.[9]

If the sciences of diagnosis made the non-normative body visible as a social problem, that fact was recorded in literature through what Sharon Snyder and David Mitchell have called a "narrative prosthesis."[10] They argue that representations of disability in literature often serve as a "crutch upon which literary narratives lean for their representational power, disruptive potentiality, and analytical insight."[11] The appearance of a "different body" in a literary work assists the narrative's larger goal of restoring the community to health by reigning in excess and ridding society of deviance. The protagonist's disability, as exemplified by Oedipus, Richard III, or Ahab, becomes the outward sign of internal moral and ethical flaws. Such examples suggest that narrative prosthesis is a general feature of all literature, but it has particular salience within modernist works composed during periods of intense scrutiny of citizenship, biological health, and racial identity.

Biofuturity

In order to think about the cultural logic of disability in modernism we might look at parallels between the *derangement of the senses* ("*le dérèglement de tous les sens*") that the French poet Arthur Rimbaud saw as modern poetry's goal and disability's unsettling of bodily and sensory normalcy. A common theme in discussions of modernist literature is that the literary work makes the familiar strange, that it disrupts conventional forms of communication thereby revealing language in its material, linguistic, and textual nature. This "defamiliarization," as the Russian formalist critics called art's disruptive power, has a particular relevance for the way that disability unsettles conventional ideas about the body and cognition. Ato Quayson speaks of what he calls "aesthetic nervousness" occasioned when "the dominant protocols of representation within the literary text are short-circuited in relation to disability."[12] Quayson is speaking about a literary encounter between able-bodied and disabled characters, but he alludes to a larger social anxiety produced by the nontraditional body in a society that presumes normative ideas of health, autonomy, and rationality. The experience of physical or mental impairment reveals the body's contingent nature, challenging the presumed normalcy of embodiment. Deviations from this model are subject to scrutiny and stigma that, in the eugenically tinged Progressive Era of the early twentieth century, led to repressive forms of social engineering, which included institutionalization, criminalization, and sterilization.

Such practices were hardly considered crackpot ideas during the early twentieth century. One of the more problematic aspects of any consideration of modernism is its investment in eugenic ideas of biological perfection and racial purity – what we might call ideas of "biofuturity" since they promise a better life through an improved gene pool. Many authors and intellectuals took seriously the writings of Francis Galton, Otto Weininger, Charles Davenport, and Max Nordeau who applied Darwinian ideas of natural selection and breeding to humans. Among the most obvious adherents were Charlotte Perkins Gilman, W. B. Yeats, Gertrude Stein, Virginia Woolf, T. S. Eliot, D. H. Lawrence, Ezra Pound, Margaret Sanger, Jane Addams, F. T. Marinetti, and Thomas Mann. What inspired such forward-looking thinkers to take eugenics seriously is perhaps aligned with their aesthetic interest in repudiating past models to "make it new." When a poet like Ezra Pound speaks of a need for poetic "hygiene" or when W. B. Yeats despairs of "Base-born products of base beds," or when D. H. Lawrence calls for a "lethal chamber" in which to euthanize the "sick, the halt, and the maimed," we see the close connection between vanguard aesthetic formations and ideas of bodily health and ability.[13]

Fears of such dysgenic or degenerative futurity were particularly acute in the case of mental disability or what was then called "feeble-mindedness." Whereas Romantic poets could celebrate the simple fool or mad prophet, modernist writers tended to treat mental disability as pathological counterpart to cultural decay. The developmentally disabled Benjy Compson, in Faulkner's *The Sound and the Fury* (1929), embodies in his discontinuous, fragmentary narrative the South's capitulation to entrepreneurial capital and cultural sterility. William Carlos Williams's mentally disabled servant Elsie expresses with "broken brain" modern America's dedication to cheap "gauds" and excitements.[14] Joseph Conrad's anarchists in *The Secret Agent* all appear to be derived from one of the period's criminal catalogues, especially the innocent Stevie who is variously described as a "slobbering idjut," "crazy," "degenerate," half-witted," and "weak-minded."[15] John Steinbeck's indictment of Depression-era economic powerlessness is figured in *Mice and Men* (1937) by his mentally disabled character, Lennie Small, whose inadvertent violence justifies euthanasia by his fellow migrant worker, George. In each case, mental disability marks biological degeneration and social disorder that the narrative seeks to contain and transform.

Among artists of the avant-garde, representations of futurity, rather than expressing fears of genetic or racial decline, are embodied through utopian bodies forged in an ideal of technology, speed, and athletic prowess. F. T. Marinetti's first Futurist manifesto celebrates a new human type, "the man at the wheel who hurls the lance of his spirit across the Earth" and excoriates "the city of Paralysis with its henhouse cackle, its impotent prides of truncated columns, its bloated domes that give birth to mean little statues."[16] There is little room in the futurist program for bodies incapable of "aggressive action . . . the racer's stride, the mortal leap" (41). Marinetti's most notorious proposal, his glorification of war and militarism, is directly tied to a "scorn for women" and by implication feminine associations with Catholic Italy (42). In Marinetti's rhetorically bombastic manifestos, "futurism" promises a world free of domestic obligation and religious authority.

Women futurists who responded to Marinetti's misogyny attacked his hierarchical gender divisions by claiming an equality that nevertheless perpetuated eugenicist principles. Mina Loy's "Feminist Manifesto" attacks the economic base of marriage and exalts better breeding: "Every woman of superior intelligence should realize her race-responsibility, in producing children in adequate proportion to the unfit or degenerate members of her sex."[17] Valentine de Saint-Point in her "Manifesto of Futurist Women" stresses the equality of the sexes and scorns the cult of domesticity: "Women are Furies, Amazons, Semiramis, Joans of Arc, Jeanne Hachettes, Judith and Charlotte Cordays, Cleopatras, and Messalinas: combative women who fight more ferociously than males."[18] Futurist manifestos, needless to say, did not trade in reasoned debate or nuanced distinctions; their function was to cajole and declaim, imagine a collective future that did not yet exist. The movement's eventual alliance with Italian Fascism made concrete the social implications of a purified body politic.

On Being Ill

> "It would have been nice if he could have been taken with fever all alone at his hotel, and she could have come to look after him, to write to his people, to drive him out in convalescence. *Then* they would be in possession of the something or other that their actual show seemed to lack."[19]

In Henry James's story, "The Beast in the Jungle" (1903), John Marcher imagines he is reserved for something "rare and strange." He figures his destiny throughout the story as a romantic confrontation with a lurking beast, but his egotism, manifested in remarks such as the one above, prevents any such encounter. In Marcher's imagination, illness and convalescence would afford him the illusion of sociality – provided by his companion May Bartram – thus giving him the "something or other that their actual show seemed to lack." Convalescence becomes for Marcher (and for James whose entire family lived with a number of ailments) not a site of painful solitude but an alternative form of social intercourse that his solipsism denies him.

The title of Virginia Woolf's essay, "On Being Ill" (1926), describes a cultural trope that applies not only to the author's own history of mental breakdowns and depression but to nervous disorders experienced by many modernist artists.[20] In the late nineteenth century, the phrase "nervous disorders" was applied to a variety of psychological and physical conditions whose clinical diagnoses often referred to the stress and complexities of modern life. Kate Chopin, Theodore Dreiser, Henry Adams, Henry James, Frank Lloyd Wright, Alice James, Charlotte Perkins Gilman, and many others suffered from what George M. Beard defined as "neurasthenia." Symptoms varied from individual to individual and across genders, but appeared variously as exhaustion, sick headaches, nausea, depression, and psychosis. To some extent neurasthenia was regarded as an inevitable, perhaps honorific, product of modern civilization, appearing specifically among "brain workers" and educated, independent women. According to Beard, "no age, no country, and no form of civilization, not Greece, nor Rome, nor Spain, nor the Netherlands, in the days of their glory, possessed such maladies."[21] Beard utilized economic metaphors, appropriate to an age of expanding capitalism, to explain how neurasthenia manifested itself. When an individual's quotient of "nerve force" is expended through overwork or stress, the individual could become "bankrupt" and needed to "reinvest" nervous energy either through bed rest or vigorous exercise. Tom Lutz notes that dissipation "eventually led to 'decadence', the death and decay of nerve centers in the individual and the death and decay of civilization at the social level."[22] Therapeutic solutions to neurasthenia were differently applied to women and men. The physician S. Weir Mitchell prescribed a "rest cure" for women, requiring complete and total elimination of all stimulation, whereas overworked males were instructed to engage in manly activities of hunting, hiking, and horseback riding – the infamous "West Cure" experienced by Theodore Roosevelt, Thomas Eakins, and Owen Wister.

In Charlotte Perkins Gilman's "The Yellow Wall-Paper," the unnamed narrator is undergoing a rest cure imposed by her doctor and her physician husband in a large vacation home near the seashore.[23] As readers of the story, we are the recipients of her first-person journal entries as she attempts to rationalize the medical necessity for her imposed bed rest. She writes under duress; her journal must be hidden from her husband and sister-in-law, who both feel that writing itself is too stimulating. Forbidden access to social life, her children, and creative pursuits, the narrator becomes increasingly unhinged and begins to interpret the pattern of the wallpaper in her sick room as depicting a woman trapped in its complicated design. The longer the narrator stays in her asylum prison, the more fervent her desire to free the imagined women from the wallpaper. Denied access to paper in her journal, she transfers her story to the paper on the wall, thus turning the borders of her prison into a text. By the end of the story, she imagines that she has successfully freed the woman from the room while being discovered by her husband crawling on the floor around its perimeter.

Most critics read "The Yellow Wall-Paper" as a feminist critique of Mitchell's rest cure (to which Gilman had been subjected) and the treatment of nervous disorders in women in the late nineteenth century. It is also, I would add, a study of the close proximity of illness and the aesthetic for the new woman. The narrator is a writer who must tell her own story against the medical story narrated by her doctor husband. Thwarted in her attempt to give narrative form to her life, she transfers her art to another form of paper – wallpaper – so that she may "write" in a different medium. She becomes, we might say, a literary critic, interpreting her own condition as a narrative projected onto the wall like a nineteenth-century phantasmagoria. Although it is a tragic tale of madness, it is also a story about the will to art against narrative containment in rigid gender categories.

For Virginia Woolf, unlike Gilman, illness implies a state of acute awareness in which "undiscovered countries" are disclosed and one's own mortality revealed. For Woolf, who lived with many illnesses, besides neurasthenia, illness challenges the tendency to privilege mind over body and brings the latter into a proper relation with intellectual endeavor. She wonders at the absence of novels and epic poems devoted to influenza or typhoid or pneumonia, but she acknowledges, "literature does its best to maintain that its concern is with the mind; that the body is a sheet of plain glass through which the soul looks straight and clear."[24] Woolf's essay is less about illness than the acute consciousness that illness brings.[25]

Such consciousness is the domain of another modernist type, the invalid aesthete, a figure of refined taste and sensibility who lives in an artificial paradise of heightened sensations and whose artistic pursuits create an alternative nature to the dominant scientific (Darwinian, positivist) version of the day. Among many modernist writers the aesthetic and invalid state are elided as paired "cures" for social ills; they are not ends in themselves but stages on the way to recovery. We tend to look upon aesthetes like Oscar Wilde's Dorian Gray, Joris-Karl Huyssman's des Esseintes, Walter Pater's Marius, Marcel Proust's Marcel, or Evelyn Waugh's Sebastian Flyte through their cultivation of exquisite sensibilities that provide a barrier against modernist progress and bourgeois rationality. Their ennui is embodied in the term "languor," a word derived from the French that refers to conditions of wastage and lassitude but which is revived among fin de siècle decadents to suggest, as Ellis Hanson says, a mood of "immoral and voluptuous bittersweetness of erotic fatigue, often with a degree of ironic detachment."[26] Not quite an illness, not quite an affect, languor captures the mood of decadent writing as well as its voluptuous stylistic qualities. It also captures the way that physical wastage is linked to erotic desire – an excess that cannot be expressed in heteronormative terms.

The figure of the invalid is a common feature of Victorian literature, from the writings of Harriet Martineau, Elizabeth Barrett Browning, and Alice James, to heroines like Esther Summerson in *Bleak House* (1853) and, somewhat later, Milly Theale in *The Wings of the Dove* (1902).[27] What often differentiates women invalids from their male counterparts is that in most cases, the former die or go mad by the end, whereas male invalids often rise like Lazarus from the sickbed and write with renewed vigor. It is not in sickness that the aesthete is defined so much as in his convalescence. Arthur Symon's invalid aestheticism empowers his coming out as homosexual, author of his *Memoirs*. Kierkegaard's Constantine Constantius develops his theory of repetition after recovering from a long illness. In Nietzsche's chapter of *Thus Spake Zarathustra* (1883–91) entitled "The Convalescent," the titular narrator gathers the animals of nature around him to hear his prophecy and then promptly falls into a seven-day illness, during which time, "pale and trembling ... he would neither eat nor drink." When at last he rises, the animals question him: "Did perhaps a new knowledge come to you, a bitter, grievous knowledge? Like leavened dough lay you, your soul rose and swelled beyond all its bounds." Whereupon Zarathustra delivers a sermon:

> Everything goes, everything returns; eternally rolls the wheel of existence. Everything dies, everything blossoms forth again; eternally runs on the year of existence.
>
> Everything breaks, everything is integrated anew; eternally builds itself the same house of existence. All things separate, all things again greet one another; eternally true to itself remains the ring of existence.[28]

After this speech, he remembers his sickness with disgust, but the animals prevent him from dwelling on the past: "Do not talk further... rather, you convalescent prepare for yourself first a lyre, a new lyre!" (236). Nietzsche calls that lyre the myth of eternal return, the idea that time does not move progressively forward (the modern ideology of progress and Darwinian selection) but repeats past events eternally. The idea of cyclic or repetitive time, derived from Eastern philosophy, inspired subsequent modernists, from Henri Bergson and William James to Marcel Proust, T. S. Eliot, and Gertrude Stein, but the strings of Zarathustra's lyre were strung in a sickbed.

Perhaps the most succinct link between convalescence and creativity occurs in Poe's "The Man of the Crowd" (1840), in which the unnamed narrator is recovering from a serious illness. He sits in a coffeehouse, staring at the bustling crowd through a window. He becomes interested in one man who appears to be both part of the crowd yet detached from it. The narrator leaves the café and follows this mysterious figure through an entire night of wandering through the streets, arcades, and shopping districts of the city, never unraveling the man of the crowd's secret.[29] Baudelaire describes the narrator's convalescence as being "like a return towards childhood. The convalescent, like the child, is possessed in the highest degree of the faculty of keenly interesting himself in things."[30] If the man of the crowd abjures such interest, his convalescent observer is interested in everything. In a sense, the man of the crowd is the double of his observer, a figure who only exists through the convalescent's consciousness.

Baudelaire's interest in Poe's story derives from the French writer's concern for what it means to paint "modern life" without becoming reified by it. If modernity is the ephemeral and contingent, as Baudelaire said it was, how best to capture it without succumbing to its surface allure? What astonishes the narrator about the man of the crowd's desultory tour is that although he enters emporia of commercial and cultural exchange, he does not participate in them, never pausing to buy a product, eat a meal, or watch a play. Nineteenth-century invalids like Poe's narrator exist in a dialectical relationship to work and activity. If one is *not* active, he may justify inertia by thinking of the invalid state as permitting reflection and introspection. To convalesce and remove from the sickbed is to realize the force of bodily infirmity and make out of it a story of eternal return, of repetition as growth.

As the century progressed, however, this rearticulation of idleness as an alternative form of labor was no longer tenable. The romance of the sickroom as a site of consolation and reflection gives way to a darker allegory of the body reified into capital. We can see this dynamic in Henry James's *The Portrait of a Lady* (1881) through the figure of Ralph Touchett, the son of a wealthy American businessman living in England who is dying of consumption. He becomes entranced with a distant cousin, Isabel Archer, who comes to visit. Although he is not erotically interested in Isabel, Ralph comes to see her as a type of independent, self-reliant American, and he desires to "put wind in her sails," as he puts it, by diverting a large portion of his considerable inheritance to her upon his – inevitable – death.[31] His long, lingering illness is to some extent the necessary complement to Isabel's youth, beauty, and imagination. But as it turns out, the wind he puts in *her* sails at the expense of the wind draining from his lungs becomes her downfall. Instead of using her new wealth to achieve the independence Ralph believes she deserves, she marries the Machiavellian aesthete, Gilbert Osmond, and becomes ensnared in a diabolic plot between her husband and his lover, Madame Merle. While Ralph's illness is not the centerpiece of the novel, it facilitates several important features of the narrative's sexual politics, not the least of which is to justify his lack of heterosexual desire on the basis of his "condition." It also serves as a link between consumption as a bodily infirmity and consumption as an economic disease that destroys self-reliance and independence. It is James's subtle critique of the cash nexus to make Ralph's disease the source of Isabel's imprisonment.

James expands the Victorian era's treatment of invalidism among the wealthy as a kind of alternative labor. Ralph's illness becomes, in Madame Merle's terms, his career:

> But the men, the Americans; *je vous demandez un peu*, what do they make of it over here? I don't envy them, trying to arrange themselves. Look at poor Ralph Touchett: what sort of a figure do you call that? Fortunately he has got a consumption; I say fortunately, because it gives him something to do. His consumption is his career; it's a kind of position. You can say, "Oh, Mr. Touchett, he takes care of his lungs, he knows a great deal about climates." But without that who would he be, what would he represent? "Mr. Ralph Touchett – an American who lives in Europe." That signifies absolutely nothing – it's impossible that anything should signify less. (171)

Madame Merle articulates, however cynically, something important about disability and national identity: having an illness "signifies," whereas being an "American who lives in Europe" and has no profession signifies nothing. She joins the energetic journalist Henrietta Stackpole in deploring Ralph's inactivity as a specifically "American" failing. But Ralph does have an important function thematically by occupying a parallel relationship to his nemesis Osmond, who *is* positioned as an aesthete, a collector of fine china and bibelots. And just as Ralph capitalizes on what he imagines to be Isabel's autonomy, freeing her to exist outside of economic dependency, so Osmond seeks to turn her into an artwork. He is quite specific about this, comparing her at one point to a new acquisition in his collection of fine china. Isabel is necessary to sustain his sexual relationship with Madame Merle and secure a mother for their illegitimate daughter, but his arid collecting, belief in social proprieties, and sedentary boredom are the aesthetic equivalent of Ralph's invalidism. Both are joined by the capitalist desire to turn Isabel into a "profit," of which Ralph's invalidism is a marker.

Disability and the "Great War"

Any account of disability in modernism must include the traumatizing effects of World War I that exerted perhaps the most dramatic impact on postwar art and literature. Ezra Pound's excoriation of a war in which "died a myriad, / And of the best, among them ... For two gross of broken statues, / For a few thousand battered books" is typical of artists who mourned the war's wastage of lives in the name of a defunct civilization.[32] Writers who participated in the Great War or the Spanish Civil War saw carnage and injury at levels unimaginable in previous conflicts, and those images were etched into many of their poems and novels. Furthermore, the fact of new technologies of war (aerial bombing, chemical weapons) and medical science – surgical innovations in amputation, transfusion, and prosthetics – all provided images of bodily fragmentation that demanded new formal and rhetorical strategies.

Disability was a significant theme in war poetry composed by British poets who participated in the war effort. Siegfried Sassoon, Wilfred Owen, Rupert Brooke, Richard Aldington, Robert Graves, and others saw action in World War I and recorded their impressions in poetry. Owen's "Disabled" (1917) is the most disturbing, both for its depiction of war's violence but also for its pathos:

> He sat in a wheeled chair, waiting for dark,
> And shivered in his ghastly suit of grey,
> Legless, sewn short at elbow. Through the park
> Voices of boys rang saddening like a hymn,
> Voices of play and pleasure after day,
> Till gathering sleep had mothered them from him.[33]

Owen regards the disabled veteran as a de-sexed, pathetic figure destined to spend "a few sick years in institutes, / And do what things the rules consider wise" (521). Whatever heroics serving his country offered to the young man, has become a cruel joke: "Now he will never feel again how slim; Girls' waists are, or how warm their subtle hands. / All of them touch him like some queer disease" (520). Owen's poetry was hardly modernist in the sense of linguistic fragmentation, but it marks an important transition from the emotional pathos of late Victorian and Georgian verse into the charged and violent world that the war bequeathed to the next generation.

Owen's poem reinforces a pervasive treatment of impotence that one finds in postwar novels in which formerly vigorous males become, through their participation in the trenches, sexless, feminized caricatures. Sir Clifford Chatterley in D. H. Lawrence's *Lady Chatterley's Lover* (1928) lives as a paraplegic in a wheelchair. He becomes a negative foil to the hypermasculine groundskeeper Mellors, the titular lover of the novel. The same goes for Jake Barnes in Hemingway's *The Sun Also Rises* (1926), whose sexual impotence due to war wounds contrasts with the vigorous masculinity of Robert Cohn or the matador Romero, or, alternately, the promiscuous Lady Brett Ashley. A subtler rendering of postwar trauma occurs in Virginia Woolf's *Mrs. Dalloway* (1925), through her depiction of Septimus Smith, a shell-shocked veteran who "went to France to save an England which consisted almost entirely of Shakespeare's plays and Miss Isabel Pole in a green dress walking in a square."[34] In his experiences in war, "he developed manliness; he was promoted; he drew the attention, indeed the affection of his officer" (94). But when he returns, he suffers from hallucinations and paranoia. Woolf is scathing in her denunciation of Smith's doctors, whose diagnosis of his condition is that he "had nothing whatever seriously the matter with him but was a little out of sorts" and who suggest that he should "take an interest in things outside himself" (23). Smith's suicide at the end of the novel provides idle chatter among Clarissa's party guests, but it marks the haunted presence of a war that marked the loss of innocence for a generation.

Conclusion

Modernism's early goal of achieving artistic autonomy, the "word as such," a "book about nothing," through the material medium is often seen as an attempt to escape bodily contingency and personal biography. But as Tobin Siebers observes, "aesthetics suppresses its underlying corporeality only with difficulty."[35] Siebers suggests that attempts to jettison the body in favor of disinterested appreciation belie the body that is often the necessary condition for ideas of beauty and corporeal perfection. One might say that disability is the uncanny other of the modernist aesthetic, a necessary figure of damaged embodiment against which the statistically normal body may be compared. When the disabled or mentally ill body appears in modernist art, it often foregrounds those aspects of modern life that cannot be contained by claims to improvement, progress, and independence.

It was precisely this frontal display of grotesque bodies in cubism or expressionism that led to the Third Reich's attacks on modernist art through its *entarte kunst* exhibitions during the 1930s. In these exhibitions the work of Egon Schiele, Arthur Kokoshka, Otto Dix, Emile Nolde, Ernst Kirchner, and others were regarded as signs of modernist disease. Against the "healthy" heroic and muscular Aryan figures presented in Goebbels's parallel German exhibits, the distorted faces and bodies in paintings by these artists were paraded before the German public as examples of a diseased aesthetic. The words "disease," "infection," "invalid," and "pathological" are common descriptors in the exhibit's catalogue. If the claustrophobic display of cubism, expressionism, and surrealism were not enough of a dismissal, placards on the wall reminded viewers of the Jewish and Bolshevist character embodied in this work. The cultural logic of disability in the *entarte kunst* exhibitions served to provide an image of degeneration around which a brave new world could be imagined.

By referring to the cultural logic of disability in modernism, I am emphasizing the way that metaphors of illness, disability, invalidism, and contagion help to "produce narrative" around anxieties connected with modern life. Such metaphors are often enlisted in justifying aesthetic innovation: when art is sick, it needs a cure; when language is stale, it requires refreshing. But these metaphors are produced *within* a modernity dedicated to a perfectible body and improved mind. Modernist literature in its attack on bourgeois domesticity, positivist science, and mass culture drew on disabled figures as examples of a deracinated body politic. By the example of aesthete and invalid, illness offered a counterdiscourse to a rationalized, "healthy" Darwinian futurity, a form of introspection productive of reflection and clarity. At the same time, the increased representation of nontraditional bodies and psychological conditions helped make visible the corporeal and psychological self. As Samuel Beckett's Molloy ruefully admits, "To decompose is to live, too."[36]

NOTES

1. Athena Vrettos, *Somatic Fictions: Imagining Illness in Victorian Culture* (Stanford, CA: Stanford University Press, 1995), p. 2.
2. Beckett's characters often exist in tragicomic relations of codependence that seem to mock communitarian ideals of charity and mutual aid while exposing the limits of liberal individualism. Hamm and Clov (*Endgame*), Mercier and Camier in the novel of that name, Pozzo and Lucky (*Waiting for Godot*), Winnie and Willie (*Happy Days*), Vladimir and Estragon (*Waiting for Godot*) – and if we extend codependence more broadly – Molloy and Moran (*Molloy*), Malone and his reader (*Malone Dies*), old Krapp versus younger Krapp (*Krapp's Last Tape*) – all rely on each other to "go on." Their formulaic routines and dialogues often seem parodic versions of a rational discourse whose content has been evacuated, leaving interlocutors to exchange empty signs. Many of these characters are disabled and form tenuous alliances for mutual aid. In *Endgame* (1957), to take the obvious example, Hamm is blind and lacks the use of his legs; Clov has a stiff leg and is losing his sight; Nagg and Nell have lost their limbs in a bicycling accident and have been relegated to trashcans. See Stuart Murray's chapter in this volume for further discussion of Beckett's disability representations.

3. Maria Frawley quotes Arthur Symonds describing his sojourn in Davos, Switzerland: "The cure of lung disease by Alpine air and sun and cold was hardly known in England at that time. When I found my health improve beyond all expectation the desire to remain where I was, to let well alone, and to avoid that fatiguing journey to Cairo, came over me." Maria Frawley, *Invalidism and Identity in Nineteenth-Century Britain* (Chicago, IL: University of Chicago Press, 2004), p. 142.
4. Matthew Arnold, "The Scholar Gypsy," in *The Norton Anthology of Poetry*, 4th edn., ed. by Margaret Ferguson, Mary Jo Salter, and Jon Stallworthy (New York: Norton, 1996), p. 993; Søren Kierkegaard, *The Sickness Unto Death*, trans. by Walter Lowrie (Princeton, NJ: Princeton University Press, 1941).
5. Describing Baudelaire's sonnet, "A une passante," Benjamin says that the sonnet "deploys the figure of shock, indeed of catastrophe. But the nature of the poet's emotions has been affected as well." Walter Benjamin, "On Some Motifs in Baudelaire," in *The Writer of Modern Life*, ed. by Michael Jennings (Cambridge, MA: Harvard University Press, 2006), pp. 170–212 (p. 185).
6. "This does not mean that I consider [Wagner's] music healthy . . . My objections to the music of Wagner are physiological objections: why should I trouble to dress them up in aesthetic formulas? After all, aesthetics is nothing but a kind of applied physiology." "Nietzsche Contra Wagner," in *The Portable Nietzsche*, ed. by Walter Kaufmann (New York: Penguin, 1985), pp. 661–83 (p. 664).
7. T. S. Eliot, "The Waste Land," in T. S. Eliot, *The Complete Poems and Plays 1909–1950* (New York: Harcourt, Brace & World, 1962), pp. 37–55.
8. Michel Foucault, *The History of Sexuality: An Introduction*, vol. 1, trans. by Robert Hurley (New York: Random House, 1990), p. 139.
9. Ian Hacking, *Mad Travelers: Reflections on the Reality of Transient Mental Illnesses* (Cambridge, MA: Harvard University Press, 1998).
10. David T. Mitchell and Sharon L. Snyder, *Narrative Prosthesis: Disability and the Dependencies of Discourse* (Ann Arbor: University of Michigan Press, 2000).
11. Ibid., p. 49.
12. Ato Quayson, *Aesthetic Nervousness: Disability and the Crisis of Representation* (New York: Columbia University Press, 2007), p. 15.
13. "The cult of beauty is the hygiene, it is sun, air and the sea and the rain and lake bathing. The cult of ugliness, Villon, Baudelaire, Corbière, Beardsley are diagnosis." Ezra Pound, "The Serious Artist," in *Literary Essays of Ezra Pound* (New York: New Directions, 1968), pp. 41–57 (p. 45). W. B. Yeats, "Under Ben Bulben," in *W. B. Yeats: The Poems* (New York: Macmillan, 1983), p. 327. D. H. Lawrence, "Letter to Blanche Jennings (1908)," in *The Letters of D. H. Lawrence*, vol. 1, ed. by James Boulton, (Cambridge: Cambridge University Press, 1979), p. 81.
14. William Carlos Williams, "To Elsie," in *The Collected Poems of William Carlos Williams*, vol. 1, ed. by A. Walton Litz and Christopher MacGowan (New York: New Directions, 1986), p. 218.
15. Joseph Conrad, *The Secret Agent: A Simple Tale*, ed. by Michael Newton (London: Penguin, 2007), pp. 192, 218, 235, 168, 173.
16. F. T. Marinetti, *Selected Writings*, ed. by R. W. Flint (New York: Farrar, Strauss, and Giroux, 1971), pp. 41, 47. Further page references to primary texts will be given parenthetically in the body of the chapter.

17. Mina Loy, "Feminist Manifesto," in *The Lost Lunar Baedeker: Poems*, ed. by Roger L. Conover (New York: Farrar, Strauss, and Giroux, 1996), p. 155.
18. Valentine de Saint-Point, "Manifesto of Futurist Woman," in *Manifesto: A Century of Isms*, ed. by Mary Ann Caws (Lincoln: University of Nebraska Press, 2001), pp. 213–16 (p. 214).
19. Henry James, "The Beast in the Jungle," in *Selected Tales*, ed. by John Lyon (London: Penguin, 2001), pp. 426–61 (p. 429).
20. Virginia Woolf, *On Being Ill* (Ashfield, MA: Paris Press, 2012).
21. Quoted in Tom Lutz, *American Nervousness, 1903: An Anecdotal History* (Ithaca, NY: Cornell University Press, 1991), p. 6.
22. Ibid., p. 4.
23. Charlotte Perkins Gilman, "The Yellow Wall-Paper," in *The Yellow Wall-Paper and Other Stories*, ed. by Robert Shulman (Oxford: Oxford University Press, 2009), pp. 3–19. For further discussion of "The Yellow Wall-Paper," see Chapter 12 in this volume.
24. Woolf, *On Being Ill*, p. 4.
25. In this discussion of neurasthenia, it is worth remembering that illness and disease, until recently, have not been included in disability studies research. Susan Wendell describes the problematic relationship between the two areas, noting that chronic disease seems fatally linked to a medical model that considers disability as an "individual misfortune," an association that led disability rights activists to argue that although they may be disabled, they are not "sick." As Wendell argues, "some people with disabilities *are* sick, diseased, and ill," while participating actively in the disability rights movement. Susan Wendell, "Unhealthy Disabled: Treating Chronic Illnesses as Disability," in *The Disability Studies Reader*, 4th edn., ed. by Lennard J. Davis (New York: Routledge, 2013), pp. 161–76 (p. 162; emphasis in original).
26. Ellis Hanson, "The Languorous Critic," *New Literary History*, 43.3 (2012), 547–64 (p. 548).
27. Ann Douglas Wood notes that illness among Victorian authors approached the condition of fashion statement. "Among many nineteenth-century women ill health in women had become positively fashionable and was exploited by its victims and practitioners as an advertisement of genteel sensibility and an escape from the too pressing demands of bedroom and kitchen." Ann Douglas Wood, "'The Fashionable Diseases': Women's Complaints and Their Treatment in Nineteenth-Century America," in *Clio's Consciousness Raised*, ed. by Mary S. Hartman and Louis Banner (New York: Harper and Row, 1974), pp. 1–22 (p. 22).
28. Friedrich Nietzsche, *Thus Spoke Zarathustra*, trans. by R. J. Hollingdale (Baltimore, MD: Penguin, 1969), p. 234.
29. Edgar Allan Poe, "The Man of the Crowd," in *The Fall of the House of Usher and Other Stories* (London: Penguin, 1986), pp. 131–40.
30. Charles Baudelaire, "The Painter of Modern Life," in *The Painter of Modern Life and Other Essays*, trans. by Jonathan Mayne (New York: Phaidon, 1965), pp. 1–40 (p. 7).
31. Henry James, *The Portrait of a Lady*, ed. by Jonathan Bamberg (New York: Norton, 1975), p. 160.

32. Ezra Pound, "Hugh Selwyn Mauberley," in *Personae* (New York: New Directions, n.d.), p. 191.
33. Wilfred Owen, "Disabled," in *The Norton Anthology of Modern Poetry*, ed. by Richard Ellman and Robert O'Clair (New York: Norton, 1973), p. 520.
34. Virginia Woolf, *Mrs. Dalloway* (London: Penguin, 1992), p. 94.
35. Tobin Siebers, *Disability Aesthetics* (Ann Arbor: University of Michigan Press, 2013), p. 1.
36. Samuel Beckett, *Molloy*, ed. by Shane Weller (London: Faber and Faber, 2009), p. 22.

7

STUART MURRAY

The Ambiguities of Inclusion

Disability in Contemporary Literature

It is arguable that no period in history has seen greater understanding of, and support for, people with disabilities than the contemporary. In Europe and North America in particular, the civil rights movements in the 1960s and 1970s that transformed social acceptance of race and gender identities laid the base and provided momentum for similar developments within disability communities in the 1970s and 1980s. Activists for independent living and other disability rights gave visibility to those with disabilities in ways that had not existed before, and advocated for substantial changes in law to protect rights, while many governments enacted legislation (the 1990 Americans with Disabilities Act in the United States; the 1995 UK Disability Discrimination Act, for instance) that spoke for those with disabilities when before they had often been explicitly marginalized and excluded. In the literary and cultural spheres, the rise of new publishing outlets focused on disability titles (such as Jessica Kingsley in the UK) and the popularity of memoirs from the 1990s onwards created both the space to articulate disability experience and an audience – both disabled and not – for those stories. Novels and plays featuring protagonists with disabilities or disability-focused themes and topics have never been more prevalent.

And yet for all of these changes, there is a real sense that, within majority social and cultural constructions of citizenship, narrative, or community, people with disabilities are still subject to misrepresentation and prejudice, still patronized, feared, or relegated to the margins. Lennard J. Davis, whose work on normalcy is referenced in Chapter 1 of this volume, has argued in his more recent writing that the idea of the normal as a social yardstick has been replaced by a concept of diversity, where ideas of which *kinds* of subjects are now included in civil society are framed within value judgments made around readings of "positive" diversity. As Davis notes, however, even while it might be expected that disability is precisely the kind of diversity that will be valued within such schema, it is still all too common that those with disabilities fall outside the parameters created by these particular versions of inclusion. Disabled difference, it appears, is not frequently seen to be the kind of difference that societies value.[1]

This chapter will explore the ways in which post-1945 writing has captured, reflected, and perpetuated this ambiguity, noting the ways in which literary cultures have been striving for openness and inclusion yet frequently produce stories that reduce the lived experience of disability through simplistic and stereotypical symbols and structures. It will use examples from a range of Anglo-American writers, and will discuss questions of agency, metaphor, narrative form, technology, the disabled hero, and the rise of the "neuronovel," all during a period in which everyday life has been increasingly medicalized. It will conclude by highlighting the precarious nature of disability in contemporary writing, emphasized and explored as never before, but still often contained within frames of sentimentality and melodrama in particular.

As Michael Davidson points out in his essay in this Companion, disability in modernist literature and culture was seen through the lenses of developing technologies in both the social and scientific realms. Medical knowledge shaped new ideas of psychiatry, psychology, and surgery that reconfigured understandings of mental and physical health, and the social sciences reworked ideas of "the human" that, for all their productive consequences, also created the eugenic movements of the modern period. In literary texts, modernists focused on the difference such changes brought: the postwar trauma of Septimus Smith in Virginia Woolf's *Mrs. Dalloway* (1925) outlined ideas of psychological damage; Clifford Chatterley's wheelchair in D. H. Lawrence's *Lady Chatterley's Lover* (1928) symbolized that character's impotence, sterility, and absence of passion; while William Faulkner's *The Sound and the Fury* (1929) presented arguably the most complex representation of disability in modernist writing, with the portrayal of Benjy Compson's learning disabilities in particular represented in innovative combinations of language and form that displayed a profound psychological interiority.

The transition between modern and contemporary writing was in fact saturated with disability contexts. World War II had not only created disabilities in millions of people, it had also emphasized the idea of "broken" societies, especially in Europe, traumatized by a war that had reduced lives and communities to rubble. The onset of the nuclear age promised further devastation, and the growing awareness of the specific disabilities that would be produced by radiation came to haunt much literary production as the 1940s turned into the 1950s. Samuel Beckett's work of the period offers the most comprehensive depiction of how this idea of disability was built into the structures of literary narrative. It can be argued that in a very real sense, all of Beckett's characters are disabled, as all seem caught in contexts in which both physical and cognitive activities appear restricted. This is true of those figures who are physically trapped in his drama, such as Hamm in *Endgame* (1957), unable to move or leave his chair for the whole of that play; Winnie, "embedded" up to her waist at the opening of *Happy Days* (1961) (and then, in Act Two, up to her neck); or the central unnamed protagonist in *Act Without Words* (1957) who, despite all his efforts, is unable to leave the stage, being continually flung back as he tries to exit. Even Vladimir and Estragon in *Waiting for Godot* (1952), Beckett's most famous play, are subjected to such restrictions, unable to abandon their seemingly endless hiatus, stuck on pause and committed to repeat their present in a manner reminiscent of anterograde amnesia.

The presentation of such evident disability is even more true of Beckett's characters who have physical impairments, such as both Molloy and Moran, the central figures in his 1951 novel *Molloy*, a text in which the idea of a forward trajectory implicit in a journey is offset by an ongoing process of disablement. Molloy, a vagrant who sets out to find his mother at the start of the novel, is incapacitated by leg pain that continues as his journey develops. Carrying crutches as well as pushing a bicycle, Molloy notes that "my two legs are as stiff as a life-sentence," and that "my progress, slow and painful at all times, was more so than ever, because of my short stiff leg."[2] Molloy's feeling that his legs are "shortening" creates a literal lack of balance in his sense of self: "For the suffering of the leg at rest was constant and monotonous. Whereas the leg condemned to the increase of pain inflected by work knew the decrease of work dispensed by work suspended, the space of an instant" (72). All progress is "slow and painful," Molloy observes, and here his disability powers the classic Beckettian capture of contradiction within a character's speaking voice: "Yes, my progress reduced me to stopping more and more often, it was the only way to progress, to stop" (72–73). As he goes on, Molloy's body continues to fall apart.

By the end of his section of the novel, Molloy is reduced to a figure "flat on my belly, using my crutches like grapnels," who "plunged them ahead of me into the undergrowth and [...] pulled myself forward, with an effort of the wrists." His body, "all swollen and racked by a kind of chronic arthritis probably," produces a level of "decrepitude" that leaves Molloy stuck in a ditch and barely able to move (84). What follows in the novel offers a mirroring twist: Jacques Moran, the detective who appears to be instructed to track and find Molloy, finds his own body caught in a process of physical decline that leads, in a clear parallel to Molloy's story, to his being reliant on crutches. Moran's legs stiffen – "I despaired at first of ever bending my leg again" (133) – and he resorts to taking morphine to alleviate the pain caused by the increasing "heaviness" of his leg (139). As readers, we are unsure of the real motivations of each of the central characters, and there is a sense that Moran may in fact be the author of the Molloy section because of the similarities in their experiences and the looping narrative structure; a voice tells Moran to "write the report" (170) while the novel opens with Molloy reflecting on a "man who comes every week" to take "away the pages" he appears to be writing (3). But, whatever the complexities of the story itself, *Molloy* presents a world in which to forget (both characters experience amnesia), and to experience both psychological and chronic physical pain, is an everyday occurrence.

In Beckett's work disability undoubtedly figures ideas of *reduction*, both of the capabilities of the body and the capacity of the self to conceive of a productive place in the world. The "decrepitude" of Molloy and Moran in *Molloy* is matched by the psychological voids and wastelands that form the locations of many of the plays (the stage directions of *Happy Days* set up an "expanse of scorched grass" subjected to "[b]lazing light"),[3] complete with their trapped or restricted protagonists. All can be read in terms of metaphors of a postwar world in which the very idea of subjectivity and belonging is threatened from without and stretched to the point of breaking. But it is equally the case that the all-pervasive nature of disability in Beckett's work means that bodily and cognitive difference actually become *central* to the narratives that explore self, place, and the language and forms that express them. In this sense, Beckett's imagined worlds are textual spaces where disability proliferates and is a norm rather than an exception. This appears true even when alternative explanations might exist for the texts' representations of physical or cognitive differences. In *Endgame*, Hamm tells a story of knowing "a madman who thought the end of the world had come," whom Hamm would visit in an asylum: "I'd take him by the hand and drag him to the window. Look! There! All that rising corn! And there! Look! The sails of the herring fleet! All that loveliness!"[4] But the man's reaction is to reject such possibilities of bounty: "He'd snatch away his hand and go back into his corner. Appalled. All he'd seen was ashes" (28). Here it is the "reality" of the man's apparent hallucination that is meaningful, not the potential in the fecundity and "bounty" that Hamm is attempting to display.

Beckett's "ashes" are symptomatic of a contemporary postwar period in which technology assumed the capacity to destroy the globe. Within such a context, many writers found it impossible to assume a sense of ongoing progress, whether individual or social, and the disabled body or mind became more frequent in literature from the 1950s and 1960s that challenged ideas of personal or social cohesion. Anne McCaffrey's 1969 science fiction novel *The Ship Who Sang* (a version of which was first published as a short story in 1961) tells of a future world in which children born with severe physical disabilities but cognitive powers can become "shell people," beings encased in "life-support" systems with multiple computer/technological connections, who then work to provide services for the societies responsible for their transformation.[5] Helva, the cyborg protagonist of both the novel and short story versions of the narrative, works as the cognitive center of a spaceship – a "brainship" – in an example of McCaffrey's fusion of ideas of disability and labor: other instances of such "brain" activity in the novel lie in cyborg input into buildings and cities. In the context of its writing in the 1960s, *The Ship Who Sang* explores disability within the complexities of an emerging contemporary intersection of technology and capitalism.

Such an intersection persisted, especially in science fiction, in the literature of the decades that followed. In William Gibson's Sprawl Trilogy (*Neuromancer, Count Zero*, and *Mona Lisa Overdrive*), disabilities produced through technological change are ubiquitous. In the future world of *Neuromancer* (1984), for example, developments in genetic engineering, neurosurgery, and synthetic organ production create multiple possibilities for bodily adaptation that suffuse the novel. Case, the central protagonist, begins the narrative with his nervous system deliberately damaged "with a wartime Russian mycotoxin" after he is caught stealing from his employers,[6] while Molly, the femme fatale of the story and central female character, has mirror glasses that are, in fact, "surgically inset, sealing her sockets," and "ten double-edged, four-centimeter scalpel blades" that emerge from her nails to be used as weapons (36–37). In Gibson's trilogy, physical or cognitive enhancement is a given, and it is often rather the quality or value of the work that has been undertaken that is the relevant issue. While an idea such as "enhancement" might not seem to suggest issues of disablement, there is often an associated quality of impairment that comes with the adaptation: the changes to Case's nervous system, for example, stop his ability to access the novel's cyber-world matrix. In addition, the very banality and ease of such "updates" creates an everyday spectrum of physical and cognitive identities that echoes the ideas of variation that a critical disability perspective brings to the representation of subjects, selves, and communities. As Kathryn Allan has noted, "SF has long explored deviant and disabled bodies [and] is inhabited by people (and aliens) whose embodiments are situated along the entire spectrum of ability."[7] While this can mean a focus on ideas of technology as cure for disabilities, it can also make for disability-rich narratives in which difference becomes the norm.

But disability was also a core component of postwar realist fiction and often associated with storytelling that highlighted social and political concerns. Harper Lee's *To Kill a Mockingbird* (1960) established (particularly because of its phenomenal popularity) a complex link between notions of disability and justice, as Boo Radley's (unspecified) learning disability/mental health condition appears integral to Lee's positioning of him on the side of truth in her account of racism and intolerance in the 1930s American South.[8] When Boo saves the Finch children from an attack by Bob Ewell at the end of the novel, his status as savior owes much to a wondrous idea of his disabled difference: the agoraphobic recluse who has "haunted" the childhoods of Scout and Jem suddenly intervenes as a vital element in the novel's moral climax. Here disability equates to innocence, part of Lee's wider exploration of ideas of loss. Whatever "absence" Boo appears to have, the novel's characterization of his "natural" sense of justice and morality allows him, as he carries Jem home after Ewell's attack, to be part of the narrative restitution of community order. With Boo, the "simple" man is positioned on the side of moral goodness, a clearly problematic portrayal of disability subjectivity.

In subtle ways, *To Kill a Mockingbird* contextualizes disability within a frame of racial politics and notions of violence. Michelle Jarman's essay in this volume outlines the processes through which the bodies and minds of women and men of color were targeted by what she terms "white structures of power." Such structures ranged from slavery and its legacy to eugenics, medical and welfare policies, and the representations of black characters by white authors. But equally, the writing of figures such as Toni Morrison and Octavia Butler, to name just two authors, challenges such structures and reclaims imaginative spaces for the representation of black disabled subjectivities in, for example, the "between worlds" character of Beloved in Morrison's *Beloved* (1987), or Butler's 1980s Xenogenesis trilogy (1987–89) with its focus on transspecies genetic modification. More generally, however, disability interacted with a range of identity positions in literature from both sides of the Atlantic. British writer Alan Sillitoe conceived of his two most well-known works – the novel *Saturday Night, Sunday Morning* (1958) and short story *The Loneliness of the Long Distance Runner* (1959), narratives in which young male protagonists are forced to confront the drudgery and oppression of postwar life – while on a military disability pension granted because of his tuberculosis. Yet Sillitoe is rarely, if ever, considered as a disabled writer, despite the added complexity such a perspective gives to his stories of hardship in the face of class barriers and social change. Both of Sillitoe's works can, in fact, be read in terms of a disability-informed critique of capitalist notions of work and progress. In *The Loneliness of the Long Distance Runner*, for example, the protagonist Smith is sentenced to a brutal regime in a junior detention center following an act of petty crime.[9] He escapes the drudgery through running and is subsequently entered in a cross-country race with the promise of a reduced workload if he wins. But, though he is leading up until the very end of the race, Smith pauses just before the finishing line, letting others pass him in a defiant statement of independence. This statement is noticeably a refusal to define his sense of self in terms of standard notions of physical capability and achievement. He chooses to stop rather than run, to idle rather than win, knowing that this will consign him to harder meaningless physical work in prison. From the vantage point of his own disability, Sillitoe undermines the idea of success being a byproduct of physical activity. Smith's body is not disabled, but he challenges the idea of progress that physical ability purportedly brings.

Such a reading of Sillitoe's work, while it highlights the ways in which mid-century writing outlined and developed ideas around subject-based identity positions, also prefigures the place of disability in the more contemporary world of neoliberal work demands and patterns, a society sociologist John Tomlinson has characterized as a "culture of speed" in which a 24/7 idea of "immediacy" dominates ideas not only of work, but also of selfhood.[10] The seeming need to be active, indeed the notion that activity is an end in itself, creates a world – of labor especially – in which disability is understood to be a problem because it is seen not to embrace multitasking and productivity as norms in work contexts. In many contemporary media accounts, disability is seemingly inexorably linked to questions of welfare and benefits, with individual subjectivity understood primarily in economic terms.[11] Viewed in this way, those with disabilities will inevitably be seen in terms of deficit, apparently lacking some required element for full participation in civil society, and such conceptions have become one contemporary manifestation of the ways in which disability is figured within a long historical language of absence or loss.

And yet, in a range of fiction – both popular and literary – that represents disability experience with insight and sensitivity, it is precisely this aspect of "work" that functions to express the value of disabled difference. In crime fiction in particular (as Ria Cheyne shows in her essay in this volume) the exceptionality of the disabled detective reconfigures ideas of insight and perception. While this is true of popular crime fiction, it is also apparent in novels by authors, such as Jonathan Lethem and Mark Haddon, not usually associated with crime writing. Lethem's *Motherless Brooklyn* (1999) and Haddon's *The Curious Incident of the Dog in the Night-Time* (2003) both weave detective narratives through their storylines, and in each novel it is the disability of the central protagonist that provides the means by which the mystery is solved. Lionel Essrog, the main character of *Motherless Brooklyn*, has Tourette's and is widely ridiculed by others in the novel as a spectacle and "freakshow" for his outbursts: "Me, I become a walking joke, preposterous, improbable, unseeable," as he puts it.[12] But it is precisely his Tourettic ability to make links and associations, as well as the presumption by others that he cannot be intelligent, that allows him to find the killer of Frank Minna, his employer and friend. Lionel notes that his compulsions help him to focus when on stakeout duty, for example, while a dying Minna passes on a clue, in the form of a joke, that he knows only Lionel will be able to decode because of his ability with language. It is "precisely because you were crazy that everyone thought you were stupid," the story's femme fatale Julia tells Lionel near the end of the novel (300). But Lionel is anything but stupid. Though his Tourette's frequently overwhelms him – "My mouth won't quit" as he puts it (1) – and he recounts numerous occasions where he has "no control in my personal experiment of self" (131), the novel maneuvers Lionel into a position as "successor and avenger [...] a detective on a case" (132) where he is clearly highly capable. This capability extends to his narration. For much of the novel Lionel speaks out to us, as readers, describing his condition and the ways in which it creates a disabling world. But, at the end of the novel when describing a particular compulsion – "the wild call of symmetry" – as he fights a hitman who attacks him, he ends a paragraph by saying simply: "It's a Tourette's thing – you wouldn't understand" (283). Gone is the need to explain himself to others. Here, whether Lionel is a "freakshow" or not is immaterial. His is doing things his own way.

Haddon's narrator, fifteen-year-old Christopher Boone, has autism, and while he tends to dislike fiction – "I don't like proper novels" he notes,[13] "because they are lies about things which didn't happen" (25) – he appreciates detective writing: "I do like murder mystery novels [...]. In a murder mystery novel someone has to work out who the murderer is and catch them. It is a puzzle" (5). *The Hound of the Baskervilles* is Christopher's "favourite book" (88), and "I like Sherlock Homes and I think that if I were a proper detective he is the kind of detective I would be" (92). Christopher's own detection lacks the glamor of many of Holmes's cases, but in his search for his mother, whom he presumes has died, he – like Lionel – evidences a work practice that centers on the nature of his condition. Christopher's literalism and attention to detail allow him to piece together the circumstances that led to his mother leaving the family home, and his single-mindedness leads to his being able to travel alone across London to find her. Christopher's autism is, in the novel, a filter that allows him to discriminate – as he sees it – between the essential and irrelevant. His detective abilities fill him with confidence.

As he imagines a future full of academic success at university he notes: "And I know I can do this because I went to London on my own [. . .] and I found my mother and I was brave and I wrote a book and that means I can do anything" (268). Earlier in the novel, Haddon has Christopher problematize the biblical associations of his name; he does not want to be associated with what he calls the "apocryphal story" of carrying Christ across a river. Rather, he asserts, "I want my name to mean me" (20). In allowing such fidelity to Christopher's own sense of self, Haddon creates a fiction that aligns itself with disability experiences conceived as having validity and integrity. By making Christopher the novel's narrator, Haddon extends these ideas of selfhood and integrity to formal issues of narration, aesthetics, and connections to the reader. As Alice Hall says, "Christopher's first-person perspective does seek to render an autistic point of view normal; as readers we are complicit with his way of seeing the world."[14] Crucial to the representation of Christopher's condition, then, is the understanding that it is mediated through a specific literary lens.

Both Lethem and Haddon are aware of the trappings of many disability narratives in which stories are resolved through sentimental or melodramatic interventions, and in each novel these are resisted. Neither Lionel nor Christopher is, for example, allowed straightforward personal or family resolutions at the stories' end (Lionel alienates and then loses his girlfriend while Christopher's parents are separated and he is living in an unglamorous small apartment with his mother at the novel's conclusion). Equally, for all their achievements, neither Lionel nor Christopher is specifically heroic in the context of the worlds in which they live. Lionel grew up in "St. Vincent's Home for Boys, in the part of downtown Brooklyn no developer yet wishes to claim for some upscale, renovated neighborhood" (36), and Haddon's choice of the nondescript satellite town of Swindon as the setting for *Curious Incident* indicates a desire to make Christopher's day-to-day life reflect a suburban ordinariness. Both novels stress disability is an everyday occurrence, even as they create mysteries that are solved.

Motherless Brooklyn and *The Curious Incident of the Dog in the Night-Time* are also examples of another notable new feature of contemporary disability fiction, namely a concentration on cognitive conditions and neurobehavioral syndromes. Writing in 2009, Marco Roth termed this a move to "the neurological novel," a process that sought to reject the workings of "the novel of consciousness or the psychological or confessional novel" that had dominated fictional representations of states of mind for most of the twentieth century.[15] Suspicious of the psychologizing that accompanies literary accounts of mind, writers – Roth asserts – have moved to portray issues such as identity, motivation, or behavior through a scientific prism that values neurological brain makeup as a superior way of articulating personhood. Both Tourette's and autism, neurobehavioral conditions that have received much media attention in the last few decades, exemplify this new cultural/literary turn, and Roth lists a number of other writers (Ian McEwan and Richard Powers, among others) who have produced recent fiction that seeks to explore what Nikolas Rose and Joelle Abi-Rached term "the management of the mind."[16] As Rose and Abi-Rached note, "As the twenty-first century began, there was a pervasive sense, among the neuroscientific researchers themselves, among clinicians, commentators, writers of popular science books, and policymakers that advances in our understanding of the human brain were nothing short of revolutionary."[17] Fiction that followed such heady strains of revolution found, in neurological/disabled difference, both new topics and new ways to tell old stories.

In Joshua Ferris's 2010 novel, *The Unnamed*, Tim Farnsworth, a successful Manhattan lawyer, suddenly develops a condition that causes him, against his will, to have to walk without stopping. The condition's origins baffle clinical expertise, while Farnsworth can only describe its manifestations and sensations in "nonmedical and not very useful ways"; he talks of feeling "jangly, hyperslogged, all bunched up," noting that "he spoke a language only he understood."[18] In a clever analysis of the poverty of medical knowledge surrounding many neurobehavioral conditions, Ferris has Farnsworth subjected to multiple opinions from doctors with different medical specialisms: he is, varyingly, referred to neurologists, psychiatrists, and environmental psychologists; is subjected to multiple MRI scans; has group therapy suggested because of possible problems with compulsion; is given a list of urban toxins as a possible cause; is prescribed muscle relaxants; and has rebirthing recommended. One clinician tells him that, given that there is "no laboratory examination to confirm the presence or absence of the condition" it might not "even exist at all"; while another diagnoses "benign idiopathic perambulation," a nod to the idea that, in a world governed by new neurological knowledge, any unusual activity can be seen as a syndrome (41). Although "the health professionals suggested clinical delusion, hallucinations, even multiple personality disorder" Farnsworth is skeptical of their expertise. He believes that "his mind was intact, his mind was unimpeachable. If he could not gain dominion over his body, that was not 'his' doing. Not an occult possession but a hijacking of some obscure order of the body" (24). For Farnsworth, the possibility that such an "obscure order," affecting the body but located in the brain, is the cause of the walking allows him to admit to a disability while preserving the sense that, psychologically, his mind is intact.

The subtle unpicking of the paucity of medical understanding in *The Unnamed* allows Ferris to use debates surrounding psychology and neurology (the "mind versus brain" argument) as a disability optic to examine central elements of American society.[19] As Farnsworth walks away from both his work and his family, the novel questions the formation of each institution: the relentless demands of the 24/7 work culture in which he locates much of his sense of self, and the expectations surrounding a "loving" family structure (much of the novel focuses on how Farnsworth's wife and daughter are forced to adapt to his condition). Crucially, it is his experience of disability that provides this critical insight and, for all the seemingly exotic nature of the condition at the heart of Ferris's novel, it is its everyday manifestations and intersections with life events that are most revealing.

The suggestions provided by new neurological research as to the constitution of minds and selves at the end of the twentieth century and beginning of the twenty-first were significant and profound. They created new possible subject matters for writers (such as Lethem, Haddon, and Ferris) seeking to make subtle disability stories about the makeup of individuals and their relationships to communities. But it would be a mistake to think that such subtlety has been the norm in contemporary writing about disability. For every novel such as the three described above there were numerous others that continued those practices recognizable from the long history of disability representation: narratives of overcoming or sentimentality; crude stories in which disability is equated with criminality or social difference; wondrous tales in which physical or cognitive difference produces awe in fellow characters (and indeed readers). The turn to neurology in fiction opened the door for numerous accounts, both first- and third-person, of characters with behavioral difference, and so offered endless problematic metaphors in which disability might be couched. In *The Way Things Look to Me*, a 2009 novel by British Pakistani writer Roopa Farooki, for example, autism is used to showcase a classic set of disability stereotypes. Yasmin is the youngest child of three siblings who have lost their parents, and her difference is figured throughout the novel either as evidence of a set of personal idiosyncrasies, or as challenges for brother Asif (whose duty as primary carer is seen to inhibit his own life) and sister Lila (who resents Yasmin for the manner in which she was the object of their mother's attention).[20] In a manner recognizable from any number of disability narratives from the nineteenth century onwards, Yasmin becomes the conduit through which ideas of family solidity, personal sacrifice, and social (non)acceptance are explored, with her non-normal status as a "problem" figure allowing for the discussion of a host of these and other non-disability tropes. Farooki's twist on this is, following on from figures such as Haddon and Lethem, to give Yasmin her own voice, but this voice frequently descends into cliché and the bizarre, as with her assumption, attributed to the idea that autism is a condition associated with logic, routine, and rational thinking, that a "normal" response to finishing high school is to contemplate suicide. *The Way Things Look to Me* was received with critical acclaim, and long-listed for both the 2010 Orange Prize for fiction and the 2011 Impac Dublin Literary Award. Such status reveals the extent to which problematic disability representation can still pass without comment in the world of contemporary writing.

Thinking about representations of disability in contemporary writing then, it becomes clear that there is no one trajectory that defines or illustrates commonalities in the ways stories are told. As G. Thomas Couser has shown in his essay in this volume, the proliferation of disability life writing since the 1990s has given an urgent voice to experiences that might have been left unexpressed (and unread) while, as the above has shown, there are examples in recent fiction where the lived difference of disability informs and structures narratives of all different kinds. Yet the age-old tendency to configure disability as absence, lack, loss, problem, or tragedy shows no signs of disappearing. Between February and March 2015, Brad Fraser's play *Kill Me Now* ran at the Park Theatre in London. Fraser, a queer Canadian Metis from British Columbia, has been writing for the theater since the 1970s and is known for staging controversial topics, including AIDS, steroid abuse, and the sex industry, in an abrasively comic fashion. In *Kill Me Now*, father Joey gives up a promising career as a writer to look after his disabled son Jake, who has spinal stenosis. In a dramatic twist, Joey develops a disability himself and, unable to face a future of seeming hardship, commits suicide.

The play drew a furious response from critic Dea Birkett, herself the parent of a child with disabilities. Writing in the British *Guardian* newspaper, Birkett asked,

> Why can't theatre, which is supposed to be about creativity, imagine what it's like to be me? Perhaps the best way to do that would be to include at least one disabled actor in the cast. But that might risk showing the life of a family which lives with disability as messy, flawed, joyous, human – and we wouldn't want that. Because the title is *Kill Me Now*. And in the end, the father, becoming disabled himself – developing a creeping disabling condition – and with the terrible burden of Joey, hates life so much he kills himself, then the audience applauds.

She went on:

> Still, the play disturbingly rings true to the non-disabled audience because it gives voice and panders to all their preconceptions and fears about what it's like to be in a family like ours. It presumes that we're both consumed by disability

> and nobly fight it – yet still pities us. When the audience gives a standing ovation, they're applauding this prejudice.[21]

Birkett's critique of *Kill Me Now* comes from within the experience of the subject the play presents as fiction but, as she makes clear, her criticism derives as much from a sense of Fraser's theater perpetuating wide cultural stereotypes as it does from an interaction with her personal circumstances. Birkett concludes her review with "sorry – I'm still here," an assertion of presence and a refusal to be subsumed in Fraser's narrative of pity and tragedy. Potentially the more telling point though, as she realizes, is that the attitudes and sentiments in *Kill Me Now*, a drama awarded four and five stars in reviews across North America and Europe, come not as a particular surprise. It is still, it seems, acceptable to explore ideas pertaining to "the human condition," even considerations of extremities such as suicide and death, through prejudicial notions of disabled bodies and minds.[22]

With the kinds of ambivalence displayed in the representation of disability in contemporary writing, it is inevitable that there will continue to be the sort of tensions noted in this essay. If individual appreciation of the experience of disabled lives and the nature of their distinctiveness has never been greater, structural and systemic conditions in the contemporary period have not only maintained discrimination, they have increased it. Whether in the neoliberal world of work or state vocabularies of categorization, the parameters of much contemporary life serve to work against the ways in which people with disabilities live. The social narratives such systems produce will undoubtedly influence the kinds of literary stories that are told about disability, and as long as this is the case, the representations that result will continue to be volatile and ambiguous.

NOTES

1. Lennard J. Davis, *The End of Normal: Identity in a Biocultural Era* (Ann Arbor: University of Michigan Press, 2014), Chapter 1.
2. Samuel Beckett, *Three Novels: Molloy, Malone Dies, the Unnameable* (New York: Grove, 2009), pp. 56, 71. Further page references to primary texts will be given parenthetically in the body of the chapter.
3. Samuel Beckett, *Happy Days* (London: Faber and Faber, 2010), p. 1.
4. Samuel Beckett, *Endgame* (London: Faber and Faber, 2009), p. 28.
5. Anne McCaffrey, *The Ship Who Sang* (London: Corgi, 1982).
6. William Gibson, *Neuromancer* (London: Harper Voyager, 1995), p. 12.
7. Kathryn Allan (ed.), *Disability in Science Fiction: Representations of Technology as Cure* (Basingstoke: Palgrave Macmillan, 2013), p. 2.
8. Harper Lee, *To Kill a Mockingbird* (London: Arrow, 2010).
9. Allan Sillitoe, *The Loneliness of the Long Distance Runner* (London: Harper Perennial, 2007).

10. John Tomlinson, *The Culture of Speed: The Coming of Immediacy* (London: SAGE, 2007). See also Robert Hassan, *Empires of Speed: Accelerations of Politics and Society* (Leiden and Boston: Brill, 2009); and Jonathan Crary, *24/7: Late Capitalism and the Ends of Sleep* (London: Verso, 2014).
11. See, for example, Frances Ryan, "Poverty Has Been Rebranded as Personal Failure," *The Guardian*, April 22, 2014, https://www.theguardian.com/society/2014/apr/22/disability-poverty-crisis-government-policies, accessed October 10, 2016.
12. Jonathan Lethem, *Motherless Brooklyn* (London: Faber and Faber, 1999), p. 2.
13. Mark Haddon, *The Curious Incident of the Dog in the Night-Time* (London: Jonathan Cape, 2003), p. 5.
14. Alice Hall, *Literature and Disability* (London and New York: Routledge, 2016), p. 118.
15. Marco Roth, "The Rise of the Neuronovel," *N+1*, 8 (2009), https://nplusonemag.com/issue-8/essays/the-rise-of-the-neuronovel/, accessed August 17, 2016.
16. Nikolas Rose and Joelle M. Abi-Rached, *Neuro: The New Brain Sciences and the Management of the Mind* (Princeton and Oxford: Princeton University Press, 2013).
17. Rose and Abi-Rached, *Neuro*, p. 5.
18. Joshua Ferris, *The Unnamed* (Harmondsworth: Penguin, 2011), p. 126.
19. See Nikolas Rose, "Neuroscience and the Future for Mental Health?," *Epidemiology and Psychiatric Sciences*, 25 (2016), 95–100; and Raymond Tallis, *Aping Mankind: Neuromania, Darwinitis and the Misrepresentation of Humanity* (Durham: Acumen, 2011).
20. Roopa Farooki, *The Way Things Look to Me* (London: St. Martin's Press, 2011).
21. Dea Birkett, "Why Can't Theatre Imagine What It's Really Like to Be the Parent of a Disabled Child?" *The Guardian*, February 26, 2015, http://www.theguardian.com/commentisfree/2015/feb/26/theatre-parent-disabled-child-kill-me-now, accessed April 12, 2015. Fraser responded to Birkett in *The Stage* magazine: Brad Fraser, "Did I get my play about disability wrong? No, but we need to talk about this," *The Stage*, March 9, 2015, https://www.thestage.co.uk/opinion/2015/brad-fraser-get-play-disability-wrong-no-need-talk/, accessed April 12, 2015.
22. The 2016 release of Thea Sharrock's film *Me Before You*, based on the novel by Jojo Moyes, received criticism from disability groups similar to that directed at *Kill Me Now*. See Cavan Sieczkowski, "*Me Before You* Criticized for Its Portrayal of Disability," *Huffington Post*, May 25, 2016, http://www.huffingtonpost.com/entry/me-before-you-criticized-for-portrayal-of-disability_us_574602b3e4b0dacf7ad3ca13, accessed August 28, 2016.

8

CLARE BARKER

"Radiant Affliction"
Disability Narratives in Postcolonial Literature

When Derek Walcott's poet-narrator describes the "head-wound" and subsequent trauma sustained in World War II by Major Plunkett, one of the central characters in *Omeros* (1990), he states that "He has to be wounded, affliction is one theme / of this work."[1] A poem set on Walcott's beloved Caribbean island, St. Lucia, and covering in epic scope the long history of the African diaspora and the manifold legacies of slavery and colonialism – including poverty, environmental damage, and the degradations of tourism in the contemporary Caribbean – the "wounds" in *Omeros* are indeed plentiful, and are physical and mental, literal and allegorical, human and ecological. A focal point for this trope of affliction lies in Philoctete, the "hobbling" (20) fisherman whose painful leg wound, caused in realist terms by "a scraping, rusted anchor" (9), is figuratively linked to the historical inheritance of the slave trade:

> He believed the swelling came from the chained ankles
> of his grandfathers. Or else why was there no cure?
> That the cross he carried was not only the anchor's
> but that of his race[.] (19)

Philoctete's understanding of his wound positions the poem's Caribbean setting as a space still somehow "crippled" by the violent heritage of slavery, and his wound performs an important narrative function as an access point to the partial and fragmented story of slavery that is one of Walcott's major preoccupations in the poem. In its visceral representation and recurring imagery, Philoctete's "putrescent shin" (247) becomes a visible and powerful symbol of this history of colonialism and violence.

The central disability in *Omeros* is far more than a stigmata in a "poetics of affliction,"[2] however. Even while it is both a source of agony that makes work and daily functioning difficult for Philoctete, and a symbol of historical shame drawing attention to the embodied nature of slaves' suffering, it undergoes many poetic transfigurations in the text and is also frequently aestheticized as something beautiful, a "radiant anemone" (9) rooted in the poem's natural environment. Read in this way, the disability that is "given by the sea" (242) becomes a natural feature of the Caribbean land- and seascapes, part of the beauty of the island, and in this respect it becomes valuable. The text opens on the shore with the image of Philoctete acting as guide for a group of tourists and showing them his now-healed scar for "some extra silver":

> It has puckered like the corolla
> of a sea-urchin. He does not explain its cure.
> "It have some things" – he smiles – "worth more than a dollar." (4)

The wound with "no cure" *is* eventually healed through the traditional medicine of the "sibyl, the obeah-woman" (245), Ma Kilman, who draws on the power of African deities while bathing Philoctete's leg in a brew made from the island's roots and leaves. As Philoctete asserts, the secret of his cure has a worth beyond tourist dollars as it combines traditional medicinal knowledge, African religious practices, and the resources of the Caribbean environment. Right from the start of the text, then, the scar exceeds its association with colonial suffering and also sets in motion more positive stories of knowledge, care, and cultural strength. Philoctete's wound is a "radiant affliction" (323), as it is described at the poem's end, which tells a complex and multifaceted story of suffering and resilience, damage and renewal, pain, beauty, wisdom, and pleasure.

This notion of "radiant affliction" captures fittingly how disability features in ambivalent and exciting ways in many works of postcolonial literature.[3] Given the painful nature of much (post)colonial experience, "affliction" is inevitably "a theme" of much postcolonial writing, and we find disabled characters appearing as a matter of course. Their so-called afflictions may be represented as direct consequences of colonization. European imperialism throughout the past few centuries, which peaked with the rapid expansion of colonial territories in the nineteenth century, was accompanied by many horrific and debilitating acts of violence. This included physical violence as "native" inhabitants of the colonies were forcibly subdued and subjected to hard labor, sexual abuse, imported diseases, and slavery; but also what Gayatri Spivak calls "epistemic violence," the privileging of "western" knowledge systems to justify the subjugation of cultures and communities around the globe.[4] Colonization caused untold numbers of physical injuries as well as large-scale mental distress.[5] In the present day, the wars, debt, migrations, and disasters brought about by decolonization, as well as neocolonial activities such as economic sanctions and western military interventions in the Middle

East, persist in disabling postcolonial citizens. To tell a story about colonialism or its aftermath, it is often necessary to tell a story about disability.

It is important to note, though, that even in the kinds of social realist postcolonial texts where disability is linked straightforwardly to (post)colonial injury or trauma, disabled characters also have narrative and aesthetic functions. They provide tropes that give writers ways of accessing themes and experiences such as loss, suffering, and dispossession. "Broken" bodies may signify partitioned countries, troubled minds represent a nation's collective trauma, and blindness might stand in for a refusal of leaders to "see" the lives and circumstances of their subjects. In *Omeros*, Philoctete's wound is a disability that is clearly used to perform narrative functions in this way. It is what disability theorists David Mitchell and Sharon Snyder term a "narrative prosthesis," a "crutch" that provides the text's central patterns of imagery and, as the arc of the poem moves from the trope of woundedness toward tentative healing, generates the impetus for narrative.[6]

Such functions are characteristic of many postcolonial disability narratives, and some postcolonial writing may cause concern for disability critics since disability is undoubtedly used to express the extremes of disorder, dysfunction, suffering, and damage that constitute colonialism's legacies. But it is also the case – as in *Omeros* – that "radiance" figures in many postcolonial disability representations. Postcolonial images of disability are incredibly rich and diverse, and disabled characters in postcolonial texts are complex and ambivalent – sometimes disempowered, oppressed, bitter, or suffering, but also brilliant, fierce, subversive, resilient, funny. We may find disability celebrated as positive difference, or simply represented as mundane, rather than being a tragic condition or the "master metaphor for social" (or in this case, colonial) "ills."[7] In the context of (post)colonial formations, "affliction" often sets the scene for generating agency, wisdom, empathy, care, pleasure, responsibility, creativity, social critique. As the following examples show, to read postcolonial literature in light of disability studies criticism requires us to engage critically with the narrative functions and wider political implications of disability representation, but also to seek out and celebrate the "radiance" of disability.

Can the Subaltern Speak?

There are certain impairments or disabling conditions that appear with regularity in postcolonial literature and have particular resonance with postcolonial concerns, either due to historical realities (such as the scarred back of the slave), or through their metaphorical aptness.[8] One such recurrent trope is muteness. Characters who are nonverbal or who have other forms of non-normative speech feature in a wide range of postcolonial narratives, including – to name just a few – Anita Desai's *Clear Light of Day* (1980), Keri Hulme's *the bone people* (1983), J. M. Coetzee's *Foe* (1986) and *The Life and Times of Michael K* (1983), Brian Friel's *Translations* (1981), and Alexis Wright's *The Swan Book* (2013). This abundance is perhaps not surprising given that a lack of speech is also the central motif in one of the most famous texts of postcolonial theory. Gayatri Spivak's foundational essay "Can the Subaltern Speak?" is now a cornerstone of the postcolonial literary critical field and offers a hugely influential analysis of subalternism and the possibilities and strategies that exist, within politics and art, for representing the powerless. The essay's titular question does not refer to actual muteness or speech impairment, of course, but asks whether oppressed (post)colonial subjects have the means to represent themselves, whether their speech acts are recognized in dominant discourses, and, if they are effectively "silenced" by inequalities, who is authorized to speak on their behalf and in what ways.[9]

The prolific debate prompted by Spivak's deceivingly simple question demonstrates how crucial the issue of voice is to postcolonial literary studies.[10] For a politicized field centrally concerned with power and oppression, questions such as "who has the authority to speak?," "who is listening?," and "how do we ethically represent (speak for or on behalf of) another?" are among the most pressing for scholars to address, and they encourage constant vigilance and self-reflection regarding creative and critical writing – particularly when educated and cosmopolitan writers choose to depict disenfranchised communities in the Global South. We often see postcolonial texts grappling with the same questions as Spivak, creatively theorizing in their own ways voice, agency, and aesthetic power relationships. And if one project of postcolonialism (in the broadest terms) is to recover the silenced voices and suppressed stories of colonized "others," what better way to explore these possibilities than through the trope of muteness?

A stark example of just how powerful muteness can be as a marker of postcolonial dispossession occurs in M. NourbeSe Philip's poetry collection *She Tries Her Tongue, Her Silence Softly Breaks* (1989). A Canadian writer with roots in the Caribbean, Philip employs the motif of speechlessness to explore the ambivalent legacies and tyrannies of the English language for African Caribbean subjects descended from slaves. In "Discourse on the Logic of Language," the poetry is interspersed with "edicts" on slave-keeping, describing how slaves were punished severely for speaking in their native languages, including by removal of the tongue.[11] This image of "verbal crippling"[12] through mutilation of the tongue recurs compulsively throughout the collection as a metaphor for colonial violence and the containment of African culture. Philip contrasts the severed "mother tongue" of African languages (intimate, natural, loving) with the alien "foreign language" – or, as she puts it with characteristic wordplay, "foreign anguish" – English:

> I have no mother
> tongue [. . .]
> I must therefore be
> tongue
> dumb
> dumb-tongued
> dub-tongued
> damn dumb
> tongue
> ("Discourse on the Logic of Language," 30)

This tongue-twisting passage perfectly embodies the speaker's frustration: the words make the tongue heavy and impede expression so are, in effect, disabling. The tone of self-disgust this provokes is mirrored in "She Tries Her Tongue; Her Silence Softly Breaks," where the "withered," "petrified," "blackened stump of a tongue" is described in terms of "monstrosity" and "obscenity" (66). Throughout this elegiac collection, mourning the losses of colonialism, there is a sense of the subject and her community being almost irredeemably damaged, stunted, unwhole, and barred from self-expression. It is ultimately colonial acts of violence – including the enforcement of the English language – that are represented as obscene and monstrous, but their victims' disablement that provides the imagery powerful enough to express such an excess of violation and suffering.

In a very different way, Friel's three-act play *Translations* also uses a character's speechlessness to telescope its concern with the English language as an instrument of imperialism. Set in the Irish-speaking Baile Beag/ Ballybeg community in 1833, the play opens with a scene in which Sarah, a local woman with a significant "*speech defect*,"[13] is being taught to say her name by Manus, the schoolteacher. Although a relatively minor character, Sarah plays a prosthetic role upon which the play's symbolism hinges. The action revolves around the intrusion into the village of British soldiers tasked with mapping the Irish countryside as part of the Ordnance Survey. As they embark upon Anglicizing place names – so "Bun na hAbhann" becomes "Burnfoot" (35) and "Druim Dubh" is renamed "Dromduff" (38) – it becomes increasingly clear how imperative toponymy (place-naming), and language imposition more broadly, are to the colonial enterprise. As the community resist against the sounds of their language and the nuances of their places and histories being erased, the play reflects on what is lost in translation and on the power that accompanies the freedom to name. In the climactic scene of the play, Captain Lancey demands of Sarah "Who are you? Name!" (62), and although her "*face becomes contorted*" and she "*tries frantically*" (62; emphasis in original), she cannot speak. In the face of imperial power, this suggests, the possibility of self-expression for the subaltern is erased.

Within this context where language has become a tool of violence, however, *Translations* also more hopefully explores other modes of expression. Sarah's ability to communicate effectively using sounds and gestures, as well as other details such as the love affair across language barriers between Maire and Lieutenant Yolland, unsettle the dominance and singularity of the English language and emphasize possibilities for interaction beyond speech. Likewise, a hint of radiance enters Philip's poetry at the end of "She Tries Her Tongue; Her Silence Softly Breaks," where the body is willed to find modes of expression, including singing, music, and dance, that bypass formal language. The speaker is allowed to imagine, very tentatively, a voice of a different kind:

> Might I... like Philomela... sing
> continue
> over
> into
> ... pure utterance (72)

The sense of transcendence here comes from the intimation that communication is possible beyond conventional speech; like the mythological Philomena's metamorphosis into a nightingale following her rape and mutilation,[14] here colonial injury does not preclude the potential for expression, joy, and connectivity. So while these texts use muteness metaphors as powerful symbols of violence and dispossession, they also destabilize the authority of speech and remind us to think more freely and creatively about what constitutes communication.

In terms of the ethics of representation, nonverbal characters present postcolonial writers with a conundrum, as they inevitably magnify the Spivakian dilemma about speaking for the "other." The complicated power relations this engenders are themselves the subject of some postcolonial writing. Coetzee's *Foe* is a postmodernist rewriting of Daniel Defoe's *Robinson Crusoe* (1719) – a paradigmatic text of colonial encounter and dominance – which uses metafictional devices to explore the "problem" of representing the subaltern. In doing so, I would argue, it also finds ways to avoid objectifying or speaking for its mute central character. Defoe's Friday is famously taught to speak English, enabling him to call Crusoe "Master" and therefore to articulate (and implicitly consent to) his own state of slavery. Coetzee's Friday has had his tongue cut out, meaning firstly that this submissive act of naming cannot take place, but also that although Friday is a significant presence in the novel, the story of his enslavement and mutilation is irrecoverable. As Susan Barton, one of the text's narrators, exclaims, "the only tongue that can tell Friday's secret is the tongue he has lost!"[15] Successive characters and narrators (Crusoe himself, Barton, the writer Foe) *desire* Friday's story, but it remains withheld at the novel's close. This subaltern disabled character is ultimately *not* spoken for; Friday's muteness is one way of the author refusing the power implied in the act of narrating subaltern lives. The text's preoccupation is not so much with Friday's tale itself – or with his disability – but with the desires, the representational limitations, and the ethical imperatives it exposes, especially for writers and readers. In refusing to speak for the silenced slave, or force him to *mean* something comprehensible, Coetzee also resists turning Friday into a prosthesis; while his muteness *could* mean many things in the text, it elides any confident act of interpretation.

At the very end of the text, Friday appears to us in a slave ship buried at the bottom of the ocean. He is not dead and does not provide any sense of closure to the novel; instead, "His mouth opens. From inside him comes a slow stream, without breath, without interruption" (157). This resembles the "pure utterance" that Philip invokes; in a similar vein, this text affirms the survival and expressive ability of the mute and mutilated character without ventriloquizing his voice. This text demonstrates how, in some ways, postcolonial narrative *needs* the metaphor of voicelessness to represent subalternity, and yet how politically engaged and self-reflexive postcolonial writing also takes care to trouble the metaphor. In the process, some of the best works of postcolonial literature stage a productive exploration of the ethics of representation for both disabled and subaltern subjects.

Whose Normality?

In disability studies scholarship in the Global North, disability tends to be understood as a minority subject position, and normalcy to be the ideological category against which it is defined.[16] But disability studies also teaches us that normalcy is a constructed idea rather than a fixed property of certain bodies and minds, and is continually shaped and reshaped by factors such as the medical knowledge available at any given time; the degree of political and economic stability in a country or community; labor conditions; media representations; and the body-focused products sold to us by consumer culture. Postcolonial literature is a space where the relativity of normalcy becomes very apparent. Crucial to the ethical maneuvers in texts such as *Foe* and *Translations* is the fact that they represent disability experience as bound up with specific historical moments, cultural practices, and socioeconomic contexts. In doing so, they offer disability studies rich conceptual resources through their explorations of how key ideas such as "normalcy," "ability," and "disability" are constructed across cultures – but also by representing these as unstable categories that respond to local, national, and global geopolitical events. As postcolonial literature highlights the western-centrism of many values and practices that we may casually assume to be universal, it also productively decenters widely accepted ideas about the body, health, ability, and healing.

Aminatta Forna's *The Memory of Love* (2010) is a novel about the mental health effects of the 1991–2002 civil war in Sierra Leone, a context of ongoing emergency that exposes established medical categories of psychiatric "disorder" and "normalcy" to scrutiny and even ridicule. It follows a British psychologist, Adrian Lockheart, to Freetown, where he aims to revitalize his career by working with traumatized survivors of the war. Adrian sets up group therapy sessions to help young men who were perpetrators of extreme violence regain some level of peace and social functionality. But the novel paints a damning portrait of how foreign doctors like Adrian understand their role in Sierra Leone. In one telling scene, Adrian encounters the local psychiatrist, Attila, who asks,

> "What do you aim to achieve with these sessions?"
> The cat pawing the mouse.
> "To return the men to normality, to some degree of normality. So they can live their lives. Achieve everything anyone else could expect to achieve."
> "And what is that?"
> "Sorry?"
> "What is it they can expect to achieve?"
> "To hold down a job. To enjoy a relationship. To marry and have children."[17]

For Attila, normalcy is not the self-evident category that it is for Adrian, measurable by broad lifestyle indicators. He shows Adrian what he means by driving him out to one of the city's slum districts, where the dwellings are tin huts, there is no drainage or waste disposal, and residents perform backbreaking unpaid labor such as scavenging for scrap metal. Attila chooses this backdrop to tell Adrian about a team of medical researchers who surveyed the population a few years ago:

> "They were here for six weeks. They sent me a copy of the paper. The conclusion they reached was that ninety-nine per cent of the population was suffering from post-traumatic stress disorder. [...]
>
> "When I ask you what you expect to achieve for these men, you say you want to return them to normality. So then I must ask you, whose normality? Yours? Mine? So they can put on a suit and sit in an air-conditioned office? [...]
>
> "This is their reality. You call it a disorder, my friend. We call it *life*."
>
> (319; emphasis in original)

Attila's pointed question – whose normality? – exposes how Adrian's understanding of psychiatric disorder is founded on assumptions about levels of safety, stability, and privilege that are immaterial when transferred to a troubled and impoverished society. And, we can extrapolate, the categories of "normalcy" and "disorder" in which Adrian and the researchers are invested may have potentially damaging effects: the PTSD diagnosis normalizes ideas about mental health that are generated in Europe and America, purporting that trauma is expressed uniformly and eliding its culturally specific manifestations.[18] In turn, "disability" seems to be an insufficient term for describing or categorizing the experience of traumatized war survivors in this novel, given that they make up the majority of the population and their ordinary life, as Attila emphasizes, plays out in conditions of extreme hardship and precarity. Jasbir Puar's notion of "debility," according to which disability is "rethought in terms of precarious populations,"[19] is more apposite here since it allows space for mental distress to be the norm – a proportional response to local circumstances – rather than the exception, and recognizes how poor people's bodies in Freetown are more vulnerable to injury or ongoing strain in their debilitating environmental conditions. In its interrogations of "normalcy," "trauma," and "disorder" in this particular African context, *The Memory of Love* shows us that other discourses of disability are needed.

It is not only texts depicting "real" events and conflicts that offer insights into conditions of debility and put pressure on our disability vocabularies. To take a very different example, Margaret Atwood's *The Handmaid's Tale* (1985) is a speculative fiction novel set in the imaginary Republic of Gilead (formerly the United States) in a dystopian near-future – a foreboding take on where conservative politics and aggressive foreign policy in 1980s America might have led to. This text is not ostensibly "about" disability at all, but among other things its satirical perspective challenges the notion of "ability" in interesting ways. In doing so, it has much to say about how political events may render the body's functions vulnerable to radical new interpretations, and about how states of debility may be perpetuated to serve oppressive social orders.

In *The Handmaid's Tale*, a group of ultra-conservative Christian fundamentalists has seized power from the US government following a period of global upheaval in which the neocolonial military and industrial practices of western powers have caused massive environmental damage. Gilead's unspecified "Colonies" are now uninhabitable wastelands, dumping grounds for hazardous pollutants, and it is gradually revealed that a combination of "nuclear-plant accidents, shutdowns, [...] leakages from chemical and biological-warfare stockpiles and toxic-waste disposal sites, [...] the uncontrolled use of chemical insecticides, herbicides, and other sprays,"[20] along with a "mutant strain of syphilis" (122) and the toll on young lives taken by AIDS, have led to widespread infertility and plummeting birth rates in western society. The context in Gilead is one in which the population is dwindling and reproductive impairment has become the norm, with the consequence that fertility is overtly reframed as a valuable and desirable "ability."

The regime's slogan – a bastardization of Marxist thought that is recited like a prayer at the dinner table – states, "*From each [...] according to her ability; to each according to his needs*" (127; emphasis in original). Women are allocated to labor roles on the basis of their fertility status, with fertile women like the protagonist Offred deemed a "national resource" (75) and put to work as Handmaids, assigned to the regime's Commanders to provide them with offspring. Men's "needs" are identified completely with the state here, while women's so-called ability to reproduce becomes highly consequential: those Handmaids who deliver healthy babies enjoy protected status, while those who do not are reclassified as Unwomen and deported to the Colonies to undertake dangerous labor, cleaning up radiation spills and disposing of bodies after battles (260). "Discards, all of [them]" (261), the Unwomen are officially stripped of their gender and personhood, reduced to a state of "bare life," where their sacrifice by grueling labor is entirely acceptable to the regime.[21]

Although very different from the Sierra Leone of *The Memory of Love*, Atwood's Gilead could equally be read as a location where ideas about bodily "normality" have been unmoored: infertility is experienced by the majority, the "ability" to reproduce reframed as labor, and the population crisis used to justify the dehumanizing treatment of those whose bodies fail to perform as required by the state (with discomfiting echoes of the Nazis' T4 euthanasia program). While Atwood engages most explicitly with the raging 1980s debates about feminism and reproductive rights, her satire emphasizes how closely these intersect with "ideologies of ability" (Tobin Siebers' term), combining to categorize and control human populations.[22] And this policing of bodily functions and activities creates unbearable conditions of debility, obviously so in the "disabling environment" of the Colonies,[23] but also in the majority culture where the status of Handmaid is privileged yet terrifyingly precarious. Both *The Handmaid's Tale* and *The Memory of Love*, then, portray contexts of postcolonial unrest where bodily norms are deeply unstable and vulnerable to manipulation by those in positions of power, whether well-funded western research teams or totalitarian governments. Reading postcolonial literature with an alertness to representations of normalcy, ability, disorder, and debility, and asking questions of texts such as "whose normality" is depicted, can be productive strategies that help to expose the constructed nature of our social realities and enable us to reach more incisive critiques of power structures and systems of control.

"Tomorrow There Will Be More of Us": Eugenic Endings, Crip Futurity

With so many postcolonial texts depicting states of disorder, debility, and trauma, we might wonder what kinds of futures are projected for their disabled and vulnerable characters. The notion of futurity is a fraught one within literary disability studies, since in many texts (novels in particular), closure and resolution are reached at the end of the story through the death or cure of a disabled character,[24] with the implication that disability, in all its difference and unpredictability, cannot be tolerated beyond the end of a text. Disabled characters are sometimes ultimately reduced to plot resolution devices and their fates to narrative strategy, but when disability is written out of the story in this way, disability critics argue, a kind of narrative eugenics is at work,[25] reinforcing the notion that disability is unthinkable in our collective imagined futures.

In this sense, endings are important to the politics of disability representation because they function as a transition point between the storyworld and the world beyond the text. In postcolonial literature, endings can be particularly charged because so many postcolonial texts engage with events and situations that are far from resolved. Elleke Boehmer points out that endings serve to "open [. . .] the storyline onto the real-life action that will follow" and offer "prognoses," "a set of choices for thinking about the future."[26] Boehmer finds a tendency toward "suspended endings" in postcolonial literature produced in conditions of political turmoil when it is difficult to foresee what might come next: escapes without destinations, characters "caught in a void," the "closing down or narrowing of possibility."[27] When disabled characters are involved, postcolonial endings are perhaps especially meaningful in terms of the kinds of futures that we might want to imagine.

The death and cure of disabled characters does occur frequently in postcolonial texts, but we also see other alternatives – such as *Foe*'s surreal ending – and significant complications of the "Cure-or-kill story endings [connected] to logics of eugenics,"[28] which may unsettle rather than fortify ideas about corporeal normalcy and the disposability of postcolonial bodies. *The Handmaid's Tale* has, in effect, two endings. The first, utterly ambiguous, leaves Offred, possibly illegally pregnant by the Commander's servant Nick, poised on the brink of either escape to freedom or capture and punishment for her transgressions. This leaves open the slim possibility that a baby might be born beyond the ending of Offred's narration, and that that baby might survive, and might be disabled: due to the polluted environment, "[t]he chances are one in four," Offred tells us, of giving birth to "an Unbaby" (122), a child with unusual embodiment who in Gilead is subject to eugenic disposal, "put somewhere, quickly, away" (123). While the ending of the novel is almost unbearably indeterminate, the possibility of Offred's pregnancy, escape, and survival hints at the tentative chance of a disabled child escaping declassification and death, of this child living and being loved. *The Handmaid's Tale* ends suspended between a eugenic conclusion for this potential unborn child and a fragile but more hopeful future, in which disability exists, thrives, and is valued.

Atwood's novel was published just months after a gas leak from a pesticide factory created a real-life toxic environment for residents of the central Indian city of Bhopal. Indra Sinha's 2007 novel *Animal's People* is a fictional retelling of the aftermath of the 1984 Bhopal disaster (shifted here to the imaginary city of Khaufpur), another narrative of environmental catastrophe and one that is deeply concerned with the figure of the unborn disabled child. The novel's protagonist is a nineteen-year-old boy called Animal who is severely disabled as a result of the gas explosion. He walks on all fours due to the "smelting in [his] spine," which has twisted the bones in his back "like a hairpin,"[29] and he also experiences what could be interpreted as the psychological after-effects of trauma such as hallucinations and voice hearing. Animal is haunted by the voices of those killed in the disaster – and especially by those who were denied the opportunity to live. He befriends the "Khã-in-the-Jar," a miscarried fetus with two heads whom he encounters in a doctor's office, a surreal figure who yearns to be freed and who speaks to Animal with "great bitterness," protesting that "at least you are alive. Me, I'm still fucking waiting to be born" (58).[30] The Khã-in-the-Jar and his companions are essentially the Unbabies of Khaufpur, deprived of the opportunity to live by the negligence of the "Kampani" (the chemical manufacturing company that caused the disaster). In this text, the disabled unborn are importantly given a voice, acting as a kind of conscience to Animal and a chorus to his life and the city's fortunes.[31]

At the very end of the novel, Animal decides against going to America for an operation to straighten his back, unsettling any straightforward equation of cure with better quality of life through his assessment that he is highly mobile on all fours and better adapted to the rough roads of the *bastis* (slum districts) than he would be with walking sticks or a wheelchair. He asserts his uniqueness as a positive difference – "Stay four-foot, I'm the one and only Animal" (366) – and ends his narrative with these ambiguous words: "All things pass, but the poor remain. We are the people of the Apokalis [apocalypse]. Tomorrow there will be more of us" (366). This is at once a protest against the debilitating "slow violence" of environmental damage that continues to disable and disenfranchise new generations,[32] a warning to the unheeding Kampani about the political potency of the grassroots activist movement in Khaufpur, and a powerful affirmation of disabled presence and longevity within the slum community. Paradoxically evoking a future beyond apocalypse, Animal's narrative resists a tragic resolution; disability is not an endpoint in the text but an ongoing fact of life for the majority of Khaufpuris. A future in which the toxic environment is cleaned up, preventing the disablement of more, as yet unborn, Khaufpur residents, is absolutely to be desired – the health problems faced in the city should never have happened – but this sentiment, driven by a desire for justice, is very different from the eugenic impulse to *eradicate* disability for the sake of a "better future."[33] In rejecting what Alison Kafer describes as a "curative imaginary," in which "intervention" is the only conceivable response to disability,[34] and in projecting into the future a vision of an increasing population of affected people, Animal's last words resemble Kafer's notion of "a politics of crip futurity, an insistence on thinking these imagined futures – and hence, these lived presents – differently."[35] Disability is here to stay in Khaufpur and the text affirms the value and agency of disabled lives, reflecting the unresolved situation in the "real life" Bhopal, where survivors are still waiting – for compensation, for remediation of environmental damage, and for targeted healthcare. Sinha's assertion of "crip futurity" performs two significant functions: it demonstrates an alternative to normative narrative denouements that write disability out of the text, and provides an absolutely necessary validation of disabled presence given the reality onto which the novel's storyworld opens.

Reading postcolonial literature's ambiguous endings from a crip perspective allows us to see how central disability is to projections of the future in many postcolonial contexts. There are many crip futures awaiting in the texts discussed here and many others – some faced triumphantly, some with trepidation – and what these texts often have in common is a demonstration of care about disability's place within these futures, and a concern to listen out for the voices (however unconventional) of even the most unlikely subaltern disabled subjects, such as the Khã-in-the-Jar. In *Omeros*, Philoctete's wound has a "mouth" (18), while Animal describes his tale as a "story sung by an ulcer" (12), referencing an anecdote about a local poet whose leg ulcer allegedly begins to recite "sweet verses," as if "his poems were trying to burst their way out of him" (12). It is a commonplace in disability studies that disability generates storytelling,[36] but many postcolonial texts are notable for the creative ways that disability experience is articulated. The disability stories bursting out of postcolonial narratives are urgent and ethically complex, many concerned with the extreme deprivations faced by disabled people in the developing world, but like the improbable juxtaposition of the ulcer with lyrical poetry, they often access the transcendent as well as the mundane, the beauty and value of disability experience as well as hardships and exclusions. "Afflictions" are plentiful in works of postcolonial literature, but the ethical engagements of postcolonial writing mean that more often than not a tentative yet "radiant" politics of crip futurity – a commitment to a more secure place for disabled postcolonial citizens – can be glimpsed within the aesthetics of postcolonial storytelling.

NOTES

1. Derek Walcott, *Omeros* (London: Faber and Faber, 1990), pp. 25, 28. Further page references to primary texts will be given parenthetically in the body of the chapter.
2. Jahan Ramazani, "The Wound of History: Walcott's *Omeros* and the Postcolonial Poetics of Affliction," *PMLA*, 112.3 (1997), 405–17.
3. I use the term "postcolonial literature" to refer not only to literature produced in the former colonies of the British Empire, set in contexts of colonialism and decolonization, or written by "ethnic minority" writers in the global North, but also as a way of describing literature that engages critically with past and present colonialisms and the continuing uneven redistributions of power in the contemporary, globalized world.
4. See Gayatri Chakravorty Spivak, "Can the Subaltern Speak?," in *Marxism and the Interpretation of Culture*, ed. by Cary Nelson and Lawrence Grossberg (Urbana: University of Illinois Press, 1988), pp. 271–313.
5. On postcolonial trauma see Stef Craps, *Postcolonial Witnessing: Trauma Out of Bounds* (Basingstoke: Palgrave Macmillan, 2013).
6. David T. Mitchell and Sharon L. Snyder, *Narrative Prosthesis: Disability and the Dependencies of Discourse* (Ann Arbor: University of Michigan Press, 2000), p. 49. See Chapter 1 of this volume for further discussion of "narrative prosthesis."
7. David T. Mitchell, "Narrative Prosthesis and the Materiality of Metaphor," in *Disability Studies: Enabling the Humanities*, ed. by Sharon L. Snyder, Brenda Jo Brueggemann, and Rosemarie Garland-Thomson (New York: Modern Language Association of America, 2002), pp. 15–30 (p. 24).
8. On such tropes see Mark Sherry, "(Post)colonising Disability," *Wagadu: A Journal of Transnational Women's and Gender Studies*, 4 (2007), 10–22; Michael Davidson, "Universal Design: The Work of Disability in an Age of Globalization," in *Concerto for the Left Hand: Disability and the Defamiliar Body* (Ann Arbor: University of Michigan Press, 2008), pp. 168–96; Clare Barker, *Postcolonial Fiction and Disability: Exceptional Children, Metaphor, and Materiality* (Basingstoke: Palgrave Macmillan, 2011); and Clare Barker, "Disability and the Postcolonial Novel," in *The Cambridge Companion to the Postcolonial Novel*, ed. by Ato Quayson (Cambridge: Cambridge University Press, 2015), pp. 99–115.

9. The first version of Spivak's theoretically complex essay, published in 1985, famously concluded that "The subaltern cannot speak." Spivak, "Can the Subaltern Speak?," p. 308. The "History" chapter of *A Critique of Postcolonial Reason: Toward a History of the Vanishing Present* (Cambridge, MA: Harvard University Press, 1999) constitutes an extended and reconsidered account of the essay where she revises her position somewhat.
10. See, for example, Rosalind C. Morris (ed.), *Can the Subaltern Speak? Reflections on the History of an Idea* (New York: Columbia University Press, 2010).
11. M. NourbeSe Philip, "Discourse on the Logic of Language," in *She Tries Her Tongue, Her Silence Softly Breaks* (Middletown, CT: Wesleyan University Press, 1989), pp. 29–33 (p. 32).
12. M. NourbeSe Philip, "She Tries Her Tongue; Her Silence Softly Breaks," in *She Tries Her Tongue*, pp. 58–73 (p. 68).
13. Brian Friel, *Translations* (London: Faber and Faber, 1981), p. 11; emphasis in original.
14. See Book VI of Ovid's *Metamorphoses*.
15. J. M. Coetzee, *Foe* (London: Penguin, 1986), p. 67.
16. See Lennard J. Davis, *Enforcing Normalcy: Disability, Deafness, and the Body* (London: Verso, 1995), and Lennard J. Davis, *The End of Normal: Identity in a Biocultural Era* (Ann Arbor: University of Michigan Press, 2014).
17. Aminatta Forna, *The Memory of Love* (London: Bloomsbury, 2010), p. 318.
18. In contrast, in its representation of Adrian's patient Agnes, the novel depicts an expression of trauma that is entirely shaped by local contexts and personal experience. See also China Mills, *Decolonizing Global Mental Health: The Psychiatrization of the Majority World* (New York: Routledge, 2013).
19. Jasbir Puar, "The Cost of Getting Better: Ability and Debility," in *The Disability Studies Reader*, 4th edn., ed. by Lennard J. Davis (London: Routledge, 2013), pp. 177–84 (p. 181).
20. Margaret Atwood, *The Handmaid's Tale* (London: Vintage, 1996), p. 317.
21. See Giorgio Agamben, *Homo Sacer: Sovereign Power and Bare Life*, trans. by Daniel Heller-Roazen (Stanford, CA: Stanford University Press, 1998).
22. See the introduction to Tobin Siebers, *Disability Theory* (Ann Arbor: University of Michigan Press, 2008).
23. See Anthony Carrigan, "Postcolonial Disaster, Pacific Nuclearization, and Disabling Environments," *Journal of Literary and Cultural Disability Studies*, 4.3 (2010), 255–72.
24. See Lennard J. Davis, "Who Put the *the* in *the Novel*? Identity, Politics, and Disability in Novel Studies," in *Bending over Backwards: Disability, Dismodernism, and Other Difficult Positions* (New York and London: New York University Press, 2002), pp. 79–101; and Mitchell and Snyder, *Narrative Prosthesis*.
25. Sharon L. Snyder, "Infinities of Forms: Disability Figures in Artistic Traditions," in *Disability Studies: Enabling the Humanities*, ed. by Sharon L. Snyder, Brenda Jo Brueggemann, and Rosemarie Garland-Thomson (New York: Modern Language Association of America, 2002), pp. 173–96 (p. 181). See Michelle Jarman's chapter in this volume for more detail on disability and eugenics.
26. Elleke Boehmer, "Endings and New Beginning: South African Fiction in Transition," in *Writing South Africa: Literature, Apartheid, and Democracy,*

1970–1995, ed. by Derek Attridge and Rosemary Jolly (Cambridge: Cambridge University Press, 1998), pp. 43–56 (p. 46).

27. Ibid., p. 45.
28. Snyder, "Infinities of Forms," p. 181.
29. Indra Sinha, *Animal's People* (London: Simon and Schuster, 2007), p. 15.
30. On the night of the Bhopal disaster, large numbers of pregnant women suffered spontaneous miscarriages, and in the three decades since 1984, residents of the slum areas adjoining the factory site have experienced serious reproductive disorders, among a wide range of other impairments and diseases.
31. On this aspect of the novel see Anthony Carrigan, "'Justice Is on Our Side'? *Animal's People*, Generic Hybridity, and Eco-Crime," *Journal of Commonwealth Literature*, 47.2 (2012), 159–74.
32. Rob Nixon, *Slow Violence and the Environmentalism of the Poor* (Cambridge, MA: Harvard University Press, 2011).
33. Alison Kafer, *Feminist, Queer, Crip* (Bloomington and Indianapolis: Indiana University Press, 2013), p. 2.
34. Ibid., p. 27.
35. Ibid., p. 3.
36. See for example, Davis, *Enforcing Normalcy*, Chapter 1.

PART II

Across Critical Methods

9

ALISON KAFER AND EUNJUNG KIM

Disability and the Edges of Intersectionality

"Intersectionality" is a big fancy word for my life.
Mia Mingus, *Leaving Evidence*[1]

What does it mean to do intersectional work? Although Audre Lorde does not use the term "intersectionality," she guides our response to this question.[2] Her writings demonstrate that gender cannot be fully extricated from race, or race from class, or class from sexuality; intersectionality refers to the theoretical approach that foregrounds such connections. In her 1984 essay "Age, Race, Class, and Sex: Women Redefining Difference," Lorde argues that the US women's movement has been harmed by its overarching focus on gender. Not only does this focus prevent feminists from recognizing the differences among women, it also establishes gender as operating separately from, or even in competition with, race and sexuality.[3]

We begin with Lorde's essay because its title reveals that doing intersectional work in disability studies means addressing gaps in existing theories. Disability studies scholars and activists note that disability – like age, race, class, and sex – is a category with a contested history and material effects; as such, it merits attention within other analyses of intersectionality. Ableism does, too: disability activists and scholars have detailed the workings of ableism and its conjunction with other structures of oppression. This intervention is not merely a matter of "adding" disability to the list, but rather a critical examination of how disability is fully enmeshed in the histories, experiences, and meanings of age, race, class, and sex, as well as sexuality, citizenship, nation, religion, health status, and other categories of difference. Recognizing that gender performances are inseparable from cultural constructions of disability, for example, alters our theorizations of gender, opening up new lines of inquiry.[4] A disability studies-inflected intersectionality recognizes disability as an essential component of intersectional work.

Reading in the other direction, Lorde's title reveals what is missing from some disability scholarship and activism: an awareness that categories such as age, race, class, and sex intersect with or create experiences of disability. There is no monolithic "disabled person" or universal experience of disability, but rather experiences, conceptualizations, and manifestations of disability that vary widely by cultural, historical, and global context. Just as scholarship that fails to attend to disability is complicit in maintaining ableism, scholarship that attends *only* to disability, casting it as separate from processes of racialization or histories of colonialism, reproduces oppressive norms.

But this kind of "bidirectional" reading – what Jasbir Puar describes as "the mutual interruptions of theory X by theory Y" – obscures the *relational* dimensions of intersectionality.[5] Lorde highlights the importance of relationality throughout her work, and "Age, Race, Class, and Sex" is no exception; it ends with a poem about solidarity: "We have chosen each other / and the edge of each other's battles."[6] By calling attention to "the edge of each other's battles," Lorde urges us to recognize that our struggles do not align neatly; not only does working in solidarity require working across differences, but sometimes it means working under extreme duress or uncertainty. Significantly, she frames this solidarity in terms of commitment and desire – "we have chosen each other" – positioning reciprocity and affective ties as necessary to intersectional work. Intersectionality means not only reading disability alongside race, or bringing disability theory to bear on queer theory, but investing in each other and "each other's battles." It requires more than shifting the direction of our theories, but also shifting the orientation of our desires and relationships, refusing to distance ourselves from other movements, theories, and histories of resistance.

In this chapter, we explore disability in relation to theories of intersectionality (particularly in US-based disability studies), demonstrating how experiences and representations of disability are always inflected by other categories, and providing examples that suggest how students and scholars may utilize intersectional approaches in their analysis of literature. Rather than "adding" our way toward a "complete list" of categories, we focus on transformative, critically reflective, and affective investments that emphasize relationality while acknowledging the inevitable incompleteness of intersectionality.

We begin with an examination of disability studies, unpacking assumptions about the relations – or lack thereof – among disability, ableism, and other structures of oppression. Next, we turn our attention to two writers who have informed our own understandings of intersectionality. Michelle Cliff's 1982 essay "If I Could Write This in Fire, I Would Write This in Fire" explores the politics of skin color, sexuality, coloniality, and class in Jamaica and England. It describes disability in terms of failed relations or encounters, and we use it to track the difficulty of separating oppressive structures and their effects. We then return to Audre Lorde. As feminist disability studies scholars whose work has been significantly influenced by Lorde, we want to encourage a deeper engagement with her work, especially in the context of an introduction to intersectionality. Introductions can do important political and epistemological work: the histories they name, the genealogies they trace, the identifications and practices they highlight can potentially undermine the very work of intersectionality, perpetuating a disability studies isolated from other movements for social justice. We want to acknowledge both fissures and relationships, recognizing the multiple kinds of investment that undergird intersectional scholarship. By foregrounding work from the 1980s, work that predates much of literary disability studies, we hope to offer an expanded genealogy and intellectual history for the field, one that owes much to feminist of color theorists. What might the insights and gaps in Lorde's work teach us about disability, or how might they reshape disability studies? How might her work provide us with the tools for crafting an intersectional approach to the field?

Intersectionality and/in Disability Studies

"What does it mean," asks Lorde, "when the tools of a racist patriarchy are used to examine the fruits of that same patriarchy?"[7] Lorde aims her question at (white, middle- and upper-class) feminist academics in the United States, urging them to recognize the limitations of a movement that focuses only on women like themselves: "the absence of these considerations [race, sexuality, class] weakens any feminist discussion of the personal and political." She goes on to assert, famously, that "the master's tools will never dismantle the master's house," insisting that existing theories, those that fail to attend to differences between women, inevitably fail to deconstruct the workings of power.[8] Lorde urges scholars to consider whether our methodologies and frameworks can help us dismantle the structures we purport to oppose.

Guided by her query, we begin by highlighting some approaches to intersectionality that can make intersectional analysis more difficult. We focus more on larger patterns in the field than on the work of a few scholars. Our goal is to make clear how pervasive these approaches are; they are embedded in the field's founding assumptions as well as in current academic and activist attempts to address disability. We recognize ourselves in these practices, and we delineate them here as a way to shift, extend, and reorient our own patterns.

One of these patterns is to describe disability as "the missing term" as a way of arguing for its inclusion.[9] We have engaged in this practice in our own work, urging feminist theorists to attend more fully to disability, but this approach has its limits. If it is used to position disability as a category that can be "added" to existing theories, the ways those theories are grounded in ableist assumptions or frameworks go unexplored; including disability in queer or postcolonial theory, for example, will necessitate changes in those very theories. Moreover, an additive approach fails to consider that *disability* will likely need to be reconceptualized when colonial relations or histories of sexuality are addressed.

Another pattern is to treat disability as "like" or even "the same as" race, sexuality, or class, even going so far as to insert disability terminology directly into existing frameworks: remove "race," insert "disability"; remove "sexuality," insert "disability"; and so on. The risk with such substitutions is that they proceed as if the terms are fully separate and separable – as if disability were not already present in constructs of race or sexuality – and as if the concepts do not have their own histories and logics; substitutive practices keep us from uncovering which differences come to matter and how.[10] As Jennifer James and Cynthia Wu urge, "In place of claims that 'disability is like race', we stress the importance of understanding how disability has always been racialized, gendered, classed and how racial, gender, and class difference have been conceived of as 'disability'."[11] Lorde herself cautions against such substitutive moves, warning: "When language becomes most similar, it becomes most dangerous, for then differences may pass unremarked. [...] But it is an error to believe that we mean the same experience, the same commitment, the same future, unless we agree to examine the history and particular passions that lie beneath each other's words."[12]

Sometimes the logic of substitution is taken further, so that it is not merely a matter of using a theorization of gender to theorize disability, but of casting disability as a necessary replacement for gender (for example, disability as "the new gender").[13] Here, disability and disability studies are cast as the successors of fields and categories that are played out, appearing just in time to correct their mistakes. In many of these approaches, disability is deployed to demonstrate the errors of identity politics; because disability is such a fluid category, or because differences between disabilities are so great, disability is said to reveal the instability of identity itself and the relative insignificance of race, class, or sexuality. The problem with such approaches is that they ignore the fluidity of critical work happening in other interdisciplines and movements (for instance, queer theory's critical approach to identity), implying that such theories have no bearing on disability theory and politics, and again position disability in isolation from race, class, nation, and sexuality.

More to the point, "intersectionality" seems to signal the pursuit of the "new," representing an ever-expanding search for the "right" or "complete" list of categories. Sara Ahmed notes that the call to intersectionality can be used as a method of deflection, closing down critical interrogations of power. "When I give talks on race and racism," she explains, "a common question is 'but what of intersectionality?' or 'what about gender/sexuality, class?'"[14] In such moments, systems of "gender/sexuality [and] class" are mentioned not in order to engage with Ahmed's inquiry but to brush it aside as incomplete and therefore dismissible, as if one need not engage with her critique of race and racism because it engages too deeply with race and racism. We mention this example not to promote a single-issue approach, but to point to how intersectionality can be invoked to foreclose deep engagements in *particular* structures of power and oppression.

Even as Ahmed offers a sustained analysis of race and racism, she does not position race as the foundational category or the most important oppression; she demonstrates that it is possible to focus on one dynamic of inequality while still being critically aware of its entanglement in – rather than priority over – other dynamics. Yet some disability studies scholarship assumes that focusing on disability requires isolating it from wider cultural contexts. Ableism is presented as foundational, such that it undergirds other systems of oppression (for instance, disability as "the master trope of human disqualification"); or as most oppressive, such that the disabled body serves as the ultimate other ("a much more transgressive and deviant figure").[15] In both cases, the relationship of disability studies to other critical theories is less one of relation and more one of prioritization. Disability is considered to "trump" race, or disabled people are understood as the "most discriminated against" category.[16]

While many might pause at the notion of one oppression "trumping" another, it is common to position disability as a kind of "master trope." In this framing, scholars reveal how "disability" has been used to justify other forms of oppression, leading other oppressed groups to distance themselves from disability as a way of refusing their own marginalization. We, too, have criticized this ableist use of "disability," but we want to caution that such critiques can easily position disability as the only or primary discourse of disqualification. On the contrary, however, race, gender, class, and species have also been used to justify the inferior status of other groups. Ascriptions of femininity, for example, have been used to justify the marginalization of, among others, indigenous peoples, colonial subjects, and disabled people; similarly, sexual othering does not always occur in terms of disability, but often relies on nationalist, racist, and colonialist imaginaries. Disability, in other words, is not the only justification for or instrument of oppression, and the attribution of incapacity is far from the only way in which oppressions operate. The prioritization of disability as the one difference that surpasses others hinders, rather than encourages, intersectional analysis.

For example, once disability is framed as "the ultimate other," then differences among disabled people are erased. All disabled people fall into the category of "most oppressed," obscuring not only differences of race, class, or gender, but also differences of impairment. This monolithism makes it difficult to recognize how some disabled people are more marginalized than others or how some disabled people may benefit from the conditions that hinder others. People of color and poor people, for example, are more likely to become disabled through their encounters with state violence, a class- and race-stratified health care system, and global capitalism. The benefits of disability rights legislation are rarely spread equally across all populations but, rather, have exacerbated existing inequalities, with wealthier areas more likely to reap the benefits of accessible institutions; such policies cannot simply be hailed as improvements without examining *for whom* or *in what context*.

However, while it is essential to draw attention to these disparities, such framing can ironically reinforce a separation between movements rather than fostering greater affective ties and commitments. Take, for example, the assumptions embedded in the notion of "overrepresentation," as in "disability is overrepresented in communities of color." Even as such framing highlights the need to examine the relationships among disability, race, and class, semantically it takes white, owning-class people as the norm. More to the point, it can depoliticize these patterns, as if simply noting the disparities were all that needed to be done, instead of interrogating what comes before and after being identified as having a disability. Discussions of overrepresentation can also serve to generalize the experiences of disability in different global contexts or minoritized communities. While "disability" as a universal, unmarked category (that is, in the Global North, in white people, in neoliberal western democracies) is conceptualized as a potential source of pride, disability as associated with other oppressions (among poor people, in the Global South, in communities of color) is seen only as the "real" consequence of violence, unable to be reclaimed as difference or identity.

Such homogenizing is made easier when intersectionality is conceptualized only in terms of identity and, specifically, marginalized identities, such that "intersectionality" becomes code for "black women." In this formulation, intersectional analysis looks only to minoritized figures: the immigrant of color, the working-class lesbian, the person with HIV/AIDS living in the Global South. Yet this very list belies the problem with such formulations: the working-class lesbian is also a racialized figure, the immigrant of color circulates in a heteronormative sexual economy, and the person with HIV/AIDS is a gendered being. Intersectional analysis, then, cannot be limited to marginalized identities and subject positions, but must also be applied to dominant positions and the structures that create them.

Treating intersectionality as a characteristic that some people have and others don't not only fails to address how white people are bound up in white supremacy or how cisgender men have a gender, but it also removes intersectionality itself from the realm of critical analysis. Intersectionality is reduced to being about identity rather than systems and structures of oppression. Moreover, it fixes identities in place, stabilizing them, as if we all know and agree what "disability" or "disabled/nondisabled person" means. In other words, intersectional disability studies scholarship requires us to look not only at disabled characters or figurations of disability, but also, and especially, at ideologies of ability and health. How do these ideologies play out in people's lives, in the organization of capital, or in the structure of society?

"Lines of Denial and Rejection"

Although she does not explicitly address these questions, Michelle Cliff offers insight into theories and practices of intersectionality. We encounter disability in her work not as master trope or static consequence of injustice, but rather as an embodiment and orientation that demands relationality, reciprocity, and contact. In "If I Could Write This, I Would Write This in Fire," Cliff discusses her private all-girls school in Jamaica, where she was taught by "white Englishwomen" and "pale Jamaicans." Students and teachers engaged in a ritual of singing English hymns for an hour each day. "Once," Cliff writes,

> a girl had a grand mal seizure. To any such disturbance the response was always "keep singing." While she flailed on the stone floor, I wondered what the mistresses would do. We sang "Faith of Our Fathers" and watched our classmate as her eyes rolled back in her head. I thought of people swallowing their tongues. This student was dark – here on a scholarship – and the only woman who came forward to help her was the gamesmistress, the only dark teacher. She kneeled beside the girl and slid the white web belt from her tennis shorts, clamping it between the girl's teeth. When the seizure was over, she carried the girl to a tumbling mat in a corner of the gym and covered her so she wouldn't get chilled.[17]

Reflecting back, Cliff asks, "Were the other women unable to touch this girl because of her darkness? I think that now. Her darkness and her scholarship." Cliff links these women's refusal to touch the girl to their status as "ladies," explaining that "we were constantly being told that we should be ladies also" (18–19). She highlights how the "white Englishwomen" and "pale Jamaicans" taught the students to adhere to lines of color and class, but this story reveals intertwined lessons about disability as well. The colonial imposition of cultural otherness and white femininity delegitimized students' sense of justice; the girl remained untouchable, and the students were pressured to deny any connection. Cliff echoes the ladies' refusal to acknowledge the presence of a poor, dark, disabled body in the structure of her narrative itself. She simply marks the disappearance and moves on: "The girl left school that day and never returned" (19).

Although Cliff never returns to the girl in the essay, a few paragraphs later she ruminates, "Lines of color and class. Lines of history and social context. Lines of denial and rejection" (19). Surely such lines were at work in this prohibition of contact and the girl's disappearance from the institutional colonial space. The placement of this story in the narrative suggests that it was a moment in which Cliff and her classmates learned denial and rejection as strategies for survival; there was no room for darkness, poverty, or illness. It seems clear that the permanent removal of the girl from the school hinged on her disability as much as her color and class, but Cliff states that "darkness [was] usually enough for women like those to hold back" (18). Perhaps "the lines of history and cultural context" and "of denial and rejection" remind us not to dissect the lives in question into discrete categories in search of causes of oppression but, rather, to remain focused on the structural power generated by such divisions.

Indeed, Cliff's essay refuses simple categorizations. As she asks in this same passage, "When did *we*, the light-skinned middle-class Jamaicans, take over for *them* as oppressors?" (19; emphasis in original). Later Cliff offers another example of failed contact that resists easy classification:

> In a middle-class family's home one Christmas, a relation was visiting from New York. This woman had brought gifts for everybody, including the housemaid. The maid had been released from a mental institution recently, where they had "treated" her for depression. This visiting light-skinned woman had brought the dark woman a bright red rayon blouse, and presented it to her [. . .]. The maid thanked her softly, and the other woman moved toward her as if to embrace her. Then she stopped, her face suddenly covered with tears, and ran into the house, saying, "My God, I can't, I can't." (30)

Falling in the middle of a discussion on colorism in Jamaica, a system in which "dark and light people [rarely] comingle" or "achieve between themselves an intimacy" (28), it is clear again that the "lines of color and class" are "lines of denial and rejection," and disability hovers along these lines, too. The woman's tears of shame for failing to embrace the othered body make visible the separation that operates through seemingly unconscious bodily responses.

The essay is filled with fury at the colonial injustices of Cliff's early life, but it is also brutally honest about her own shifting relations to power and privilege. Although she does not attend to the presence of able-bodied privilege compared to the unnamed schoolgirl, might we view her essay as a resource for disability studies scholars trying to analyze not only racism and classism but also *ableism* within disability communities? Cliff's exploration of how her status as a light-skinned Jamaican meant she was both marginalized and privileged strikes us as a useful tool for disability scholars and activists who want to challenge a reliance on state-, diagnosis- or identity-based claims, recognizing that legal protections and social supports have uneven effects across different populations. Intersectional disability studies can entail exploring how differences within the category of "disabled" – or differences in the application of the label "disabled" – can lead to "uneven incorporation" in the public and academic spheres.[18]

We find similar insights in the work of Audre Lorde, another writer of Caribbean descent who was suspicious of "Coca-Cola democracy" and the promises of incorporation into the capitalist state.[19] Lorde's work, like that of Cliff, opens the possibility of engaging with disability and disability studies differently, and we continue to highlight moments of relationship and contact, or lack thereof, in the final section of our essay.

The Edges of Intersectionality

Lorde's work on breast cancer has been a welcome resource for disability scholars seeking to challenge the normalizing demands of the medical-industrial complex. Lorde is critical of the cultural imperative to overcome illness and disability by "looking on the bright side of things," noting that such imperatives lead to "blame-the-victim thinking" while obscuring "realities of life"; she is equally critical of those who cast her only as an object of pity.[20] She condemns the economic stratifications of contemporary healthcare, wondering, "What would it be like to be living in a place where [. . .] this crucial part of our lives was not circumscribed and fractionalized by the economics of disease in America? Here the first consideration concerning cancer is [. . .] how much is this going to cost" (*A Burst of Light*, 99).

Each of these passages demonstrates Lorde's relevance to disability studies: not only does she uncover the personal and structural violence of the medical-industrial complex, but she models how to oppose curative imaginaries while desiring a cure for one's illness. These examples also demonstrate Lorde's usefulness in developing a disability studies more attuned to intersectionality; cognizant of how black women received different treatment than white women, she was similarly aware of how her own class privilege and cultural capital afforded her better care than many other women of color. She knew that breast cancer could not be discussed separately from race, class, gender, or nation; nor could we develop an anti-cancer agenda without movements for environmental, economic, and racial justice and decolonization.

One of the ways Lorde exhibits intersectional thinking is through the (seemingly) simple act of naming. She makes clear, through her self-descriptions, that she cannot be reduced to any single identity; she is always more than one thing. In *The Cancer Journals* (1980), she calls herself "a woman, a black lesbian feminist mother lover poet" (24); later, in *Zami: A New Spelling of My Name: A Biomythography* (1982), she describes growing up "fat, Black, nearly blind, and ambidextrous in a West Indian household" (24). But these are not her only namings; she recombines these identities, naming and renaming herself as a way of refusing monolithic, singular identities. She stresses the politically generative power of naming oneself in multiplicity even when it feels dangerous: "I identified myself as a Black Feminist Lesbian poet although it felt unsafe, which is probably why I had to do it. [...] I identified myself as such because if there was one other Black Feminist Lesbian poet in isolation somewhere within the reach of my voice, I wanted her to know she was not alone" (*A Burst of Light*, 100–01). Lorde shifts the meanings of the labels that have been attached to her; she seeks to transform the meaning of difference by naming it for herself.

Yet even as she insists upon naming as an act of self-definition, Lorde recognizes that the practice is not innocent. Carriacou, where Lorde's mother was born, is a small island off the coast of Grenada, yet Lorde never saw it on a map until she was twenty-six. Not being able to locate this "magic place," Lorde doubted its existence, dismissing her mother's sense of geography as "a fantasy or crazy or at least too old-fashioned" (*Zami*, 14). When Lorde finally discovered Carriacou in the *Atlas of the Encyclopedia Britannica*, she knew that the book's accurate cartography served the colonial enterprise. We hear resonances here with disabled people's ambivalent relationships to diagnosis, a system of authoritative classification that can simultaneously bring recognition and misrecognition. Naming, like mapping, can be a way of claiming one's differences, but it also defines and constrains how those differences are understood.

Take the label of "disabled." Although Lorde wrote extensively about her experiences with cancer and repeatedly referred to herself as an "almost blind" child, she did not identify herself as a "person with disabilities." We are wary, then, of too easily naming Lorde as "disabled" or "crip" – political identities she did not claim – or of too seamlessly incorporating her "into" disability studies in the name of intersectionality. As disability justice activists and theorists have noted, the main current of disability studies has not always been available to disabled people of color. Gloria Anzaldúa – another queer woman of color who had disabilities but did not identify as "disabled" – expressed concern about the homogenizing and compressing effect of identifying with "one particular form of 'Otherness'," namely disability, and thereby "allowing issues of class, cultural diversity, ethnicity, and gender to be ignored."[21] Ruminating on Anzaldúa's refusal, Aurora Levins Morales suggests that such identification might have required the presence of "a strong, vocal, politically sophisticated disability justice movement led by queer working class women and transpeople of color [...], and it wasn't there yet."[22] Following Levins Morales, we want to argue that while Lorde's writing is essential to an intersectional disability studies, we must reckon with the possibility that she would not have identified with the field as it is. In other words, to claim writers such as Lorde as disabled or as parts of disability studies can, ironically, be a way of shutting down intersectionality if such moves are not accompanied by an analysis of what makes it impossible for some people and communities to recognize themselves in, and be recognized by, disability studies and disability movements.

Theorizing disability intersectionally means shifting the terrain of disability studies, being open to both identification and disidentification with the field's terms.[23] Just as, in Lorde's terms, "Black feminism is not white feminism in blackface,"[24] Black disability studies, Asian American disability studies, Chicana/o disability studies, and transnational feminist disability studies, as well as the claim of crip or the focus on debility and precarity, may take different forms than white Western disability studies.[25] Similarly, a disability studies that recognizes "illness" and "disability" as racialized categories, or that explores the workings of "ability" and "normalcy" in constructions of gender, sex, and class, will be a different disability studies than the largely unmarked (white, Anglo-European) disability studies at work historically. When we approach potential sites of analysis – such as a text by Audre Lorde – we cannot look only for signs of politicized disability identities or disability critiques as they have been articulated by white people. Critiques of ideologies of ability and health that do not take up the language of disability or make disability identity claims are not to be dismissed but rather can be regarded as sites for mutually transformative connections.

In *Zami*, Lorde's blindness never appears alone or at the center of her self-definition; she describes herself as "nearly blind" (24) and "legally blind"

(21) but such descriptors surface as part of a longer string of identifications, as in "Fat Black Female and almost blind" (*Cancer Journals*, 40). While her visual impairment clearly had an impact on her life and self-definition, it does not serve as the foundation of her narrative or as the primary determinant of her experiences. The book's prologue, for example, focuses on how she "always wanted to be both man and woman," and the first chapter opens with her parents' immigration story; neither mentions Lorde's sight. The rest of the book follows a similar pattern; while she describes experiences of visual impairment, her grapplings with sexuality, gender, race, and class occupy more central roles. Reading intersectionally might mean looking not only at stories in which disability plays a starring role, but also at those where race, indigeneity, or immigration are more centrally featured.

Doing so can allow for an exploration of how disability is used to illuminate other oppressions. In *Zami*, anecdotes of Lorde's visual impairment occur alongside explorations of gender, race, and class. In one such story, she links the whiteness of her vision to the whiteness of Washington, DC, where her family spent the Fourth of July in 1947:

> I was squinting because I was in that silent agony that characterized all my childhood summers, [...] brought about by my dilated and vulnerable eyes exposed to the summer brightness.
>
> I viewed Julys through an agonizing corolla of whiteness and I always hated the Fourth of July, even before I came to realize the travesty such a celebration was for Black people in this country. (69)

Lorde closes the chapter by returning to the overwhelming sensation of whiteness, noting that the "white heat and the white pavement and the white stone monuments [...] made me sick to my stomach" (71). In linking the whiteness of the nation's capital to the pained brightness of her vision, Lorde presents an embodied experience of racism; whiteness is all-encompassing, affecting one's whole field of vision, structuring one's being in the world. Lorde's language here is both metaphorical and literal: her experience of blurred, painful vision facilitates her understanding of the violence of white supremacy.

Lorde recognized that disability and race were often used to justify oppression or disqualification. In describing her mother as a "very powerful woman," she notes:

> This was so in a time when that word-combination of *woman* and *powerful* was almost unexpressable in the white american common tongue, except or unless it was accompanied by some aberrant explaining adjective like blind, or hunchback, or crazy, or Black. Therefore when I was growing up, *powerful*

woman equaled something else quite different from ordinary woman, from simply "woman." (15)

Lorde reveals how attributions of disability ("blind," "hunchback," and "crazy") were used alongside attributions of race ("Black") as delegitimizing forces. Race and disability, while not the "same," can be put to similar cultural work. Moreover, this passage suggests that normative gender performance requires both whiteness and ableness; being disabled or being black meant one could not be a real woman. This incompatibility between "aberrancy" and conventional womanhood becomes, in turn, a source of power. Although Lorde's focus is not on disability per se, she does offer examples of how to understand disability in relation to other power dynamics.

Yet, while Lorde seemed aware of how race and disability labels could be used to justify the oppression of other groups, as evidenced by her rumination on "powerful women," she drew heavily on disability metaphors herself. In a discussion of the inseparability of oppressions, she describes racism, sexism, heterosexism, and homophobia as "forms of human blindness."[26] "Blindness" surfaces repeatedly in her work as a way of describing ignorance or the willful refusal to "see" oppression (for example, the "arrogant blindness of comfortable white women"); so, too, do deafness and muteness, both signaling a failure to speak out against injustice (*Cancer Journals*, 10, 21). While Lorde condemned the violent normalizing imperative that all women have "the 'right' color, shape, size, or number of breasts," she unreservedly used disability as a metaphor to condemn racist and sexist society. How are we to understand her reliance on such metaphors, or her failure to imagine people who are deaf, mute, and blind as part of her work? How should we respond to her use of now outdated language that may feel violent to contemporary readers (for instance, referring to disabled children as "retarded")? As Levins Morales suggests, Lorde may not have had communities of disabled women of color to help her rethink this use of language. Moreover, her own embodied experiences of impaired vision and muteness (she reports that she did not talk until she was five) may have made such metaphors particularly evocative to her. Yet as disability scholars have demonstrated, such metaphors are embedded in ableist structures of thought, casting illness, disability, and impairment as the things that must be overcome for oppression to end.

These failures of imaginative relation coexist with Lorde's brilliant theorizations of relations between movements. Not only did she refuse to separate race from gender, or to accept the bifurcation of feminism from racial justice, she continually stressed the political dimensions of illness and disability. Part of her argument was that we must challenge the classism and racism undergirding the medical-industrial complex, condemning the targeting of particular populations for debilitation. But it was also about naming the interconnectedness of different movements for social justice. Both *The Cancer Journals* (1980) and *A Burst of Light* (1988) are accounts of her illness, but they are simultaneously indictments of racism, capitalism, sexism, and colonial violence. She moves seamlessly from describing her use of herbs for her liver to stories of apartheid violence in Soweto. She challenges the "idea that the cancer patient should be made to feel guilty about having had cancer" by underscoring the pervasiveness of injustices such as "when 12 year old Black boys are shot down in the street at random by uniformed men who are cleared of any wrong-doing" or "when ancient and honorable citizens scavenge for food in garbage pails," suggesting that all of these battles are related (*A Burst of Light*, 59–60; *Cancer Journals*, 76–77). She invests her strength as much in her recovery as in struggles over sovereignty for indigenous peoples. Her criticism of cuts to programs educating disabled children occurs alongside her condemnation of the "spread of radiation, racism, woman-slaughter, chemical invasion of our food, pollution of our environment, [and] the abuse and psychic destruction of our young" (*Cancer Journals*, 77).

We understand this coexistence as evidence of the important, yet incomplete, work of intersectionality. One of the promises of some interpretations of intersectionality is that we will eventually name all the categories of oppression and fully map their operations; adding disability brings us closer to that goal. We want to stress instead the *incompleteness* and *relationality* of intersectionality. Doing intersectional work requires not only examining material realities and injustices, but also questioning how our theories may actually *produce* unjust realities; moments of tension between and within movements help illuminate such productions. In other words, these tensions – the edges of intersectionality, "the edges of each other's battles" – are the real promise of intersectionality, as they prompt us not only to challenge multiple structures of oppression, but to do so in relation to other movements for social justice – even when such solidarity feels difficult or risky. As Lorde and Cliff demonstrate, intersectional analysis can allow us to critique multiple categories without taxonomizing or stabilizing them. We can address illness and disability as sites for mutually transformative relations rather than prioritizing or isolating disability and disability studies.

NOTES

1. Mia Mingus, "'Intersectionality' Is a Big Fancy Word for My Life," *Leaving Evidence* blog, February 25, 2010, https://leavingevidence.wordpress.com/2010/02/25/%E2%80%9Cintersectionality%E2%80%9D-is-a-big-fancy-word-for-my-life/, accessed October 12, 2016.

2. Kimberlé Crenshaw introduced the "intersection" framing in 1989, but intersectionality's roots extend deeper; nineteenth-century feminist Anna Julia Cooper, for example, recognized that race and gender are intertwined. Kimberlé Crenshaw, "Demarginalizing the Intersection of Race and Sex: A Black Feminist Critique of Antidiscrimination Doctrine, Feminist Theory and Antiracist Politics," *The University of Chicago Legal Forum*, 1.8 (1989), pp. 139–67; Vivian M. May, "Intellectual Genealogies, Intersectionality, and Anna Julia Cooper," in *Feminist Solidarity at the Crossroads: Intersectional Women's Studies for Transracial Alliance*, ed. by Kim Marie Vaz and Gary L. Lemons (New York: Routledge, 2011), pp. 59–71. Moreover, attributing the theory to a single scholar "fixes the concept," removing it from "the collaborative context in which it emerged." Santa Cruz Feminists of Color Collective, "Building on 'the Edge of Each Other's Battles': A Feminist of Color Multidimensional Lens," *Hypatia*, 29.1 (2014), pp. 23–40 (p. 33).
3. Audre Lorde, "Age, Race, Class, and Sex: Women Redefining Difference," in *Sister Outsider: Essays and Speeches by Audre Lorde* (Freedom, CA: Crossing Press, 1984), pp. 114–23.
4. See also Sami Schalk's chapter in this volume.
5. Jasbir Puar, "Disability," *TSQ: Transgender Studies Quarterly*, 1.1–2 (2014), pp. 77–81 (p. 80).
6. Lorde, "Age, Race, Class, and Sex," p. 123.
7. Audre Lorde, "The Master's Tools Will Never Dismantle the Master's House," in *Sister Outsider*, pp. 110–13 (pp. 110–11).
8. Ibid., p. 112.
9. Lennard J. Davis, "Introduction: Disability, the Missing Term in the Race, Class, Gender Triad," in *Enforcing Normalcy: Disability, Deafness, and the Body* (London: Verso, 1995), pp. 1–22.
10. Ellen Samuels warns of the pitfalls of substituting disability for gender in her essay, "Critical Divide: Judith Butler's Body Theory and the Question of Disability," *NWSA Journal*, 14.3 (2002), pp. 58–76 (pp. 62–65).
11. Jennifer C. James and Cynthia Wu, "Editors' Introduction: Race, Ethnicity, Disability, and Literature: Intersections and Interventions," *MELUS*, 31.3 (2006), pp. 3–13 (p. 8).
12. Audre Lorde, *A Burst of Light: Essays by Audre Lorde* (Ithaca, NY: Firebrand Books, 1988), p. 70.
13. Nancy J. Hirschmann, "Disability, Feminism, and Intersectionality: A Critical Approach," *Radical Philosophy Review*, 16.2 (2013), pp. 649–62 (p. 661).
14. Sara Ahmed, *On Being Included: Racism and Diversity in Institutional Life* (Durham: Duke University Press, 2012), p. 195, n. 18.
15. David T. Mitchell and Sharon L. Snyder, *Narrative Prosthesis: Disability and the Dependencies of Discourse* (Ann Arbor: University of Michigan Press, 2000), p. 3; Davis, *Enforcing Normalcy*, p. 5.
16. Lennard J. Davis, "Foreword," in *Blackness and Disability: Critical Examinations and Cultural Interventions*, ed. by Christopher M. Bell (Münster: LIT Verlag, 2011), pp. viii–xi (pp. ix, x).
17. Michelle Cliff, "If I Could Write This, I Would Write This in Fire," in *Home Girls: A Black Women's Anthology*, ed. by Barbara Smith (New York: Kitchen Table Women of Color Press, 1983), pp. 15–30 (p. 18). Further

page references to primary texts will be given parenthetically in the body of the chapter.

18. Jasbir Puar, *Terrorist Assemblages: Homonationalism in Queer Times* (Durham, NC: Duke University Press, 2007), p. xiii.
19. Audre Lorde, *Zami: A New Spelling of My Name: A Biomythography* (Freedom, CA: Crossing Press, 1994), p. 86.
20. Audre Lorde, *The Cancer Journals: Special Edition* (San Francisco: Aunt Lute, 1997), pp. 76–78; Lorde, *A Burst of Light*, p. 79.
21. Gloria Anzaldúa, "Disability & Identity: An E-mail Exchange and a Few Additional Thoughts," in *The Gloria Anzaldúa Reader*, ed. by AnaLouise Keating (Durham, NC: Duke University Press, 2009), pp. 298–302 (p. 302).
22. Qwo-Li Driskill, Aurora Levins Morales, and Leah Lakshmi Piepzna-Samarasinha, "Sweet Dark Places: Letters to Gloria Anzaldúa on Disability, Creativity, and the Coatlicue State," in *El Mundo Zurdo 2: Selected Works from the Society of the Study of Gloria Anzaldúa*, ed. by Sonia Saldívar Hull, Norma Alarcón and Rita Urquijo-Ruiz (San Francisco, CA: Aunt Lute, 2012), pp. 77–97 (pp. 78–79).
23. Sami Schalk, "Coming to Claim Crip: Disidentification with/in Disability Studies," *Disability Studies Quarterly*, 33.2 (2013) n. pag., http://www.dsq-sds.org/article/view/3705/3240, accessed October 12, 2016.
24. Marion Kraft, "The Creative Use of Difference," in *Conversations with Audre Lorde*, ed. by Joan Wylie Hall (Jackson: University Press of Mississippi, 2004), pp. 146–53 (p. 150).
25. See Therí Pickens, "Outliers and Out Right Lies; or How We 'Do' Black Disability Studies," *tpickens.org* blog, August 9, 2012, http://www.tpickens.org/2012/08/09/outliers-and-out-right-lies-or-how-we-do-black-disability-studies/, accessed October 12, 2016; Mel Y. Chen, "Asian American Speech, Civic Place, and Future Nondisabled Bodies," *Amerasia Journal*, 39.1 (2013), pp. 91–105; Julie Avril Minich, *Accessible Citizenships: Disability, Nation, and the Cultural Politics of Greater Mexico* (Philadelphia: Temple University Press, 2014); Nirmala Erevelles, *Disability and Difference in Global Contexts* (New York: Palgrave Macmillan, 2011); Carrie Sandahl, "Queering the Crip or Cripping the Queer?: Intersections of Queer and Crip Identities in Solo Autobiographical Performance," *GLQ: A Journal of Lesbian and Gay Studies*, 9.1–2 (2003), pp. 25–56; Robert McRuer, *Crip Theory: Cultural Signs of Queerness and Disability* (New York: New York University Press, 2006); Julie Livingston, *Debility and the Moral Imagination in Botswana* (Bloomington: Indiana University Press, 2005); Puar, "Disability."
26. Audre Lorde, "Scratching the Surface: Some Notes on Barriers to Women and Loving," in *Sister Outsider*, pp. 45–52 (p. 45).

10

ROBERT MCRUER

The World-Making Potential of Contemporary Crip/Queer Literary and Cultural Production

Like "queer," "crip" has been, historically, a pejorative word that has been reclaimed by the very people it was meant to wound. Derived in English from "cripple," "crip" has been used as a more radical and defiant word than disability over the past few decades, similar to the ways in which queer has been used by LGBT people. Because of the edginess and defiance of the two reclaimed words, "crip" and "queer" have also been very closely related terms. This chapter will examine some of the processes of contemporary crip/queer cultural and literary production, examining both works that use these terms directly and some of their predecessors that share their outspoken boldness, even if they use somewhat different language.

Culture, as Raymond Williams famously suggested, is in one sense about shared values or norms, about "the particular way of life ... of a people, a period, a group, or humanity in general."[1] To suggest, however, that the *production* of culture or cultures might be somehow "crip" or "queer" (or both) is to imply, perhaps paradoxically, either that particular people, periods, or groups might have characteristics that identify them as crip or queer or that some forms of cultural production, whether tied to identity or not, might generatively de-form or pervert "particular ways of life," transforming, in potentially world-making ways, that which is normative.

In his groundbreaking 1999 memoir *Exile and Pride: Disability, Queerness, and Liberation*, Eli Clare reflects at length on the generative power of queer and crip as descriptors. In the process, he provides a glimpse of the origins of crip/queer cultural production:

> *Queer*, like *cripple*, is an ironic and serious word I use to describe myself and others in my communities ... I adore its defiant external edge, its comfortable internal truth. *Queer* belongs to me. So does *cripple* for many of the same reasons. *Queer* and *cripple* are cousins: words to shock, words to infuse with pride and self-love, words to resist internalized hatred, words to help forge

a politics. They have been gladly chosen – *queer* by many gay/lesbian/bi/trans people, *cripple*, or *crip*, by many disabled people.[2]

Although by the early twenty-first century it was virtually impossible to be well-versed in disability theory without an understanding of how it was thoroughly intertwined with sexuality studies or queer theory, Clare's words predate the rise of scholarly work that might be called crip/queer. Clare's words, moreover, locate the terms "crip" and "queer" in more broadly communal or political realms. Indeed, the rise of academic crip/queer theory should be understood as indebted to the vibrant cultural and political production that has taken place largely outside of the academy. Clare's analysis makes clear that "queer," "crip," and "cripple" have frequently been intended to shock or wound. Although they originated as terms of abuse, however, disability and lesbian/gay/bisexual/transgender (LGBT) communities have resignified them in order to materialize something in excess of that origin, a defiant and expansive politics and culture.

The transformative promise that attends the development of queer/crip literatures and cultures is the focus of the remainder of this chapter. In 2003, Carrie Sandahl published an important article spotlighting four figures (all performance artists) whom she read as participating, flamboyantly and in various ways, in that work.[3] In some ways, this foundational essay theorizing crip and queer cultural production in disability performance studies echoed the work of José Esteban Muñoz, who understood the power of queer by imagining "one queer standing onstage alone ... bent on the project of opening up a world of queer language, lyricism, perceptions, dreams, visions, aesthetics, and politics."[4] Solo autobiographical performance work, for Sandahl, given its public and communal setting and its Muñozian reveling in generative spectacle, affords an arena for performative play, crip/queer play that might be understood as "bent" in capacious ways beyond that which Muñoz intended with his use of the word.[5] This performative play makes use of the edginess, shock, pride, and love that Clare noted as always being in circulation around ways of living identified as crip and queer. The paradox I identified at the outset, whereby "crip" and "queer" are attached to certain people or groups as identities at the same time that they function less as identities and more as processes working to undo the power of able-bodied (and able-minded) normativity and heteronormativity,[6] is also very much in evidence in the performances Sandahl analyzes.

In her article, Sandahl surveyed the work of Greg Walloch, Robert DeFelice, Julia Trahan, and Terry Galloway, arguing that these performers "experiment with the cultural meanings of crip and queer in theory, practice, and representation."[7] This experimentation, for Sandahl, allowed for "crip," in particular, to function not just as a noun but as an active, critical verb: cripping as performative practice "spins mainstream representations or practices to reveal able-bodied assumptions and exclusionary effects. Both queering and cripping expose the arbitrary delineation between normal and defective and negative social ramifications of attempts to homogenize humanity, and both disarm with a wicked humor, including camp."[8] All of Sandahl's crip/queer subjects deploy humor of this sort in some way: Walloch, for example, uses his position within both disabled and gay communities to craft comedic performances that expose and critique heterosexist assumptions in disabled communities and ableist assumptions in LGBT communities. When he is expected to perform the role of "the made-for-television image of the inspirational crip," Sandahl explains, he steps into it with "a drag queen's flair," inhabiting the stereotype queerly in a way that mocks and ultimately explodes it.[9] Similarly, as a deaf performer who does not sign, Galloway uses her always-shifting and contradictory identifications as crip and queer both to challenge intragroup norms and to work the system. In one sketch remembering her childhood, for example, she performs a deafness obviously not grounded in pride (a significant intragroup norm for most members of Deaf culture) in order to access hearing aids from Rehabilitation Services: "The fate of my ears hinges on whatever performances of deafness I come up with," Galloway recalls in the performance. "So I went into that office and ping! I . . . got all meek and uncertain and my speech got blurry and I sat there silent, unfunny and glum."[10] She got the hearing aids she needed, however, and Sandahl's point is that the crip/queer space of solo autobiographical performances like Galloway's provides a site where innovative and humorous stories of navigating ableist and homophobic assumptions can be shared and extended in the interest of generating new queer/crip ways of knowing, and of collectively surviving and thriving.

In what follows, I survey crip and queer cultural production of various sorts. I have emphasized performance in this opening; I move, in the following sections, from literary to visual cultural production. I conclude briefly, in the final section of this chapter, with visual and linguistic activism – or, put differently, with reflections on what Clare, Sandahl, and many others have identified as the world-making possibilities of new crip/queer languages or vocabularies. These new languages are "world-making" because they imagine, and help to construct, a world apart from the intertwined homophobia and ableism that structure the world we currently inhabit. Taken cumulatively, the cultural production on display in this chapter represents a virtual crip/queer renaissance, beginning in the last part of the twentieth century and continuing with no signs of stopping into the twenty-first.

Crip Lit

Something that perhaps might be termed "crip lit" goes back several decades, and is (not surprisingly) thoroughly queer, in all its valences. The category would likely include edgy memoirs such as Lorenzo Milam's *The Cripple Liberation Front Marching Band Blues* or Connie Panzarino's *The Me in the Mirror*, both published in 1984.[11] Milam, who would later (in 1993) author a book titled *CripZen: A Manual for Survival* (about the importance of, and strategies for, ending high rates of suicide among disabled people),[12] explicitly echoes with the title of his earlier memoir the name of the Gay Liberation Front, the radical activist movement that emerged in 1969 and that stressed both collective pride and struggle against institutionalized oppression. Gay liberationists were not so much stressing coming out *of* the closet to a clearly delineated identity but rather coming out *to* a vibrant and collective movement that would, conceivably, reinvent the world.[13] The crippled or crip liberation front, in all of the texts under consideration here, rejects mainstream culture's ableist belief that disability is neither desirable nor desiring.

Milam represents literal institutions intended to control and confine disability in *The Cripple Liberation Front Marching Band Blues* as he details his experiences of polio, including the rehabilitation unit he terms "Hopeless Haven," where a boy named Randall (who had osteomyelitis) would come "to the bed next to me, his warm body threatening, by its very presence, to consume my own in a pure blue flame which seems to emanate, by magic, from his pores" (42). Although such incidents were not explicitly sexual, or not explicitly "queer" as Milam terms it in his memoir or understood it at the time, they were suffused with a homoeroticism that remade the sterile isolation of Hopeless Haven. This world-making moment created an imaginative and sensual space of community for Milam.

Panzarino does not include the word crip explicitly – although she does write about resisting "the stereotype of the 'helpless cripple'" (178) – but *The Me in the Mirror* nonetheless sets the stage for some of the more openly crip work that followed it in more recent decades. As with Milam, Panzarino moves toward queerness as a space for ending isolation and imagining new possibilities. She tells the story of becoming lesbian, particularly stressing her encounter with Maura, an attendant who validated Panzarino's belief in the beauty of vulvas by beginning "to do four-by-five paintings of vulva flower-like abstracts" (203). Panzarino would later become a well-known figure in Boston Gay Pride marches, where she would attach to her wheelchair a sign reading "Trached Dykes Eat Pussy Without Coming Up for Air," an undeniably (and even literal) in-your-face assertion of disabled/crip and queer sexual freedom and agency.

Like solo autobiographical performance, memoir is a genre that allows for self-experimentation and (re)invention.[14] Milam's and Panzarino's earlier memoirs make clear that Clare is just one of a range of creative writers who have used memoir over recent decades to explore crip/queer cultural experiences and to forward crip/queer cultural production. Clare's own memoir is, as implied above, more explicitly or openly crip (and queer) than the earlier texts and is important for numerous reasons. It has a doubled publication date that is itself queer – the reissued version of *Exile and Pride* was published, in 2009, after Clare openly claimed a transgender identity and shifted the pronouns he most commonly used to identify himself.

The ways in which trans sits easily alongside the other defiant identities Clare writes about in his memoir is a good testament to how queer/crip cultural production is actively coalitional. *Exile and Pride* opens with an analysis of the ways in which "the mountain" functions metaphorically in disabled lives. Disability activists have critiqued some narratives for suggesting that disabled individuals should strive for spectacular achievements that appear to "overcome" disability; such stories of super achievement have been deemed overcoming narratives and the individuals at the center of such stories have sometimes been labeled supercrips.[15] Supercrips, in the dominant imagination, should be able to scale every mountain with ease. In a powerful narration of the experience of navigating (by choice) an actual mountain and making decisions about when to continue and when to stop based on the actual, embodied experience of a climb with a friend, Clare critiques these ubiquitous ableist demands. Clare also, through this story, arguably positions genuine crip/queer friendship as at odds with the compulsory individualism of the overcoming narrative. Over the course of *Exile and Pride*, it is repeatedly clear that community (beginning with the community of two on the mountain) is for Clare the condition of possibility for such critiques. The memoir in fact ends with a beautiful alternative image of many different subjects sitting on a wall and telling each other stories of survival (the wall is quite notably a flat surface and not a mountain peak that an individual should master):

> I will sit on the wide, flat top of my wall . . . with butch women, femme dykes, nellie men, studly fags, radical faeries, drag kings and queens, transsexual people who want no more than to be women and men, intersexed people, hermaphrodites with attitudes, transgendered, pangendered, bigendered, polygendered, ungendered, androgynous people of many varieties and trade stories long into the night. (138)

Galloway also wrote a memoir, *Mean Little deaf Queer* (2009), with the uncapitalized "deaf" signifying that she never learned sign language and was thus invariably not an ideal or proper representative of Deaf culture.[16] *Mean Little deaf Queer* is one of the more explicitly sexual queer/crip memoirs, although as should be clear in this exploration of crip lit, sex is quite often a key component of them, allowing for the resistance of both homophobic and ableist assumptions that would cast certain bodies and pleasures as either undesirable or unthinkable. As she represents in narrative her path through a non-normative adolescence, Galloway makes clear that it is filled with longing: "The dictionary mentioned desire and that's how I imagined homosexual – as being in the throes of longing" (90). Galloway does not remain in the throes of longing forever, although openly accepting her own queerness does take a while: "It strikes me funny now that of all the things I was doing then – the threesomes, the foursomes, the sixsomes, with the tinker, the tailor, the mescaline maker – the one thing I dreaded my parents discovering was that I was sleeping with women" (130). As in her solo autobiographical performances, however, *Mean Little deaf Queer* ultimately represents Galloway as moving toward a position where it is possible to find meaning and sustenance (and queer/crip love, a key value toward which Galloway writes) in open affiliation with misfits of all sorts.

Merri Lisa Johnson's memoir *Girl in Need of a Tourniquet* (2010) also does not use the term crip explicitly but contains many of the elements that would make it "crip lit" for the purposes of this overview: it represents both an inhabiting and an explosion of a diagnostic category (it is in fact subtitled *Memoir of a Borderline Personality*) and it displays a range of sometimes messy or slippery queer desires (as well as a Galloway-like yearning toward, and affinity with, a range of misfits).[17] It is also formally experimental, incorporating various news items, medical reports, email communications, and other kinds of writing (in a range of fonts and typefaces) in order to explore and experiment with ways of living with and through mental disability. "Beneath the facades of distraction, debauchery, denial, and diagnosis," Johnson muses, "a deeper level of unsolved heartsore questions about mental health flows. Here is where the hard work truly begins. I set out to make friends with my borderline personality. I set out to teach my borderline personality to play well with others" (203). *Girl in Need of a Tourniquet* arguably also set the stage for Johnson's more explicitly theoretical work, again indicating that the paths between creative and political work and more openly academic or theoretical work are multidirectional. Following the publication of *Girl in Need of a Tourniquet*, Johnson coined the term "cripistemologies" to signify ways of "knowing and unknowing disability, making and unmaking disability epistemologies, and the importance of challenging subjects who confidently 'know' about 'disability', as though it could be a thoroughly comprehended object of knowledge."[18] Two special issues of the *Journal of Literary and Cultural Disability Studies*, both published in 2014, became a platform for a range of crip, queer, and queer/crip scholars, artists, and activists to collectively explore how such generative knowing and unknowing, making and unmaking, might proceed. The essays included focus on borderline personality, anxiety, chronic pain, HIV/AIDS, trans identity, and a range of other embodiments or states of being not usually understood as "representative" of disability in the way that the universal access symbol for disability makes the wheelchair user representative. Crip lit in general exhibits this will toward a more expansive understanding of what disability can mean.

Crip Visual Production

Literary production is only one form of crip/queer cultural production; crips and queers have been extensively producing visual culture as well over the past few decades. The production of visual images often directly counters stereotypical or two-dimensional images of disabled people – images, for example, that quickly elicit pity or awe from presumedly able-bodied viewers.[19] In 1997, David Mitchell and Sharon Snyder released a short film that represents well this cultural work of generating alternative representations, explicitly calling that work both "vital" and "crip" and suggesting that, in the process of speaking in its own voice, crip culture actively speaks back to the hegemonic forms of cultural production that would limit or short-circuit it. *Vital Signs: Crip Culture Talks Back*, largely filmed at a disability studies gathering held at the University of Michigan a few years before its release, includes poetry, performance, interviews, and some direct footage of activism.[20] *Vital Signs*, as a title, in many ways functions with a double-edged signification similar to crip or queer. It is saturated in medical languages, since "vital signs" are generally taken by a trained medical practitioner in a clinical setting; the title thus gestures toward the record of an individual and objectified patient being monitored by medical authorities. Simultaneously, however, it gestures toward the collective production of new subjects and of a new culture resistant to being defined solely or predominantly in medical terms.[21]

Clare, DeFelice, Trahan, and Sandahl are among the several participants in *Vital Signs*. Sandahl's performance in the film makes the dual signification of "vital signs" most explicit, as she is represented in a museum space in a white costume upon which is written all the many medicalized terms that have been used to describe her by medical authorities over the course of her life. She takes language that in an ableist culture generally speaks univocally ("what's wrong with you, exactly?") and makes that language speak, in the context of a defiant crip culture, in multiple ways. The performance can be interpreted as suggesting "My life is art; I am part of a political and cultural movement; I cannot be reduced to the terms you would use to contain me."

Vital Signs announces itself as producing crip culture, but it is queer in multiple ways, not least in its simple refusal to abide by the dictates of normalcy or normalization.[22] The artists, activists, and academics in the film inhabit and delight in the very queer categories that would place them beyond the limits of normalcy. DeFelice, for example, announces in a performance included in the film (and to the delight of his crip/queer audience), "'Broken down' I do not need to be called. 'Crippled' was good. Cripples have class. It sounds like Victorian back bedrooms. I like that. It's got mystery." In a more straightforward interview about discovering disability culture in California in the 1970s, Simi Linton likewise links disability to hitherto unknown pleasures: "And I went off and went back to my apartment and spent the next four months in Berkeley just exploring the pleasure and fun of life as a disabled woman." Linton would go on to write an important memoir of her own in 2006, *My Body Politic*, which again proudly affirms a range of sexual pleasures (and includes stories of Linton's time as a counselor specifically concerned with emphasizing disabled people's sexual freedom).[23]

Sexuality and queerness have thus been central to this visual form of cultural production, just like its literary counterpart. In the wake of *Vital Signs*, Loree Erickson has been among those artists and activists working to generate bold and sexually explicit crip/queer visual cultures. Indeed, Erickson produces crip/queer pornography: she is a self-described "porn star academic," and uses her own productions to fill the void of positive visual representations of queer/crip desire. "My work is a synthesis of theoretical engagement and critical artistic creation," she writes, "both of which are motivated and shaped by personal experience and activist ideals. I want to replace the gawking, gazing, and glaring people with disabilities encounter on a daily basis with beholding, recognizing, and reacting when people with disabilities are red fucking hot."[24] Erickson's emphasis on "*when* people with disabilities are red fucking hot" does not simply imply that disabled people are *sometimes* sexually attractive and compelling so much as insist that they *always* are. Mainstream cultures, Erickson's work suggests, have simply not generated representations that affirm that basic fact sufficiently.

Want is Erickson's most well-known video; the ten-minute film was awarded a Feminist Porn Award in 2008.[25] What is most notable about *Want*, from its title to the intimate and sexual images it provides, is its yearning for something else, a yearning that can be connected in this particular representation to a *transnational* crip (and queer) sharing of ideas and images that continually asks for more than specific national or institutional contexts provide. *Want* takes place in Canada, a country that is perhaps at times naively romanticized south of the border, given the relative availability of social services when healthcare and many other basic rights remain so precarious or inaccessible to many in the United States. Erickson's film debunks any easy romanticization, and partly uses queerness as a tool for that debunking. The film is about everything Erickson wants and that "want" is largely articulated through a seemingly insatiable and sexualized hunger. Over images of her in various sexual positions with a queer or trans figure and engaged in intimate and nonintimate activities with a range of others, Erickson tells viewers that she wants to be the girl you laugh with, wants to be the girl you have fun with, wants to be the girl you make cum so hard she can't scream, wants, wants, wants, wants (she repeats the verb over and over again). Erickson wants, she insists, to be the girl with *access* to both sexual pleasure and collectivity, concepts that the film articulates, both in the sense of speaking (sexual pleasure and collectivity are talked about) and joining together (sexual pleasure and collectivity have some perhaps-not-specified but palpable connection). The film explains that Erickson's life is a collective one, patched together with and by friends, lovers, and queers who both attend to each others' needs and fulfil each others' pleasures. And here *Want* articulates the deromanticization of Canada: this collective crip existence has been forged because of a *lack* of social services and, even more important, because of the structural homophobia endemic to the services that do exist.

Queer/crip yearnings or desires can now be traced in numerous other national and transnational locations and networks. In Barcelona, a documentary was produced and directed in 2015 by Antonio Centeno and Raúl de la Morena entitled *Yes, we fuck!* The documentary emphasized the sexual freedom that accompanies independent living and spotlighted both physical and cognitive disabilities; one of the highlights of the film is a conversation among a group of intellectually disabled young adults about their sexual fantasies and pleasures.[26] *Yes, we fuck!* quickly became not just a documentary but a movement, generating conversations and activism across Spain and Latin America. The symbol for *Yes, we fuck!* is a queer/crip adaptation of the universal access symbol for disability. The (nongendered) universal access figure, seated in a wheelchair, is joined by another figure seated in her/his lap; the two are clearly engaged in some sort of (unspecified) intimate, erotic connection.

Back in Canada, in 2012, Danielle Peers organized an exhibit that also (as with Erickson's yearning and the first-person plural of *Yes, we fuck!*) implicitly stressed the importance of sharing crip and queer ideas and experiences (including erotic experiences), as well as the importance of producing crip and queer culture across borders. The exhibit, held in Edmonton, was called

FIG. 10.1: Logo for the 2015 documentary *Yes, we fuck!* (dir. Antonio Centeno and Raúl de la Morena).

"CripTease: An Evening of Irreverent Art," and included painting, sculpture, film, and performance by artists from across the United States and Canada. Sculptor Shelley Wright displayed her abstract pieces, designed to represent the experience of living with a cleft lip and palate. Wright's work is strongly influenced by indigenous North American traditions that affirm the body as it is and do not position it as something to be "fixed." Melissa Brittain and Lucas Crawford presented their film *Elephant in the Room* (2012).[27] "Do you have slender trouble?" the film opens, and proceeds to represent fatness as an identity to accept and celebrate. The parodic film uncovering the problem of "slender trouble" in the process makes clear connections among queer, crip, fat, and trans activism.[28] Peers herself is also a filmmaker; her eight-minute film *G.I.M.P Boot Camp* (2008) parodies the ableist demand that crips be inspirational. It is a satirical gimp's guide to survival, representing both the fictitious "crip awards" for the most inspirational disabled person and a boot camp training on how to be a proper (and nonthreatening) disabled subject in an able-bodied world.[29]

One of the most important and well-known artists generating crip/queer visual culture is Riva Lehrer, whose work was also included in "CripTease." Lehrer has been the subject of another film by Sharon Snyder and David Mitchell, *Self-Preservation: The Art of Riva Lehrer* (2005).[30] This film surveyed much of Lehrer's work through the early 2000s, particularly focusing on portraits of disabled individuals from her series *Circle Stories* (2004). A painting of Clare is perhaps the most famous portrait from this series, representing a disabled and trans identity in a state of "magical transformation," as the disability theorist Tobin Siebers describes it in the film. Clare, who is well-known for his environmental politics and activism, is represented in a forest intertwined with a tree that seems to be growing up and through his body. In no way reducible to flat, pitiful, two-dimensional representations of disability (or queerness), the painting is a puzzle that gestures toward new ways of living as crip and queer (and, importantly for Clare, in harmony with the environment).

Since *Circle Stories* and *Self-Preservation*, Lehrer has begun to write as well, composing queer and crip autobiographical pieces that mix prose, poetry, and art. This lyrical writing gestures toward lovers and affirms bisexuality in different ways: the portraits Lehrer uses to accompany her writing (including a range of nudes) are of both men and women, and – in at least one recent piece – the pronouns for the unnamed lover are left ambiguous ("you").[31] She was part of the important 2014 collection *Criptiques*, an anthology that includes a wide range of affirmative crip/queer writing (and that in fact opens with yet another piece exploring sexuality and disability, an evocative essay titled "Criplesque," written by blind burlesque dancer Elsa Henry).[32] Lehrer's own contribution, in which a new and vital relationship is marked by pronouns explicitly gendered female, is a provocative meditation on beauty. "Simple Beauty," which for Lehrer "conforms to cultural standards," is opposed to "Informed Beauty," which comes across as something legible as queer and crip: "Informed Beauty can cause a change in all your senses. My beloved's features become more delicious; her voice grows musical; her skin is a shock to my fingertips. I don't hold these as conscious opinions, but enjoy a rising visceral, aesthetic and sexual pleasure."[33]

It is arguably such Informed Beauty that electrifies the important work of Sins Invalid, a group of performers famous for celebrating what they term "Beauty in the Face of Invisibility." Sins Invalid represents one of the most significant forums for exploring disability and sexuality that has emerged in the twenty-first century: "Sex and disability," one performer notes in their 2014 documentary, *Sins Invalid: An Unashamed Claim to Beauty in the Face of Invisibility*, "are two words that you don't often hear together. And if you do, it's like huh!? [puts her hand mockingly to her face] Those people have sex?" Founded in 2006, the troupe's performances, and their 2014 documentary, centralize artists of color and queer and gender-variant disabled people. The film, produced by Patty Berne, represents performers such as Leroy Moore, Nomy Lamm, Mat Fraser, Maria Palacios, and others talking about and exploring through music, dance, dramatic vignettes, interviews, and monologues multiple queer/crip meanings for sensuality and sexuality.[34] The camerawork, as it focuses on bodies in motion or alone, on body parts (such as stumps) lovingly embraced and caressed, or wheelchairs put into beautiful and unexpected positions through dance, only accentuates what is already the point of Sins Invalid's performance: to develop new and erotic ways of perceiving disability, race, and sexuality, and the beauty that is actively generated when the desirability of all bodies is affirmed.

Love, Loss, and Longing: New Crip Vocabularies

All of these forms of crip/queer cultural production are about imagining otherwise, of replacing the impoverished representations we have been bequeathed by an ableist and homophobic culture with something more generative.[35] This generation of alternatives has sometimes taken the form of explicit queer/crip visual activism. In August 2012, for example, in the wake of supercrip and sentimentalized images of disability circulating globally due to the spectacle of the London 2012 Paralympics (most famously, a sentimental image of Oscar Pistorius running alongside a little girl newly fitted with prosthetic legs), self-described "badass lawyer-turned-sexologist" Bethany Stevens posted an image of herself and friend Robin Wilson-Beattie, along with Stevens's service dog Sully, as part of a "visual culture" campaign designed to change how we look (in both senses of "how we look") via Facebook. The black-and-white photo, by Stan Bowman, shows both women looking directly at the camera. Stevens is seated in her wheelchair with her legs crossed (revealing her high femme shoes); Wilson-Beattie stands behind her, her cane in one hand and a disability tattoo (the universal access symbol merged with a heart) clearly visible on the other arm. The dog, also looking at the camera, stands in front. "This Is What Disability Looks Like" is written across the top; "F*cking Awesome" across the bottom.

After posting her own image with Wilson-Beattie, Stevens began to collect and post images of others; the campaign quickly spread with dozens of disabled people participating and thousands of people viewing the images around the world. The comedienne Stella Young, for example, participated from Australia with a similar tagline, "F*cking Irreverent." Merri Lisa Johnson participated with the tagline "Invisible," making clear that "disability" sometimes includes readily visible signs such as a wheelchair or cane, and as often does not. As news about the This Is What Disability Looks Like project spread, it was taught in a number of disability studies classrooms, profiled in various news magazines, and displayed as part of a mobile mural project in Toronto.[36]

What is arguably crip and queer about the creative campaign is its sociality and *potentiality*. It is tied to, but not exactly defined or restricted by, a certain identity politics. Disability as clearly delineated and two-dimensional object is soundly rejected, replaced by something that Stevens terms "real," but that can be interpreted as a realness of process rather than substance. "I am tired of images of disabled folks that are supposed to inspire or incite fear," she argues. "People are bloody hungry for images of disabled people that are glimpses of our real lives, not just flattened boring stereotypes of what we are supposed to be."[37] It is both the collective mode (what Michael Hardt and Antonio Negri might call the "swarm intelligence")[38] of the project – making the "this" and "is" that "disability looks like" necessarily nonunitary and nonidentical – and the mode in which the repeated "this is" necessarily and perpetually gestures toward ways of being-in-common *currently being invented* that generate potentiality. The clearest cognate for "this is what disability looks likes" is the longstanding global activist chant, "this is what democracy looks like." Although threading through a range of world-transformative movements (from the anticapitalist protests as part of the Battle of Seattle in 1999 to reporting on the politically revolutionary Arab Spring of 2011), "this is what democracy looks like" has no necessary content even though its content is always sufficient for both marking a "realness" of the multitude and gesturing elsewhere. "This is what disability looks like" functions similarly and echoes the earlier slogan.

For Leslie Freeman Taub, those new crip/queer vocabularies can be accessed in dance. Dance, indeed, provides a fitting conclusion to this brief overview of crip and queer cultural production, since it is the fine art that uses the body to reach for world-making ways of thinking or modes of being that perhaps cannot yet be expressed in words. For Taub, Lisa Bufano was a dance partner whose body in many ways mirrored Taub's own (their

FIG. 10.2: Crip/queer dancer Leslie Freeman Taub.

hands ending in very similar stumps) and whose movements allowed them to find an aesthetic of sexuality and disability together. Bufano committed suicide in 2013, and Taub continued and continues to dance in Bufano's absence, moving through her grief to express both the loss of, and ongoing (unending) desire for, queer/crip community and love. This is, perhaps, an affect that is always at the heart of queer and crip cultural production: a yearning for the connection that is always vanishing, but a yearning that nonetheless captures the conviction both that queer and crip lives and experiences matter, and that the artistry generated through and across those lives can somehow point us toward new horizons beyond ableism and homophobia.

NOTES

1. Raymond Williams, *Keywords: A Vocabulary of Culture and Society*, rev. edn. (New York: Oxford University Press, 1983), p. 90.
2. Eli Clare, *Exile and Pride: Disability, Queerness, and Liberation* (Boston: South End Press, 1999), p. 70. Further page references to primary texts will be given parenthetically in the body of the chapter. Although the 1999 edition of *Exile and Pride* discussed Clare's lesbian identity, in the prologue to the reissued tenth anniversary edition of *Exile and Pride* (2009), Clare made clear that male pronouns were appropriate for discussing his work. Clare's transgender politics are discussed later in this chapter.
3. Carrie Sandahl, "Queering the Crip or Cripping the Queer? Intersections of Queer and Crip Identities in Solo Autobiographical Performances," *GLQ: A Journal of Lesbian and Gay Studies*, 9.1–2 (2003), pp. 25–56.
4. José Esteban Muñoz, *Disidentifications: Queers of Color and the Performance of Politics* (Minneapolis: University of Minnesota Press, 1999), p. 1.

5. *Bent: A Journal of CripGay Voices* was in fact the title of a magazine for disabled gay men that ran for most of the first decade of the twenty-first century.
6. "Heteronormativity" is now in wide circulation as a term to describe the ways in which the institutions of contemporary culture both position heterosexual identities and desires as more desirable and subsequently enforce that prioritization of heterosexual normativity (through, for example, stigmatization and policing of nonheterosexual modes of being).
7. Sandahl, "Queering the Crip or Cripping the Queer?," p. 25.
8. Ibid., p. 37.
9. Ibid., p. 39.
10. Ibid., p. 41.
11. Lorenzo Wilson Milam, *The Cripple Liberation Front Marching Band Blues* (San Diego, CA: MHO & MHO Works, 1984); Connie Panzarino, *The Me in the Mirror* (Seattle, WA: Seal Press, 1984).
12. Lorenzo Wilson Milam, *CripZen: A Manual for Survival* (San Diego, CA: MHO & MHO Works, 1993).
13. For a discussion of these varied meanings of "coming out," see Robert McRuer, *The Queer Renaissance: Contemporary American Literature and the Reinvention of Lesbian and Gay Identities* (New York: New York University Press, 1997), pp. 32–68, and Sandahl, pp. 40–44.
14. See also G. Thomas Couser's essay in this volume.
15. On the term "supercrip," see Sami Schalk, "Reevaluating the Supercrip," *Journal of Literary and Cultural Disability Studies*, 10.1 (2016), pp. 71–86.
16. Terry Galloway, *Mean Little deaf Queer: A Memoir* (Boston: Beacon Press, 2009). Deaf with a capital D is widely used to indicate membership in a linguistic group that communicates in American Sign Language (ASL) or another signed language.
17. Merri Lisa Johnson, *Girl in Need of a Tourniquet: Memoir of a Borderline Personality* (Seattle: Seal Press, 2010).
18. Merri Lisa Johnson and Robert McRuer, "Cripistemologies: An Introduction," *Journal of Literary and Cultural Disability Studies*, 8.2 (2014), pp. 127–47 (p. 130).
19. For a discussion of varied modes for viewing disability that often reduce disabled subjects to flattened dimensions, see Rosemarie Garland-Thomson, "Seeing the Disabled: Visual Rhetorics of Disability in Popular Photography," in *The New Disability History: American Perspectives*, ed. by Paul K. Longmore and Lauri Umansky (New York: New York University Press, 2001), pp. 335–74.
20. Sharon L. Snyder and David T. Mitchell, *Vital Signs: Crip Culture Talks Back* (Marquette, MI: Brace Yourself Productions, 1997).
21. For more extended considerations of *Vital Signs*, see Mitchell and Snyder, "Talking about Talking Back: Afterthoughts on the Making of the Disability Documentary *Vital Signs: Crip Culture Talks Back*," *Michigan Quarterly Review*, 36.2 (1998), pp. 316–36; and Robert McRuer, *Crip Theory: Cultural Signs of Queerness and Disability* (New York: New York University Press, 2006), pp. 48–53.
22. For a discussion of the history of "normal" that explicitly traces the ways in which that history similarly targeted populations with non-normative desires/

sexualities or non-normative embodiments, see Robert McRuer, "Normal," in *Keywords for American Cultural Studies*, 2nd edn., ed. by Bruce Burgett and Glenn Hendler (New York: New York University Press, 2014), pp. 184–87.

23. Simi Linton, *My Body Politic: A Memoir* (Ann Arbor: University of Michigan Press, 2006). See Sami Schalk's chapter in this volume for further discussion of *My Body Politic*.
24. Loree Erickson, "Loree Erickson ... Porn Star Academic," http://www.femmegimp.org, accessed March 19, 2015.
25. Loree Erickson, *Want* (Toronto: Femmegimp Productions, 2008).
26. Antonio Centeno and Raúl de la Morena, *Yes, we fuck!* (Barcelona: Barcelona Independent Living, 2015).
27. Melisa Brittain and Lucas Crawford, *Elephant in the Room* (Edmonton: KingCrip Productions, 2012).
28. "Slender trouble" is an ironic allusion to philosopher Judith Butler's notion of "gender trouble," which suggests that gender is not natural, but rather constituted through repeated performances that are always destined to generate incoherence and contradiction. See Butler, *Gender Trouble: Feminism and the Subversion of Identity* (New York: Routledge, 1990).
29. Danielle Peers, *G.I.M.P Boot Camp* (Edmonton: KingCrip Productions, 2008). Like "crip," "gimp" is a derogatory word that has been reclaimed by the people it was meant to offend.
30. Sharon L. Snyder and David T. Mitchell, *Self-Preservation: The Art of Riva Lehrer* (Chicago: Brace Yourself Productions, 2005).
31. Riva Lehrer, "Golem Girl Gets Lucky," in *Sex and Disability*, ed. by Robert McRuer and Anna Mollow (Durham, NC: Duke University Press, 2012), pp. 231–55.
32. Elsa S. Henry, "Criplesque," in *Criptiques*, ed. by Caitlin Wood (Lexington, KY: May Day Publishing, 2014), pp. 5–10.
33. Riva Lehrer, "Beauty in Exile," in *Criptiques*, pp. 155–56.
34. Patty Berne and Sins Invalid, *Sins Invalid: An Unashamed Claim to Beauty* (San Francisco, CA: New Day Films, 2014).
35. The material in the first three paragraphs of this section is adapted from Robert McRuer, *Crip Times: Disability, Globalization, and Resistance* (New York: NYU Press, 2018).
36. Caitlin Wood, "Tales from the Crip: This Is What Disability Looks Like," *Bitch Media*, http://bitchmagazine.org/post/tales-from-the-crip-this-is-what-disability-looks-like-feminist-magazine-facebook-disabilities-visibility, accessed March 31, 2015.
37. Quoted in Wood, "Tales from the Crip."
38. Michael Hardt and Antonio Negri, *Multitude: War and Democracy in the Age of Empire* (New York: Penguin Books, 2005), p. 92.

11

MICHELLE JARMAN

Race and Disability in US Literature

In "Introducing White Disability Studies: A Modest Proposal" (2006), Chris Bell challenged the field to recognize its pervasive whiteness, in large measure by addressing its dearth of engagement with concerns of disabled people of color, and by critically integrating and participating in race and ethnic scholarship more broadly.[1] Over the past decade since this critique, a good deal of work has been done in this area. Bell's 2011 edited book, *Blackness and Disability*,[2] was an early contribution, and many scholars such as Jennifer James, Sami Schalk, Anna Mollow, Therí Pickens, Cindy Wu, and Ellen Samuels, to name a few, have made substantive contributions to literary analyses of disability and race. Nirmala Erevelles, working in education, has been a driving force in disability studies to push for greater attention to the intersecting material effects of race, ethnicity, class, and disability in national and global contexts.[3] In a recent meditation upon the growth of the field, rather than hoping for something more abstract or edgy, Erevelles dreams of a "future that is simply more accountable" to the complex material intersections of disability and race.[4] In this spirit of accountability, and in an effort to return to Bell's critique, I ground my approach to disability studies in critical race, especially black feminist, theories. Disability studies owes a great debt to civil rights activism and critical race theories, and while this debt is largely acknowledged, it is often more gestural than substantive. Also, although disability studies scholars have rightly called attention to ableism embedded at times in racial justice activism and theory, we need to extend these critiques toward relational, not oppositional, approaches to disability and race, approaches that highlight new knowledge but also engage with pain, suffering, and the violent production of disability.

Because the fault line of racial tension falls so explicitly along a black/white divide in the United States, this essay focuses heavily on blackness and disability, and draws largely from African American literature. The urgency of material accountability is also shaped by contemporary racial injustice. In light of intensifying protests against police violence since the 2014 deaths of Eric Garner in Staten Island and Michael Brown in Ferguson, Missouri (to list only a few), and over the senseless deaths in 2015 of Freddie Gray and Sandra Bland while in police custody, I ask how disability studies in general, and our engagement with literature more specifically, can be more accountable to such material realities of race? How do we attend to the danger people of color experience on the street, especially knowing disabled people of all races and ethnicities are also at risk, vulnerable to being (mis)read as threatening and targeted as a result? Indeed, in some of these cases, disability has been used to diffuse charges of racism: Eric Garner's asthma, obesity, and cardiovascular condition were cited as contributing factors in his death; Sandra Bland's suicide was attributed by some to depression and epilepsy rather than to police harassment. Such troubling intertwinings of disability and race have a long history in the United States, and this chapter reads those material realities within literary analysis.

Mapping a chronology of sorts, I turn first to slave narratives as a framework for disability and blackness, one insistent upon reckoning with disablement in a context of captivity and loss. In the early to mid-twentieth century, with the rise of eugenics, race and disability become interconnected through diagnostic systems and rhetorical overlays. Through these periods, and into contemporary texts, I focus upon the unique vulnerability and exploitation of female bodies, the cultural power and endurance of the figure of the "demonic" black male, while also tracing an epistemology of healing forged through relational disabled subjectivity.

Slave Narratives and Economies of the Flesh

As Clare Barker and Stuart Murray point out in their work on postcolonialism and disability, because the various global histories of colonialism are constituted by "mass disablement" and "wider patterns of dispossession," there is "a pressing need . . . to resist the too-easy censure of narratives that construct disability as loss."[5] In slave narratives, loss in relation to disability is interconnected with larger forces of oppression. Instead of pushing against loss, we might ask how disability shapes or transforms loss? Or, how are pain and loss mediated through disability? In an effort to contribute to a "more robust and inclusive theorization" of loss,[6] I focus on three themes: first, drawing from Hortense Spillers, I suggest reading the violent production of disability within the context of an economy of the flesh; second, within this context, I suggest a more nuanced engagement between disability and healing; and third, acknowledging the impossible ruptures in kinship and care, I also consider how relations, within and beyond family, become sites of resistance.

Slave narratives were intended, in many ways, to detail the horrors of captivity. Living conditions, lack of food, overwork, and the brutal violence of many slaveholders, all contributed to corporeal and psychic suffering. *Narrative of Sojourner Truth* (1850), for example, recounts the "dismal chamber," built beneath the white family's home, where all the slaves were forced to dwell.[7] Truth and fellow captives slept upon loose boards, spread over an uneven dirt floor, where they endured cold, splashing mud, and "noxious vapors" (6). She details these conditions as disabling: "she wonders not at the rheumatisms, and fever-sores, and palsies, that distorted the limbs and racked the bodies of those fellow slaves" (6). Indeed, illness and disability among captives, often produced by slavery, were also treated with brutality or cruel neglect. In *Narrative of the Life of Frederick Douglass* (1845), the author describes an incident working in the field, when, nauseous from heat stroke, he fell to the ground. Douglass was living at this time with the notorious Mr. Covey, a man with a reputation for "breaking" slaves, whose response was to beat Douglass horribly with a "hickory slat," ultimately inflicting a "heavy blow upon the head."[8] Risking permanent *damage* to *property*, white slaveholders attempted to balance the violence they deemed necessary for control with the economic imperative of maintaining able-bodied laborers.

We might better understand the relationship between disability, loss, and blackness by contextualizing slavery within economies of the flesh. In her seminal essay, "Mama's Baby, Papa's Maybe" (1987), Hortense Spillers distinguishes between the "body" and "flesh," arguing, in fact, that this distinction should be marked as "the central one between captive and liberated subject-positions."[9] Captives, caught up in the Middle Passage and for generations after, were severed from individualized domains of gender, maternity, paternity, kinship, language, or community; they were bodies made "flesh." In this rubric, Spillers figures "the 'flesh' as a primary narrative" of blackness (206). Further, the dehumanizing alchemy of transforming bodies to flesh deeply intertwines race to disability. In contemplating the corporeal violence prevalent in descriptions of plantation life, Spillers provides more texture to her theory of the flesh:

> The anatomical specifications of rupture, of altered human tissue, take on the objective description of laboratory prose – eyes beaten out, arms, backs, skulls branded, a left jaw, a right ankle, punctured; teeth missing ... These undecipherable markings on the captive body render a kind of hieroglyphics of the flesh whose severe disjunctures come to be hidden to the cultural seeing by skin color. We might well ask if this phenomenon of marking and branding actually "transfers" from one generation to another, finding its various *symbolic substitutions* in an efficacy of meanings that repeat the initiating moments?
>
> (207; emphasis in original)

The scarring, destruction, and branding of the flesh marked captives as nonsubjects, and provided visual support to position black flesh as always subjugated to white bodies. Further, the presence of disability buttressed racial hierarchies; corporeal and psychic markings were absorbed into the overarching "cultural seeing by skin color."

Addressing Spillers' "disjunctures of the flesh," Toni Morrison's *Beloved* (1987) provides a template for imagining how captives engaged in a process of transforming objectified flesh into subjective bodies. Baby Suggs, who acts as spiritual healer in her community, sees loving the flesh as a process of reclamation and resistance: "Here," she preaches, "in this here place, we flesh; flesh that weeps, laughs; flesh that dances on bare feet in grass. Love it. Love it hard. Yonder they do not love your flesh. They despise it ... *You* got to love it, *you*!"[10] Baby Suggs names body part after body part, all wounded or stolen by the violence and hatred of "whitefolks" (89). This process of loving one's flesh, of piecing back together bodies and minds, attempts to address and soothe the trauma of bondage. Dancing "with her twisted hip" (89), she demonstrates the most powerful resistance comes in reclaiming – in loving anguish – every scar, pain, and sorrow.

Such contradictory forces surrounding bodies, flesh, captivity, and resistance are prevalent in literature about slavery. Disability, in and of itself, is rarely the central focus; instead, it figures into captivity and the ultimate promise of emancipation. For example, in *Incidents in the Life of a Slave Girl* (1861), Harriet Jacobs (as Linda Brent), conceals herself in a tiny garret for seven years, where she willingly endures life-threatening illness and disability to avoid recapture. She and friends "feared I should become a cripple for life."[11] This fear was not simply ableism, but reflected the material danger disability would likely cause: discovery, capture, and horrible punishment for herself and family members. Katherine McKittrick, working at the intersections of human geography and black feminism, suggests reading the garret as a "usable and paradoxical space" where Jacobs/Brent is able to provide insight into a unique black geography of resistance. McKittrick calls attention to the "disabling confines" of the garret, to the fact that the site of struggle for Jacobs/Brent is deeply inscribed by bodily pain and permanent impairment.[12]

Building upon McKittrick's conceptualization of the garret, I wonder how our analysis might change if we position Jacobs'/Brent's garret as a resistant space of race and disability, as a disabled, black geography? One of the key impulses for Jacobs/Brent in accepting the confines of the garret is maintaining her relationship with family. From her hiding place, she negotiates with the father of her children, strategizes with family members, and keeps careful watch over her children and pursuer, Dr. Flint. In this space, disability becomes integral to transforming object to subject; being disabled and free is in every way preferable to being an able-bodied captive. Jacobs'/Brent's determination to remain garreted to sustain her kinship relations is a key act of resistance.

Refusing slavery's destruction of kinship bonds was not always possible, but desperate acts of defiance and resistance populate slave literature – especially those of women refusing to become sexual objects or surrender their children. As Anna Julia Cooper wrote, "there is hardly a daughter of a slave mother who has not heard of the ... heroic soul of some maternal ancestor that went home to God ... rather than live a life of enforced infamy."[13] Thinking about the legacies of ruptured kinship returns us to Spillers' inquiry as to the generational impact of being marked as object/flesh. Using her framework, we might ask how "initiating moments" of violence and oppression still haunt contemporary theoretical and material relations between disability and race.

The Eugenic Turn: Overlapping Diagnostics of Disability and Race

In the early twentieth century, disability and race become increasingly interwoven within eugenic discourse. Focused on improving the quality of human heredity, and specifically interested in (white) racial progress, eugenicists applied biological solutions to increasingly complex social problems such as racial relations (miscegenation), poverty, immigration, non-normative sexuality, addiction, and criminal behavior. In *Cultural Locations of Disability* (2006), Sharon Snyder and David Mitchell situate the emergence of eugenics as a pivotal historical formation of modernism, organized around "diagnostic regimes," which were largely based upon cognitive disability.[14] Eugenicists used many terms to specify levels of impairment such as "idiocy," "low-" to "high-grade imbecility," and "moron," but "feeblemindedness" soon became a catch-all phrase for mental deficiency. Although targeting intellectual impairment specifically, eugenicists described its characteristics "on physiognomic grounds."[15] In this way, all manner of sensory, cognitive, physical, and psychological difference fell under this overarching term.

Part of the success of eugenic rhetoric was its adaptability: conservatives used eugenic arguments to support oppressive structures of white supremacy; progressive reformers used eugenic rationale to promote social progress. In either case, specific groups or behaviors were targeted as biologically inferior, and "progress" for one group often depended upon surveillance and control of another. As Snyder and Mitchell explain, eugenicists were mindful of social context, but their solutions slipped to the biological: "While nearly all eugenicists explicitly identified the social environment as the causal agent of displacement, eugenicist actions continually targeted individuals rather than environments as that which needed to be fixed."[16]

Mitchell and Snyder also pay critical attention to the deeply intertwined and imbricated rhetoric of race and disability in eugenic discourse. However, I worry that their positioning of disability as the "master trope" of human disqualification actually puts race and disability into unnecessary competition.[17] More accurately, this insight should be acknowledged as a necessary critical demand for cultural and race theorists to pay more attention to the specific oppression and violence enacted on disabled bodies; further, disability studies scholars could attend to coupling this critique with direct engagement with racialized locations of disability and the material complexities of disabled people of color.

Eugenic social controls impacted on people in widely diverse ways, depending upon class, race, gender, ethnicity, and geography. For example, although eugenic sterilization had been legalized in several states, the 1927 Supreme Court decision in *Buck* v. *Bell* authorized eugenic sterilization at the federal level, making the numerous inmates in state institutions newly vulnerable. By the 1920s, mental institutions housed nearly 275,000 inmates nationwide,[18] making people with disabilities particularly exposed to medical intervention. Early institutions largely targeted poor whites and disabled people from all classes, but racial precursors should be ever kept in mind. As legal and race scholar Dorothy Roberts argues, "Forced sterilizations, eugenicists' favorite remedy for social problems, were an extension of the brutality inflicted on black Americans. Slaveholders' total dominion over the bodies of enslaved Africans – including ownership of enslaved women's wombs, which they exploited for profit – provided an early model of reproductive control."[19] Earlier forms of racial domination cannot be separated from eugenic social programs.

Indeed, growing institutionalization and eugenic social influence took place alongside intensifying racial violence and entrenched segregation, violence that did not always depend upon disability rhetoric. Keeping in mind the enduring process of bodies made flesh, I turn to the racialized construct of the "menacing" black man. In their meticulously researched book, *Unspeakable: The Story of Junius Wilson* (2007), Susan Burch and Hannah Joyner piece together an important singular history of the intersecting materialities of blackness, disability, and masculinity. Junius Wilson was born in 1908 outside Wilmington, North Carolina. Deaf from childhood, he and his family struggled to communicate without any shared sign language. However, his state had one of the few deaf schools for African American children, which he attended from age eight to sixteen.[20] Here, Wilson gained community, language, and a small level of written literacy; however, instead of ASL, students were taught a form of "Black Signs," and the one he learned was specific to his school in Raleigh. As a result, although he could communicate with peers and teachers, his signs would have been indecipherable beyond the context of his school.[21]

In 1924, young Junius Wilson was forced to leave school. After being home for less than a year, Arthur Smith, a close family friend, had him arrested for a fabricated charge of rape – of an African American woman. Because no one established effective communication with officials, he was judged insane, committed to a state hospital, and castrated for his "crime." In this case, we witness the easy displacement of one disability (deafness) for another (insanity), both of which fell under the larger rubric of "feeble-minded." Wilson spent the next seventy-six years within the mental hospital system, until his death in 2000. Although the details leading up to his arrest remain unclear, Burch and Joyner suggest that Junius Wilson's tenuous place within the family was likely exacerbated by the cost of supporting him and the increasing racial hostility in the region.

Indeed, during this period, white racial violence, fueled in reaction to African American success, was erupting in the region; the open activities of the Ku Klux Klan and the threat of lynching were ever present. Philip Bruce, Harvard historian and son of a plantation owner, had originated the idea that black men found white women "strangely alluring and seductive," and had "a penchant for rape."[22] *Harper's Weekly* called this the "New Negro Crime" in the 1890s,[23] and the idea proliferated so regularly over the next decades that even progressives such as Frederick Douglass and Jane Addams accepted lasciviousness among many African American men as real. Within this milieu, the risks of being (fatally) misread as a disabled black man were profound. The injustices suffered by Junius Wilson are impossible to calculate, but, ironically, institutionalization may have saved his life.

I pivot from Junius Wilson's history across the Canadian border to an Ojibway reserve town of Cape Croker to shift from the black/white racial materiality to Basil Johnston's 1999 memoir, *Crazy Dave*, which traces a family history centered around his uncle, David McLeod, who was born with Down syndrome in 1920. Although McLeod lived in Canada, his narrative has roots in the indigenous territories of the Saugeen-Nawaush peoples, which extended from Minnesota to parts of Quebec. Johnston's memoir provides a rare glimpse into disability history from an indigenous perspective, and notably, the author critically connects the disability stigma experienced by his Uncle Dave with white people's disparaging perceptions about North American Indians more broadly. Misconceptions about the Ojibway were grounded in disability-inflected, paternalistic rhetoric: "they were wild"; "they belonged in an institution"; they "were as children," needing "guidance and protection."[24] White officials on the reserve applied this logic to David, putting pressure on Rosa Johnston, his mother, and tribal officials to institutionalize him. However, his mother resisted and kept him at home throughout his life. Ironically, Rosa Johnston was unable to stop the removal of her nondisabled sons, all of whom were taken to white-run Indian schools. The reserve community, while they saw David as different, also cared for and accepted him; they socialized with him, disciplined him at times (when he stole from his mother, for example), helped him find work, and protected him as needed.

Reading David McLeod's history with that of Junius Wilson, I highlight a singular event, the only time David encountered the world outside the reserve. Through an odd combination of events, near the end of World War II, David was driven off the reserve and left in a nearby town. He was dressed in a Canadian army uniform, given to him by his brother, but as he walked in town, speaking in utterances unrecognized by locals, he was misidentified as a "Jap soldier" (294–320), beaten severely by a civilian white man, and thrown in jail. News spread rapidly, and by chance, two Ojibway soldiers on furlough lined up to see the prisoner. These men immediately recognized David McLeod and demanded his release. The incident was an embarrassment to local officials, but also a harsh reminder to the soldiers that their military service did not make them part of the wider Canadian society – a sentiment echoed by African American and indigenous veterans in the United States.

Enduring Enfleshment and Mapping Healing

Toni Morrison's 2012 novel, *Home*, set in the 1950s, provides provocative thematic connections to enduring eugenic practices and racialized distortions of men of color. In the opening pages, readers meet Frank Money, an African American Korean War veteran, handcuffed to a bed in a Seattle mental hospital. Struggling with emotional trauma from the war, Frank tries to recall what he had done to end up in this situation: "peeing on the sidewalk," "hollering curses," "banging his head on a wall"?[25] More important, Frank concentrates on executing an escape to rescue his sister, Ycidra (Cee), from the surgical experimentation of a corrupt white doctor. Sarah, a servant in the doctor's home, had called Frank days before. "Come fast," she told him, "She'll be dead if you tarry" (13). Forced to escape the hospital without shoes, he knows this will be his most urgent problem, not because of the cold but because he risks arrest for being barefoot and black – for "vagrancy," a crime, he thinks, overly applied to people of color for "walking without clear purpose" (9). As a tall, young, black man, haunted by memories of war, and unable to fully manage his thoughts and behavior, Frank is uniquely marked for white surveillance. After his escape, however, he gains aid from the AME Zion church nearby, and journeys homeward. Morrison's characterization of Frank pushes readers to think through the material complications of intersectional embodiment. Disability is not prop or prosthetic to race, but interwoven into his seeing of the world.

Cee's situation centers on loss through the racialized production of disability. Cee is hired by the white supremacist, eugenic doctor, Beauregard Scott, "Dr. Beau," as an assistant; however, her real role soon becomes medical specimen. In his basement "laboratory," Dr. Beau performs life-threatening experiments on poor women and girls of color – to his mind expendable bodies in endless supply. Dr. Beau's daughters were born with cognitive impairments, then institutionalized, so his motivation to medical research is connected to disability. In this construct, Morrison exposes the ways preventing and treating illnesses and disabilities in white bodies have justified producing illness and disabilities in bodies of color. When Frank finally reaches Cee, she is near death. Dr. Beau has destroyed her uterus, performed untold surgeries, and left her to die quietly in her basement room.

Through Cee, Morrison captures the ways white structures of power, from slavery and eugenics to medical apartheid, have injured, disabled, and rendered disposable women of color. Disability studies must attend to the production of disability in multiply oppressed communities, and to the resistant insights forged in these spaces. Cee's healing, which comes under the attentive nursing of a powerful group of black women in Lotus, Georgia, is also collective resistance. As Miss Ethel and her friends attend to Cee, they also admonish her: "Who told you you was trash?" they ask; "You ain't a mule," "You have to stay awake" to guard against "misery" (121). When Cee recovers, she learns she can no longer have children, but the time with Miss Ethel and the other women has made her more fierce and resolute. This healing is not an erasure of disability or loss, but an integration. Sobbing, she tells Frank, "It's just as sad as it ought to be and I'm not going to hide from what's true just because it hurts" (131). As Anna Mollow has suggested, it is important to attend to the "suffering impairments can cause and the role of politics in producing them."[26] Cee's healing engenders resilience and strength through acknowledging loss – and demands that readers reckon with the racialized economy of flesh that produced her impairment.

The Asylum and the Street

Indeed, the need to address structural racism has been in graphic relief as activism against police violence has taken place across the United States.

The grand jury decision on November 24, 2014 not to indict officer Darren Wilson in Michael Brown's shooting spurred intense protests in Ferguson, Missouri. In that highly controversial case, Wilson's imagery describing Michael Brown in his grand jury testimony brashly evoked distorted racial and disability imagery. Wilson described Brown's large stature, like "Hulk Hogan," saying he felt the size of a child in comparison. His depiction of the final moments before shooting are especially telling: "The only way I can describe it, it looks like a demon, that's how angry he looked. He comes back towards me again with his hands up."[27] This is the moment other witnesses described as Brown putting his hands in the air in surrender, to show he was not armed; this moment provided the symbolic gesture and mantra, "Hands up, don't shoot" for protests against the shooting.

In evoking a large, menacing, angry, black youth, *a demon*, Wilson calls forth a long history of oppressive images. From slaveholders' attempts to diagnose escaped captives as mentally ill, from white supremacist production of black men as "rapists," from Junius Wilson and David McLeod, caught up in webs of misidentification, to black youth still overrepresented as threatening – emotionally disabled – these legacies haunt and animate current racial tensions. The presence of demons, historically, has been used to explain dangerous, violent, or even cruel behaviors. From a disability studies perspective, the demonic calls forth the figurative and material legacies of linking madness (defined broadly), cognitive disability, autism/neurodiversity, and myriad other types of disabilities to spiritual possession, to extra-human evil and violence, and in the modern era, to the diagnostic regimes of psychopathology. In many ways, the demonic, as a term, functions as a powerful negative nexus, an alchemical intertwining of disability and race.

Not only was Michael Brown imagined by his killer as demonic/mentally unstable, his death is also haunted by numerous deaths of disabled people, especially those with mental disability, at the hands of police. We might recall Kajieme Powell, a man with a mental illness diagnosis shot to death after stealing two cans of soda by St. Louis police, just days after Brown was killed. Indeed, prior to the Ferguson protests over Brown's death, activists in New Mexico were protesting police violence against citizens diagnosed with mental illnesses, citing numerous avoidable deaths, mostly of men of color, at the hands of police.

To expand upon these connections, rather than dismiss the term, I suggest a theoretical usefulness of the *demonic*. Sylvia Wynter, whose work in black diaspora studies is widely known, uses the term *demonic ground* as a productive space of theory and praxis; in her framing, demonic ground refers to knowledge and perspectives that emerge from the liminal spaces produced by dominant power configurations. By insisting on incorporating colonial, racialized histories into so-called master narratives, Wynter's work attempts to map more inclusive, radical, human geographies. Wynter does not exclude disability or use it as a borderline category of the human; however, disability is often mentioned then immediately displaced by seemingly more salient issues of race and class. Ultimately, Wynter's use of the demonic insists upon an engagement with disability studies, especially an analysis of how bodyminds are constructed as threatening and of the danger of using the term *demonic* as primarily metaphorical – standing in for race/ethnicity, gender, sexuality, class, nation – and blurring over phenomenological insights of disability.

A productive strategy along these lines would be interconnecting Wynter's "demonic ground" with Merri Lisa Johnson's and Robert McRuer's "cripistemology."[28] Johnson and McRuer see cripistemology as an umbrella term for crip ways of knowing and doing, intrinsically tied to crip ways of *unknowing* and *undoing*. Cripistemology recognizes the situated knowledge of disabled people and seeks to push the boundaries of the disabled/nondisabled binary to a wider sphere of people situated by social or bodily debility.[29] Mindful of identity-based theory and activism, cripistemology also challenges the limits of identity. The term offers a place where "varied, unstable crip positions" might push against each other to map new theoretical approaches, questions, and practices.[30]

In order to think about the relationship between these many themes – the demonic, racial violence on the street, and cripistemologies, I turn to Victor LaValle's 2012 novel, *The Devil in Silver*. An African American author from Queens, New York, LaValle has a personal connection to madness – with diagnoses of bipolar disorder and schizophrenia across both sides of his family. *The Devil in Silver* is a cross between *One Flew Over the Cuckoo's Nest* and *Dr Jekyll and Mr Hyde* – a twenty-first century horror story set in an underfunded state mental hospital (aptly called New Hyde) in Queens. I focus briefly on two key elements of the novel – the figuration of the "Devil" and the violent death of Kofi Acholi at the hands of the police – to bring together contemporary racialized crip geographies of the street and the asylum.

LaValle features a material/metaphorical "Devil" within the hospital, a patient who has been isolated for years within a repurposed stairwell, who occasionally escapes his chamber to violently attack other patients on the main ward. This figure, later identified as long-time patient Mr. Vesserplien, is cast as demon but also figured to expose myriad dehumanizing structural abuses within New Hyde. Readers first encounter Mr. Vesserplien through Pepper, a forty-two-year-old white man who has been put on a locked ward, not because of mental illness, but for expediency in processing. A few weeks in, Mr. Vesserplien enters Pepper's room from the ceiling, and physically assaults

Pepper, who is tethered to his bed. His description is overtly animalistic: feet like "horseshoes," a massive head, "covered in matted fur."[31] Frail looking, the man is shockingly strong; he rips the restraints, throws Pepper to the floor, and stomps on his chest. When staff members finally arrive, the Devil is still in the room. This makes it more terrifying – "No delusion. No dream. It was real" (108).

Mel Chen's rich concept of "animacy" explores how discursive gestures to animals have defined humanity – especially in terms of race, sexuality, and disability.[32] Physically buffalo-esque, the Devil/Mr. Vesserplien evokes a story recounted in the novel of US army troops driving massive herds of buffalo over cliffs to deprive indigenous people of livelihood. Against this backdrop, the Devil functions metaphorically and materially; however, rather than inhabiting the clichéd madness = demon = animal, like the buffalo, he is caught up in the destructive, violent powers of conquest. At the same time, Mr. Vesserplien *is*, in fact, torturing people on the ward. His materiality is crucial, because, within the hospital, patients' testimonies are always already silenced. Inhabiting a state hospital, a "mad place," causes one to be, in Margaret Price's words, "*obliterated* as a speaking subject."[33] The real, the delusional, the material, and the metaphorical are on slippery ground in the psych ward.

In order to avenge attacks of patients on the ward, Pepper and three other inmates – Loochie, a teenage African American girl, Kofi, a middle-aged Guinean immigrant, and Dorry, an older white, motherly woman – plot a mini-takeover to confront the Devil. They pull off a surprisingly effective revolt, where they lock the two staff in a conference room. After that, however, the plan falls apart in spectacular fashion. The nurse ultimately calls the police, who enter to a chaotic struggle. Loochie is fighting with Mr. Vesserplien. In the tumult, Kofi, with a handful of syringes, comes to her aid, but at the last moment, Dorry turns on Kofi to protect Vesserplien. This is the moment the police enter, guns drawn:

> An old white woman fighting off an armed black attacker? That's not a difficult equation to solve. You can do it at home, without a calculator ... One of the officers ran forward and tackled the old woman out of the way. The rest fired on the crazed man. Then the cops fired forty-one shots. The assailant was hit nineteen times. (210)

The specific details, forty-one shots, hit nineteen times, directly reference the infamous police shooting of Amadou Diallo, an unarmed West African man who was gunned down in the doorway of his Bronx apartment in 1999. The officers misidentified Mr. Diallo as a rape suspect, and when he reached for his ID, thinking he was reaching for a gun, they opened fire. Like the murder of Michael Brown, this case set off massive protests; the officers, while charged, were ultimately acquitted.

LaValle's reanimation of Diallo's shooting implies that the coercive, violent logics, so easily concealed in the confines of the locked ward, are mirrored and active on the street. Within the demonic ground of New Hyde, Pepper gains important, situated insight. When he sees Kofi's picture in the paper, and the media coverage of an "aggressive inmate" (210), Pepper realizes anyone in the asylum could be produced as *demonic*. This realization reorients him toward the other inmates, not through identification but crip affiliation. It is through Pepper's relationship with Loochie, especially, that LaValle develops a cripistemology of sorts, especially what Johnson and McRuer describe as "disability-in-relation."[34] Pepper comes to understand Loochie's volatility and self-destructive tendencies; however, as their relationship deepens, Pepper reorients to these characteristics as strengths – as her feisty resourcefulness, her instinctual rebelliousness – and ultimately helps her escape, confident she will be able to survive on the outside. Crucially, Pepper's transformation of consciousness, through friendships with Loochie, Kofi, and other inmates, represents an *unlearning* of white masculinity, of transforming self-oriented aggression through racial and disability insight, to relational resistance.

Conclusion

The interrelationship between race and disability in United States literature is complex, multiple, and borne out of distinct yet connected pasts. In tracing specific histories of slavery, eugenic practices, and contemporary injustice with related literary representations, this analysis attends to several dimensions of disability and race: material economies that produce disabilities; the representation and experience of disabled people of color; and the way discourses of race and disability buttress, overlap, or displace each other. In many contemporary works of fiction, authors are rendering more nuanced disabled subjectivities, and within this context, we can uncover insights shaped by racial geographies and cripistemological perspectives, including processes of "unlearning" and learning disability-in-relation. At the same time, we must attend to tensions between disability and race. For example, analyses should critically trace and dismantle both ableist and racist justifications of violence—such as deploying the term "demon"—*and* resist constructing false divisions or hierarchies between racial and disability justice. Finally, I suggest looking to multi-ethnic literature for more expansive, sociopolitical engagement with healing, not to reject or overcome impairment, but to work toward mapping more complex, relational approaches to disability.

NOTES

1. Chris Bell, "Introducing White Disability Studies: A Modest Proposal," in *The Disability Studies Reader*, 2nd edn., ed. by Lennard J. Davis (New York: Routledge, 2006), pp. 275–82 (p. 278).
2. Christopher M. Bell (ed.), *Blackness and Disability: Critical Examinations and Cultural Interventions* (Berlin: Lit Verlag, 2011).
3. For a discussion of disability and intersectionality, see Alison Kafer and Eunjung Kim's chapter in this volume.
4. Nirmala Erevelles, "Thinking with Disability Studies," *Disability Studies Quarterly*, 34. 2 (2014), n. pag., http://dsq-sds.org/article/view/4248/3587, accessed November 21, 2014.
5. Clare Barker and Stuart Murray, "Disabling Postcolonialism: Global Disability Cultures and Democratic Criticism," *Journal of Literary and Cultural Disability Studies*, 4.3 (2010), pp. 219–36 (p. 230).
6. Ibid., p. 231.
7. Olive Gilbert, *Narrative of Sojourner Truth* (Toronto: HarperTorch Classics, 2014), p. 6. Further page references to primary texts will be given parenthetically in the body of the chapter.
8. Frederick Douglass, "Narrative of the Life of Frederick Douglass," in *The Classic Slave Narratives*, ed. by Henry Louis Gates, Jr. (New York: Penguin, 1987), p. 289.
9. Hortense J. Spillers, "Mama's Baby, Papa's Maybe," in *Black, White, and in Color: Essays on American Literature and Culture* (Chicago: University of Chicago Press, 2003), pp. 203–29 (p. 206).
10. Toni Morrison, *Beloved* (New York: Penguin, 1988), p. 88 (emphasis in original).
11. Harriet A. Jacobs, *Incidents in the Life of a Slave Girl: Written by Herself* (Cambridge, MA: Harvard University Press, 2000), p. 127.
12. Katherine McKittrick, *Demonic Grounds: Black Women and the Cartographies of Struggle* (Minneapolis: University of Minnesota Press, 2006), e-book, loc. 262.
13. Quoted in Paula J. Giddings, *When and Where I Enter: The Impact of Black Women on Race and Sex in America* (New York: HarperCollins e-books, 1984), p. 87.
14. Sharon L. Snyder and David T. Mitchell, *Cultural Locations of Disability* (Chicago: University of Chicago Press, 2006), p. 82.
15. Ibid., p. 79.
16. Ibid., p. 85.
17. Ibid., p. 127. See Chapter 9 in this volume for a similar argument.
18. Susan Burch and Hannah Joyner, *Unspeakable: The Story of Junius Wilson* (Chapel Hill: University of North Carolina Press, 2007), p. 43.
19. Dorothy Roberts, *Fatal Invention: How Science, Politics, and Big Business Re-Create Race in the Twenty-First Century* (New York: New Press, 2011), p. 37.
20. Burch and Joyner, *Unspeakable*, p. 20.
21. Ibid., p. 23.
22. Quoted in Paula J. Giddings, *When and Where I Enter*, p. 27.
23. Ibid.

24. Basil Johnston, *Crazy Dave* (St. Paul: Minnesota Historical Society Press, 1999), p. 11.
25. Toni Morrison, *Home* (New York: Scribners, 2012), p. 13.
26. Anna Mollow, "'When *Black* Women Start Going on Prozac': Race, Gender, and Mental Illness in Meri Nana-Ama Danquah's *Willow Weep for Me*," *MELUS*, 31.3 (2006), pp. 67–99 (p. 68).
27. Damien Cave, "Office Darren Wilson's Grand Jury Testimony in Ferguson, Mo., Shooting," *New York Times*, November 25, 2014, www.nytimes.com/interactive/2014/11/25/us/darren-wilson-testimony-ferguson-shooting.html?_r=0, accessed October 13, 2016.
28. Merri Lisa Johnson and Robert McRuer, "Cripistemologies: Introduction," *Journal of Literary and Cultural Disability Studies*, 8.2 (2014), pp. 127–47 (p. 127).
29. In their discussion of "debility," Johnson and McRuer are drawing from Jasbir Puar's work specifically.
30. Ibid., p. 133.
31. Victor LaValle, *The Devil in Silver* (New York: Spiegel and Grau, 2012), p. 103.
32. Mel Y. Chen, *Animacies: Biopolitics, Racial Mattering, and Queer Affect* (Durham, NC: Duke University Press, 2012).
33. Margaret Price, *Mad at School: Rhetorics of Mental Disability and Academic Life* (Ann Arbor: University of Michigan Press, 2011), p. 27; emphasis in original.
34. Johnson and McRuer, "Cripistemologies: Introduction," p. 141.

12

SAMI SCHALK

Disability and Women's Writing

Disability studies has a long relationship with feminist theory and gender studies. Several texts in early disability studies, such as Michelle Fine and Adrienne Asch's *Women with Disabilities* (1988) and Susan Wendell's *The Rejected Body* (1996), emphasize the need to explore disability in women's lives as well as the intersection between feminist and disability politics.[1] As a result, feminist disability studies is a recognized and important area of study that can inform any reading of women's literature. In her foundational essay, "Integrating Disability, Transforming Feminist Theory," Rosemarie Garland-Thomson argues that disability studies and feminist theory can have a mutually beneficial relationship because both have something to learn from and contribute to the other. Garland-Thomson writes that integrating disability into feminist theory does not limit the focus to women with disabilities nor foreclose engagement with race, class, sexuality, or other vectors of power; rather, "[i]ntegrating disability clarifies how this aggregate of systems operates together, yet distinctly, to support an imaginary norm and structure the relations that grant power, privilege, and status to that norm."[2] Feminist disability theory, therefore, uses a universalizing, rather than minoritizing view of disability, understanding it as part of a broad system of privilege and oppression, based on notions of ability and disability, which interprets, defines, disciplines, and produces bodily and cognitive variation.

Feminist disability theory can also draw attention to ableism within women's literature and feminist scholarship. For example, Alison Kafer notes that Marge Piercy's feminist utopian novel *Woman on the Edge of Time* (1976) envisions a future in which disabled bodies do not exist. In fact, in order to imagine a world without oppression, Piercy does away with racial, class, sexuality, and ability differences altogether, suggesting an inability for society to contain difference without creating hierarchy and prejudice. Equality in the text is produced through sameness: similar light brown skin tones, no gendered labor, equal access to resources, and everyone is able-bodied. Kafer argues that the erasure of disability particularly is emblematic of a larger social bias. She writes, "In both the novel and the interpretation of the novel, it is assumed that disability has no place in feminist visions of the future, and that such an assumption is so natural, so given, that it does not merit public debate."[3] The common-sense nature of ableism in our culture, the belief that a disabled life is inherently a lesser life and that nondisabled people represent the ideal, often goes unnoticed and unquestioned. Feminist disability studies is, therefore, an essential counterpoint to the nondisabled privilege and ableism prevalent even in other social-justice-based fields like feminist and gender studies.

As a whole, feminist disability theory is an expansive critical lens for researching a variety of cultural domains, including literature. This approach not only helps us understand how ability/disability intersects and interacts with other social systems like gender, but also how such systems are mutually constitutive. Understanding the intersectional and mutually constitutive relationship between disability and gender is essential to reading representations of disability in women's writing. From Aristotle's assertion that females are merely mutilated males to Sigmund Freud's theory of penis envy, women have long been constructed in Western thought as deformed and inferior versions of men, both physically and cognitively. Women have been represented as bound and limited by their lesser bodies and minds, particularly in regard to menstruation and pregnancy. These rhetorics of gender difference as inferiority are simultaneously rhetorics of disability, as they rely on the notion that bodily and cognitive differences can and should be valued and ranked. Such theories have long shaped cultural perceptions and treatment of women and have thus been the object of protest and criticism in generations of women's writing. As a result, feminist disability theory provides a crucial lens for the interpretation of women's literature from different time periods, cultures, and genres.

Representations of the Madwoman

Prior to the development of feminist disability studies, disability was already a common aspect of women's writing. Often, disability appeared as a metaphor for other larger social issues and concerns, such as in Mary Shelley's *Frankenstein* (1818), in which Dr. Frankenstein's monster is often read as symbolizing the potential for failures in the human quest for scientific advancement, or in Emily Brontë's *Wuthering Heights* (1847), in which various chronic and mental illnesses represent the interiority and morality of different characters in the novel.[4] Within the first wave feminist movement, which sought to gain women the right to vote, and the second wave feminist movement, which sought broader cultural changes for gender equality such as equal pay for equal work, reference to disability was often a vexed undertaking. In some instances, feminists sought to distance themselves from rhetorics of disability which were used against women to justify their oppression. For example, people opposed to the feminist movement argued that women are inherently mentally and physically weak – in other words, disabled in comparison to men – and that the activities of public life typically reserved for men, such as working outside the home, advanced education, and voting, would further strain if not break women's delicate constitutions. Historian Douglas Baynton explains that early feminists' responses to such arguments included explicit distancing from disability in one of three ways. They argued, "one, women were not disabled and therefore deserved the vote; two, women were being erroneously and slanderously classed with disabled people, with those who were legitimately denied suffrage; and three, women were not naturally or inherently disabled but were *made* disabled by inequality – suffrage would ameliorate or cure these disabilities."[5] The last argument, that women were disabled by patriarchal oppression, became a regular and prominent theme in women's literary texts, especially in the late nineteenth and early twentieth centuries.

The representation in women's literature of women disabled by sexist inequality and oppression often manifests through the figure of the "madwoman." This figure appears in Virginia Woolf's *A Room of One's Own* (1929) through the imaginary tale of Shakespeare's equally talented sister, Judith, who is driven to suicide by the limits society places upon her genius as a woman, and in Charlotte Brontë's depiction of Bertha, the woman locked away in the attic by her husband, Rochester, in *Jane Eyre* (1847).[6] Late twentieth-century feminist literary criticism, such as Sandra M. Gilbert and Susan Gubar's *The Madwoman in the Attic* (1979), reclaimed representations of the madwoman as symbols of rebellion against patriarchal oppression rather than as victims disabled by it.[7] In an article on this figure, Elizabeth J. Donaldson traces how the interpretation of the madwoman as rebel has become a ubiquitous reading in feminist criticism, often in conjunction with research which reveals the history of the pathologization of women in psychiatry and theories which suggest that madness is the only reasonable response for women to the strictures of a patriarchal society. Donaldson argues that though turning the madwoman into a metaphor seems to combat some of the stigma associated with psychiatric disability, it actually "indirectly diminishes the lived experience of many people disabled by mental illness."[8] Other disability studies scholars have similarly critiqued the tendency, especially within feminist theory, queer theory, and critical race theory, to represent and interpret disability as a metaphor for gender, sexuality, and racial oppression, rather than investigating the material and discursive relationship of disability and other systems of oppression or identities.

One well-known example of the figure of the madwoman in women's literature is in Charlotte Perkins Gilman's "The Yellow Wall-Paper" (1892).[9] This highly anthologized short story, narrated by the "madwoman" herself through journal entries, depicts a woman's mental deterioration over the course of several months as she is essentially confined in a room in a summer house, under the supervision and direction of her physician husband, to recover from her nervous condition. The narrator obsesses over the ugly patterned yellow wallpaper in her room, which she begins to believe moves and changes. Later, she is convinced that the wallpaper contains bars confining a woman who creeps about the room trying to escape. By the end of the text, the narrator represents herself as the woman who escaped from within the wallpaper. Throughout these changes, the narrator's physician-husband patronizes her, treating her like a child and calling her "a blessed little goose" (32) and "little girl" (36). He remains convinced that she has a nervous ailment that will be cured with food, rest, fresh air, and little to no excitement or exertion. Scholars have interpreted this text as a feminist story that critiques various aspects of gender politics in the United States, including the confinement of women to the domestic sphere, the power of husbands over their wives, the pathologization of women's bodies and minds, and the infantilization of women, all while asserting the power – if not necessity – of women's creative expression.[10] The madwoman narrator, therefore, has been read in numerous ways as symbolic of the psychological impact of patriarchal oppression on women as well as women's resistance to patriarchal oppression. By bringing in disability studies, however, readers can ground these metaphoric interpretations in the lived experience of mental disability and in the historical and discursive relationship of womanhood and disability in the late nineteenth century.

Disability studies scholars David Mitchell and Sharon Snyder argue that "the storyteller's strategy upends the controlling medical model of femininity's excessive frailty and emotional instability" which was prevalent in the time Gilman was writing.[11] What Mitchell and Snyder's interpretation suggests is that the pathologization of femininity is part and parcel of the history of the medical model of disability, which defines bodily and cognitive differences as individual medical problems to be treated and cured by professionals and obscures the various ways that society influences how bodily and cognitive differences are interpreted, valued, and treated. This demonstrates how a disability studies perspective allows readers to interpret the story as not only a critique of sexism, but of ableism as well. The narrator's insistence on her worsening condition, despite her doctor-husband's assertions that she is getting well, encourages readers to question the narrator's treatment. For example, the husband states, "you really are better, dear, whether you can see it or not. I am a doctor, dear, and I know. You are gaining flesh and color, your appetite is better," but the narrator responds "I don't weigh a bit more ... nor as much; and my appetite may be better in the evening when you are here, but it is worse in the morning when you are away!" (36). This moment reveals how the dual role of physician and spouse gives the husband total control over his wife-patient. This control goes unquestioned by others, including, at least initially, the narrator herself, who early in the story states "If a physician of high standing, and one's own husband, assures friends and relatives that there is really nothing the matter with one but temporary nervous depression – a slight hysterical tendency – what is one to do?" (29). Here, it is further evident that the husband receives his authority and power over her not merely due to his gender and their marriage, but also due to his position as a respected doctor. Disability studies' challenge to the medical profession's control, expertise, and decision-making power over those deemed sick and disabled enhances a reading of the story's feminist critique of both husbands' control over wives and the influence of sexism on the medical and psychological treatment of women. Disability studies allows readers to go beyond a solely metaphoric interpretation of the text to also take into consideration the historical context and material elements of the story in regard to mental disability and women.

Empowered Disabled Women Characters

Thanks in part to the influence of the feminist and disability rights movements, contemporary women writers are creating more complex and empowered disabled women characters, characters who cannot as easily be interpreted as pure metaphors for oppression. In *Extraordinary Bodies: Figuring Physical Disability in American Culture and Literature* (1997), Rosemarie Garland-Thomson devotes the last chapter to representations of powerful disabled women in the work of Ann Petry, Audre Lorde, and Toni Morrison. Garland-Thomson writes that these authors "use the extraordinary body in the discourse of positive difference ... [as] a physical testimony to individual and collective experience."[12] Changes in society stemming from the disability rights movement mean that people with disabilities are increasingly being represented as complex, powerful characters rather than as simply villains or victims.

Octavia E. Butler, the first black woman science fiction writer, is another example of a woman writer who frequently represents empowered disabled women characters,[13] but whose work has only recently been interpreted in conjunction with disability studies theories. Butler's books engage explicitly with issues of disability, race, gender, and class. One of the most notable aspects of Butler's work is her representation of complex power dynamics which make right and wrong less easy to distinguish. Butler's ability to engage disability in this often unique and complicated fashion comes in part from her position in the nonrealist genres of science fiction and fantasy.[14]

While science fiction and fantasy literature is sometimes dismissed as juvenile or escapist, many texts in this genre have explicitly political content. In Butler's *Parable of the Sower* (1993) and *Parable of the Talents* (1998), the young black heroine, Lauren Olamina, lives with a nonrealist disability called hyperempathy. Hyperempathy causes Lauren to feel the pain and pleasure of people around her. Although, in the world of the novels, this disability has been deemed a psychological delusion, the bodily impact is nonetheless really felt by those born with the disease, colloquially referred to as "sharers." Lauren lives in a near-future California in which global warming, war, and economic depression have resulted in a dystopian setting where violence, poverty, and chaos have become the norm. In this particular time period, hyperempathy becomes a difficult and dangerous disability because of how often one witnesses pain. If Lauren was living in some utopian future where pain was rare and she could regularly share the pleasure of others, hyperempathy might be more manageable and desirable than it is in the texts. Instead, readers regularly encounter Lauren sharing the pain of others and attempting to survive when witnessing severe pain. When she sees a person being shot, for instance, it makes her pass out from shared pain, leaving her vulnerable to being robbed, raped, or kidnapped in this dystopian society. In many ways, hyperempathy in the *Parable* books is a useful example of the social construction of disability – how time, place, location, and culture collectively determine the meaning of bodily and cognitive differences as well as how those differences are experienced.

The *Parable* series also presents a strong, black, disabled woman protagonist who creates a new belief system called Earthseed. Lauren develops the tenets of Earthseed, writes its verses, and establishes its first community of believers through preaching and relationship building. It is possible to interpret Lauren's disability as influencing her development of Earthseed. In *Parable of the Sower*, reflecting on recent violent events, Lauren writes,

> If hyperempathy syndrome were a more common complaint, people couldn't do such things . . . if everyone else could feel everyone else's pain, who would torture? Who would cause anyone unnecessary pain? I've never thought of my

> problem as something that might do some good before, but the way things are, I think it would help. I wish I could give it to people. Failing that, I wish I could find other people who have it, and live among them. (115)

Lauren's desire to live among people with hyperempathy can be read as a yearning for a disability community or a community informed by politics and ethics arising from experiences of disability. We can then see how Lauren's disability and her desire for a disability community influences her development of Earthseed. One of the major emphases of Earthseed is change, as expressed in the first verse of Lauren's book *Earthseed: The Books of the Living*:

> All that you touch
> You Change.
>
> All that you Change
> Changes you.
>
> The only lasting truth
> Is Change.
>
> God
> Is Change. (3)

Embracing change is a primary aspect of the Earthseed communities that seek to create a new life for humanity in outer space. Earthseed also values adaptability, which is a central value of the contemporary disability rights community, as a component of embracing change. It is important to read Lauren's disability, as well as her gender, race, class, and education, as having an impact on this belief system and network of communities she helps build. In the end, Lauren is a complex heroine who makes hard decisions. She is not always likeable, but she is nonetheless humanized, powerful, and compelling – and her disability is a part of all this. In Butler's papers at the Huntington Library, early notes on Lauren's character reveal that one of her models was the Underground Railroad leader Harriet Tubman, whom Butler describes as a "black woman, illiterate, physically handicapped, who managed to do so incredibly much through her long life."[15] These notes reveal not only Butler's knowledge of Tubman's often forgotten disability – a traumatic brain injury resulting in symptoms similar to narcolepsy – but also Butler's awareness of how attention to disability alongside race and gender is critical to comprehending the entirety of a person's life.[16] Butler developed Lauren's character inspired by Tubman's legacy as a successful and empowered black disabled woman. Therí A. Pickens argues that "the stories [Butler] tells do not seek to neatly erase disability or difference writ large, but to live with it."[17] It is important, therefore, to read the multiple differences represented in Butler's work together and not ignore the role of disability as an identity or lived experience. As people with disabilities continue to fight for equality, representation, and power in contemporary society, as more disabled people take on visible roles in the public sphere, it is likely we will continue to see more empowered disabled women characters in contemporary women's writing. As this discussion of Octavia E. Butler's *Parable* books demonstrates, this kind of work requires readers to think about the intersection of disability, gender, race, class, sexuality and other social systems in our contemporary world.

Disabled Women Writers

Finally, any exploration of women writing disability would be incomplete without a discussion of how disabled women themselves have written about disability, not only as life experience and identity, but also in relation to culture and politics. One of the primary locations for disabled women's representations of disability culture and politics is in disability life writing.[18] Garland-Thomson argues that feminist standpoint theory is most effective when grounded in life writing; disabled women's life writing therefore provides another excellent location for bringing together feminist and disability studies literary criticism.[19] Disabled women have been writing autobiographies and memoirs since well before the advent of the disability rights movement in the late twentieth century. In addition to the well-known life writing of Helen Keller, including her 1903 text *Story of My Life* and *Midstream: My Later Life* (1929), other disabled women also published memoirs and autobiographies, including Katharine Butler Hathaway's *The Little Locksmith* (1943), an autobiographical tale of love, art, faith, and independence for a physically disabled woman; Louise Baker's *Out on a Limb* (1946), a lighthearted memoir of life as a female amputee; and Frances Warfield's *Cotton in My Ears* (1948), a memoir of deafness that confronts stereotypes about women with disabilities.[20] This history of disabled women's life writing demonstrates how disabled women writers have long crafted literary representations of their lives, many of which exhibit critical awareness of the intersection between disability and gender.

More recent disabled women's life writing, such as Nancy Mairs's *Waist High in the World* (1996) and Simi Linton's *My Body Politic* (2006),[21] have increasingly represented disability not merely as an individual experience, but as a community, culture, and political movement.

Linton, for example, spends a portion of her memoir discussing the atmosphere and community at the Society for Disability Studies annual conference, including the now infamous dance that concludes the conference each year. She writes,

> It is not only the local and immediate pleasure of these events that excited me, it is that on the dance floor at SDS something is happening that has never happened – at least publicly – before. Beyond being a significant social and political moment – a coming-out dance and celebration of our newfound liberties – it is also a cultural moment .... Our bodies in motion insist that the terms *dance* and *dancer* be redefined. Our bodies on stage challenge every assumption about the shame and displeasure that supposedly shadow disabled people's lives. (152–53; emphasis in original)

Linton's discussion of the SDS dance as a cultural moment that redefines our understanding of dance demonstrates how disability community and culture can create change beyond the confines of that community alone, but instead has significant meaning for society at large. This attention to the creation, role, and impact of disability community and culture is essential to disability studies and critical to any interpretation of contemporary writing by disabled women writers.

Nonfictional life writing is not, however, the totality of disabled women writers' work. There are many contemporary disabled women poets, playwrights, and fiction writers, such as Laura Hershey, Jillian Wiese, and Susan Nussbaum, whose work warrants engagement from a feminist disability studies perspective. One prominent disabled woman writer is Anne Finger, who has published both life writing and fictional texts. Finger's 2009 short story collection, *Call Me Ahab*, is an excellent example of how contemporary disabled women writers incorporate disability culture and politics into their work. *Call Me Ahab* reimagines the lives and experiences of various disabled people from history and literature, such as Captain Ahab of *Moby Dick*, Marxist philosopher Rosa Luxemburg, and Maria Barbola, the little person depicted in Diego Velázquez's painting *Las Meninas*. Finger takes several approaches to representing these figures, including imagining them in more contemporary time periods, placing figures who could have never met in conversation with one another, and allowing once-secondary literary characters to now narrate their own stories. Throughout the collection, Finger uses irony, juxtaposition, humor, and hyperbole to comment upon the role of ableism in the lives of disabled people, socially, interpersonally, and internally.

Call Me Ahab opens with the short story "Helen and Frida." In this story, a young girl narrator, sitting on the couch in front of the television with a leg cast on, imagines a Hollywood movie featuring Helen Keller and Frida Kahlo, two famous disabled women who occupy very different spaces in the public imagination. The narrator asserts early on that "[t]his isn't going to be one of those movies where they put their words into our mouths," citing older problematic films like *Johnny Belinda* (1948), *Magnificent Obsession* (1954), and *A Patch of Blue* (1965), but rather "in this movie the blind women have milky eyes that make the sighted uncomfortable. The deaf women drag metal against metal, oblivious to the jarring sound, make odd cries of delight at the sight of the ocean, squawk when we are angry."[22] Here the narrator uses the collective noun "we" to demonstrate her – and perhaps even the reader's – alliance with disabled people. Her insistence upon a narrative created by and focused on disabled women as they are – not as able-bodied people wished they would be – permeates the entire story. One of the most prominent themes is sexuality for disabled women. Finger uses explicitly sexual language throughout, for example, describing a wound on Frida's leg as "cunt-like" (5), but the intersection of disability and sexuality becomes most explicit when the narrator, describing Frida, insists "but she can't be Disabled, she's Sexual" (5). Here the girl narrator voices the social stereotype that disabled people are incapable of sexual interactions and this is particularly emphasized by the capitalization of "Disabled" and "Sexual," making them proper noun identities that are, for the young narrator, incongruent.

As the story continues on, Frida and Helen discuss their love lives – Frida's active and open with her husband Diego, Helen's chaste and constricted by her mother. Soon the sexual tension between them becomes apparent as Frida "strokes gently" (7) as she signs into Helen's hand "in its infinite, unpassive receptivity" (10). Again here, the language is sensual, building the sexual tension, eventually even drawing the reader into the mood through direct address. The narrator instructs readers to close their eyes and cover their ears to experience touch without distraction, as blind-deaf Helen Keller might have, stating that "you feel your body with the same distinctiveness as a lover's touch makes you feel yourself. You fold into yourself, you know the rhythm of your breathing, the beating of your heart ... Your cunt, in all its patient hunger" (12). Here the text interpolates the reader into its sensuality, specifically in respect to the female body, before culminating in a kiss between Helen and Frida. Though the text's word choices have suggested such an interaction was imminent, the narrator herself states that she is "not ready for the way that Helen's tongue probes into Frida's mouth, the tongue that seems to be not so much interested in giving pleasure as in finding an answer in the emptiness of her mouth" (12). The sexual nature of a probing tongue, combined with the desperation of trying to find an answer in an empty mouth, together prove too much for the young narrator's own imagination. She shouts "cut" to her imagined film, but the scene continues on until the narrator, in the penultimate paragraph of the story, "will[s] the screen to snow, the sound to static" (13).

Back on the couch with her cast, the narrator wonders if she is a lesbian, not just for imagining this scene, but because she is "not like the women on television" nor like the mothers she knows, asking "and what else can there be?" (13). Here, the story succinctly critiques the damaging and limiting nature of the social construction of femininity and "proper" womanhood for the young narrator by revealing how this normative notion of gender is intertwined with compulsory heterosexuality and compulsory able-bodiedness.[23] The story ends with a paragraph depicting how Helen and Frida's images begin to merge on the screen, describing them as "the one who will be disabled and nothing more, the other who will be everything but" (13), returning readers, in the end, to the limits of the social construction of a disability identity which forecloses the possibility of sexuality.

Feminist disability studies theory aids in tracing the relationships of multiple social systems of oppression within a text – even when those social systems seem to be operating in contradictory ways. In her discussion of the wheelchair-using Barbie doll, Share-a-Smile Becky, Rosemarie Garland-Thomson notes that disabled women have been generally excluded from the confines of normative womanhood and yet, "[b]anishment from femininity can be both a liability and a benefit."[24] Share-a-Smile Becky, Garland-Thomson argues, presents a feminist challenge to the strictures of femininity because she wears practical, comfortable shoes and clothing and is "one of the few [Barbie] dolls with flat feet and legs that bend at the knee" which "suggests that disabled girls might be liberated from those oppressive and debilitating scripts" of patriarchal society.[25] Feminist disability studies allows readers to trace the normative systems of femininity and able-bodiedness and thereby consider how exclusion from one might result in freedom from another. By exploring this issue in regard to literary characters, the reader can explore the costs and benefits of such exclusion and freedom to individuals. The contradictory nature of systems of oppression appears in "Helen and Frida" in regard to disability, feminine appearance, sexuality identity, and sexual expression, mirroring Garland-Thomson's observations about Share-a-Smile Becky.

This reading of Finger's short story underscores the dual nature of Garland-Thomson's previously discussed theorization of feminist disability studies: that integrating disability studies transforms feminist theory and including feminist theory improves disability studies. Regarding Finger's work especially, focusing on disability without gender or gender with disability would do great disservice to the creative and critical ways in which "Helen and Frida" explores the mutually constitutive and contradictory nature of disability, sexuality, and womanhood. While a feminist reading of the text would be attuned to the story's critique of heterosexuality and femininity, especially as these two are linked in popular representations such as films, without a disability studies analysis, such a reading would miss the story's engagement with the desexualization of disabled people and how it particularly impacts disabled women. The story's critique of gendered expectations of sexuality and femininity, therefore, is one grounded in both feminist and disability politics.

Conclusion

There are many ways in which disability studies theory can enhance and nuance analysis of women's writing. Discourses of disability have been and continue to be used against women as a form of patriarchal oppression. This is apparent in the diminishment and dismissal of women's emotions through accusations of mental disability – that is, being called "hysterical" – and in the pathologization, hiding, and shaming of bodily functions associated with women, such as breastfeeding and menstruation. Disability remains, therefore, an integral aspect of women's writing both historically and contemporarily. Disability appears in women's literature as a metaphor for oppression and rebellion, as an aspect of characters' lives and identities, and as a culture and political movement. As a result, disability studies provides a necessary added perspective to feminist literary analysis which allows readers to be more aware and critical of the various ways disability is represented in women's literature. By utilizing the combined approach of feminist disability studies theory, literary scholars can be attuned to the ways in which a text engages with and represents ableism, the intersectional experience of disabled women, and the mutually constitutive nature of disability and gender as larger social systems that impact us all. Baynton argues that "[d]isability is everywhere in history, once you begin looking for it" and a similar statement might be made about disability in women's literature.[26] Given the frequent engagement with issues of the body and oppression in women's writing, representations of disability – as metaphor, identity, experience, culture, and politics – are incredibly prevalent in this area of literature. One only needs to know how to look for them and how to analyze them. Disability studies provides the perspective and theories necessary to enhance feminist understandings of well-known and well-discussed women's literature and to expand the possibilities for interpreting newer and lesser-known texts as well.

NOTES

1. Michelle Fine and Adrienne Asch (eds.), *Women with Disabilities: Essays in Psychology, Culture, and Politics* (Philadelphia, PA: Temple University Press, 1988); and Susan Wendell, *The Rejected Body: Feminist Philosophical Reflections on Disability* (New York: Routledge, 1996). For more recent examples of feminist disability theory, see Bonnie G. Smith and Beth Hutchinson (eds.), *Gendering Disability* (New Brunswick, NJ: Rutgers University Press, 2004); and Kim Q. Hall (ed.), *Feminist Disability Studies* (Bloomington: Indiana University Press, 2011).
2. Rosemarie Garland-Thomson, "Integrating Disability, Transforming Feminist Theory," in *Feminisms Redux: An Anthology of Literary Theory and Criticism*, ed. by Robyn Warhol-Down and Diane Price Herndl (2002; New Brunswick, NJ: Rutgers University Press, 2009), pp. 487–513 (p. 489).
3. Alison Kafer, *Feminist, Queer, Crip* (Bloomington: Indiana University Press, 2013), p. 73.
4. Mary Wollstonecraft Shelley, *Frankenstein: The 1818 Text, Contexts, Criticism*, 2nd edn., ed. by J. Paul Hunter (New York: Norton, 2012); Emily Brontë, *Wuthering Heights: The 1847 Text, Backgrounds and Contexts, Criticism*, 4th edn., ed. by Richard J. Dunn (New York: Norton, 2003).
5. Douglas Baynton, "Disability and the Justification of Inequality in American History," in *The New Disability History: American Perspectives*, ed. by Paul Longmore and Lauri Umansky (New York: New York University Press, 2001), pp. 33–57 (p. 43; emphasis in original).
6. Virginia Woolf, *A Room of One's Own* (San Diego: Harcourt Brace Jovanovich, 1989); Charlotte Brontë, *Jane Eyre: An Authoritative Text*, ed. by Richard J. Dunn (New York: Norton, 2000).
7. Sandra M. Gilbert and Susan Gubar, *The Madwoman in the Attic: The Woman Writer and the Nineteenth-Century Literary Imagination* (New Haven: Yale University Press, 1979).
8. Elizabeth J. Donaldson, "The Corpus of the Madwoman: Toward a Feminist Disability Studies Theory of Embodiment and Mental Illness," *NWSA Journal*, 14.3 (2002), pp. 99–119 (p. 102).
9. Charlotte Perkins Gilman, *Charlotte Perkins Gilman's "The Yellow Wall-Paper" and the History of Its Publication and Reception*, ed. by Julie Bates Dock (University Park: The Pennsylvania State University Press, 1998). Further page references to primary texts will be given parenthetically in the body of the chapter. For more discussion of "The Yellow Wall-Paper" see Michael Davidson's chapter in this volume.
10. For examples of these types of interpretations, see Elaine R. Hedges, "Afterword," in Charlotte Perkins Gilman, *The Yellow Wallpaper* (New York: Feminist Press, 1973), pp. 37–67; Beth Brunk-Chavez, "If These Walls Could Talk: Female Agency and Structural Inhabitants in Charlotte Perkins Gilman's 'The Yellow Wallpaper' and the Paintings of Remedios Varo," *Popular Culture Association in the South*, 26.2 (2003), pp. 71–87; and María Teresa González Mínguez, "Charlotte Perkins Gilman's 'The Yellow Wallpaper': On How Female Creativity Combats Madness and Domestic Oppression," *Babel A.F.I.A.L.*, 23 (2014), pp. 51–59.

11. David T. Mitchell and Sharon L. Snyder, *Narrative Prosthesis: Disability and the Dependencies of Discourse* (Ann Arbor: University of Michigan Press, 2001), p. 27.
12. Rosemarie Garland-Thomson, *Extraordinary Bodies: Figuring Physical Disability in American Culture and Literature* (New York: Columbia University Press, 1997), p. 130.
13. In addition to the character Lauren in Octavia E. Butler, *Parable of the Talents* (New York: Warner Books, 2000) and *Parable of the Sower* (New York: Grand Central Publishing, 2007), see also Dana in *Kindred* (Boston, MA: Beacon Press, 2003), Shori in *Fledgling: A Novel* (New York: Seven Stories Press, 2005), and Lynn in "The Evening, the Morning, and the Night," in *Bloodchild and Other Stories*, 2nd edn. (New York: Seven Stories Press, 2003), pp. 33–71.
14. See Ria Cheyne's chapter in this volume for further discussion of disability in genre fiction.
15. Octavia E. Butler, "OEB 1702," Octavia E. Butler Papers, The Huntington Library, San Marino, California.
16. For more on Tubman's disability, see Jean McMahon Humez, *Harriet Tubman: The Life and the Life Stories* (Madison: University of Wisconsin Press, 2003), pp. 14–15, 175–78.
17. Therí A. Pickens, "Octavia Butler and the Aesthetics of the Novel," *Hypatia*, 30.1 (2015), pp. 167–80 (p. 175).
18. On disability life writing, see G. Thomas Couser's chapter in this volume.
19. Rosemarie Garland-Thomson, "Feminist Disability Studies," *Signs*, 30.2 (2005), pp. 1557–87 (p. 1569). Feminist standpoint theory pays attention to the experiences of women and girls, arguing that specific and important knowledge arises from such experiences. For more on how feminist standpoint theory has been developed and used in feminist studies, see Susan Hekman, "Truth and Method: Feminist Standpoint Theory Revisited," *Signs*, 22.2 (1997), pp. 341–65.
20. Helen Keller, John Albert Macy, and Annie Sullivan, *The Story of My Life* (New York: Doubleday, Page & Company, 1903); Helen Keller, *Midstream: My Later Life* (Garden City, NY: Doubleday, Doran & Company, 1929); Katharine Hathaway, *The Little Locksmith* (New York: Coward-McCann, 1943); Louise Baker, *Out on a Limb* (New York: Whittlesey House McGraw-Hill, 1946); and Frances Warfield, *Cotton in My Ears* (New York: Viking Press, 1948).
21. Nancy Mairs, *Waist-High in the World: A Life among the Nondisabled* (Boston, MA: Beacon Press, 1996); and Simi Linton, *My Body Politic: A Memoir* (Ann Arbor: University of Michigan Press, 2006).
22. Anne Finger, "Helen and Frida," in *Call Me Ahab: A Short Story Collection* (Lincoln: University of Nebraska Press, 2009), pp. 1–14 (pp. 4, 5).
23. Adrienne Rich defines compulsory heterosexuality as the unquestioned societal assumption that heterosexuality is the sexual preference of all or most women, which does not take into account the various ways in which heterosexuality is imposed upon women within patriarchal oppression so that no other options appear valid or possible. See Adrienne Cecile Rich, "Compulsory Heterosexuality and Lesbian Existence (1980)," *Journal of*

Women's History, 3 (2003), pp. 11–38. Inspired by this concept, Robert McRuer defines compulsory able-bodiedness as the societal assumption that "able-bodied identities, able-bodied perspectives are preferable and what we all, collectively, are aiming for" while once again obscuring the ways in which disciplines of normality provide the appearance of choice without actually allowing for multiplicity or preference at all. Robert McRuer, *Crip Theory: Cultural Signs of Queerness and Disability* (New York: New York University Press, 2006), p. 9.

24. Garland-Thomson, "Integrating Disability, Transforming Feminist Theory," p. 501.
25. Ibid., p. 502.
26. Baynton, "Disability and the Justification of Inequality in American History," p. 52.

13

RIA CHEYNE

Disability in Genre Fiction

> A visually impaired hero is unable to recognize the woman he meets as his lost love. Through her intervention, his sight is restored, and the couple live happily ever after.
>
> A young girl with autism is threatened by a supernatural monster, but is protected by a nondisabled boy.
>
> A man with a disfiguring genetic condition commits a series of murders, eventually attacking the detective working on the case.
>
> A disabled girl is transformed into a cyborg, and teaches those around her – and the reader – about what it means to be human.[1]

Genre fiction has always told stories about disability. Literary genres, like their counterparts in film, television, and other media, present and re-present characteristic disability tropes and narratives, such as the disabled horror monster, the romance hero who is cured by the love of a good woman, and the cognitively exceptional detective. These images reflect disability discourses and stereotypes circulating in wider culture, but they are also refracted by the demands of the genres in which they are located.[2] As Ato Quayson observes, "generic conventions serve to situate the disabled characters differently from genre to genre."[3] Genre affects how disabled people are depicted, and how those depictions are interpreted; it influences how frequently people with impairments are portrayed, which impairments those characters possess, and whether they appear in primary, secondary, or marginal character roles.

Despite the manifest importance of genre to disability representation, it is only very recently that cultural disability scholars have begun seriously to consider genre fiction, and genre scholars to embrace disability-informed perspectives.[4] Clare Barker notes the "limited literary range" of scholarly work on disability representation, and the ways in which such works have tended to overlook factors such as "genre, period and context of production, or political orientation," while Rebecca Mallett and Katherine Runswick-Cole write that there is still "much work to be done on the importance of impairment and disability to genres such as sci-fi, romance and crime fiction."[5] Scholars have examined disability in works of genre fiction, and their historical precursors, but such works have rarely been read *as* genre fictions, meaning that the interplay between disability and genre, and the way that it shifts over time, remains largely unexplored. For genre fiction, perhaps more than any other type of literature, the narratives of the past shape the narratives of the present: genre fiction is always meta-genre fiction, as genre fictions write back, either directly or indirectly, to previous works in that genre. Brooks Landon argues that "science fiction is perhaps the most recursive and most self-reflexive of all major literary movements," while John Scaggs observes that "individual works of crime fiction are built from the devices, codes and conventions established by previous works of crime fiction."[6] The same holds true for romance, horror, and fantasy fiction, the other genres dominant in the contemporary marketplace. The literary inheritance of today's genre fiction is a complex and shifting network of rules, conventions, tropes, and motifs – including those directly affecting the depiction of disability. Identifying and examining these conventions opens up new insights into the workings of genres, as well as into disability's literary history.

Examining disability thus enables a greater understanding of genre,[7] but genre fiction can also do productive cultural work in the ongoing struggle against the marginalization and oppression of disabled people. The intersection of disability and genre can encourage readers to think differently about disability, and to reflect upon their own assumptions and preconceptions. The conventions of individual genres enable particular types of disability narrative, and while some of these genre-shaped stories of disability shore up dominant discourses, others challenge them. By analyzing two exemplary texts – Abigail Padgett's crime novel *Strawgirl* (1994) and Fay Robinson's romance *A Man Like Mac* (2000) – this chapter demonstrates how genre frameworks can facilitate the creation of narratives of disability that trouble reductive beliefs about disabled people. These two novels offer particularly good examples of how texts can work with, and against, genre conventions to encourage readerly reflection upon disability, but the potential to do so is inherent in all genre fictions.

Crime, Stigma, and Deviance

Padgett's *Strawgirl* is part of a fictional tradition that can be traced through the history of crime, detective, and mystery fiction: the "disabled detective" story.[8] In particular, Padgett's novel, whose investigator protagonist has bipolar disorder, prefigures a boom in crime fictions with neurodiverse or cognitively exceptional investigators that began in the late 1990s and continues to the present day.[9] In such texts, disability is called into service partly as a shortcut to the creation of a memorable protagonist, as in the larger tradition of "disabled detective" fictions. However, the upsurge in neurodiverse detectives also arises from their status as a compelling variant upon a core crime convention: the detective protagonist with an unusual or exceptional mind. Though fictional detectives require a range of other qualities, it is conventional in the genre for the investigator protagonist to be possessed of an extraordinary mind – indeed, for the possession of such a mind to be necessary for the apparently insoluble case to be cracked. Whether the solution is found in a moment of epiphanic insight, or by a painstaking chain of logical deductions, uncovering whodunnit (or *why* or *how* it was done) requires a detective with an uncommon mind. Conditions of cognitive exceptionality, such as autism, depression, and bipolar disorder, provide a ready source of such unusually minded protagonists.

In *Strawgirl*, the second in a series of novels featuring San Diego Child Protective Services investigator Bo Bradley, Bo is assigned the case of the Franer family. Three-year-old Samantha Franer has been raped, and dies of her injuries; her mother's suicide follows soon after. Bo must work against the bureaucracy she represents to protect Samantha's emotionally fragile older sister, Hannah, which includes preventing Hannah's father-figure Paul Massieu from being wrongly convicted. Because of her bipolar disorder, Bo has an intense sensitivity to subtlety and detail; she "just sees deeper" and is highly attuned to "the little twitches that hide lies, mask deception."[10] She is therefore almost always able to tell when a person is lying. Having spoken with Paul, Bo is convinced of his innocence, and while the police focus on finding evidence that will convict him, Bo investigates other possibilities.

Bo, like the "neurotecs" discussed by Stuart Murray, is "a productive detective because of, not in spite of"[11] her "different" brain (51). The novel does not present a rose-tinted view of bipolar disorder, but Bo's condition is positioned not as a burden, obstacle, or impediment – as per dominant cultural discourses – but as something that enhances her investigatory skills. While the larger tradition of crime fictions with disabled protagonists is not unproblematic,[12] it is nonetheless significant, for a number of reasons. The genre's narrative pattern of crime, investigation, and resolution means that the reader both anticipates and encounters the detective's success. Disabled people are positioned by default as successful achievers, and as contributing to the social good. Such fictions also locate disabled people as active agents: genre convention requires that the fictional detective be a person with *agency*, acting to gather clues, analyze them, and solve the mystery. These works therefore directly contradict dominant perceptions of disabled people as passive and lacking in agency.

Bo's bipolar disorder makes her a better investigator, but the novel also highlights the stigma associated with the condition. Of Bo's coworkers, only her best friend Estrella knows about Bo's diagnosis, because Bo knows from experience that being open will negatively affect how others perceive her: "The minute anybody knows about the manic depression, they feel compelled to watch me like a mutating virus and provide unsolicited opinions about medication on the hour. No matter what I do, it's suspect" (140). When Bo disregards departmental procedure to help Hannah, Estrella, who knows that Bo is off her medication, questions her judgement, much to Bo's frustration: "The only way to protect this child is to break the rules. I'm sick of hearing how I should be on medication every time I exercise what amounts to simple common sense . . . it's not your job to measure every decision I make for symptoms of madness" (150).

Bo's reflections upon her experience of surveillance and suspicion are only one part of a broader exploration of the stigma attached to mental health conditions. Social worker Rombo Perry reflects that "To say that nobody cared about people with psychiatric problems . . . was to put it kindly. What people really wanted, he suspected, was for the neurobiologically ill simply to vanish" (104). In particular, *Strawgirl* emphasizes and problematizes a representational trope that appears in a range of cultural forms, but is frequently mobilized in crime fiction: the mentally ill criminal or perpetrator. Such depictions shore up perceived associations between mental illness and violence or criminality; the perpetrator of awful acts is positioned as a psychopath or "crazy" by default, or mental illness is viewed as in itself a sufficient explanation for criminal behavior. Investigating the daycare center Samantha attended, Bo meets Zolar, a young man with schizophrenia. Familiar with the symptoms from her own experience of the psychiatric system, which has also left her "comfortable chatting with madmen," Bo is able to connect with Zolar, who leads her to crucial evidence (199). Bo is painfully aware, though, that if she tells the police, Zolar will be scapegoated: "the young man who'd led Bo to the truth would be crucified. She could see the headlines – 'Canyon Crazy Arrested in Child Rape'" (206). Bo knows that the police will interpret Zolar's schizophrenia as sufficient evidence of wrongdoing, because "everybody would recall that mentally ill people are universally prone to unspeakable crimes, overlooking the fact that mentally ill people are almost invariably victims, not perpetrators" (206). Bo eventually does tell the police, and it is only the fact that a neighbor is able to provide an alibi that saves Zolar. Padgett highlights and calls into question the association of mental illness with criminal deviance, as well as the ways in which genre conventions might be culpable in reinforcing stigmatizing beliefs.[13] Bo herself is initially afraid of Zolar, wondering if he is "[t]he stock lunatic of countless horror stories, lurking in shadows like a half-remembered nightmare" (201). The "stock lunatic" is equally a convention of crime fiction, but one that the novel decisively rejects: Zolar is harmless, and the fact that he provides crucial information about the case aligns him with the investigators, not the perpetrators, of crime.

Strawgirl refutes the association between mental health conditions and criminal acts in both its vindication of Zolar and its positioning of Bo as investigator protagonist. Also relevant is the depiction of Paul Massieu. Paul is the prime suspect not only because he was Hannah's mother's boyfriend, but because he had what he believes to be an alien abduction experience. The same flawed inferential chain that interprets Zolar's schizophrenia as evidence of guilt also applies to Paul: Paul's beliefs are taken as de facto evidence that he is mentally ill – "wacko" (23) and "crazy" (86) – which is in turn understood as proof of wrongdoing. Despite the fact that Paul voluntarily sought psychiatric advice after his experience, and was found to have "no evidence whatever of thought or affective disorder" (59), his beliefs are nonetheless interpreted as indicating that he probably committed the crime. As Bo comments, Paul is not in jail because there is any real evidence that he raped Samantha, he is "in jail because he thinks he saw little men from outer space in upstate New York" (176).

Though the reader knows that Paul is innocent for most of the novel, he is publicly vindicated in the penultimate chapter, a chapter that highlights, in multiple ways, some of the problems with how disability is conventionally represented and interpreted – in the crime genre and beyond. Threatened with losing her job, Bo is forced to testify in court that her department believes Paul is a danger to children. Bo does so, but arranges with Paul's lawyer to reveal her psychiatric history on the stand, on the assumption that her testimony will be dismissed as unreliable. Ironically, the scheme fails because the judge, unlike many of the characters in the novel, does not stigmatize mental health conditions, and rules that her testimony should be accepted. Symbolically, it is not just Bo herself but all people with psychiatric disabilities who are on the stand, and the judge's verdict that Bo "appears perfectly competent" (297) is an implied vindication of all people with mental illness.

Paul's innocence is publicly established just a few pages later, due to new evidence that Bo played a crucial if indirect role in obtaining. Though the novel's primary focus is on challenging the stigma attached to minds perceived as abnormal, the manner in which Paul is cleared constitutes a broader challenge to how disabled bodies, as well as minds, are conventionally interpreted and represented. As Lennard J. Davis writes, in literature "more often than not villains tend to be physically abnormal: scarred, deformed, or mutilated."[14] Paul has a badly scarred hand and is missing a finger, something that gives him a "sinister quality that was misleading" (58). Padgett immediately challenges the equation of physical disability with villainy, a representative tradition common in narrative in general but which is mobilized particularly frequently in crime fiction; as Irving Kenneth Zola notes, "from the earliest crime-fiction writing as well as in illustrations and silent films," the villain is "often scarred or disfigured."[15] In the novel's final pages, Padgett inverts the genre convention under which "[d]eformity of body symbolizes deformity of soul," in the most public of settings.[16] New evidence in the form of a video of the attack on Samantha is shown in court, and though the perpetrator cannot be identified from it, his hands are clearly visible. As a video still of the perpetrator's (undamaged) hands is displayed in court, Paul holds up his hands so that everyone in the courtroom can "see the right one, scarred and bent. Missing its little finger" (300). Paul's disfigured hand might conventionally signify guilt, but in the court it is incontrovertible proof of his innocence.[17] His disabled body testifies that he is not guilty of the crime.

Strawgirl foregrounds and refutes conventional interpretations of disabled bodies and minds as suggesting villainy or criminality. External form does not signify inner character, and the association of mental illness with criminality is decisively rejected: Zolar is innocent, while the actual perpetrator is positioned as "quite sane," with "none of the major psychiatric disorders" (231). The novel is able to develop this exploration of the way in which disability is commonly misunderstood or misinterpreted precisely because of the genre's intense focus on the process of deduction and interpretation. As Gill Plain writes, "detection is about the reading of bodies."[18] Crime, more than any other type of literature, encourages the reader to interpret bodies and behaviors. Though contemporary crime fictions generally pay little heed to the rules of "fair play" codified in the early twentieth century (under which the author must make it possible for the alert reader to solve the mystery before the solution is revealed), crime fictions nonetheless always invite readers to join the protagonist in deducing and interpreting. In crime fiction, objects and appearances are always potential or actual signifiers of something other than themselves; clues that can be decoded to indicate guilt or innocence. The bodies and behaviors of the characters are just another potential clue or piece of evidence. The genre is thus ideally suited to problematizing how we read – and misread – disabled bodies and minds in the wider world.

Romance, Sexuality, and the Barrier

Plain suggests that "under the comfortable cover of genre, writers can display narratives that would not otherwise see the light of day."[19] The next genre

I examine takes readers *under* the covers: the popular romance novel. Though romance novels vary widely in their levels of sexual explicitness, a mutually satisfying sexual relationship is generally a key element of the requisite happily-ever-after ending, meaning that romance novels frequently entail either implicit or explicit exploration (and often celebration) of sexuality and sexual pleasure. Dominant discourses of disability and sexuality view the pairing of the terms sex and disability as "if not antithetical ... then certainly incongruous," with disabled people rarely "regarded as either desiring subjects or objects of desire."[20] In contrast, romance novels featuring disabled heroes or heroines allow a different kind of story to be told, one in which disabled people's sexual experiences are not absent or deviant, but expected and celebrated.

Fay Robinson's *A Man Like Mac* (2000) is in some ways an extremely conventional romance. Keely, the heroine, finds her happily ever after with Mac, her former athletics coach, and the novel ends not just with the couple united but with a "babylogue" indicating that they are expecting their first child. However, this conventional framework enables a story to be told that positions disabled people as both desiring and desirable, and the novel recognizes and values forms of sexual activity and sexual pleasure not conforming to the norm of penile-vaginal sex leading to orgasm.[21] Mac is depicted as sexually active and sexually desirable despite lower-body paralysis resulting from a spinal cord injury. Meeting Mac again after a gap of several years, Keely is unaware of the impairment he has acquired in the interim. Initially disturbed, she is quickly attracted to him, and is clear that her desire is not based on memories of the nondisabled Mac: "it wasn't that other Mac she wanted, the Mac from ten years ago who had ... been so physically perfect. It was *this* Mac. ... She wanted the Mac in the wheelchair."[22] Keely is not the only one to find "the Mac in the wheelchair" desirable. Early in the novel, Mac comes home to find messages on his answering machine from women he dates, wanting to know "why he hadn't called" (38) and he has acquired the nickname "the Mouth" (70) for his prowess at giving oral sex. Mac does not have any other sexual partners after Keely comes back into his life – in line with romance conventions under which the hero either does not have other sexual partners after meeting the heroine, or finds such encounters unsatisfying – but the novel makes it clear that his postimpairment sexual life is an active and pleasurable one.

The novel situates its central couple amongst a community of disabled people, many of whom are in sexual relationships. Vicki, the wife of Mac's friend Alan, who also has a spinal cord injury, is aware of the attraction between Keely and Mac before Keely admits it to herself. Vicki offers Keely a primer on sex with a man with a spinal cord injury: "Even though the traditional stuff is sometimes out of the question with a para or a quad, sex can be terrific as long as you understand what they can and can't do" (93). Vicki and Alan are depicted as having an active and satisfying sexual relationship. Rather than being victims of cultural stereotypes that would position them as nonsexual, the college wheelchair athletes Keely meets exploit their impairments to attract her touch, pretending that they need her to apply their sunscreen. The pleasure this produces is presented specifically as sexual pleasure, because of enhanced sensitivity on their upper bodies: "If she rubs him just right, she's liable to make that old dead pecker of his stand up and salute" (43). After enlightening Keely, Alan commiserates with her for being taken in but suggests it was inevitable: "the first things you learn in rehab are how to hit on women and how to get laid" (44). These young men are aware of the associations of impairment in the public imaginary, and actively exploit them to gain sexual pleasure. While not unproblematic in feminist terms, these actions position them as active agents, rather than as passive victims of negative stereotypes. The novel's default position is that its characters with spinal cord injuries are sexual beings, just as its nondisabled characters are. While they might access sexual pleasure in different ways, that pleasure is not positioned as inferior or lacking.

Because of his impairment, Mac is unable to maintain an erection, and cannot orgasm or ejaculate. That Mac and Keely develop a sexual relationship in which both find extreme pleasure is already a challenge to normative notions of sexual pleasure, but the novel goes further than this. After Mac and Keely first make love, Mac reflects: "He had been with a lot of women, before and after his injury, and enjoyed every experience, but none had given him as much pleasure as this woman had last night" (164). It is conventional in romance novels for the central couple to reach previously undreamed-of levels of pleasure in the sexual encounter with the right partner.[23] In *A Man Like Mac*, though, the use of this standard romance trope requires the reader to accept that Mac, as a paralyzed man who cannot maintain an erection or ejaculate, has found his sexual encounter with Keely not just pleasurable but *more* enjoyable than all his previous sexual experiences – including his experiences of "normal" intercourse. A type of sexual encounter that the nondisabled reader (at least) is likely to perceive as limited, restricted, and inferior is positioned as better than "unrestricted" sex.

A Man Like Mac, then, illustrates the potential of romance novels to offer counternarratives of disabled sexuality. The positioning of a disabled character within a standard set of conventions and tropes enables a story to be told that, while conforming to the expectations of the genre, is radical in its exploration and celebration of disabled sexuality. Because of the status of these works as part of a mass-market, popular genre, they can reach an audience that might be unwilling to engage with more overtly didactic works. Romance novels with disabled central characters can therefore challenge a range of negative preconceptions about disability and disabled people; they "require the reader to enter into an imaginative engagement with a world where disabled people love and are loved."[24] Thus both genre conventions and the popular audience for genre fiction create the potential for important cultural work in problematizing entrenched beliefs about disability.

Just as there are genre-specific conventions for disability representation in crime, such as the psychopathic perpetrator, the cognitively exceptional detective, or the disabled witness who possesses but cannot reveal key information, romance has its own set of disability-related tropes. Motifs such as the blow to the head which restores a visually impaired character's sight,[25] or the kissing of a scar to symbolize acceptance of the "imperfect" body,[26] have attained the status of naturalized conventions in the genre, familiar and anticipated. A recurring trope in romance novels featuring a disabled protagonist is a belief on the part of the disabled character that they are unworthy of their nondisabled partner's love – a trope that Robinson's novel reworks in productive ways.

Pamela Regis identifies the *barrier* as one of the eight essential narrative elements of a romance novel. The barrier prevents the union of the central couple, and it often leads directly to another of the essential elements, the "point of ritual death," at which the union of the lovers seems "completely impossible."[27] In romances with a disabled hero or heroine, the barrier and the point of ritual death are almost universally related to disability, though not necessarily in the manner that might be anticipated in an ableist culture. The impairment itself is generally not the issue; rather, because of internalized oppression,[28] the disabled person comes to perceive that s/he is unworthy of their nondisabled partner, and that s/he will become a burden upon them if the relationship continues. This realization is often triggered by the arrival on the scene of a nondisabled rival, and leads to the point of ritual death. In Tami Hoag's *Rumor Has It* (1989), for example, the mobility-impaired heroine decides to break up with the hero after watching him dance with another woman, saying "you deserve more than I can give you. You deserve someone who's strong and whole" (162). In an echo of romance urtext *Jane Eyre*, in which the disabled Rochester requires not one but four affirmative responses to his proposal before he believes Jane really wants to marry him,[29] disabled characters in contemporary romance novels believe that their impairment renders them unworthy of the loved one. They therefore renounce the nondisabled partner, ending the relationship. This plot element is almost universal in romance novels featuring disabled heroes or heroines. It generally occurs in the latter stages of the novel, after it has been firmly established in the reader's mind that the couple *should* be united, and functions to increase the dramatic tension by making the happy ending seem impossible. While this obstacle is always, ultimately, overcome, its consistent appearance as a plot device positions disability as a problem in need of a solution, and risks implying that disabled characters *should* feel unworthy of nondisabled partners.

A Man Like Mac reworks this trope to powerful effect. Mac initially resists his attraction to Keely because of internalized oppression, highlighting the ways in which his impairment makes him different from the ideal romantic partner – noting ironically: "I'm sure her idea of the perfect man is a paraplegic in a wheelchair. A guy who can't get it up and can't hold his bladder half the time" (54). As their relationship develops, Mac actively resists becoming closer to Keely (both emotionally and sexually) because of these beliefs. The night that they first make love, Mac falls asleep without remembering to catheterize, and wakes to find that he has wet the bed – and Keely. Despite having just realized that he is in love with her, Mac attempts to break up with her, stating "[y]ou deserve more out of a relationship than a paraplegic can give you" (165). At this point, however, the novel diverges from the conventional pattern, under which the nondisabled partner reluctantly accepts the disabled partner's dismissal, creating distance between them. Keely simply refuses to accept Mac's rejection of her; in fact, she refuses his repeated requests for her to leave his house, stating bluntly "You're not getting rid of me" (167). When, after several pages of dialogue, Mac refuses to accept that he is the man she wants, Keely acts decisively to settle the argument:

> "What if I was the one who'd wet on you? . . . Would you allow me to be so embarrassed that I ended our relationship?"
>
> "No, but that's not the situation here. And you didn't wet on me, so you have no way of knowing how I feel." [. . .]
>
> Before he could push her off his lap the crazy sweet wonderful woman wet on him. (167–68)

Mac is "shocked . . . into submission" (169), and the reader is likely to be too: urinating on your partner is definitely not within the realm of expected behaviors in a mainstream romance novel. Keely's act conclusively resolves the disagreement, but it is also a metafictional commentary on the conventions of romance novels with disabled protagonists. She literally pisses upon the idea that a disabled person should think that their impairment renders them unworthy of a nondisabled person's – or anyone's – love.

Conclusion

Both *A Man Like Mac* and *Strawgirl*, then, work with and against genre-specific disability tropes and narratives in ways that speak to wider prejudices and assumptions, encouraging the reader to reflect on disempowering representational habits. These works illustrate how popular genre texts can urge readers to consider their assumptions about disability. Eric S. Rabkin suggests that there are four distinct ways of constructing genre definitions: *characteristic* definitions "list the characteristics of the thing in question. Those that have the characteristics are in; those that don't are out"; *prototypical* definitions involve the evaluation of texts against a prototypical example of the genre; *operational* definitions identify "an operation the result of which is the thing defined"; while *social* definitions specify the role of that genre in society.[30] What these different ways of approaching genre share is that they are all normative, with the text judged against a "normal" list of features, social function, operative result, or prototypical example. As Heta Pyrhönen writes, "A genre functions as a norm or an expectation guiding writers in their work and readers in their encounter with texts."[31] In contrast to the school of thought that views the potential for subversion in genre texts as directly correlated to the extent to which they deviate from the norms of that genre, I suggest that genre norms are not inherently limiting or oppressive, and that authors can work with – as well as against – those norms to subvert dominant perceptions of disability. In *A Man Like Mac* Robinson works within romance conventions to tell a story of disability and sexuality that radically differs from conventional narratives in which "pleasurable *sexual* sensations are generally dissociated from disabled bodies and lives"[32] – one in which disabled people's sexual pleasures are depicted as not just equal but in fact potentially superior to the pleasures of nondisabled people.

Both Robinson and Padgett foreground established genre conventions for the depiction of disability, denaturalizing them. In doing so, they offer a metacritical commentary not just on genre norms but on the ways disability is represented and interpreted in wider culture. Robert Eaglestone observes that genre fiction is always limited fiction, "shaped by its own self-chosen restrictions."[33] These restrictions arise from the normative nature of genres. The paradox of genre fiction is that it is these very restrictions – the web of conventions and associations that adhere to particular genre traditions – that enable narratives not found elsewhere. The vindication of Paul Massieu and Zolar in *Strawgirl* is effective precisely because it occurs within the context of a genre where disability has conventionally suggested villainy. That convention is undoubtedly problematic, as is the tendency for disabled characters in romance to assume that they are unworthy of love. In *Strawgirl* and *A Man Like Mac*, though, it is the very existence of these problematic conventions and associations that opens up a space in which readers' expectations and beliefs can be challenged.

Like literary disability studies, genre fiction studies has had to fight for recognition from a literary-critical establishment that perceives its subject matter as marginal and niche. Though both fields are now flourishing, the textual bodies of genre fiction are still frequently devalued, with genre fiction positioned as fiction which is functionally impaired in comparison to (some construct of) literary or mainstream fiction. Insights from disability studies remind us, though, that notions of "normal" function are always constructed and contingent, and that what the wider world perceives as restricting or limiting can in fact be a source of new insights and potentials. Genre fiction can be conceptualized in the same way that Michael Davidson, in *Concerto for the Left Hand*, views the concertos composed by Ravel for one-handed pianist Wittgenstein. Davidson suggests that in composing for Wittgenstein, "Ravel disables Ravel, imposing formal demands on composition that he might not have imagined had he not had to think through limits imposed by writing for one hand."[34] Implicit in this statement is the idea of demands or restrictions as productive, and Davidson explores how "a consideration of works written for a one-armed pianist" might "resituate both music and disabled performer."[35] Simultaneously abnormal and normative, genre fiction allows for the re-situation of disability, even as a disability-informed approach opens up new ways of thinking about genre.

NOTES

1. While many texts can be found with similar tropes and narratives, these examples are from Victoria Gordon, *Blind Man's Buff* (Toronto: Harlequin, 1984); Dean Koontz, *77 Shadow Street* (London: HarperCollins, 2012); Patricia Cornwell, *Black Notice* (London: Little, Brown and Company, 1999); and Anne McCaffrey, *The Ship Who Sang* (London: Corgi, 1980).
2. In *Aesthetic Nervousness: Disability and the Crisis of Representation* (New York: Columbia University Press, 2007), p. 36, Ato Quayson argues that all literary representations of disability are "refractions," since "disability in the real world already incites interpretation." Here, I suggest that genre fiction involves a further level of refraction or transformation that has not generally been acknowledged.
3. Ibid., p. 35.
4. Genre fiction has been analyzed in a number of critical works on disability in literature, but genre context has rarely played a central role in that analysis. For discussions that foreground genre context see Kathryn Allan (ed.), *Disability in Science Fiction: Representations of Technology as Cure* (New York: Palgrave Macmillan, 2013); Ria Cheyne, "Disability Studies Reads the Romance," *Journal of Literary and Cultural Disability Studies*, 7.1 (2013), pp. 37–52; and Lucy Burke, "Genetics at the Scene of the Crime: DeCODING *Tainted Blood*," *Journal of Literary and Cultural Disability Studies*, 6.2 (2012), pp. 193–208.

5. Clare Barker, *Postcolonial Fiction and Disability: Exceptional Children, Metaphor, and Materiality* (Basingstoke: Palgrave Macmillan, 2011), pp. 22, 21; Rebecca Mallett and Katherine Runswick-Cole, *Approaching Disability: Critical Issues and Perspectives* (London: Routledge, 2014), p. 51.
6. Brooks Landon, *Science Fiction after 1900: From the Steam Man to the Stars* (New York: Routledge, 2002), p. xviii; John Scaggs, *Crime Fiction* (London: Routledge, 2005), p. 3.
7. For more on this argument see Ria Cheyne, "Freaks and Extraordinary Bodies: Disability as Generic Marker in John Varley's 'Tango Charlie and Foxtrot Romeo'," in Kathryn Allan (ed.), *Disability in Science Fiction*, pp. 35–46.
8. From this point on I use "crime fiction" as an umbrella term for crime, detective, and mystery fiction. On disabled detectives, see Gary Hoppenstand and Ray B. Browne, "'I'd Kiss You Sweetheart, But My Lips Are Missing': The Defective Detective in the Pulps," in *The Defective Detective in the Pulps*, ed. by Gary Hoppenstand and Ray B. Browne (Bowling Green: Bowling Green State University Popular Press, 1983), pp. 1–7; Irving Kenneth Zola, "'Any Distinguishing Features?' – The Portrayal of Disability in the Crime-Mystery Genre," *Policy Studies Journal*, 15.3 (1987), pp. 485–513; and Frederic W. Hafferty and Susan Foster, "Decontextualizing Disability in the Crime-Mystery Genre: The Case of the Invisible Handicap," *Disability and Society*, 9.2 (1994), pp. 185–206.
9. Literary examples include Jonathan Lethem's *Motherless Brooklyn* (London: Faber and Faber, 2000), Mark Haddon's *The Curious Incident of the Dog in the Night-Time* (London: Vintage, 2004), and Karin Slaughter's *Triptych* (London: Random House, 2006) and its sequels. See Stuart Murray, "Neurotecs: Detectives, Disability and Cognitive Exceptionality in Contemporary Fiction," in *Constructing Crime: Discourse and Cultural Representations of Crime and "Deviance,"* ed. by Christiana Gregoriou (Basingstoke: Palgrave Macmillan, 2012), pp. 177–89.
10. Abigail Padgett, *Strawgirl* (London: Headline, 1994), pp. 276, 118. Further page references to primary texts will be given parenthetically in the body of the chapter.
11. Murray, "Neurotecs," p. 186.
12. See Hafferty and Foster, "Decontextualizing Disability," and Murray, "Neurotecs."
13. For a similar framing of schizophrenia, see Colin Dexter, *The Silent World of Nicholas Quinn* (London: Pan, 1978). The central detective creates an elaborate theory in which a young man's schizophrenia is central, but his theory is proved to be entirely wrong.
14. Lennard J. Davis, *Enforcing Normalcy: Disability, Deafness, and the Body* (London: Verso, 1995), p. 41.
15. Zola, "Any Distinguishing Features?," p. 488.
16. Paul K. Longmore, "Screening Stereotypes: Images of Disabled People in Television and Motion Pictures," in *Why I Burned My Book: And Other Essays on Disability* (Philadelphia, PA: Temple University Press, 2003), pp. 131–46 (p. 133).
17. Examples of crime novels where disability functions as evidence of guilt include Patricia Cornwell, *Postmortem* (London: Warner, 1993) and P. D. James, *Death in Holy Orders* (London: Faber and Faber, 2014).

18. Gill Plain, *Twentieth-Century Crime Fiction: Gender, Sexuality and the Body* (Edinburgh: Edinburgh University Press, 2001), p. 96.
19. Ibid., p. 94.
20. Anna Mollow and Robert McRuer, "Introduction," in *Sex and Disability*, ed. by Robert McRuer and Anna Mollow (Durham, NC: Duke University Press, 2012), pp. 1–34 (p. 1).
21. In some ways the depiction of disabled sexuality in *A Man Like Mac* still falls within the boundaries of dominant conceptions of "normal" sexuality, in that it is heterosexual, happens within the context of a monogamous relationship, and is (as far as the reader can ascertain) vanilla. Though LGBTQ romance novels are increasingly popular with romance readers, the vast majority of mainstream popular romances focus on a heterosexual couple, and BDSM and other non-culturally sanctioned forms of sexual activity are generally the preserve of erotica rather than romance. However, given that disabled sexuality, where it is acknowledged, is often coded as freakish or excessive, this normative framework may itself perform an important function.
22. Fay Robinson, *A Man Like Mac* (Toronto: Harlequin, 2000), p. 119.
23. See Sarah Wendell and Candy Tan, *Beyond Heaving Bosoms: The Smart Bitches' Guide to Romance Novels* (New York: Fireside, 2009), pp. 37–38, 86.
24. Cheyne, "Disability Studies," p. 41.
25. See for example Gordon, *Blind Man's Buff*; Teresa Medeiros, *Yours Until Dawn* (New York: Avon, 2004); Christina Dodd, *Candle in the Window* (New York: HarperCollins, 2009); and (for incipient blindness) Pamela Britton, *The Wrangler* (Richmond: Harlequin, 2009).
26. See for example Tami Hoag, *Rumor Has It* (Toronto: Bantam, 1989), and Elle James, *Dakota Meltdown* (Richmond: Mills and Boon, 2007).
27. Pamela Regis, *A Natural History of the Romance Novel* (Philadelphia: University of Pennsylvania Press, 2003), p. 14.
28. Donna Reeve, "Negotiating Psycho-Emotional Dimensions of Disability and Their Influence on Identity Constructions," *Disability and Society*, 17.5 (2002), pp. 493–508.
29. Charlotte Brontë, *Jane Eyre* (London: Penguin, 1996), p. 494.
30. Eric S. Rabkin, "Defining Science Fiction," in *Reading Science Fiction*, ed. by James Gunn, Marleen S. Barr, and Matthew Candelaria (Basingstoke: Palgrave Macmillan, 2009), pp. 15–22 (pp. 16, 19).
31. Heta Pyrhönen, "Genre," in *The Cambridge Companion to Narrative*, ed. by David Herman (Cambridge: Cambridge University Press, 2007), pp. 109–24.
32. Mollow and McRuer, "Introduction," p. 1.
33. Robert Eaglestone, *Contemporary Fiction: A Very Short Introduction* (Oxford: Oxford University Press, 2013), Kindle edition.
34. Michael Davidson, *Concerto for the Left Hand: Disability and the Defamiliar Body* (Ann Arbor: University of Michigan Press, 2008), pp. 2–3.
35. Ibid., p. xvi.

14

G. THOMAS COUSER

Signifying Selves
Disability and Life Writing

As numerous scholars have pointed out – not least in this volume – disability has been a prominent topos in the Western literary tradition from antiquity to the present. Think of Oedipus, Richard III, and Ahab. Disability has figured prominently in popular culture as well, especially in the modern era. Some of the first motion pictures exploited physical anomaly for its value as spectacle in the new, inherently voyeuristic, visual medium. Indeed, one reason horror films so often feature visible disabilities, such as facial scars, amputated limbs, and limps, is that by their nature, visual media display disability in a way that writing cannot. As media have emerged and representation has evolved, Western culture has capitalized on disability, quite literally, for millennia.

But despite its pervasiveness, diachronically and synchronically, in the literary and popular culture of Western Europe, disability has not always been recognized as: a product of social and cultural arrangements; a basis for personal, communal, and political identity; and an existential condition. Rather, disability has usually functioned as a code according to which visible flaws body forth inner faults, allowing character to be read off the body. Functioning this way, disability has served Western culture profitably, but it has served those with disabilities ill – reducing them to a single dimension, denying their complexity, and eliding the contextual factors that oppress them. Disabled characters are usually viewed from outside; when they are not tragic, doomed, and stigmatized protagonists, they are often foils. Consider the juxtaposition in Herman Melville's *Moby-Dick* (1851) of a sympathetic, reflective Ishmael against an obsessive, self-destructive, and masochistic Ahab. Ishmael survives to tell his tale; Ahab is sent to a death he not only deserves but seems to desire. So while disability has been a persistent, even prominent, presence in Western culture, it has also, paradoxically, been a conspicuous *absence*. That is, its prominent *representation* has all too often amounted to *mis*representation.

Until quite recently, then, the subjectivity of disabled people has rarely been foregrounded, rarely understood in depth and in full context. But if we turn from "creative writing" – those genres presently regarded as literary (poetry, fiction, and drama) – to nonfiction, especially to life writing, we find a counterdiscursive movement over at least the last half-century, culminating in the current "memoir boom." Like other marginalized groups, disabled people have much to gain from taking the means of literary production into their own hands. But this is a fraught and precarious move. In everyday life, they are considered responsible for self-narration as examples of misfortune, often asked bluntly by complete strangers: "What happened to you?" To this question, the desired answer is one that offers a medical diagnosis or a story somehow reassuring to the inquisitor. Like other minorities historically represented largely by members of dominant groups, disabled people come to literary production from within the same culture that marginalizes them; they are vulnerable to infection with the very prejudices that oppress them. Thus, disabled people come to life writing from a position of preinscription: they are already "known" as defective, deficient, interpellated as fundamentally alien. In life writing, their charge is to undo, and/or overwrite, their prior representation: to offer compelling counterrepresentation. The challenge is to do this without deploying rhetorics already in circulation that simply reinforce stigma or condescension. Furthermore, as we shall see later, unlike other marginalized statuses, disability may interfere with, or even preclude, self-narration; for disabled people, self-representation may involve obstacles not faced by gender, racial, or ethnic minorities.

There is much work to be done to excavate and recuperate works that initiated the practice of counterdiscursive self-representation by disabled people. One milestone was the 1754 publication of "Deformity: An Essay" by British Member of Parliament William Hay, a hunchback disfigured by smallpox. Hay's title echoes that of Sir Francis Bacon's essay "Of Deformity," written nearly a century and a half earlier. Bacon seems to have had in mind his hunchbacked cousin, a successful courtier, and he theorized in an impersonal way about deformity (arguing that is it not a sign of divine disfavor but rather a physical trait that shapes character).[1] In contrast, Hay boldly and unapologetically wrote of his own deformity, affirming it as a source of positive identity even though it subjected him and people like him to public ridicule.[2] With the advantages of class and gender, Hay was able to challenge cultural preconceptions about deformity; indeed, his essay may constitute the first disability memoir in English.

Nineteenth-century precedents for contemporary counterdiscursive life writing may be found in narratives by survivors of institutionalization for mental illness: for example, Anna Agnew's *From under the Cloud; or,*

Personal Reminiscences of Insanity (1887), Hiram Chase's *Two Years and Four Months in a Lunatic Asylum* (1868), and Moses Swan's *Ten Years and Ten Months in Lunatic Asylums in Different States* (1874).[3] Their titles' specification of the duration of institutionalization likens it to other forms of involuntary confinement, incarceration, and slavery. Long obscure, these narratives have recently been examined by scholars including Mary Elene Wood and Sara Newman.[4] But there is a long hiatus between this flurry of late nineteenth-century testimony and contemporary narratives of mental illness, especially depression.

Another milestone in this tenuous tradition would be the writing of Helen Keller, especially her autobiography, *The Story of My Life* (1903).[5] Keller's writing is noteworthy as issuing from a woman with significant disabilities – blindness and deafness – that can compromise literacy and communication, as well as for reaching a very broad audience. One of the distinctive characteristics of some disability memoir is that it functions as "performative utterance," that is, a statement that does not merely describe a state of affairs but effects it (like a referee's call announcing a goal or penalty): its very production confirms its message that the subject/author is more capable than might be presumed. Its mere existence challenges stigma and stereotype. Thus, Keller's authorship demonstrated that blind people could read and deaf people could communicate at a high level of literacy. Perhaps as important, it advanced the fundamental work of modern disability life writing by exposing how much of Keller's disability was a function of obstacles in the environment, rather than in her significantly impaired body:

> It was necessary for me to write algebra and geometry in class and solve problems in physics, and this I could not do until we bought a braille writer, by means of which I could put down the steps and processes of my work. I could not follow with my eyes the geometrical figures drawn on the blackboard, and my only means of getting a clear idea of them was to make them on a cushion with straight and curved wires, which had bent and pointed ends.[6]

In Keller's work, we encounter a critique of a world designed, built, and maintained for the nondisabled. The fundamental distinction in critical disability studies between impairment, which is found in the body, and disability, which is located in the environment, has begun to be exposed in life writing.

Despite these notable precedents, disability life writing did not reach critical mass until the late twentieth century. In North America at least, successive rights movements – the civil rights movement, the women's liberation movement, the gay rights movement – were accompanied by discrete memoir booms. These memoir booms did not merely parallel the rights movements; they *advanced* them. There was a reciprocal relationship between the political and literary. As rights movements expanded the audience for minority memoirs, counterdiscursive life writing reinforced the political critiques being made by rights advocates. In the 1990s, there was an upsurge in narratives of HIV/AIDS and of breast cancer – each niche genre being linked to a respective rights movement. Similarly, a spike in the number of disability memoirs accompanied the disability rights movement, whose major achievement was the passage of the Americans with Disabilities Act in 1990.

Lorraine Adams has made a fundamental distinction between "somebody memoirs" (written by celebrities) and "nobody memoirs" (written by individuals who were not public figures before publishing their memoirs).[7] Somebody memoirs have the advantage of a preexisting audience: the narrative is a consequence of and a capitalization on their fame. In contrast, nobody memoirs have to earn their audiences on their own merits: if their hitherto anonymous authors achieve fame, it is a function of their stories attracting readers. Piggybacking on Adams's distinction, I coined the term "*some body* memoirs" to denote nonfiction narratives of living in, with, or as an anomalous body. (A more technical term for these would be autosomatographies.)[8] These can be sorted roughly into two categories. On the one hand, a few conditions – such as breast cancer, HIV/AIDS, blindness, deafness, and recently depression – have generated many narratives. The cultural "selection" of these conditions is worth investigation, because it is not the case that the most deadly and dangerous conditions produce the most narratives. (If it were, women would write more narratives of lung cancer than of breast cancer.) Similarly, there are relatively few narratives of common conditions like heart disease or diabetes. Obviously, other factors are at work: breast cancer in women (it also affects men, though far fewer) is memoir-worthy because it affects an organ closely associated with beauty, sexual desirability, and female identity. And it was not merely the virulence of HIV/AIDS but its association with early death in gay men that accounted for so many narratives being written.

On the other hand, many conditions have generated a few narratives each. Over the years I have developed a constantly growing list of conditions, some quite rare, that have produced small numbers of memoirs: these include, in alphabetical order, amputation, amyotrophic lateral sclerosis (also known as Lou Gehrig's disease), anorexia, anxiety, asthma, bipolar illness, borderline personality disorder, cerebral palsy, chronic fatigue syndrome, chronic pain, cystic fibrosis, deformity, diabetes, epilepsy, insomnia, locked-in syndrome, multiple sclerosis, Munchausen syndrome by proxy, obesity, obsessive-compulsive disorder, Parkinson's, prosopagnosia ("face-blindness"), schizophrenia, stroke, stuttering, Tourette syndrome, and vitiligo. Today as never before, at least in North America, having an unusual impairment or illness is considered an appropriate basis for a full-length memoir. The literary marketplace seems to have room for a vast array of such conditions. In the internet age, the ease, decreased cost, and increasing respectability of self-publishing encourage such testimony. And of course, beyond the realm of print, there is cyberspace, which hosts blogs, online support groups, and other forms of self-representation. As a result, disability life writing proliferated dramatically around the turn of the millennium.

In addition to mirroring the disability rights movement, however, the incidence of disability narrative also reflects the public's fears: a distinguishing feature of disability is that it constitutes the only minority that members of the majority can join at any time. Disability is often treated as though it were communicable in the medical sense: kept at a psychological distance for fear that it might contaminate the "healthy" and unimpaired. Insofar as it may disarm irrational fears of disability, the contemporary boom in disability life writing should be welcomed. But the relation between disability memoir and the impulse to "quarantine" disability is somewhat problematic.

The production of their own first-person nonfictional narratives is certainly a key development in the history of disabled people, but it is far from an uncomplicated phenomenon. As I have suggested earlier, preinscription challenges disabled memoirists to undermine common preconceptions about disability; and unfortunately some disability memoirs seem instead to offer (false) reassurance to the nondisabled. In *Signifying Bodies*, my book on disability and contemporary life writing, I identified several common rhetorical patterns in disability memoir that do just that, or mostly that.[9] One is what I call the rhetoric of triumph, as manifested in the popularity, and thus the prevalence, of narratives of overcoming. Whereas disabled protagonists in Western drama and fiction are often subjected to scorn, destruction (including self-destruction), and/or sentimental condescension, disabled memoirs tend to have comic plots that recount their protagonists' triumph over adversity. Granted, happy endings are typical of most autobiography and memoir, because few people relish writing self-narratives with downward narrative arcs. Narratives that offer up unlikely supercrips (a disparaging term for disabled people who overcompensate for their supposed deficiencies) are often referred to by disabled people as "inspiration porn" because in *life*, as distinct from life writing, such triumph is the exception rather than the rule. But narratives of overcoming disability are particularly valued in the literary marketplace.

Narratives of overcoming are insidious not only because they grossly misrepresent the real world, in which poverty and unemployment are endemic among disabled people, but also because they suggest that the environment is not so hostile that an impaired person cannot succeed through sheer determination. After all, what is overcome in such narratives is usually not what disability scholars call *disability*, but rather *impairment*. The protagonist/narrator manages to achieve something thought unlikely or impossible for a person with a particular condition: the blind person learns to ski; the amputee masters some activity that would seem to require all four limbs. Not surprisingly, Jim Abbott, who became a major league baseball pitcher despite being born with only one hand (and went on to become an inspirational speaker), produced an autobiography titled *Imperfect: An Improbable Life*.[10] The plot of overcoming seems calculated to reassure, not others with the same impairment, who know well what they are up against, but rather the nondisabled, whose fear of disability may be somehow assuaged, at least temporarily, by a best-case scenario. In short, the overcoming memoir is not counterdiscursive: its message is that things are all right as they are. The disabled can succeed like the nondisabled if only they have sufficient spunk.

A related discourse characterizes impairments in terms of the tropes and rhetoric of Gothic fiction ("horror" in popular culture). This rhetoric openly plays on the fear of disability. Like overcoming narratives, Gothic narratives have comic plots: the narrator is able to imbue an acquired impairment with horror precisely because it has been escaped, left in the past. A classic example of Gothic rhetoric can be found, ironically, in *A Leg to Stand On* (1984), an early narrative by the neurologist Oliver Sacks, who has made a career of writing literary case studies of people with various neurological anomalies. *A Leg to Stand On* recounts Sacks' experience of temporary paralysis, the result of an injury suffered while mountain climbing alone. Here is how he characterizes it:

> I had imagined my injury (a severe but uncomplicated wound to the muscles and nerves of one leg) to be straightforward and routine, and I was astonished at the profundity of the effects it had: a sort of paralysis and *alienation* of the leg, reducing it to an "*object*" which seemed unrelated to me: an *abyss of bizarre, and ever terrifying, effects*. I had no idea what to make of these effects and entertained *fears that I might never recover*. I found the *abyss a horror*, and recovery a wonder: and I have since had a deeper sense of the *horror* and wonder which *lurk* behind life and which are concealed, as it were, behind the usual surface of health.[11]

The italicized terms convey Sacks' utter revulsion at the effects of a seemingly straightforward soft-tissue injury, and he can deploy them only because he has been quite miraculously delivered from his paralysis. This passage reveals how Gothic disability narrative taps the emotional dynamics of Gothic literature generally: it activates, only to assuage, a fear that is repressed by most people, most of the time. This text speaks powerfully to the majority attitude toward paralysis, and it may also speak to the particular revulsion of many medical doctors toward disabling conditions, especially those that seem resistant to medical treatment.

Narratives like these are akin to those of overcoming insofar as they recount an escape from, or a transcendence of, impairment. They often coincide, then, with what Arthur Frank terms "narratives of restitution,"[12] in which an illness is cured or an impairment corrected. In such scenarios, the narrator has the luxury of glorying in his release from the dreaded condition. Here the hero is not the protagonist, because his triumph is not a function of determination and effort, but rather the medical professional who manages to resolve the problem and restore the narrator to his previous state of health or lack of impairment.

This is not the case in Sacks' narrative, however. Although his recovery is reminiscent of the sudden transformation of his Parkinson's patients on L-dopa, as recounted in *Awakenings*,[13] his account of how and why he regained his sensation and function is entirely nonclinical; rather, it veers toward the mystical: "A true miracle was being enacted before me, within me. Out of nothingness, out of chaos, measure was being made ... My soul was transfixed in a rapture of wonder" (140–41). At this point, his narrative morphs into a conversion narrative: "The reality of my leg, and the power to stand and walk again, had been given to me, had descended upon me like grace" (147). While this may be true to Sacks' experience, and may convey some of the mysterious resilience of the body and brain, such rhetoric not so subtly reinforces common responses toward paralyzed people: revulsion and pity. When the protagonist escapes the condition of impairment, this is fortunate for him or for her, but the condition's stigma is left in place. Such rhetorics – of the Gothic, of conversion – reinforce the dominant discourse.

Such rhetorics are not limited to those who manage to overcome or escape their impairments. The position of the narrator whose condition is permanent or even progressive is more problematic; this might seem to rule out the comic plot, the happy ending. Such conditions are less amenable to narratives of the sort that succeed in the literary marketplace. A positive narrative arc is not out of the question even with a chronic condition, however, if the arc traced is not that of physical, but of moral or spiritual, progress. This pattern, the rhetoric of spiritual compensation, is quite common in disability memoir; indeed, it sometimes deploys explicitly religious language. Ruth Cameron Webb's *Journey into Personhood* (1994) is an intriguing text in this regard.

Webb has a congenital disability, cerebral palsy; despite encountering considerable discrimination, especially when she was young, she earned a doctorate in psychology and had a successful career counseling others with disabilities. In recounting past discrimination, her narrative moves at times toward the social model,[14] but her narrative is shaped most decisively by a midlife spiritual crisis, during which she hears these words: "Ruth, you have a special mission from the Lord, the Great Spirit . . . You are asked to reflect God's glory in your disabled body."[15] She is compensated for her physical impairment with a sense of her special spiritual status as a servant chosen by God. While this rhetoric reverses the common valence of disability, making the defective body the sign of grace rather than of sin, it does not decouple disability from morality, the body from the soul. Rather, it characterizes disability as *needing* some kind of spiritual compensation or redemption. It is thus not as counterdiscursive as it might seem.

One of the significant developments of the last several decades has been the development of more subversive narrative methods in disability memoir. One, borrowed from gay and lesbian narrative, is the story of coming out, of owning and affirming one's identity as a disabled person. This move appeals to those whose status may be liminal: those with impairments entirely invisible to casual observers, or mild enough to be hidden or masked. Here the link between disability narrative and the disability rights movement is evident, in a couple of ways. First, as the movement asserts that disabled people merit equal rights, it implicitly encourages openness about one's identity. Second, the publication (literally, the making public) of one's story alters the dynamic between the disabled and the nondisabled. Coming out, making oneself "visible" as disabled, troubles the easy division of people into two distinct categories. Making nondisabled readers realize that they already live comfortably among people with quite significant, though invisible, impairments can thwart the othering of disabled people. Contrary to narrative patterns that remove stigma from the individual while leaving it in place for the condition, the coming-out story in effect exposes the arbitrariness of the stigma by affirming the condition that it is attached to. The coming-out story changes the landscape in which most of us live. Further, emerging in print from the disability closet can encourage others with disabilities to come out. As it happens, among recent coming-out memoirs have been narratives by significant figures in disability studies: for example, Simi Linton's *My Body Politic* (2006), Georgina Kleege's *Sight Unseen* (1999), and Stephen Kuusisto's *Planet of the Blind* (1998).[16] In these narratives, life writing and advocacy merge.

Another counterdiscursive pattern is the narrative of emancipation. Here coming out may be literal rather than figurative, as in deinstitutionalization.

Examples of this may be rare – especially considering the vast numbers of people involved in this historic shift – but they are nonetheless noteworthy. One such is *I Raise My Eyes to Say Yes* (1989), by Ruth Sienkiewicz-Mercer, a woman so severely disabled by cerebral palsy that she has never been able to walk, feed herself, or speak.[17] Institutionalized by a family unable to afford a private hospital, she was assumed by medical staff to be cognitively impaired and was, in effect, warehoused. She eventually succeeded in communicating nonverbally to the extent that the staff recognized her intelligence and, after a long struggle, she was able to move out of the institution and to live on her own with assistance – autonomously, though not independently – and to marry. As my term emancipation suggests, this genre has much in common with slave narratives. There, inequality is ascribed on the basis of race; here, on the basis of a disability. What makes stories like Sienkiewicz-Mercer's particularly valuable is that they assert equality and demand freedom despite the undeniable dysfunction of the bodies in question. Her freedom and autonomy depend on the recognition that her impairment does not justify unequal treatment, let alone involuntary confinement.

The production of her narrative illustrates an issue alluded to earlier: cognitive, neurological, and physical impairments may make it difficult or impossible for disabled people to speak for themselves, much less to represent themselves in print. In cases like Sienkiewicz-Mercer's, however, assistive technology and human collaboration can empower the aspiring memoirist. The production of her narrative involved an advocate, Steven B. Kaplan, who prompted her with questions; she responded with the help of word boards, and he would then sketch out a narrative and submit it to her for her approval. An even more labor-intensive method was used in the celebrated case of Jean-Dominique Bauby, author of *The Diving Bell and the Butterfly* (1997), who was incapacitated by a stroke that left him unable to control his body except for his left eyelid. Undaunted, he blinked that eyelid to choose letters read to him by an assistant and thus painstakingly "dictated" his short memoir from passages composed in his head.[18]

Methods like these, while complicated, labor-intensive, and time-consuming, do not compromise the validity of the narrative: as long as the "author" can "authorize" his or her text by reading and approving it, the narrative should be worthy of trust. Of course, something is always lost in translation, and in the case of someone like Sienkiewicz-Mercer, who had little formal education, the "voice" of the narrative no doubt reflects the sensibility of her collaborator. But as long as the subject is in control of the text, readers should give it the benefit of the doubt. It is unfair to subject memoirists with impairments that impinge on communication to more scrutiny than is applied to nondisabled memoirists; after all, celebrity memoirists often deploy ghostwriters (typically with far less transparency). Significantly, during the current memoir boom, a period characterized by several highly publicized fraudulent memoirs involving false claims of victimhood – usually that of a Holocaust survivor – I am not aware of the discrediting of a single disability memoir.

That is not to say, however, that disability memoir entails no ethical problems. To the contrary, disabled people are among the subjects most vulnerable to exploitation when the text is *not* in their control and they are not able to assess and respond to their representation. In everyday life, the term "memoir" is often used interchangeably with "autobiography," but as the prefix suggests, *auto*biography must be self-authored, whereas memoir can be written by anyone acquainted with the subject. And therein lies an ethical issue. Before the current memoir boom, one of the most common forms of disability memoir was the parental memoir of the disabled child, and this genre continues to be popular. Obviously, *no* child is in control of a parental memoir, but few *non*disabled children are the subjects of parental memoirs. Disabled children are doubly disadvantaged, by their age and by their disability; they are especially vulnerable subjects. Parents' motives are usually noble: to "raise awareness" of a disability, to influence public policy, to celebrate a life lived in adverse circumstances. But there is always the danger that the disabled child will be presented as a parental nightmare. Such was the case, I have argued, with Michael Dorris's *The Broken Cord* (1989), which recounts the novelist's difficulty in raising an adopted Lakota son diagnosed with fetal alcohol syndrome: "He avoided work whenever possible, refused to pay attention to his appearance, was slow to motivate, and only occasionally told the truth."[19] In his fervor to limit the incidence of this syndrome, Dorris – apparently a supportive parent in everyday life – inadvertently but inevitably devalued his own son's life by presenting him as the poster child for a preventable disability, a poster whose implicit caption reads "Not Wanted."

A more positive scenario involving a subject with a cognitive impairment is Rachel Simon's *Riding the Bus with My Sister* (2002).[20] After having grown somewhat distant from her cognitively impaired sister, Rachel reacquainted herself with Beth, immersing herself in her daily routine of riding public transportation around her home town. In the process Rachel came to see what Beth finds gratifying in what might appear to most nondisabled people as a pointless and vacant activity, literally traveling in circles. Beth relished the companionship of the drivers, most of whom welcomed her presence aboard. Rachel credits her sister with *having* a life – indeed, quite a lively social life – that she created in her own idiosyncratic way. Rachel enters that life not only as a sister, but also like an ethnographer, observing her sister negotiate the demands of independent living, learning what support services she uses, and reconciling herself to Beth's aversion to boring jobs: "To Beth, every day is Independence Day . . . I love this about her, and now that I have come to see her as proudly bearing the torch of self-determination, I regard her as courageous, a social pioneer" (180). The result is a kind of rare disability (auto)ethnography. Crucially, Beth had sufficient literacy to be able to read and endorse the story.

William Dean Howells once referred to autobiography as "the most democratic province in the republic of letters" because it is by far the most accessible of literary genres.[21] That assessment is far truer now than when he uttered it over a century ago. The memoir boom has seen a marked increase in the number of published (and self-published) narratives and heightened respectability for memoir as a literary genre, which is now taught under the rubric "the fourth genre" in creative writing programs. More importantly, it has also entailed a significant change in the demographics of memoir writers. Many are female, and many write their memoirs at relatively young ages – and sometimes more than one. More to the point here, however, it is common today for people with disabilities – even ones that once seemed to preclude the writing of memoir – to produce narratives published by trade presses. The most remarkable example of this has been the proliferation of memoirs *by* autistics – rather than *about* them by parents or siblings. Not so long ago, it was "common knowledge" that autobiography and autism were incompatible. If you were autistic, you were incapable of writing your own story; if you wrote your own story, you were not truly autistic. But today, in the wake of Temple Grandin's *Emergence: Labeled Autistic* (1986),[22] there exists a substantial and rapidly growing corpus of autistic memoirs: indeed, the genre has been given its own name: autiebiography.[23] These memoirs exemplify the performative utterances referred to above. To date, self-written narratives of (early) Alzheimer's are few, but they are no longer unheard of; a notable example is Thomas DeBaggio's *Losing My Mind*.[24] The difficulties attendant on impairment are very different here, but here too the medium is the message: there is a person here. Respect must be paid.

When I entered disability studies from the field of life writing studies in the early 1990s, I encountered palpable suspicion, if not hostility, to disability life writing. Several influential scholars had dismissed such narrativization as inherently individualizing and thus in conflict with the social model's agenda of highlighting the oppression of disabled people as a cohort. The fear seemed to be that disability memoir would emphasize impairment, rather than socially constructed disability, or that it would evoke sympathy for the individual, rather than support for the cause. The situation has changed drastically. And that has been as much a credit to disability memoirists as to scholars. Over the last three decades or so, the body of disability memoir has grown not just in volume but in sophistication; early dismissals of disability memoir, never fair, seem in retrospect even more misguided. It is also true that as the field has come to recognize the limitations of the "social model,"[25] it has made more room for narratives that focus on impairment, on the very sheer bodily suffering sometimes consequent on disability. To censor that is to deny the reality of disability for many.

Overall, then, the flowering of life writing – though not without obvious problematic aspects – has been a significant development in disability literary history. As disabled lives are lived more and more in the open, thanks to legislation creating greater access, disabled lives are being more frequently written – and especially self-authored. Moreover, new ways of representing disability bid to change the way disability is understood by the public at large.

Given the devaluing of disability by the general population (and, to a troubling degree, by medical professionals) and at a time of increasing access to prenatal and genetic testing and increasing enthusiasm for legalization of physician-assisted suicide – both of which threaten the existence of people with disabilities – there is a pressing need today for disability life writing to function as what I call "quality-of-life writing":[26] testimony affirming the value of living with disability. And increasingly, disability memoir does just that. Today, as never before, disability writes.

NOTES

1. Francis Bacon, "Of Deformity," in *The Essayes or Counsels, Civill and Morall*, ed. by Michael Kiernan (Cambridge, MA: Harvard University Press, 1985), pp. 133–34.
2. William Hay, *Deformity: An Essay* (London: R. and J. Dodsley, 1754). See Essaka Joshua's chapter in this volume for further discussion of Bacon's and Hay's essays.
3. Anna Agnew, *From under the Cloud: or, Personal Reminiscences of Insanity* (Cincinnati, OH: Robert Clarke, 1887); Hiram Chase, *Two Years and Four Months in a Lunatic Asylum: From August 20th, 1863, to December 20th, 1865* (Saratoga Springs, NY: Van Benthuysen, 1868); Moses Swan, *Ten Years and Ten Months in Lunatic Asylums in Different States* (Hoosick Falls, 1874).
4. See Mary Elene Wood, *The Writing on the Wall: Women's Autobiography and the Asylum* (Urbana: University of Illinois Press, 1994); and Sara Newman, "Disability and Life Writing: Reports from the Nineteenth-Century Asylum," *Journal of Literary and Cultural Disability Studies*, 5.3 (2011), pp. 261–78.
5. Helen Keller, *The Story of My Life*, ed. by Roger Shattuck, Dorothy Herrmann, and Anne Sullivan (1903; New York: Norton, 2003).
6. Helen Keller, *The Story of My Life* (New York: Doubleday, Page, and Company, 1905), Chapter 19.

7. Lorraine Adams, "Almost Famous: The Rise of the 'Nobody' Memoir," *Washington Monthly*, April 2, 2002, www.washingtonmonthly.com/features/2001/0204.adams.html, accessed October 31, 2014.
8. I introduce this term in *Signifying Bodies: Disability in Contemporary Life Writing* (Ann Arbor: University of Michigan Press, 2009), p. 2.
9. See Chapter 3, "Rhetoric and Self-Representation in Disability Memoir," in *Signifying Bodies*, pp. 31–48.
10. Jim Abbott, with Tim Brown, *Imperfect: An Improbable Life* (New York: Ballantine, 2012).
11. Oliver Sacks, *A Leg to Stand On* (New York: Summit, 1984), pp. 13–14 (emphasis added). Further page references to primary texts will be given parenthetically in the body of the chapter.
12. Arthur W. Frank, *The Wounded Storyteller: Body, Illness, and Ethics* (Chicago: University of Chicago Press, 1995), p. 75ff.
13. See Oliver Sacks, *Awakenings* (London: Gerald Duckworth & Co, 1973).
14. On the social model of disability, see Chapter 1 of this volume.
15. Ruth Cameron Webb, *A Journey into Personhood* (Iowa City: University of Iowa Press, 1994), p. 180.
16. Simi Linton, *My Body Politic* (Ann Arbor: University of Michigan Press, 2006); Georgina Kleege, *Sight Unseen* (New Haven, CT: Yale University Press, 1999); and Stephen Kuusisto, *Planet of the Blind* (New York: Dial, 1998).
17. Ruth Sienkiewicz-Mercer and Steven B. Kaplan, *I Raise My Eyes to Say Yes* (Boston, MA: Houghton Mifflin, 1989).
18. Jean-Dominique Bauby, *The Diving Bell and the Butterfly* (London: Fourth Estate, 1998).
19. Michael Dorris, *The Broken Cord* (New York: HarperPerennial, 1990), p. 200. See Chapter 4, "Adoption, Disability, and Surrogacy: The Ethics of Parental Life Writing in *The Broken Cord*," in G. Thomas Couser, *Vulnerable Subjects: Ethics and Life Writing* (Ithaca, NY: Cornell University Press, 2004), pp. 56–73.
20. Rachel Simon, *Riding the Bus with My Sister: A True Life Journey* (Boston, MA: Houghton Mifflin, 2002).
21. William Dean Howells, "Autobiography, A New Form of Literature," *Harper's Monthly*, 119 (1909), pp. 795–98 (p. 795).
22. Temple Grandin, with Margaret M. Scariano, *Emergence: Labeled Autistic* (Novato, CA: Arena, 1986).
23. Larry Arnold claims to have coined the term in a post of January 2, 2012 to the listserv, DISABILITY-RESEARCH@JISCMAIL.AC.UK, archived at www.jiscmail.ac.uk/cgi-bin/webadmin?A2=DISABILITY-RESEARCH;f330a300.1201, accessed November 25, 2015.
24. Thomas DeBaggio, *Losing My Mind* (New York: Touchstone, 2003).
25. For critiques of the social model of disability, see Tom Shakespeare, *Disability Rights and Wrongs Revisited* (London: Routledge, 2014), pp. 17ff.
26. I introduce this term in G. Thomas Couser, "Quality-of-Life Writing: Illness, Disability, and Representation," in Miriam Fuchs and Craig Howes (eds.), *Teaching Life Writing Texts* (New York: Modern Language Association, 2008), pp. 350–58.

15

JAY DOLMAGE

Disability Rhetorics

Confronting Absence

In *Narrative Prosthesis: Disability and the Dependencies of Discourse* (2000), Sharon Snyder and David Mitchell tell a story about talking with a Japanese literary scholar at a conference, and explaining that their area of interest is disability studies. The Japanese scholar immediately responds that there are no examples of disability in Japanese literature. Then, he pauses, and surprisingly starts to create a laundry list of examples. Mitchell and Snyder identify this "'surprise' about the pervasive nature of disability" as a common response: without "developed models for analyzing" disability, we can expect many other readers to "filter a multitude of disability figures absently through their imaginations."[1]

This same filtering operates to create a sense of rhetorical history in which disability is difficult to locate. Added to this passive inability to imagine disability is the very active belief that only the most able could (or can) be rhetoricians or orators. Canonized rhetorical history asks us to accept that disability was (and is) the opposite of rhetorical facility. Rhetorical historians Brenda Jo Brueggemann and James Fredal write that in one particular version of ancient Greek rhetoric, "[r]hetoric [was] the cultivation and perfection of performative, expressive control over oneself and others. Deformity at once prevented any rhetorical achievement."[2] Students, scholars, and the general public can be easily persuaded that, wherever abnormality was in rhetorical history, it was stigmatized and silenced. The rhetorical tradition we have accepted also demands that we inherit these assumptions, that we enforce them.

Further, over time, the tradition of *using* constructions of disability to mark excess has silenced or controlled disabled bodies as it has stifled the female body, the foreign body, the racialized body, and so on. Naturally, with a definition of rhetoric as, simply, oratory and the use of the "controllable" body for persuasion, people with disabilities can be easily ignored. When the calculus of rhetorical ability always factors upon a normal body or an invisible body, marking a body's difference and excess disqualifies it from expression. So we need to question our choices about what counts as rhetoric and who counts as a rhetorician.

In this spirit, a close examination of rhetoric in antiquity and in other social, geographic, and temporal locations allows us to recover many overlooked examples of people with and without disabilities weaving disability rhetoric, and thus to challenge the idea that "abnormal" bodies can or should be silenced. This recovery then also allows us to construct new models of expressive power for disabled people across eras and geographies. We should not be "surprised" to find disability in rhetoric.

Just as in Mitchell and Snyder's example, once we start to really think about it, it is difficult to find examples from rhetorical history that are *not* touched or inflected or fired by disability. For instance, for those who have made Plato and Aristotle the center of a canon and the architects of an epistemology, the body is a distraction or, worse, a deterrence to clear thought. We believe that the focus of these "great philosophers," clearly, was on the perfection of the mind and its powers. But ironically, we might actually view the rhetorical moves of Plato and Aristotle as being hypermediated by the body – whether through Socrates's desire for Phaedrus in that famous dialogue, his sense of his own bodily difference (specifically his snub nose) that comes across in many of the dialogues, or Aristotle's obsessive categorization of deviancy in *On the Generation of Animals* – an extensive treatise on how reproduction works and how it can go wrong. As Richard Enos points out, Plato was himself a junior Olympic champion, and like many aging athletes, his work can be read as conveying a clear nostalgia for his youthful body. Socrates was honored by Athens for his accomplishments as a soldier but was also described as disabled, and Aristotle was uniquely sensitive to his own physical limitations.[3] The Socratic dialogues, in particular *Meno* and *Phaedrus*, can be read as extended meditations on the limits and challenges of memory and the benefits and dangers of madness. Take for example the famous and provocative maxim from the *Phaedrus* that "love is a serious mental disease."[4] In sum, a more complex view of Greek history reveals that, for these philosophers, the obsession with the perfectible mind does not always (or perhaps ever) fully divert attention from the body – and specifically the disabled body. And an obsession with the perfectible mind did not lead these philosophers to find one – in themselves or in others; instead, they spent most of their time exploring the mind's limitations. Yet this is not the view we have chosen to canonize. On through rhetorical history, once you begin to search, disability is everywhere: from Homer to Sequoyah, Sojourner Truth to Gloria Anzaldúa, Demosthenes to King George VI, Caliban to the X-Men. In this chapter, I will revisit some of these often neglected or ignored rhetorical exemplars and teachers.

What Is Disability Rhetoric?

Rhetoricians focus on the uses of language for persuasive ends. You might recognize rhetoric only in a negative sense, as the intentional manipulation of language to mislead and to obscure meaning. But rhetoricians also recognize the ways that rhetoric shapes not just utterances or inscriptions, but also beliefs, values, institutions, and even bodies. One simple way to define rhetoric is to say that it is the study of all of communication. But more specifically, rhetoricians foreground the persuasive potential of all texts and artifacts, questioning why meanings adhere and sediment or detach and transform; recognizing the constant negotiations between authors and audiences; linking language to power. Rhetoric can be seen as an operational, discursive means of shaping identity, community, cultural processes and institutions, and everyday being-in-the-world. Rhetoric not only impacts all of those variables in our lives that are not given and thus subject to opinion and persuasion, rhetoric also works to whittle away our sense that any part of our lives could ever truly be set and certain.

I see rhetoric as the strategic study of the circulation of power through communication. I also argue for a focus on the central role of the body in rhetoric – as the engine for all communication.[5] Aristotle famously suggested that rhetoric is "the faculty of discovering in any particular case all of the available means of persuasion."[6] I would suggest that the body has never been fully or fairly understood for its role in shaping and multiplying these available means. When cultural ideas about the body and its potential shift, rhetorical possibilities also transform and expand. Disability rhetoric is about searching for these rhetorical shifts, looking for meaningful bodies, and interrogating the entailments of these changing values. Disability rhetorics actually should impel *further* shifts in our understanding of disability and the rhetorical body.

Disability studies would mandate that rhetoricians pay close attention to embodied difference; in return, rhetorical approaches would give disability studies practitioners means of understanding the debates that in part shape these bodies. Rhetoric needs disability studies as a reminder to pay critical and careful attention to the body. Disability studies needs rhetoric to better understand and negotiate the ways that discourse represents and impacts the experience of disability. As Melanie Yergeau and John Duffy write in their introduction to a special issue of *Disability Studies Quarterly* devoted to rhetoric, "rhetoric functions as a powerfully shaping instrument for creating conceptions of identity and positioning individuals relative to established social and economic hierarchies. A function of the rhetorical scholar is to identify such powerfully shaping instruments and their effects upon individuals, including disabled individuals."[7]

While rhetoric has often been placed outside of, or as adjunct to literary studies, in this chapter I will reveal how rhetorical attention to "literary" and seemingly nonliterary texts calls up unique and important modes of analysis. We will pay attention to the ways disability, specifically, has been figured, troped, and mythologized. We will also explore how disability offers new rhetorical repertoires and possibilities. A rhetorical approach to historical and contemporary literary texts allows for an investigation not just of where and how disability is represented, but also how disability has been overwritten and overdetermined, as well as how disability makes new meaning possible. This rhetorical approach demands a layering of meanings and a focus on persuasive possibilities: how do these texts shape bodily affordances, but also how do people *use* these texts and stories to move one another? A rhetorical approach, then, moves away from close readings of the texts or stories at hand and toward a focus on the embodied impact of these narratives on audiences.

This chapter will offer a repertoire of disability rhetorics. Here I am eliding a parallel shadow archive of disability "myths" – for instance the idea that people with disabilities need to "overcome" or compensate for their disability; or that we should read disabled characters as evoking pity and charity; or that there is a hierarchy of disabilities.[8] We could view disability myths as those tropes, stereotypes, and devices that render disability one-dimensional, that allow authors to use disability to describe characters and propel plots in simple, often negative, ways.[9] Disability rhetorics, on the other hand, highlight the ways that disability creates and multiplies meaningful possibilities. Disability myths showcase the ways that a society, an author, or an institution can get disability "wrong." But disability rhetorics, like McRuer's conception of the "crip promise" or Snyder and Mitchell's conceptions of disability culture, are means of conceptualizing not just how meaning is attached to disability, but are means of conceptualizing the knowledge and meaning that disability *generates*.[10]

A Repertoire and Choreography of Disability Rhetorics

Jeanne Fahnestock defines all "rhetorical figures" as the departure from the expected order of words.[11] In this way all rhetorical figures are non-normative or "disabled": they are the abnormality that fires newness and invites novel and multiple interpretations. For instance, in disability studies we use coinages such as *cripistemology* or the *criptionary* to revive phenomenology or redefine stigmatizing labels on our own, new terms.[12] And yet all of language works this way: we break rules to make new meanings all of the time. This, then, becomes a way to understand disability rhetoric on the word-level or the sentence-level: when we break language in ways that may cause temporary confusion or misdirection, this is also a way to create new meaning, revealing the prosthetic and interdependent nature of all language.

The rhetorics in my repertoire also create what Fiona Kumari Campbell calls "disability imaginaries," reconceptualizing knowing so that we might "think/speak/gesture and feel different landscapes not just for being-in-the-world but [also for the] conduction of perception, mobilities and temporalities."[13] These disability rhetorics offer challenges to ableist normativity, challenges that range from overt to carefully nuanced. In this way, disability rhetoric reaches far beyond the word or sentence level. The rhetorics I will discuss in this chapter adhere first of all to the three master genres of rhetoric defined by Aristotle: forensic, deliberative, and epideictic. The argument here is that even within traditional genres, and certainly beyond them, an expanded rhetorical repertoire offers further available means and ways to move, ways to make meaning by recirculating power through the body. My hope is that these rhetorics are used as tools that readers will make their own, adapt, and activate. Hopefully, this inventory of rhetorics forms an accessible choreography. Use this list yourselves, but also expand this list.

Disability Forensic

As mentioned, forensic or judicial rhetoric is one of three master genres of rhetoric identified by Aristotle, and forensic deals with the truth or falsity of past events. Mitchell and Snyder recognize the literary genre of "new historical" criticism, and I would suggest that they are also discussing forensic: "historical revisionists argue that physical and cognitive difference was the rule rather than the exception of historical experience."[14] In my own work I have argued for this rule, for instance reclaiming the stories of Hephaestus, a Greek God with a disability, and arguing that the form of knowledge he symbolized – *metis*, a form of lateral, crooked, crafty thinking – was a dominant rhetorical force in Ancient Greece. The celebration of Hephaestus, his craft, his cunning, his ability, as well as the deification of his disability, is a means of challenging held perceptions about the mythical character, but also about all of us – defined as we all are by concepts or myths of ability, by rhetorics of normalcy. A forensic exploration of Hephaestus does not just question the truth or falsity of rhetorical history; this rhetorical work should shift body values and roles, as should all of disability forensic.[15]

For disability studies, work in this rhetorical genre has largely taken the form of historical work that addresses the ways that disability has been actively submerged or ignored, and the work takes dynamic shape as a rhetorical field through which not only can history be rewritten, but any method of historical approach can be generatively disabled. Disability forensic is also a key mode of literary scholarship, as we can see through Robert McRuer's work on Shakespeare, Susan Antebi's work on the fiction of Mexican eugenics, or Julie Minich's work on disability, citizenship, and Chicana/o literature and art.[16] Specific literary texts are closely re-read, but there is also a rhetorical argument being made about how these texts can and should be received in a way that constructs a less exclusionary world.

Disability forensic both rescues and defends disabled figures (in rhetoric we call this *apologia*), and recognizes and impugns a long record of disablism, oppression, and persecution (in rhetoric we call this *kategoria*). But importantly, a disability forensic would not just offer "corrections" to the historical record, but would unearth the interestedness of the record-keepers, never limiting the multiplication of meanings and archives. A disability forensic assumes that there are always hidden narratives of disability, that there are many reasons why these stories may have been hidden, and the job of the disability rhetorician is to both recirculate the hidden stories and to recognize values and power dynamics recalibrating through their submersion and their reinvocation. That is: *your* job is to unearth new readings of literature and art and public speech, searching for disability; and *your* job is to understand the ways that this unearthing can redistribute meaning and power.

The figures, texts, and artifacts of rhetorical and literary history need to be recognized as "pervasively" centering disability, to borrow Snyder and Mitchell's words. Once we get past "surprise" about the rhetorical power of disability, we can better understand all of rhetoric.[17] This reclamation can all be seen as a form of forensic rhetoric – whether this is done with literary texts or rhetorical ones. For instance, Meredith Minister's scholarship on the black female orator Sojourner Truth also lays out the stakes of disability forensic rhetoric: "by continuing to study Truth solely as an African-American woman instead of an African-American woman with a disability, scholars perpetuate an ideology of ability," ignoring the "depth of social stigmas in a variety of historical contexts" and therefore risking "repeating those social stigmas in contemporary scholarship."[18] Disability forensics creates important agentive space in the present by refusing to allow the exclusions and oppressions of the past to continue.

In Zosha Stuckey's work uncovering the stories of freak show performers Ann E. Leak and Lavinia Warren, she shows that "revisionist work around these women demonstrates the importance of situating histories of disability within rhetorical paradigms ... It also asks that we consider their unique rhetorical obstacles. Our challenge is to move beyond the notion of disability as deficit and beyond the wonder and amazement and arrive at people's social historicity as rhetorical agents."[19] Stuckey's work is one excellent example of disability forensic. Importantly, Stuckey lays out some ground rules: in putting histories together, we need to consider the power circulating around and from bodies, including the rhetorical contexts and boundaries before them, with a focus on rhetoricity and agency. Even more importantly, Stuckey is studying these women not as passive rhetorical objects, surfaces upon which meaning is projected. Instead, she studies Warren, Leak, and other freak show subjects as rhetoricians themselves. The genre of forensic rhetoric, we are told, emerged when individual citizens began to have the power to argue their own cases in the courts.[20] And Leak and Warren, as Stuckey shows, "used their bodily variations to assert rhetorical fitness and agency ... they accessed public spaces ... recognized but also resisted their othering, and ... attempted to refashion their ethos from that of a 'vulgar', laughable, and 'disgusting unfortunate' to that of a 'true' and pious Victorian woman and an esteemed public figure."[21] So it makes sense that we should view disability forensic not just as the way we recover stories of disability from the past, but also as a means to amplify the arguments that disabled people were making for themselves.

Disability Deliberation

Deliberative rhetoric (again one of Aristotle's master genres) seeks to determine what actions should be taken in the future, and the most recognizable form of this genre is the political speech. In *The King's Speech* (2008), a movie depicting King George VI and focused primarily on his efforts to "cure" himself of a stutter, the climax of the film is a deliberative speech. This is the historic moment in which the new King prepares the British public to go to war against Hitler. In rhetorical theory and history, declarations of war by kings and politicians are *the* traditional exemplars of deliberative rhetoric. This speech gestures toward overcoming, but has a dark and realistic edge:

> The task will be hard. There may be dark days ahead, and war can no longer be confined to the battlefield, but we can only do the right as we see the right, and reverently commit our cause to God. If one and all we keep resolutely faithful to it, ready for whatever service or sacrifice it may demand, then with God's help, we shall prevail.[22]

Of course, the King also "leaves in a few" stutters in the speech, perhaps mirroring the difficulty of the task with a realistically "deliberative" delivery. As Isaac Chotiner writes, the real King George VI "felt confident enough about his stammer to turn it into a verbal signature." The king's stutter is situated as a generative rhetorical device, part of his unique *ethos*.[23]

As mentioned above, forensic rhetoric emerged because in ancient Greece, citizens began to be able to – and to need to – speak for themselves in the courts. As part of the emergence of a democracy, people also began to make political speeches, and thus deliberative rhetoric could be categorized. As the rhetorical genre that deals most specifically with the future, the role of disability in deliberative rhetoric is perhaps the most vexed. Simply, disability is often seen as the very absence of futurity, or as the very least desirable future, and thus deliberative rhetoric invokes disability to characterize everything that was undesirable about the past, everything that the future must overcome.

For instance, the first use of the term "normalcy" was in a 1921 speech by American presidential candidate Warren G. Harding, who argued that "America's present need is not heroics, but healing; not nostrums, but normalcy; not revolution, but restoration; not agitation, but adjustment; not surgery, but serenity; not the dramatic, but the dispassionate; not experiment, but equipoise; not submergence in internationality, but sustainment in triumphant nationality."[24] The rhetorical construction is simple: the war, a flood of immigration, these things are disabling America. A "normal" future is one without these disabling forces (and ostensibly, these disabled people). The exact same argument, albeit played out within a drastically different context, is offered in Donald Trump's recent (2015–16) Republican presidential nomination campaign through the use of the metaphor of a *Crippled America* – the title of a book by Trump, and a campaign slogan, both gesturing to the idea that the only way to "fix" America in the future is to invoke disability as the symbol of everything undesirable about the past and present.[25]

Adding complexity to this rhetoric is the idea that, as Alison Kafer has written, the "politics of futurity easily lends itself to an ethics of endless deferral" for people with disabilities.[26] The only future worth desiring – we are told, over and over again – is a future without disability. Thus, Kafer calls for "critical maps of the practices and ideologies that effectively cast disabled people out of time and out of our futures."[27] In the face of this, as Robert McRuer suggests, disability studies might "conjure up the disability to come" and welcome it.[28] More specifically, McRuer defines this as "a crip promise that we will always comprehend disability otherwise and that we will, collectively, somehow access other worlds and futures."[29] So, the goal of disability deliberation is both to critique the practices that cast disabled people out of time and to search for and invoke disability futures that could be welcomed, that can retain the critical possibility to oppose normalcy and normativity. The recent Twitter campaign by people with disabilities seeking to critique Trump through the #CrippledAmerica hashtag is one example of this disability deliberation. The act of taking his offensive use of the term and hijacking the hashtag to relate what life really is like for disabled people in the United States not only reversed his message, but clearly showed the rhetorical power and savvy of disabled people. For many, a political future in which disabled people could hijack the mediums of meaning making was a much more desirable and profound outcome than the one that Trump was shilling.

Disability deliberation happens also at the very level of the sentence or the utterance. I have already detailed the rhetorical significance of the "stutter" in *The King's Speech*. Recent work by Zach Richter and Joshua St. Pierre brings this agenda into the present day. Their *Did I Stutter* project was "created to provide an alternative way of thinking about speech and communication disabilities [... making a] commitment to empower stuttering voices everywhere [... and to] open a conversation about how much of the anxiety related to dysfluency is produced by oppressive social structures and values."[30] St. Pierre then further argues that stuttering cues us to make space in disability studies for it and other "liminal forms of oppression which straddle boundaries and disrupt the binaries of abled/disabled, normal/abnormal."[31] This reorientation shows us that perhaps stuttering as a highly rhetorical disability – related to speech and communication – is also the example par excellence of the rhetoricity of all of disability studies, demanding that we adopt a "posture of uncertainty" and receptiveness "in order to appreciate the specific" and variegated, fluid nature of disability oppression and expression.[32]

This project, then, is powerfully rhetorical. The Greek word *pseilos*, which we translate as "faltering speech," or a stutter, can also denote bad manners or, simply, the struggle for meaning that surrounds words.[33] As Marc Shell has written, "stuttering involves spiritually and physiologically inescapable ways of human articulation. At the same time, it pertains to the problem of the unspeakable or what remains unsaid."[34] In this way, the stutter as *pseilos* can oppose the idea that any communication happens smoothly or easily. The stutter can be viewed as amplifying that which is rhetorical in every utterance or movement, every struggle to make meaning, and highlighting the power inherent in the circulation of words through bodies.

For instance, in one early scene in *The King's Speech*, when as part of his therapy, the King is asked to yell into a microphone as loud music plays, he reluctantly recites Hamlet's most famous soliloquy (the deliberative "to be or not to be ... ") at the top of his lungs before leaving the therapist's office in frustration. There is a small irony here, however. Shell notes that "several astute productions of Hamlet depict the Danish prince, whom his mother calls 'scant of breath', as a stutterer."[35] At one stage in the play, Hamlet asks the players, "Speak the speech, I pray you, as I pronounced it to you, trippingly on the tongue" (III.2). Shell suggests that the word *tripping* here has an "internal dialectic that relates to walking and talking," and means both light-footed and nimble as well as tripping up.[36] In an important scene in *The King's Speech*, the king becomes angry at his speech therapist and starts to swear. "See how defecation flows *trippingly* from the tongue?" (55), the speech therapist remarks. The repetition of the term *trippingly* here is interesting, as is the obtuse connection between the King's swearing and the scatological legacy of Shakespeare, whose work was a laboratory for swearing, profanity, and expletives.[37]

The screenwriter for the movie, David Seidler, admitted in interviews that inspiration for this scene came from his own speech therapy for his own stutter. Whether Seidler intended to draw some allusion to Hamlet's stutter or not is unclear. But even the unintentional parallel is worth remarking upon. While Shakespeare is held up as the exemplary master of language, his prose is at the same time nimble and awkward, clear and obscurant, common and elevated. To align *The King's Speech* with Shakespeare is on the surface an appeal to an Anglophile fantasy of language mastery, yet underneath this appeal lies a messier possibility: that the allusion to Shakespeare is to what is stuttering, disabled, tripping, and crip within this canon. Disability deliberation is about expanding rhetorical possibilities, moving beyond the ableist fantasies of any rhetorical or literary canon.

In the spirit of disability deliberation, then, we can look not just to subversive expressions, like King George VI's unique delivery style, but also new *forms* of expression, and thus new embodied realities. Take for example Rosemarie Garland-Thomson's most recent work examining what she calls "bioethical case studies," like Harriet McBryde Johnson's narrative of the "case for [her] life," and we can see that when Garland-Thomson argues for "conserving disability [and] for what might be called *disability gain*," we have new ways to invoke disability deliberation and to welcome the disability to come.[38] David Bolt has since taken this concept of *disability gain* and carefully applied it to George Sava's novel *Happiness is Blind* (1987), Brian Friel's play *Molly Sweeney* (1994), and Stephen Kuusisto's memoir *Eavesdropping* (2006); we can expect further fruitful work on disability gain in both rhetorical and literary disability studies.[39]

Through the lens of disability rhetoric, any debate – and any narrative – should be analyzed to question how disability is and is not constructed as a (desirable) future. Further, all deliberation must be interrogated to better understand how disability is invoked as the opposite of futurity, and how agency and rhetoricity are deferred for people with disabilities. Finally, even within literary canons (such as Shakespeare) that we have traditionally seen as being about language mastery and control, powerful meaning is generated when language breaks down or trips, and when we recognize disability as something desirable "to be" rather than "not to be."

Disability Epideictic

The final of Aristotle's three genres, epideictic rhetoric deals with praise and blame through commemoration and celebration. An epideictic speech assesses character and virtue, stacking up and measuring flaws and strengths. But this stacking up is about much more that the characters in the story – it is about the audience, who are meant to emulate what is good and avoid what is evil about these characters. Brian Vickers and others have shown that while modern readers may have a hard time recognizing the epideictic character of much literature, for Renaissance readers (as well as their classical forebears) books and narratives were approached with the expectation that "they could change [their] life, for good or evil – could lead [them] to, or confirm [them] in, right ways of living, but could also corrupt and damage [them] forever." In his work, Vickers is focusing on Renaissance epics such as *The Faerie Queene*, works that were "contaminated" by Greek and medieval chivalric romances.[40] Yet this contamination works forward as well – in particular, we can pay attention to the ways that the narratives we read today both assign praise and blame, and encourage their readers to shape their own behavior accordingly.

One way to look at epideictic is to focus on disability studies' heroes and forms of self-congratulation. Within disability studies itself we have begun to see a very careful epideictic interrogating the deification of disabled heroes like Christopher Reeve,[41] insisting that the black disability movement not be elided from the history or future of the disability rights movement,[42] and even constructing parodical counternarratives of heroes such as Helen Keller.[43]

But epideictic also closely resembles and forms a broad range of genres of normativity. Ableism itself is a valence for epideictic: a script that foregrounds flaws and abnormalities, primarily using medical and scientific grammars; and it becomes a script everyone learns to read to themselves and others. The epideictic character of disability leads to the intensification of pathology – as we see in the changing categories of the *Diagnostic and Statistical Manual of Mental Disorders* (the widely accepted standard for classification of mental disabilities), there are ever more and ever newer ways to be abnormal. Thus disability epideictic would have to recognize the interestedness of our arguments around bodily values.

I have suggested that one dominant contemporary genre of epideictic is the biopic: the biographical film. And there is perhaps no other film genre more highly populated by disabled characters. *The King's Speech* (2008) is one example, but a wide range of other (not surprisingly award-winning) biopics are also disability epideictics: *My Left Foot* (1989), *The Sea Inside* (2004), *Ray* (2005), *A Beautiful Mind* (2006), HBO's *Temple Grandin* (2010), *The Theory of Everything* (2014); I could go on and on. These films generally adhere to disability stereotypes in order to assess the virtue and honor of their disabled subjects: the characters are honorable to the degree that they overcome or compensate for their disability, flawed when the disability "causes" them to be angry, unreliable, unrelatable. Thus, many biopics are both created and read through ableism. For this reason, they are *bio*pics not just about an individual life, they are *biopolitical*. They are narrated through the flaws of the body and mind, epideictically reinforcing but also sometimes resisting what Foucault calls biopower.[44]

We thus see that there are ways to resist normativity through disability epideictic: searching for the refusal of negative disability stereotypes, praising and accentuating disability, recognizing the forces that attempt to quantify and marketize the pathologies of the body, restoring the virtue of the denigrated and restoring the flaws of the venerated. In these ways, from film to fiction to the very field of disability studies itself, disability epideictic is a crucial genre, asking us to better understand how the act of reading/receiving literature might itself be normative. This might happen through the Renaissance sense of normative self-shaping, wherein the reader expects to be changed by the virtue or vice of the protagonist. Or this might happen through contemporary notions of biopower, wherein the quantifiable pathologies of the body are symbolized or even surveilled through narrative techniques.

Conclusion

This repertoire or choreography of rhetorics presents just a few possible moves. Hopefully the reader is inspired to think of and create many more, to make greater space and opportunity for the disability rhetorics to come. As the great rhetorical teacher and exemplar Gloria Anzaldúa said, "I want to write from the body; that's why we're in a body."[45] If we see rhetoric as the strategic study of the circulation of power through communication – or, more precisely, the circulation of power through and between bodies – then we must begin to create and recognize disability rhetorics. Rhetorics, across cultures and geographies, mediums and genres, can be inherently subversive, embodied, powerfully non-normative modes of persuasion, even while they have most often been represented as the opposite.

NOTES

1. David T. Mitchell and Sharon L. Snyder, *Narrative Prosthesis: Disability and the Dependencies of Discourse* (Ann Arbor: University of Michigan Press, 2000), p. 51.
2. Brenda Jo Brueggemann and James A. Fredal, "Studying Disability Rhetorically," in *Disability Discourse*, ed. by Mairian Corker and Sally French (Philadelphia, PA: Open University Press, 1999), pp. 129–35 (p. 131).
3. Richard Enos, personal email communication with the author, December 1, 2010.
4. Plato, *Phaedrus*, in *The Collected Dialogues of Plato*, ed. by Edith Hamilton and Huntington Cairns (Princeton, NJ: Princeton University Press, 1961), p. 249 d-e.
5. See Jay Dolmage, *Disability Rhetoric* (Syracuse, NY: Syracuse University Press, 2014).
6. Aristotle, *Rhetoric*, trans. by George Kennedy (Oxford: Oxford University Press, 1991), p. 1.
7. Melanie Yergeau and John Duffy, "Guest Editors' Introduction to Special Issue on Disability and Rhetoric," *Disability Studies Quarterly*, 31.3 (2011), n. pag., http://dsq-sds.org/article/view/1682/1607, accessed October 13, 2016.
8. Jay Dolmage, "Interchapter: Disability Myths," in *Disability Rhetoric*, pp. 31–62.
9. See Mitchell and Snyder, *Narrative Prosthesis*; and Ato Quayson, *Aesthetic Nervousness: Disability and the Crisis of Representation* (New York: Columbia University Press, 2007).
10. Robert McRuer, *Crip Theory: Cultural Signs of Queerness and Disability* (New York and London: New York University Press, 2006), p. 208; Sharon L. Snyder and David T. Mitchell, *Cultural Locations of Disability* (Chicago and London: University of Chicago Press, 2006).
11. Jeanne Fahnestock, *Rhetorical Figures in Science* (New York: Oxford University Press, 1999), p. 17.
12. See Merri Lisa Johnson and Robert McRuer, "Cripistemologies: Introduction," *Journal of Literary and Cultural Disability Studies*, 8.2 (2014), pp. 127–48; Dolmage, *Disability Rhetorics*; and McRuer, *Crip Theory*.
13. Fiona Kumari Campbell, *Contours of Ableism: The Production of Disability and Abledness* (London: Palgrave Macmillan, 2009), p. 15.
14. David T. Mitchell and Sharon L. Snyder, "Representation and Its Discontents: The Uneasy Home of Disability in Literature and Film," in *Handbook of Disability Studies*, ed. by Gary L. Albrecht, Katherine D. Seelman, and Michael Bury (Thousand Oaks, CA: Sage, 2011), pp. 195–218 (p. 205).
15. See Dolmage, *Disability Rhetoric*.
16. Robert McRuer, "Fuck the Disabled: The Prequel," in *Shakesqueer: A Queer Companion to the Complete Works of Shakespeare*, ed. by Madhavi Menon (Durham, NC: Duke University Press, 2011), pp. 294–301; Susan Antebi, *Carnal Inscriptions: Spanish American Narratives of Corporeal Difference and Disability* (London: Palgrave Macmillan, 2009); Julie Avril Minich, *Accessible Citizenships: Disability, Nation, and the Cultural Politics of Greater Mexico* (Philadelphia, PA: Temple University Press, 2015).
17. Mitchell and Snyder, *Narrative Prosthesis*, p. 51.
18. Meredith Minister, "Female, Black, and Able: Representations of Sojourner Truth and Theories of Embodiment," *Disability Studies Quarterly*, 32.1

(2012), n.pag., http://dsq-sds.org/article/view/3030/3057, accessed October 14, 2016.

19. Zosha Stuckey, "Staring Back: The Rhetorical Fitness and Self-fashioning of Ann E. Leak and Lavinia Warren, 19th Century Side Show Performers," *Enculturation: A Journal of Rhetoric, Writing, and Culture*, 9 (2014), n.pag., http://enculturation.net/staring-back, accessed October 14, 2016.
20. See George Kennedy, *Aristotle on Rhetoric: A Theory of Civic Discourse* (New York: Oxford University Press, 1991).
21. Stuckey, "Staring Back," n. pag.
22. David Seidler, *"The King's Speech" Script* (London: Bedlam/See Saw Films, 2008), p. 89. Further page references to primary texts will be given parenthetically in the body of the chapter.
23. As Isaac Chotiner reveals, in 1944, in a speech disbanding the Home Guard, George VI "only stumbled over the 'w' in weapons. Afterwards, his speech therapist asked him why this letter had proved a problem. 'I did it on purpose', the King replied with a wink. 'If I don't make a mistake, people might not know it was me'." Isaac Chotiner, "Royal Mess," *The New Republic*, January 6, 2011, https://newrepublic.com/article/80948/the-kings-speech-film-royal-mess, accessed May 31, 2017. In the film, this moment is actually wrapped into his famous 1939 speech declaring war on Germany, the key moment in the plot: "I had to throw in a few [stutters], so they'd know it was me," he says after the speech has been delivered. Seidler, *"The King's Speech" Script*, p. 89. So, the chronology is intentionally stuttered by the filmmakers. The moment is transposed into a definitively more *deliberative* speech.
24. Warren G. Harding, "Back to Normal: Address before Home Market Club," Boston, May 14, 1920, in *Rededicating America: Life and Recent Speeches of Warren G. Harding*, ed. by Frederick E. Schortemeier (Indianapolis, IN: Bobbs-Merrill, 1920), pp. 223–29.
25. Donald J. Trump, *Crippled America: How to Make America Great Again* (New York: Threshold Editions, 2015).
26. Alison Kafer, *Feminist, Queer, Crip* (Bloomington: Indiana University Press, 2013), p. 29.
27. Ibid., p. 33.
28. McRuer, *Crip Theory*, p. 200.
29. Ibid., p. 208.
30. Zach Richter and Joshua St. Pierre, *Did I Stutter?* (2014), n. pag., www.didistutter.org/blog, accessed October 14, 2016.
31. Joshua St. Pierre, "The Construction of the Disabled Speaker: Locating Stuttering in Disability Studies," *Canadian Journal of Disability Studies*, 1.3 (2012), pp. 1–21 (p. 20).
32. Ibid.
33. Martha L. Rose, *The Staff of Oedipus: Transforming Disability in Ancient Greece* (Ann Arbor: University of Michigan Press, 2003), p. 57.
34. Marc Shell, *Stutter* (Cambridge, MA: Harvard University Press, 2006), pp. 2–3.
35. Ibid., p. 175.
36. Ibid., pp. 171–72.

37. See Ashley Montagu, *The Anatomy of Swearing* (Philadelphia: University of Pennsylvania Press, 2001).
38. Rosemarie Garland-Thomson, "What We Have to Gain from Disability," *Disabling Normalcy Symposium*, University of Virginia, July 29, 2014.
39. David Bolt, "Not Forgetting Happiness: The Tripartite Model of Disability and Its Application in Literary Criticism," *Disability and Society*, 30.7 (2015), pp. 1103–17.
40. Brian Vickers, "Epideictic and Epic in the Renaissance," *New Literary History*, 14.3 (1983), pp. 497–537 (p. 499).
41. Brenda Jo Brueggemann, "Delivering Disability, Willing Speech," in *Bodies in Commotion: Disability and Performance*, ed. by Carrie Sandahl and Philip Auslander (Ann Arbor: University of Michigan Press, 2005), pp. 17–29.
42. Christopher Bell (ed.), *Blackness and Disability: Critical Examinations and Cultural Interventions* (Münster: LIT Verlag, 2011); Leroy Moore, "Pushing Limits: The Black Panthers and Disability," Radio Broadcast KPFA (February 2004).
43. We witness this in Faust Films' *Annie Dearest* (2012), an epideictic reappraisal of the relationship between Helen Keller and Anne Sullivan. *Annie Dearest: The Real Miracle Worker*, dir. Terry Galloway (Faust Films, 2012); Kim Neilson, *The Radical Lives of Helen Keller* (New York: New York University Press, 2004); Susan Crutchfield, "'Play[ing] Her Part Correctly': Helen Keller as Vaudevillian Freak," *Disability Studies Quarterly*, 25.3 (2005), n. pag., http://dsq-sds.org/article/view/577/754, accessed October 14, 2016. Anne Finger's short story "Helen and Frida" similarly reimagines Keller's life; Anne Finger, "Helen and Frida," in *Call Me Ahab: A Short Story Collection* (Lincoln: University of Nebraska Press, 2009), pp. 1–14. See Sami Schalk's chapter in this volume for analysis of this story.
44. I refer here to Foucault's explanation of biopower in volume one of his *History of Sexuality*: how power invests, distributes, and controls the body, and specifically how it controls entire populations of bodies. Biopower tracks the ways that power and knowledge become transformative factors on human life. In Foucault's words, there is a "tactical polyvalence of discourses" that can be linked to the "intensification of the body," "its exploitation as an object of knowledge and an element in relations of power." The extension or systemization of biopower is biopolitics, the ways that definitions and valuations of life organize politics and economics. Michel Foucault, *The History of Sexuality, Volume 1: An Introduction*, trans. by Alan M. Sheridan-Smith (New York: Pantheon Books, 1973), pp. 93, 107.
45. Gloria E. Anzaldúa with Linda Smuckler, "Turning Points," in Gloria E. Anzaldúa, *Interviews/Entrevistas*, ed. by AnaLouise Keating (New York: Routledge, 2000), pp. 17–70 (p. 38).

16

PETRA KUPPERS

Literary Disability Culture Imaginations at Work
An Afterword

G'niimim, zaagijig akiing
wewiib, wewini,
maashko-waagiziyeg
mino-waawiinjigaazoyeg pane.

You dance, lovers of the world
quickly, carefully
your curved strength
is a celebration!

Margaret Noodin

In this afterword, I am reflecting on creating and teaching literature with disabled people. What happens when we think about teaching literature and producing literature among groups of disabled people traditionally denied access to universities? And how can what we can learn in community settings influence university classrooms?

An afterword allows for expansiveness, for a different take than the chapters in their overview of topics. An afterword's argument can be an enactment, a poesis of merger, seeing culture creation enacted among people. So let us lean together into experience, where theoretical reflection emerges out of bodyminds in space and time together.

I am in Aotearoa/New Zealand, meeting with a group of actors from A Different Light Company, a theater group of people from Christchurch deemed to have cognitive differences, led by Tony McCaffrey. Ten of us are on an outing together: a field trip, visiting the beautiful lands of Waikuku Beach, about an hour's public bus ride above the city. Locating ourselves is important: none of us own a car, or have easy access to one, most of us can't get a driving license because of cognitive difference, and two of us use wheelchairs, including myself. Accessible buses have made outdoor access an option for us, but this recent win is constantly threatened by city governments looking to cut costs in precarious times. But for now, we can manage to find access to those regions that feature on Aotearoan tourist adventure Facebook updates: the visual poetry of long lonely beaches, picturesque estuaries, and abundant wildlife. We engage with these sites in poetry, as disabled people, most of us from a Pākehā (European or white settler) background, a few with Māori indigenous roots. Our work offers an opening into the literary imagination, into who has access to canons and readings and who is seen to be part of the citizenship of this thing called literature, with its own histories of class and gender differences (see Ria Cheyne's essay on genre fiction studies and its exclusion from literary mainstreams), and with literature's colonially inflected ways of conceiving of "text" (or subaltern speech acts, as Clare Barker's chapter shows).

I have visited and worked with this theater company before, but for this one-off visit, I have prepared a workshop on the epigraph poem. Margaret (Meg) Noodin, the poet, an Ojibwe woman (or Anishinaabe kwe), gifted it to me for my last book.[1]

She gave it to me in response to my work in disability culture, and to my previous critical writing on one of her poems, where crooked trees by the side of Lake Michigan, twisted like giant bonsai by weights attached by ropes, act as signposts for wayfarers, and also as connections to Anishinaabe ancestors.[2] The shape and sounds of Meg's poem open up to rhythm in physical movement, to the movement of drums, to embodiment and the connections between mouth, page, and land.[3] Meg and I are friends and collaborators, and the exchange of poems is part of our social life.

So this is the first thing I want to bring into the workshop, and into the discussion of literature in a Cambridge Companion: poetry is not just about accessing canons and understanding dominant sensibilities, it is also about private love tokens, small glimpses into another's complex consciousness, interdependent lives linked creatively through language.

The second thing I hope to find in this workshop, and in the pages of postcolonial literary criticism, are connections between language and land. Meg Noodin writes as an indigenous woman from the Three Fires Confederacy (a swath of land encompassing Michigan and Wisconsin in the US). These lands house me now, too, a settler who grew up with deep roots in a very different land, Germany. Here, in Aotearoa/New Zealand, the bicultural heritage is much more palpable than in other English-speaking countries, and postcolonial history is more available, thematized and made visible. We are opening our workshop with links to Māori practice, because that's the way that things are done here. We acknowledge the land we stand on, and its people, and everybody is familiar and firm with this practice, whether they have Māori heritage or Pākehā background. So I bring something that aesthetically echoes the groundedness of my current home place – the Anishinaabemowin language – to this location. We greet each other with "Kia Ora" as well as "Hello," as part of contemporary Englishnesses: ways of living in language and land, together. Some of us couldn't make it: one of the actors, Isaac, couldn't get out of his McDonald's shift.

But we are here, and happy to be in creative labor. Like the contributors to the Cambridge Companion, we make a hollow together, an incubation, putting differences in contact to see what emerges. We agree on the general shape of our time together, and get down to the serious business of lunch, breaking bread together while telling kōrero, that is, stories, of what we've been up to. Which leads quite easily into the first instruction of the workshop: giving appreciation for the land, for the country we are seeing around us, for the space we traversed coming out here to this beach community. We go round the circle, and add phrases and words: "Kiwiana," Andrew offers, and when asked, he explains: things like fish and chips and tomato sauce. For Kim it's the trees, they make her feel like home. Peter adds "a nice big BBQ," and Glen wishes to appreciate "shows." He writes this down, elaborately marking a napkin on his writing tablet. So "shows" it is! After creating a little performed group poem by stringing and chanting together all the things we appreciate about being here, we are on the march. We form a little parade, down the main street, on the way to the Domain (the commons, the park), and the estuary. While walking together in our group, we learn two lines from Meg's poem. We shout out the syllables, and connect them up, till we can all chant the lines while we parade down to the sea: dancing, loving, full of curved strength, rolling the Objiwe words in our mouth and on our tongues. Rhythms form their own human connection, and songs are often the entry ways into community – as anthropologist Karen Nakamura reminds us when she writes about being initiated with a song into a Japanese home for mental health users.[4] This is literature enacted, full-mouthed, lost in rhythms and sounds, binding humans to land and finding ground together – grounding us in what Clare Barker and Stuart Murray's introduction to this volume calls "the actual lives experienced by those with disabilities."

Finally, we arrive. A large big push up the levee, to the walkway that circles the bay, and we stand face to face with the expanse of the estuary, the stuff of New Zealand postcards: full of wading birds, tufts of grass, soaring harakeke (flax) and blooming yellow flowers. The next instruction: call out what you appreciate in your field of vision. What do you see, what do you want to honor by naming it? We create another list poem together: Water, Trees, Grass, Tekoko (cabbage tree) and Harakeke, Birdsong and SeaSound, Oystercatcher. We repeat it a few times, till we get all the words in, singing them out over the landscape of earth and water in front of us. We are lined up, aware of the formal greeting we are offering – the "show" Glen asked for. When we are clear that we are all satisfied with this small performance pooling, we move on.

Our last station is by a picnic table in the woods, just above the beach. For a little while, I invite us to be alone out in nature, to go rambling a bit, with the instruction to find something that reminds you of one in the group, so you can weave an appreciation poem with it – the way Meg used the linking metaphor of the crooked trees by Lake Michigan to appreciate disability's crooked beauty in me.

I might not use the word "metaphor" to give this instruction (see Chapter 1 of this volume for a sense of the complex cringe set up by the word), but the gist of it all seems clear enough to all participants, and we set off gleefully and focused on our mission. Few have been to this beautiful beach before – for many of us, the compass is small, the places we see regularly, the paths we traverse, confined by "special needs services," and the shapes of days. There is great freedom in these little outings, fingering unusual things, picking up seashells and pine cones. Soon, Ben is standing in the marsh, shoes off, and he enjoys the squelching mud between his toes.

The final poems of appreciation involve a soft seedhead of a grass, gifted to Andrew, who is being called a big softie. Glen has signaled that a thick fallen branch with many points reminds him of Peter – when asked to clarify, he speaks of Peter's sword, a costume shop prop we had used in our last workshop together, over a year ago, when Peter dressed up as a king in ermine and crown. Ben gets bright flowers to go with his bright shirts. Peter recites his final poem for us, clear and articulate: "Shall I compare thee to a summer's day / the ground is soft beneath our feet / the moon and the sun dance internally / wee boys cry at the sound of trumpets / pulling us home / home to the land of our forefathers / we remember those who have given their lives to protect this land."

At the end of our workshop, we stand and sing together to close our time: two lines from Meg's poem, sung out in our own melodies, strong, then soft, petering out among the trees.

This is one of the ways that a literary imagination can appear in disability culture: connections, appreciation, mixed languages, remembered fragments, new constellations. Culture, and the literary imagination, works through remixing, hybridization, and the condensery. These mechanisms are at work in this workshop, too, enacting a form of disability literature living, flowing with the kind of knowledges articulated in this Cambridge Companion, and their traces in our everyday lives. Peter's poem is a remediation of what is going on around him, a filtering mechanism that encompasses traditional notions of

(Shakespearean) poetry, Anzac day (commemorating the Australian and New Zealand war dead), and the recent funeral of All Black rugby legend Jonah Lomu. We can nod as we hear it – this is a shape we recognize, a telling of our days that is a bit surprising and mysterious and yet accessible. This is a doing of literature, reflecting on our disabled lives in oral performance poetry.

The interpenetration of human and nonhuman shapes, echoes and rhymes, appear in all appreciation poems here, and the fact that we sometimes have to dig to appreciate the connections, as in Glen's stick, seems not different from "nondisabled" poetry events (where, given poetry protocol, we'd probably be less likely to dig for connections if we are not already feeling them). The core feature of this workshop is not the production of written poetry, of course, but what Glen calls "shows." Times of being together, and being in production, not in the registers of a McDonald's production line, but in creative play. Literary engagement offers a space of open play, as many of the contributors to this Companion have shown: revisiting the givens of our disabled lives, and seeing ourselves in other narratives, frames, tones, and rhythms. Literature offers this to everybody with access to literary marketplaces, and it has been an invaluable tool in creating and maintaining disability culture's thin and constrained archive, allowing us, for instance, to hold on to perspectives of New Zealand novelist Janet Frame and her asylum experiences at Seacliff Hospital, just down the coast from our workshop. Through community workshops, literary production has become part of the cultural vocabulary of more and more disabled people. Literature can affirm and unsettle, and this walk on the edge is the core of our workshop.

I note that few of us choose to focus on memoir and overcoming narratives. Working outside the traditions of modernism, our poems link more to Raymond Williams' structures of feeling than David Mitchell and Sharon Snyder's narrative prosthesis or Michael Davidson's articulation of the cultural logic of disability in modernism, as evidenced in his chapter.[5] It is hard to un-cable from the stereotypes of disability, though – an analysis of our work might lean heavily on "longing for community" as a feature of disabled outsider status. We'd point critics to the fun we are having, and to the production sites of poetry, often rendered invisible in literary criticism. To understand how poetry works, *doing it* is invaluable – and we hope that the exercises described in this Afterword might be prompts for other (class)rooms, too. In the production of literature by contemporary students, disability and difference will likely emerge in slant and complex ways: in our workshop, we enact, in our own way, what G. Thomas Couser calls for in his chapter: "quality-of-life writing," or "testimony affirming the value of living with disability." There is a defiance in our work, a talking back. At least that is how I, in the dual role of workshop leader and critic, work toward a form of Eve Sedgwick's reparative criticism, toward pleasure, hope, unknown futures.[6] In this case, it means a criticism and a practice that aligns its work in respect with indigenous structures of feeling, connecting ourselves with ancestors and land, without forgetting personal, cultural, colonial, and biopolitical pain and trauma. As Alison Kafer and Eunjung Kim make clear in their chapter in this volume, "intersectional analysis can allow us to critique multiple categories without taxonomizing or stabilizing them." No stability: we live in balances, leaning, learning, thinking.

It all remains tricky, and at all times, most disabled cultural producers are aware of the joker role we play, when we sport and have fun in public places, or when "disability," "literature," and "Cambridge" come together, companionably. Things change. At various points in the New Zealand workshop, we had to dig Glen's chair out of the soft earth, and the gouge marks remain (until the next rain). Aotearoa's park structures do not take wheeled use into account, and loose gravel is everywhere, hindering our movement. If you wish to walk barefoot, connect yourself to earth, the gravel isn't helping. We can look at the cultural shape of how "access" is conceived here, and see how cultural narratives shape land access, and with that, our creative access. Land, bodyminds, access, kōrero (stories), histories, and rhythms: it all shapes itself into form. Disability literary production: we are here, we leave traces.

NOTES

1. Petra Kuppers, *Studying Disability Arts and Culture: An Introduction* (Harmondsworth: Palgrave, 2014).
2. Petra Kuppers, "Trans-ing: Disability Poetry at the Confluence," *TSQ: Transgender Studies Quarterly*, 1.4 (2014), pp. 605–13.
3. Margaret A. Bawaajimo Noodin, *A Dialect of Dreams in Anishinaabe Language and Literature* (East Lansing: Michigan State University Press, 2014).
4. Karen Nakamura, *A Disability of the Soul: An Ethnography of Schizophrenia and Mental Illness in Contemporary Japan* (Ithaca, NY: Cornell University Press, 2013).
5. David T. Mitchell and Sharon L. Snyder, *Narrative Prosthesis: Disability and the Dependencies of Discourse* (Ann Arbor: University of Michigan Press, 2000).
6. Eve Kosofsky Sedgwick, *Touching Feeling: Affect, Pedagogy, Performativity* (Durham, NC: Duke University Press, 2003).

RECOMMENDED READING

Allan, Kathryn (ed.), *Disability in Science Fiction: Representations of Technology as Cure* (Basingstoke: Palgrave Macmillan, 2013).

Antebi, Susan, *Carnal Inscriptions: Spanish American Narratives of Corporeal Difference and Disability* (London: Palgrave Macmillan, 2009).

Baldys, Emily M., "Disabled Sexuality, Incorporated," *Journal of Literary and Cultural Disability Studies*, 6.2 (2012), 125–41.

Barker, Clare, "Disability and the Postcolonial Novel," in *The Cambridge Companion to the Postcolonial Novel*, ed. by Ato Quayson (Cambridge: Cambridge University Press, 2015), pp. 99–115.

Postcolonial Fiction and Disability: Exceptional Children, Metaphor, and Materiality (Basingstoke: Palgrave Macmillan, 2011).

Barker, Clare, and Stuart Murray (eds.), "Disabling Postcolonialism," special issue of *Journal of Literary and Cultural Disability Studies*, 4.3 (2010).

"Disabling Postcolonialism: Global Disability Cultures and Democratic Criticism," in *The Disability Studies Reader*, 4th edn., ed. by Lennard J. Davis (New York and London: Routledge, 2013), pp. 61–73.

Bar-Yosef, Eitan, "The 'Deaf Traveller', the 'Blind Traveller', and the Constructions of Disability in Nineteenth-Century Travel Writing," *Victorian Review*, 35.2 (2009), 133–54.

Bell, Chris (ed.), *Blackness and Disability: Critical Examinations and Cultural Interventions* (East Lansing: Michigan State University Press, 2011).

"Introducing White Disability Studies: A Modest Proposal," in *The Disability Studies Reader*, 2nd edn., ed. by Lennard J. Davis (New York: Routledge, 2006), pp. 275–82.

Bolaki, Stella, and Chris Gair (eds.), "Disability and the American Counterculture," special issue of *Journal of Literary and Cultural Disability Studies*, 9.2 (2015).

Bolt, David, *The Metanarrative of Blindness: A Re-Reading of Twentieth-Century Anglophone Writing* (Ann Arbor: University of Michigan Press, 2013).

Bolt, David, and Claire Penketh (eds.), *Disability, Avoidance and the Academy: Challenging Resistance* (Abingdon and New York: Routledge, 2016).

Bolt, David, Julia Miele Rodas, and Elizabeth Donaldson (eds.), *The Madwoman and the Blindman:* Jane Eyre, *Discourse, Disability* (Columbus: Ohio State University Press, 2012).

Bourrier, Karen, *The Measure of Manliness: Disability and Masculinity in the Mid-Victorian Novel* (Ann Arbor: University of Michigan Press, 2015).

Bradshaw, Michael (ed.), *Disabling Romanticism: Body, Mind, and Text* (Basingstoke: Palgrave Macmillan, 2016).

Bragg, Lois, *Oedipus Borealis: The Aberrant Body in Old Icelandic Myth and Saga* (Madison, NJ: Fairleigh Dickinson University Press, 2004).

Brueggemann, Brenda Jo, and James A. Fredal, "Studying Disability Rhetorically," in *Disability Discourse*, ed. by Mairian Corker and Sally French (Philadelphia, PA: Open University Press, 1999), pp. 129–35.

Burke, Lucy (ed.), "The Representation of Cognitive Impairment," special issue of *Journal of Literary and Cultural Disability Studies*, 2.1 (2008).

Campbell, Fiona Kumari, *Contours of Ableism: The Production of Disability and Abledness* (London: Palgrave Macmillan, 2009).

Chen, Mel Y., *Animacies: Biopolitics, Racial Mattering, and Queer Affect* (Durham, NC: Duke University Press, 2012).

Cheyne, Ria, "Disability Studies Reads the Romance," *Journal of Literary and Cultural Disability Studies*, 7.1 (2013), 37–52.

(ed.), "Popular Genres and Disability Representation," special issue of *Journal of Literary and Cultural Disability Studies*, 6.2 (2012).

"'She Was Born a Thing': Disability, the Cyborg and the Posthuman in Anne McCaffrey's *The Ship Who Sang*," *Journal of Modern Literature*, 36.3 (2013), 138–56.

Cho, Sumi, Kimberlé Williams Crenshaw, and Leslie McCall (eds.), "Intersectionality: Theorizing Power, Empowering Theory," special issue of *Signs: Journal of Women in Culture and Society*, 38.4 (2013).

Clare, Eli, *Exile and Pride: Disability, Queerness, and Liberation* (Boston: South End Press, 1999).

Coogan, Tom, and Rebecca Mallett (eds.), "Disability, Humour, and Comedy," special issue of *Journal of Literary and Cultural Disability Studies*, 7.3 (2013).

Couser, G. Thomas (ed.), "Disability and Life Writing," special issue of *Journal of Literary and Cultural Disability Studies*, 5.3 (2011).

"Quality-of-Life Writing: Illness, Disability, and Representation," in Miriam Fuchs and Craig Howes (eds.), *Teaching Life Writing Texts* (New York: Modern Language Association, 2008), pp. 350–58.

Recovering Bodies: Illness, Disability, and Life Writing (Madison: University of Wisconsin Press, 1997).

Signifying Bodies: Disability in Contemporary Life Writing (Ann Arbor: University of Michigan Press, 2009).

Vulnerable Subjects: Ethics and Life Writing (Ithaca, NY: Cornell University Press, 2004).

Craps, Stef, *Postcolonial Witnessing: Trauma Out of Bounds* (Basingstoke: Palgrave Macmillan, 2013).

Daston, Lorraine, and Katharine Park, *Wonders and the Order of Nature, 1150–1750* (New York and Cambridge, MA: Zone Books, 1998).

Davidson, Iain F. W. K., Gary Woodill, and Elizabeth Bredberg, "Images of Disability in 19th Century British Children's Literature," *Disability and Society*, 9.1 (1994), 33–46.

Davidson, Michael, *Concerto for the Left Hand: Disability and the Defamiliar Body* (Ann Arbor: University of Michigan Press, 2008).

(ed.), "Disability and the Dialectic of Dependency," special issue of *Journal of Literary and Cultural Disability Studies*, 1.2 (2007).

Davies, Jeremy, *Bodily Pain in Romantic Literature* (London and New York: Routledge, 2014).

Davis, Lennard J., *Bending over Backwards: Disability, Dismodernism, and Other Difficult Positions* (New York and London: New York University Press, 2002).

Enforcing Normalcy: Disability, Deafness, and the Body (London: Verso, 1995).

(ed.), *The Disability Studies Reader*, 5th edn. (New York and London: Routledge, 2017).

The End of Normal: Identity in a Biocultural Era (Ann Arbor: University of Michigan Press, 2013).

Deutsch, Helen, and Felicity Nussbaum (eds.), *Defects: Engendering the Modern Body* (Ann Arbor: University of Michigan Press, 2000).

Dickie, Simon, *Cruelty and Laughter: Forgotten Comic Literature and the Unsentimental Eighteenth Century* (Chicago, IL: University of Chicago Press, 2011).

Dolmage, Jay, *Disability Rhetoric* (Syracuse, NY: Syracuse University Press, 2014).

Donaldson, Elizabeth J., "The Corpus of the Madwoman: Toward a Feminist Disability Studies Theory of Embodiment and Mental Illness," *NWSA Journal*, 14.3 (2002), 99–119.

Donaldson, Elizabeth J., and Catherine Prendergast (eds.), "Disability and Emotion," special issue of *Journal of Literary and Cultural Disability Studies*, 5.2 (2011).

Dotson, Kristie (ed.), "Interstices: Inheriting Women of Color Feminist Philosophy," special issue of *Hypatia: A Journal of Feminist Philosophy*, 29.1 (2014).

Elfenbein, Andrew, "Editor's Introduction. Byron and Disability," *European Romantic Review*, 12.3 (2001), 247–48.

Erevelles, Nirmala, *Disability and Difference in Global Contexts* (New York: Palgrave Macmillan, 2011).

"Thinking with Disability Studies," *Disability Studies Quarterly*, 34.2 (2014), n. pag., http://dsq-sds.org/article/view/4248/3587.

Erevelles, Nirmala, and Andrea Minear, "Unspeakable Offenses: Untangling Race and Disability in Discourses of Intersectionality," *Journal of Literary and Cultural Disability Studies*, 4.2 (2010), 127–45.

Esmail, Jennifer, *Reading Victorian Deafness: Signs and Sounds in Victorian Literature and Culture* (Athens: Ohio University Press, 2013).

Eyler, Joshua (ed.), *Disability in the Middle Ages: Reconsiderations and Reverberations* (Farnham: Ashgate, 2010).

Ferris, Jim (ed.), "Disability and/as Poetry," special issue of *Journal of Literary and Cultural Disability Studies*, 1.1 (2007).

Fine, Michelle, and Adrienne Asch (eds.), *Women with Disabilities: Essays in Psychology, Culture, and Politics* (Philadelphia, PA: Temple University Press, 1988).

Frank, Arthur, *The Wounded Storyteller: Body, Illness, and Ethics* (Chicago, IL: University of Chicago Press, 1995).

Frawley, Maria, *Invalidism and Identity in Nineteenth-Century Britain* (Chicago, IL: University of Chicago Press, 2004).

Gabbard, Christopher, "Disability Studies and the British Long Eighteenth Century," *Literature Compass*, 8.2 (2011), 80–94.
Garland-Thomson, Rosemarie, "Byron and the New Disability Studies: A Response," *European Romantic Review*, 12 (2001), 321–27.
Extraordinary Bodies: Figuring Physical Disability in American Culture and Literature (New York: Columbia University Press, 1997).
"Feminist Disability Studies," *Signs*, 30.2 (2005), 1557–87.
"Integrating Disability, Transforming Feminist Theory," in *Feminisms Redux: An Anthology of Literary Theory and Criticism*, ed. by Robyn Warhol-Down and Diane Price Herndl (2002; New Brunswick, NJ: Rutgers University Press, 2009), pp. 487–513.
Staring: How We Look (Oxford and New York: Oxford University Press, 2009).
"The Case for Conserving Disability," *Journal of Bioethical Inquiry*, 9.3 (2012), 339–55.
Gitter, Elisabeth G., "The Blind Daughter in Charles Dickens's *Cricket on the Hearth*," *Studies in English Literature*, 39 (1999), 675–89.
Goffman, Erving, *Stigma: Notes on the Management of Spoiled Identity* (Englewood Cliffs, NJ: Prentice-Hall, 1963).
Goodey, C. F., *A History of Intelligence and "Intellectual Disability": The Shaping of Psychology in Early Modern Europe* (Farnham: Ashgate, 2011).
Goodley, Dan, *Disability Studies: An Interdisciplinary Introduction* (London: SAGE, 2011).
Hacking, Ian, *Mad Travelers: Reflections on the Reality of Transient Mental Illnesses* (Cambridge, MA: Harvard University Press, 1998).
Hafferty, Frederic W., and Susan Foster, "Decontextualizing Disability in the Crime-Mystery Genre: The Case of the Invisible Handicap," *Disability and Society*, 9.2 (1994), 185–206.
Hall, Alice, *Disability and Modern Fiction: Faulkner, Morrison, Coetzee and the Nobel Prize for Literature* (Basingstoke: Palgrave Macmillan, 2012).
Literature and Disability (New York and London: Routledge, 2016).
Hall, Kim Q. (ed.), *Feminist Disability Studies* (Bloomington: Indiana University Press, 2011).
Heetderks, Angela, "'Better a Witty Fool than a Foolish Wit': Song, Fooling, and Intellectual Disability in Shakespearean Drama," in *Gender and Song in Early Modern England*, ed. by Leslie C. Dunn and Katherine R. Larson (Farnham: Ashgate, 2014), pp. 63–75.
Hobgood, Allison, "Caesar Hath the Falling Sickness: The Legibility of Early Modern Disability in Shakespearean Drama," *Disability Studies Quarterly*, 29.4 (2009), n. pag., http://dsq-sds.org/article/view/993/1184.
Hobgood, Allison, and David Houston Wood (eds.), "Disabled Shakespeares," special issue of *Disability Studies Quarterly*, 29.4 (2009).
(eds.), *Recovering Disability in Early Modern England* (Columbus: Ohio State University Press, 2013).
Hoeniger, F. D., *Medicine and Shakespeare in the English Renaissance* (Newark, NJ: University of Delaware Press, 1992).
Holmes, Martha Stoddard, *Fictions of Affliction: Physical Disability in Victorian Culture* (Ann Arbor: University of Michigan Press, 2004).

"Victorian Fictions of Interdependency: Gaskell, Craik, and Yonge," *Journal of Literary and Cultural Disability Studies*, 1.2 (2007), 29–41.

Hoppenstand, Gary, and Ray B. Browne, "'I'd Kiss You Sweetheart, But My Lips Are Missing': The Defective Detective in the Pulps," in *The Defective Detective in the Pulps*, ed. by Gary Hoppenstand and Ray B. Browne (Bowling Green, OH: Bowling Green State University Popular Press, 1983), pp. 1–7.

Imbracsio, Nicola M., "Stage Hands: Shakespeare's *Titus Andronicus* and the Agency of the Disabled Body in Text and Performance," *Journal of Literary and Cultural Disability Studies*, 6.3 (2012), 291–306.

Iyengar, Sujata (ed.), *Disability, Health, and Happiness in the Shakespearean Body* (London: Routledge, 2015).

James, Jennifer, and Cynthia Wu (eds.), "Race, Ethnicity, Disability, and Literature," special issue of *MELUS: Multi-Ethnic Literature of the United States*, 31.3 (2006).

Jarman, Michelle, and Alison Kafer, "Growing Disability Studies: Politics of Access, Politics of Collaboration," *Disability Studies Quarterly*, 34.2 (2014), n. pag., http://dsq-sds.org/article/view/4286/3585.

Jarman, Michelle, Leila Monaghan, and Alison Quaggin Harkin (eds.), *Barriers and Belonging: Personal Narratives of Disability* (Philadelphia, PA: Temple University Press, 2017).

Johnson, Merri Lisa, and Robert McRuer (eds.), "Cripistemologies," special issues of *Journal of Literary and Cultural Disability Studies*, 8.2–3 (2014).

Johnston, Kirsty, *Disability Theatre and Modern Drama: Recasting Modernism* (London: Bloomsbury, 2016).

Joshua, Essaka, "'Blind Vacancy': Sighted Culture and Voyeuristic Historiography in Mary Shelley's *Frankenstein*," *European Romantic Review*, 22.1 (2011), 49–69.

Kafer, Alison, *Feminist, Queer, Crip* (Bloomington and Indianapolis: Indiana University Press, 2013).

Kim, Eunjung, *Curative Violence: Rehabilitating Disability, Gender, and Sexuality in Modern Korea* (Durham, NC: Duke University Press, 2017).

Kleege, Georgina (ed.), "Blindness and Literature," special issue of *Journal of Literary and Cultural Disability Studies*, 3.2 (2009).

Kleinman, Arthur, *The Illness Narratives: Suffering, Healing, and the Human Condition* (New York: Basic Books, 1988).

Kuppers, Petra, *Disability and Contemporary Performance: Bodies on Edge* (London: Routledge, 2003).

Studying Disability Arts and Culture: An Introduction (Basingstoke: Palgrave Macmillan, 2014).

Kuppers, Petra, and James Overboe (eds.), "Deleuze, Disability, and Difference," special issue of *Journal of Literary and Cultural Disability Studies*, 3.3 (2009).

LaCom, Cindy, "'It Is More Than Lame': Infirmity and Maternity in Victorian Fiction," in *The Body and Physical Difference*, ed. by David T. Mitchell and Sharon L. Snyder (Ann Arbor: University of Michigan Press, 1997), pp. 189–201.

Mallett, Rebecca, and Katherine Runswick-Cole, *Approaching Disability: Critical Issues and Perspectives* (London: Routledge, 2014).

Marchbanks, Paul, "From Caricature to Character: The Intellectually Disabled in Dickens's Novels," three-part series, *Dickens Quarterly*, 23.1–3 (2006), 3–14, 67–84, 169–80.

McCall, Leslie, "The Complexity of Intersectionality," *Signs: Journal of Women in Culture and Society*, 30.3 (2005), 1771–800.
McDonagh, Patrick, *Idiocy: A Cultural History* (Liverpool: Liverpool University Press, 2008).
McRuer, Robert, *Crip Theory: Cultural Signs of Queerness and Disability* (New York and London: New York University Press, 2006).
"Critical Investments: AIDS, Christopher Reeve, and Queer/Disability Studies," *Journal of Medical Humanities*, 23.3–4 (2002), 221–37.
"Fuck the Disabled: The Prequel," in *Shakesqueer: A Queer Companion to the Complete Works of Shakespeare*, ed. by Madhavi Menon (Durham, NC: Duke University Press, 2011), pp. 294–301.
"Normal," in *Keywords for American Cultural Studies*, 2nd edn., ed. by Bruce Burgett and Glenn Hendler (New York: New York University Press, 2014), pp. 184–97.
McRuer, Robert, and Anna Mollow (eds.), *Sex and Disability* (Durham, NC: Duke University Press, 2012).
McRuer, Robert, and Abby L. Wilkerson (eds.), "Desiring Disability: Queer Theory Meets Disability Studies," special issue of *GLQ: A Journal of Lesbian and Gay Studies*, 9.1–2 (2003).
Metzler, Irina, *Disability in Medieval Europe: Thinking about Physical Impairment during the High Middle Ages, c. 1100–1400* (London: Routledge, 2006).
Fools and Idiots? Intellectual Disability in the Middle Ages (Manchester: Manchester University Press, 2016).
A Social History of Disability in the Middle Ages: Cultural Considerations of Physical Impairment (London: Routledge, 2015).
Mills, China, *Decolonizing Global Mental Health: The Psychiatrization of the Majority World* (New York: Routledge, 2013).
Minich, Julie Avril, *Accessible Citizenships: Disability, Nation, and the Cultural Politics of Greater Mexico* (Philadelphia, PA: Temple University Press, 2015).
Mintz, Susannah B., *Hurt and Pain: Literature and the Suffering Body* (London and New York: Bloomsbury, 2013).
Mitchell, David T., and Sharon L. Snyder (eds.), *The Body and Physical Difference: Discourses of Disability* (Ann Arbor: University of Michigan Press, 1997).
Narrative Prosthesis: Disability and the Dependencies of Discourse (Ann Arbor: University of Michigan Press, 2000).
"Representation and Its Discontents: The Uneasy Home of Disability in Literature and Film," in *Handbook of Disability Studies*, ed. by Gary L. Albrecht, Katherine D. Seelman, and Michael Bury (Thousand Oaks, CA: Sage, 2011), pp. 195–218.
"Representations of Disability, History of," in *Encyclopedia of Disability*, vol. 3, ed. by Gary L. Albrecht, 5 vols. (Thousand Oaks, CA: Sage, 2006), pp. 1382–94.
Mitchell, David T., with Sharon L. Snyder, *The Biopolitics of Disability: Neoliberalism, Ablenationalism, and Peripheral Embodiment* (Ann Arbor: University of Michigan Press, 2015).
Moody, Nickianne, "Methodological Agendas: Disability-Informed Criticism and the Incidental Representation of Autism in Popular Fiction," *Popular Narrative Media*, 1.1 (2008), 25–41.

Mossman, Mark, *Disability, Representation and the Body in Irish Writing: 1800–1922* (Basingstoke: Palgrave Macmillan, 2009).
Mossman, Mark, and Martha Stoddard Holmes (eds.), "Critical Transformations: Disability and the Body in Nineteenth-Century Britain," special issue of *Nineteenth-Century Gender Studies*, 4.2 (2008).
"Disability in Victorian Sensation Fiction," in *Blackwell Companion to Sensation Fiction*, ed. by Pamela Gilbert (London: Blackwell, 2011), pp. 493–506.
Mounsey, Chris (ed.), *The Idea of Disability in the Eighteenth Century* (Lewisburg, PA: Bucknell University Press, 2014).
Murray, Stuart, *Autism* (London: Routledge, 2012).
"From Virginia's Sister to Friday's Silence: Presence, Metaphor, and the Persistence of Disability in Contemporary Writing," *Journal of Literary and Cultural Disability Studies*, 6.3 (2012), 241–58.
"Neurotecs: Detectives, Disability and Cognitive Exceptionality in Contemporary Fiction," in *Constructing Crime: Discourse and Cultural Representations of Crime and "Deviance,"* ed. by Christiana Gregoriou (Basingstoke: Palgrave Macmillan, 2012), pp. 177–89.
Representing Autism: Culture, Narrative, Fascination (Liverpool: Liverpool University Press, 2008).
Nash, Jennifer, "Re-Thinking Intersectionality," *Feminist Review*, 89.1 (2008), 1–15.
Nelson, Jennifer L., and Bradley S. Berens, "Spoken Daggers, Deaf Ears, and Silent Mouths: Fantasies of Deafness in Early Modern England," in *The Disability Studies Reader*, 1st edn., ed. by Lennard J. Davis (New York: Routledge, 1997), pp. 52–74.
Newman, Sara, "Disability and Life Writing: Reports from the Nineteenth-Century Asylum," *Journal of Literary and Cultural Disability Studies*, 5.3 (2011), 261–78.
Nussbaum, Felicity, *The Limits of the Human: Fictions of Anomaly, Race, and Gender in the Long Eighteenth Century* (Cambridge: Cambridge University Press, 2003).
Osteen, Mark (ed.), *Autism and Representation* (London: Routledge, 2008).
Parekh, Pushpa (ed.), "Intersecting Gender and Disability Perspectives in Rethinking Postcolonial Identities," special issue of *Wagadu: A Journal of Transnational Women's and Gender Studies*, 4 (2007).
Paster, Gail Kern, *The Body Embarrassed: Drama and the Disciplines of Shame in Early Modern England* (Ithaca, NY: Cornell University Press, 1993).
Paster, Gail Kern, Katherine Rowe, and Mary Floyd-Wilson (eds.), *Reading the Early Modern Passions: Essays in the Cultural History of Emotion* (Philadelphia: University of Pennsylvania Press, 2004).
Pearman, Tory Vandeventer, *Women and Disability in Medieval Literature* (New York: Palgrave Macmillan, 2010).
Price, Margaret, *Mad at School: Rhetorics of Mental Disability and Academic Life* (Ann Arbor: University of Michigan Press, 2011).
Puar, Jasbir K., "'I Would Rather Be a Cyborg Than a Goddess': Becoming-Intersectional in Assemblage Theory," *philoSOPHIA*, 2.1 (2012), 49–66.
"The Cost of Getting Better: Ability and Debility," in *The Disability Studies Reader*, 4th edn., ed. by Lennard J. Davis (New York and London: Routledge, 2013), pp. 177–84.

Quayson, Ato, *Aesthetic Nervousness: Disability and the Crisis of Representation* (New York: Columbia University Press, 2007).
"Looking Awry: Tropes of Disability in Postcolonial Writing," in *Relocating Postcolonialism*, ed. by David Theo Goldberg and Ato Quayson (Oxford: Blackwell, 2002), pp. 217–30.
Ray, Sarah Jaquette, *The Ecological Other: Environmental Exclusion in American Culture* (Tucson: University of Arizona Press, 2013).
Richardson, Kristina, *Difference and Disability in the Medieval Islamic World: Blighted Bodies* (Edinburgh: Edinburgh University Press, 2012).
Rose, Martha L., *The Staff of Oedipus: Transforming Disability in Ancient Greece* (Ann Arbor: University of Michigan Press, 2003).
Roth, Marco, "The Rise of the Neuronovel," *N+1*, 8 (2009), https://nplusonemag.com/issue-8/essays/the-rise-of-the-neuronovel/.
Row-Heyveld, Lindsey, "The Lying'st Knave in Christendom: The Development of Disability in the False Miracle of St. Alban's," *Disability Studies Quarterly*, 29.4 (2009), n. pag., http://dsq-sds.org/article/view/994/1178.
Samuels, Ellen, "Critical Divides: Judith Butler's Body Theory and the Question of Disability," *NWSA Journal*, 14.3 (2002), 58–76.
Fantasies of Identification: Disability, Gender, Race (New York: New York University Press, 2014).
Sanchez, Rebecca, *Deafening Modernism: Embodied Language and Visual Poetics in American Literature* (New York: New York University Press, 2015).
Sandahl, Carrie, "Queering the Crip or Cripping the Queer?: Intersections of Queer and Crip Identities in Solo Autobiographical Performance," *GLQ: A Journal of Lesbian and Gay Studies*, 9.1–2 (2003), 25–56.
Sandahl, Carrie, and Philip Auslander (eds.), *Bodies in Commotion: Disability and Performance* (Ann Arbor: University of Michigan Press, 2005).
Schaap Williams, Katherine, "Enabling Richard: The Rhetoric of Disability in *Richard III*," *Disability Studies Quarterly*, 29.4 (2009), n. pag., http://dsq-sds.org/article/view/997/1181.
"'More Legs than Nature Gave Thee': Performing the Cripple in *The Fair Maid of the Exchange*," *ELH*, 82.2 (2015), 491–519.
"Performing Disability and Theorizing Deformity," *English Studies*, 94.7 (2013), 757–72.
Schalk, Sami, "Metaphorically Speaking: Ableist Metaphors in Feminist Writing," *Disability Studies Quarterly*, 33.4 (2013), n. pag., http://dsq-sds.org/article/view/3874/3410.
"Reevaluating the Supercrip," *Journal of Literary and Cultural Disability Studies*, 10.1 (2016), 71–86.
Schweik, Susan M., *The Ugly Laws: Disability in Public* (New York: New York University Press, 2009).
Senier, Siobhan, and Clare Barker (eds.), "Disability and Indigeneity," special issue of *Journal of Literary and Cultural Disability Studies*, 7.2 (2013).
Shakespeare, Tom, *Disability Rights and Wrongs* (London: Routledge, 2006).
Disability Rights and Wrongs Revisited (London: Routledge, 2013).
"The Social Model of Disability," in *The Disability Studies Reader*, 4th edn., ed. by Lennard J. Davis (New York and London: Routledge, 2013), pp. 214–21.

Sherry, Mark, "(Post)colonising Disability," *Wagadu: A Journal of Transnational Women's and Gender Studies*, 4 (2007), 10–22.
Shildrick, Margrit, "The Disabled Body, Genealogy and Undecidability," *Cultural Studies*, 19.6 (2005), 755–70.
Siebers, Tobin, *Disability Aesthetics* (Ann Arbor: University of Michigan Press, 2010).
Disability Theory (Ann Arbor: University of Michigan Press, 2008).
Singer, Julie, "Disability and the Social Body," *postmedieval*, 3.2 (2012), 135–36.
Smith, Bonnie G., and Beth Hutchinson (eds.), *Gendering Disability* (New Brunswick, NJ: Rutgers University Press, 2004).
Snyder, Sharon L., "Infinities of Forms: Disability Figures in Artistic Traditions," in *Disability Studies: Enabling the Humanities*, ed. by Sharon L. Snyder, Brenda Jo Brueggemann, and Rosemarie Garland-Thomson (New York: Modern Language Association of America, 2002), pp. 173–96.
Snyder, Sharon L., and David T. Mitchell, "Ablenationalism and the Geo-Politics of Disability," special issue of *Journal of Literary and Cultural Disability Studies*, 4.2 (2010).
Cultural Locations of Disability (Chicago and London: University of Chicago Press, 2006).
Snyder, Sharon L., Brenda Jo Brueggemann, and Rosemarie Garland-Thomson (eds.), *Disability Studies: Enabling the Humanities* (New York: Modern Language Association of America, 2002).
Stiker, Henri-Jacques, *A History of Disability* (Ann Arbor: University of Michigan Press, 2000).
Stirling, Jeannette, *Representing Epilepsy: Myth and Matter* (Liverpool: Liverpool University Press, 2010).
Stoddard Holmes, Martha, *Fictions of Affliction: Physical Disability in Victorian Culture* (Ann Arbor: University of Michigan Press, 2004).
"Victorian Fictions of Interdependency: Gaskell, Craik, and Yonge," *Journal of Literary and Cultural Disability Studies*, 1.2 (2007), 29–41.
St. Pierre, Joshua, "The Construction of the Disabled Speaker: Locating Stuttering in Disability Studies," *Canadian Journal of Disability Studies*, 1.3 (2012), 1–21.
Thiher, Allen, *Revels in Madness: Insanity in Medicine and Literature* (Ann Arbor: University of Michigan Press, 2000).
Todd, Dennis, *Imagining Monsters: Miscreations of the Self in Eighteenth-Century England* (Chicago: University of Chicago Press, 1995).
Traub, Valerie, "The Nature of Norms in Early Modern England: Anatomy, Cartography, *King Lear*," *South Central Review*, 26.1–2 (2009), 42–81.
Tromp, Marlene (ed.), *Victorian "Freaks": The Social Context of Freakery in the Nineteenth Century* (Columbus: Ohio State University Press, 2008).
Turner, David M., *Disability in Eighteenth-Century England: Imagining Physical Impairment* (New York: Routledge, 2012).
Turner, David M., and Kevin Stagg (eds.), *Social Histories of Disability and Deformity* (New York: Routledge, 2006).
Turner, Wendy J., and Tory Vandeventer Pearman (eds.), *The Treatment of Disabled Persons in Medieval Europe: Examining Disability in the Historical, Legal, Literary, Medical, and Religious Discourses of the Middle Ages* (Lewiston, NY: Edwin Mellen Press, 2010).

Valente, Joseph, "Modernism and Cognitive Disability: A Genealogy," in *A Handbook of Modernism Studies*, ed. by Jean-Michel Rabaté (Chichester: Wiley-Blackwell, 2013), pp. 379–98.

Vidali, Amy, "Seeing What We Know: Disability and Theories of Metaphor," *Journal of Literary and Cultural Disability Studies*, 4.1 (2010), 33–54.

Vrettos, Athena, *Somatic Fictions: Imagining Illness in Victorian Culture* (Stanford, CA: Stanford University Press, 1995).

Wendell, Susan, *The Rejected Body: Feminist Philosophical Reflections on Disability* (New York: Routledge, 1996).

Wheatley, Edward, *Stumbling Blocks before the Blind: Medieval Constructions of a Disability* (Ann Arbor: University of Michigan Press, 2010).

Wilson, Philip K., "Eighteenth-Century 'Monsters' and Nineteenth-Century 'Freaks': Reading the Maternally Marked Child," *Literature and Medicine*, 21.3 (2002), 1–25.

Wood, Mary Elene, *The Writing on the Wall: Women's Autobiography and the Asylum* (Urbana: University of Illinois Press, 1994).

Wu, Cynthia, *Chang and Eng Reconnected: The Original Siamese Twins in American Culture* (Philadelphia, PA: Temple University Press, 2012).

Yergeau, Melanie, and John Duffy (eds.), "Disability and Rhetoric," special issue of *Disability Studies Quarterly*, 31.3 (2011), n. pag., http://dsq-sds.org/issue/view/84.

Youngquist, Paul, *Monstrosities: Bodies and British Romanticism* (Minneapolis: University of Minnesota Press, 2003).

Zola, Irving Kenneth, "'Any Distinguishing Features?' – The Portrayal of Disability in the Crime-Mystery Genre," *Policy Studies Journal*, 15.3 (1987), 485–513.

INDEX

Page numbers given in italics denote illustrations.
Notes are given as [page number]n[note number].
Works suffixed with 'A' or 'The' are sorted by the initial letter of the subsequent word.

Cambridge Companions to ...

AUTHORS

Edward Albee edited by Stephen J. Bottoms
Margaret Atwood edited by Coral Ann Howells
W. H. Auden edited by Stan Smith
Jane Austen edited by Edward Copeland and Juliet McMaster (second edition)
Beckett edited by John Pilling
Bede edited by Scott DeGregorio
Aphra Behn edited by Derek Hughes and Janet Todd
Walter Benjamin edited by David S. Ferris
William Blake edited by Morris Eaves
Boccaccio edited by Guyda Armstrong, Rhiannon Daniels, and Stephen J. Milner
Jorge Luis Borges edited by Edwin Williamson
Brecht edited by Peter Thomson and Glendyr Sacks (second edition)
The Brontës edited by Heather Glen
Bunyan edited by Anne Dunan-Page
Frances Burney edited by Peter Sabor
Byron edited by Drummond Bone
Albert Camus edited by Edward J. Hughes
Willa Cather edited by Marilee Lindemann
Cervantes edited by Anthony J. Cascardi
Chaucer edited by Piero Boitani and Jill Mann (second edition)
Chekhov edited by Vera Gottlieb and Paul Allain
Kate Chopin edited by Janet Beer
Caryl Churchill edited by Elaine Aston and Elin Diamond
Cicero edited by Catherine Steel
Coleridge edited by Lucy Newlyn
Wilkie Collins edited by Jenny Bourne Taylor
Joseph Conrad edited by J. H. Stape
H. D. edited by Nephie J. Christodoulides and Polina Mackay
Dante edited by Rachel Jacoff (second edition)
Daniel Defoe edited by John Richetti
Don DeLillo edited by John N. Duvall
Charles Dickens edited by John O. Jordan
Emily Dickinson edited by Wendy Martin
John Donne edited by Achsah Guibbory
Dostoevskii edited by W. J. Leatherbarrow
Theodore Dreiser edited by Leonard Cassuto and Claire Virginia Eby
John Dryden edited by Steven N. Zwicker
W. E. B. Du Bois edited by Shamoon Zamir
George Eliot edited by George Levine
T. S. Eliot edited by A. David Moody
Ralph Ellison edited by Ross Posnock
Ralph Waldo Emerson edited by Joel Porte and Saundra Morris
William Faulkner edited by Philip M. Weinstein
Henry Fielding edited by Claude Rawson
F. Scott Fitzgerald edited by Ruth Prigozy
Flaubert edited by Timothy Unwin
E. M. Forster edited by David Bradshaw
Benjamin Franklin edited by Carla Mulford
Brian Friel edited by Anthony Roche
Robert Frost edited by Robert Faggen
Gabriel García Márquez edited by Philip Swanson
Elizabeth Gaskell edited by Jill L. Matus
Goethe edited by Lesley Sharpe
Günter Grass edited by Stuart Taberner
Thomas Hardy edited by Dale Kramer
David Hare edited by Richard Boon
Nathaniel Hawthorne edited by Richard Millington
Seamus Heaney edited by Bernard O'Donoghue
Ernest Hemingway edited by Scott Donaldson
Homer edited by Robert Fowler
Horace edited by Stephen Harrison
Ted Hughes edited by Terry Gifford
Ibsen edited by James McFarlane
Henry James edited by Jonathan Freedman
Samuel Johnson edited by Greg Clingham
Ben Jonson edited by Richard Harp and Stanley Stewart
James Joyce edited by Derek Attridge (second edition)
Kafka edited by Julian Preece
Keats edited by Susan J. Wolfson

Rudyard Kipling edited by Howard J. Booth
Lacan edited by Jean-Michel Rabaté
D. H. Lawrence edited by Anne Fernihough
Primo Levi edited by Robert Gordon
Lucretius edited by Stuart Gillespie and Philip Hardie
Machiavelli edited by John M. Najemy
David Mamet edited by Christopher Bigsby
Thomas Mann edited by Ritchie Robertson
Christopher Marlowe edited by Patrick Cheney
Andrew Marvell edited by Derek Hirst and Steven N. Zwicker
Herman Melville edited by Robert S. Levine
Arthur Miller edited by Christopher Bigsby (second edition)
Milton edited by Dennis Danielson (second edition)
Molière edited by David Bradby and Andrew Calder
Toni Morrison edited by Justine Tally
Alice Munro edited by David Staines
Nabokov edited by Julian W. Connolly
Eugene O'Neill edited by Michael Manheim
George Orwell edited by John Rodden
Ovid edited by Philip Hardie
Petrarch edited by Albert Russell Ascoli and Unn Falkeid
Harold Pinter edited by Peter Raby (second edition)
Sylvia Plath edited by Jo Gill
Edgar Allan Poe edited by Kevin J. Hayes
Alexander Pope edited by Pat Rogers
Ezra Pound edited by Ira B. Nadel
Proust edited by Richard Bales
Pushkin edited by Andrew Kahn
Rabelais edited by John O'Brien
Rilke edited by Karen Leeder and Robert Vilain
Philip Roth edited by Timothy Parrish
Salman Rushdie edited by Abdulrazak Gurnah
John Ruskin edited by Francis O'Gorman
Shakespeare edited by Margareta de Grazia and Stanley Wells (second edition)
Shakespearean Comedy edited by Alexander Leggatt
Shakespeare and Contemporary Dramatists edited by Ton Hoenselaars
Shakespeare and Popular Culture edited by Robert Shaughnessy
Shakespearean Tragedy edited by Claire McEachern (second edition)
Shakespeare on Film edited by Russell Jackson (second edition)
Shakespeare on Stage edited by Stanley Wells and Sarah Stanton
Shakespeare's First Folio edited by Emma Smith
Shakespeare's History Plays edited by Michael Hattaway
Shakespeare's Last Plays edited by Catherine M. S. Alexander
Shakespeare's Poetry edited by Patrick Cheney
George Bernard Shaw edited by Christopher Innes
Shelley edited by Timothy Morton
Mary Shelley edited by Esther Schor
Sam Shepard edited by Matthew C. Roudané
Spenser edited by Andrew Hadfield
Laurence Sterne edited by Thomas Keymer
Wallace Stevens edited by John N. Serio
Tom Stoppard edited by Katherine E. Kelly
Harriet Beecher Stowe edited by Cindy Weinstein
August Strindberg edited by Michael Robinson
Jonathan Swift edited by Christopher Fox
J. M. Synge edited by P. J. Mathews
Tacitus edited by A. J. Woodman
Henry David Thoreau edited by Joel Myerson
Tolstoy edited by Donna Tussing Orwin
Anthony Trollope edited by Carolyn Dever and Lisa Niles
Mark Twain edited by Forrest G. Robinson
John Updike edited by Stacey Olster
Mario Vargas Llosa edited by Efrain Kristal and John King
Virgil edited by Charles Martindale
Voltaire edited by Nicholas Cronk
Edith Wharton edited by Millicent Bell
Walt Whitman edited by Ezra Greenspan
Oscar Wilde edited by Peter Raby
Tennessee Williams edited by Matthew C. Roudané
August Wilson edited by Christopher Bigsby

Mary Wollstonecraft edited by Claudia L. Johnson

Virginia Woolf edited by Susan Sellers (second edition)

Wordsworth edited by Stephen Gill

Xenophon edited by Michael A. Flower

Zola edited by Brian Nelson

W. B. Yeats edited by Marjorie Howes and John Kelly

TOPICS

The Actress edited by Maggie B. Gale and John Stokes

The African American Novel edited by Maryemma Graham

The African American Slave Narrative edited by Audrey A. Fisch

The Cambridge Companion to Theatre Histor by David Wiles and Christine Dymkowski

African American Theatre by Harvey Young

Allegory edited by Rita Copeland and Peter Struck

American Crime Fiction edited by Catherine Ross Nickerson

American Modernism edited by Walter Kalaidjian

American Poetry since 1945 edited by Jennifer Ashton

American Realism and Naturalism edited by Donald Pizer

American Travel Writing edited by Alfred Bendixen and Judith Hamera

American Women Playwrights edited by Brenda Murphy

Ancient Rhetoric edited by Erik Gunderson

Arthurian Legend edited by Elizabeth Archibald and Ad Putter

Australian Literature edited by Elizabeth Webby

The Beats edited by Stephen Belletto

British Black and Asian Literature (1945–2010) edited by Deirdre Osborne

British Literature of the French Revolution edited by Pamela Clemit

British Romanticism edited by Stuart Curran (second edition)

British Romantic Poetry edited by James Chandler and Maureen N. McLane

British Theatre, 1730–1830 edited by Jane Moody and Daniel O'Quinn

Canadian Literature edited by Eva-Marie Kröller (second edition)

Children's Literature edited by M. O. Grenby and Andrea Immel

The Classic Russian Novel edited by Malcolm V. Jones and Robin Feuer Miller

Contemporary Irish Poetry edited by Matthew Campbell

Creative Writing edited by David Morley and Philip Neilsen

Crime Fiction edited by Martin Priestman

Early Modern Women's Writing edited by Laura Lunger Knoppers

The Eighteenth-Century Novel edited by John Richetti

Eighteenth-Century Poetry edited by John Sitter

Emma edited by Peter Sabor

English Literature, 1500–1600 edited by Arthur F. Kinney

English Literature, 1650–1740 edited by Steven N. Zwicker

English Literature, 1740–1830 edited by Thomas Keymer and Jon Mee

English Literature, 1830–1914 edited by Joanne Shattock

English Novelists edited by Adrian Poole

English Poetry, Donne to Marvell edited by Thomas N. Corns

English Poets edited by Claude Rawson

English Renaissance Drama edited by A. R. Braunmuller and Michael Hattaway (second edition)

English Renaissance Tragedy edited by Emma Smith and Garrett A. Sullivan Jr.

English Restoration Theatre edited by Deborah C. Payne Fisk

The Epic edited by Catherine Bates

Erotic Literature edited by Bradford Mudge

European Modernism edited by Pericles Lewis

European Novelists edited by Michael Bell

Fairy Tales edited by Maria Tatar

Fantasy Literature edited by Edward James and Farah Mendlesohn

Feminist Literary Theory edited by Ellen Rooney

Fiction in the Romantic Period edited by Richard Maxwell and Katie Trumpener

The Fin de Siècle edited by Gail Marshall

Frankenstein edited by Andrew Smith

The French Enlightenment edited by Daniel Brewer

French Literature edited by John D. Lyons

The French Novel: From 1800 to the Present edited by Timothy Unwin

Gay and Lesbian Writing edited by Hugh Stevens

German Romanticism edited by Nicholas Saul

Gothic Fiction edited by Jerrold E. Hogle

The Graphic Novel edited by Stephen Tabachnick

The Greek and Roman Novel edited by Tim Whitmarsh

Greek and Roman Theatre edited by Marianne McDonald and J. Michael Walton

Greek Comedy edited by Martin Revermann

Greek Lyric edited by Felix Budelmann

Greek Mythology edited by Roger D. Woodard

Greek Tragedy edited by P. E. Easterling

The Harlem Renaissance edited by George Hutchinson

The History of the Book edited by Leslie Howsam

The Irish Novel edited by John Wilson Foster

The Italian Novel edited by Peter Bondanella and Andrea Ciccarelli

The Italian Renaissance edited by Michael Wyatt

Jewish American Literature edited by Hana Wirth-Nesher and Michael P. Kramer

The Latin American Novel edited by Efraín Kristal

The Literature of the First World War edited by Vincent Sherry

The Literature of London edited by Lawrence Manley

The Literature of Los Angeles edited by Kevin R. McNamara

The Literature of New York edited by Cyrus Patell and Bryan Waterman

The Literature of Paris edited by Anna-Louise Milne

The Literature of World War II edited by Marina MacKay

Literature and Disability edited by Clare Barker and Stuart Murray

Literature on Screen edited by Deborah Cartmell and Imelda Whelehan

Medieval English Culture edited by Andrew Galloway

Medieval English Literature edited by Larry Scanlon

Medieval English Mysticism edited by Samuel Fanous and Vincent Gillespie

Medieval English Theatre edited by Richard Beadle and Alan J. Fletcher (second edition)

Medieval French Literature edited by Simon Gaunt and Sarah Kay

Medieval Romance edited by Roberta L. Krueger

Medieval Women's Writing edited by Carolyn Dinshaw and David Wallace

Modern American Culture edited by Christopher Bigsby

Modern British Women Playwrights edited by Elaine Aston and Janelle Reinelt

Modern French Culture edited by Nicholas Hewitt

Modern German Culture edited by Eva Kolinsky and Wilfried van der Will

The Modern German Novel edited by Graham Bartram

The Modern Gothic edited by Jerrold E. Hogle

Modern Irish Culture edited by Joe Cleary and Claire Connolly

Modern Italian Culture edited by Zygmunt G. Baranski and Rebecca J. West

Modern Latin American Culture edited by John King

Modern Russian Culture edited by Nicholas Rzhevsky

Modern Spanish Culture edited by David T. Gies

Modernism edited by Michael Levenson (second edition)

The Modernist Novel edited by Morag Shiach

Modernist Poetry edited by Alex Davis and Lee M. Jenkins

Modernist Women Writers edited by Maren Tova Linett

Narrative edited by David Herman

Native American Literature edited by Joy Porter and Kenneth M. Roemer

Nineteenth-Century American Women's Writing edited by Dale M. Bauer and Philip Gould

Old English Literature edited by Malcolm Godden and Michael Lapidge (second edition)

Performance Studies edited by Tracy C. Davis

Piers Plowman by Andrew Cole and Andrew Galloway

Popular Fiction edited by David Glover and Scott McCracken

Postcolonial Poetry edited by Jahan Ramazani

Postcolonial Literary Studies edited by Neil Lazarus

Postmodern American Fiction edited by Paula Geyh

Postmodernism edited by Steven Connor

The Pre-Raphaelites edited by Elizabeth Prettejohn

Pride and Prejudice edited by Janet Todd

Renaissance Humanism edited by Jill Kraye

The Roman Historians edited by Andrew Feldherr

Roman Satire edited by Kirk Freudenburg

Science Fiction edited by Edward James and Farah Mendlesohn

Scottish Literature edited by Gerald Carruthers and Liam McIlvanney

Sensation Fiction edited by Andrew Mangham

The Sonnet edited by A. D. Cousins and Peter Howarth

The Spanish Novel: From 1600 to the Present edited by Harriet Turner and Adelaida López de Martínez

Textual Scholarship edited by Neil Fraistat and Julia Flanders

Travel Writing edited by Peter Hulme and Tim Youngs

Twentieth-Century British and Irish Women's Poetry edited by Jane Dowson

The Twentieth-Century English Novel edited by Robert L. Caserio

Twentieth-Century English Poetry edited by Neil Corcoran

Twentieth-Century Irish Drama edited by Shaun Richards

Twentieth-Century Russian Literature edited by Marina Balina and Evgeny Dobrenko

Utopian Literature edited by Gregory Claeys

Victorian and Edwardian Theatre edited by Kerry Powell

The Victorian Novel edited by Deirdre David (second edition)

Victorian Poetry edited by Joseph Bristow

Victorian Women's Writing edited by Linda H. Peterson

War Writing edited by Kate McLoughlin

Women's Writing in Britain, 1660–1789 edited by Catherine Ingrassia

Women's Writing in the Romantic Period edited by Devoney Looser

Writing of the English Revolution edited by N. H. Keeble